Before the Movement

ALSO BY DYLAN C. PENNINGROTH

The Claims of Kinfolk: African American Property and Community in the Nineteenth-Century South

Before the Movement

THE HIDDEN HISTORY OF BLACK CIVIL RIGHTS

Dylan C. Penningroth

Liveright Publishing Corporation

A Division of W. W. Norton & Company
Celebrating a Century of Independent Publishing

Printed in the United States of America
First Edition

Manufacturing by Lake Book Manufacturing
Book design by Chris Welch
Production manager: Lauren Abbate

ISBN 978-1-324-09310-7

Liveright Publishing Corporation, 500 Fifth Avenue, New York, N.Y. 10110
www.wwnorton.com

W. W. Norton & Company Ltd., 15 Carlisle Street, London W1D 3BS

1 2 3 4 5 6 7 8 9 0

For my mother

CONTENTS

PART IV: THE MOVEMENT ERA

INTRODUCTION

In April 1976, my twenty-seven-year-old uncle, Craig Baskerville, made a tape recording of his great-uncle, Thomas Holcomb. The tape is scratchy, and Lady, the family dog, keeps barking in the background. "My father was a runaway man," my great-great-uncle Tom says. "He was a slave" in Cumberland County, Virginia, near the Appomattox River, and "he had a boat." Sometime in the spring of 1865, after the Battle of Richmond, when Confederate soldiers were "running all through the woods," Jackson Holcomb "was down there" ferrying those "Jeff Davis men . . . across." "And everybody he put em across the river they give him money." They "paid him." On the recording, my uncle Craig sounds a little puzzled.[1] Thomas Holcomb seems to be saying that his father had a piece of property, and that he used that property to make deals that sound a lot like contracts: a promise to pay in exchange for a promise to ferry. Why would a band of heavily armed white men, who were risking

My uncle Craig's cassette tape from interviewing Thomas Holcomb.

their lives in a war to preserve slavery, treat an enslaved man as if he had *rights?*

Searching for an answer to this question sent me down the path toward this book, which reveals a hidden history of civil rights among African Americans. It's a story that begins not in 1955 but in 1830. It is not about people mobilizing to march but about what made it possible for the people to march. It is about the rights to make a church, own a home, get paid. These civil rights are like an invisible thread woven into the fabric of Black people's lives since before they even had rights, patterning how they loved, worshiped, worked, learned, and played. At bottom, this book is about how ordinary Black people used law in their everyday lives. People like my great-great-great uncle and aunt, Jackson and Louisa Holcomb.

They touched law at every step of their lives. A few years after freedom came, Jackson Holcomb made a marriage contract with Louisa Brown, who had also grown up in slavery. In 1883 they bought a hundred acres of farmland from a local white woman, with a swap of timber rights for eight months' rent. Over the next few decades, they bought and sold and mortgaged more land, and each time they had a deed recorded at the Cumberland County courthouse. Every year, Jackson Holcomb rode the ten miles up Guinea Road to the courthouse and paid their property taxes. As time passed, the Holcombs bequeathed some of that land to their children and nieces and nephews, sold some of it to a Black neighbor, and donated still more to the Cotton Town Odd Fellows Lodge and to their church, Midway Baptist, an unincorporated religious association founded in 1874, where they held the rights and privileges of membership.[2] In the 1920s, the Holcombs' youngest son, Thomas, and his wife, Annie Reaves Holcomb, moved to South Orange, New Jersey, a small town next to the city of Newark.

Like most migrants, they never really left home. They started "fellowshipping" at First Baptist South Orange but they remained members of Midway Baptist. They bought a little house and paid taxes in South Orange but they also sent home money for Thomas's brother Robert to take to the courthouse for their share of the taxes on the family's land in Cumberland. They laid plans to move back for good, buying out some of Thomas's relatives' shares of the land. They were always driving down for funerals and family visits. Sometimes they brought along their niece and nephew, Yolanda and Osborne Reaves, who lived with them in South Orange after Yolanda and Osborne's parents got divorced in the Cumberland courthouse. Later, they brought along Yolanda's children, Craig and Penelope, my mother. Uncle Tom died in 1976, five years after Aunt Annie and a few months after his interview with my uncle Craig. I was five years old. We all caravaned down from New Jersey, my little sister and I yawning in the back seat of our family's powder-blue Plymouth Valiant. The burial was at Midway Baptist, on a strip of land Thomas and Annie had deeded to the church in 1965.[3] Uncle Craig talked with lawyers to settle up the deeds, tax receipts, life insurance, and the title to the Holcombs' old Buick, using notes Thomas had penciled out sometime earlier. Then Craig put the papers back into my uncle Tom's dented, wood-grain-metal file box. I am looking at it now. It holds but a few of the millions of legal acts that are memorialized on scraps of paper in attics and basements and on a hundred thousand docket books in county courthouses all across America—the vast paper trail of "the law." Once you start looking, you realize that the history of Black civil rights is all around us.

The story of Thomas and Louisa Holcomb and their descendants is not a very special one (though it is special to me). Probably many of you, reading this now, have a similar story. Yet precisely because it is so ordinary, it challenges much of what we think we know about civil rights—and about Black people and the law more generally.

The story of civil rights that most people are familiar with goes something like this. Once, the legal system was dominated by racist state and local officials who refused to recognize not only Black people's civil rights, but their basic human dignity and even their lives. Law was a hostile, fearsome power to be avoided whenever possible: full of unknowable secrets and often deadly. Then, in the 1940s, a few brave lawyers ventured south, bent on changing the law. They confronted the system with a carefully planned series of strategic lawsuits and with the powerful symbolism of a Black lawyer in a white courthouse. Soon, ordinary African Americans, their sense of possibility awakened by *Brown v. Board of Education of Topeka* and other Supreme Court victories and galvanized by racial justice activists, coalesced into a mass movement demanding that the federal government force those racist state and local officials to recognize Black people as free, full members of American society. This is the master narrative of civil rights. It is powerful, not least because it refuses to concede to right-wing reactionaries the right to say what "freedom" is.

It is also powerful because history is not just about the past. "History is literally *present* in all that we do," James Baldwin wrote, at the height of the civil rights movement: "we carry it within us." The choices historians make—what to write about, what counts as evidence and how to interpret it—are inevitably shaped by the world around us. African American history is no different. In its modern form it grew directly out of the civil rights movement itself. Activists in the 1960s created Black history units to teach in the Mississippi Freedom Schools; at colleges, a Black student movement demanded Black history courses, faculty to teach them, and a wholesale rethinking of what our country's history is and how it should be taught. Many leading Black historians came into the field profoundly shaped by their experiences as activists in the 1960s; some explicitly said that their scholarship was a continuation of the struggle for Black freedom.[4]

Today, even as many historians remain committed to the idea of scholarship as struggle, they are debating what that struggle actually was and what lessons it holds today. Instead of looking from the top down—from the perspective of great leaders like Martin Luther King and Malcolm X, famous lawyers like Thurgood Marshall, statesmen like Lyndon Johnson, and the liberal justices of Earl Warren's Supreme Court—a "grassroots" approach has transformed our understanding of the movement by rethinking it from the perspective of "local people."[5] Others have taken a long view of the era of mass protests commonly called The Movement—the dozen years or so between the *Brown v. Board of Education* decision in 1954 and the Civil Rights Acts (1964, 1968) and Voting Rights Act (1965). Looking back to the 1930s and forward to the 1980s reveals a much bigger struggle, contend the proponents of the "long civil rights movement" view, a struggle for full citizenship, economic justice, and true grassroots democracy, a struggle that burned as fiercely in New York and Los Angeles as in Selma, Alabama. Movement activists realized that civil rights were not enough, the long-movement scholars argue. Real freedom required changing the underlying structures that kept most Black people poor, politically weak, undereducated, and abused by police. It meant transforming American democracy itself.[6]

What hasn't been rethought is the fundamental moral drama of the movement, in which civil rights—and Black history more broadly—are framed as an unfinished "freedom struggle," a battle against the forces of "plunder," a journey from humiliation to dignity, from second-class citizenship to full citizenship, from Black fear in the face of white lawlessness to Black people defiantly asserting their rights under the law.[7] That moral vision gleams bright today, as police killings mercilessly continue and as Republican politicians knowingly enact policies that systematically hurt Black people. Movement-centered scholarship is as urgent and necessary today as it was in the 1960s.

But the notion of Black history as a freedom struggle has also cost us something. It has helped make Black history almost synonymous with the history of race relations, as if Black lives only matter when white people are somehow in the picture. It has laid a moral burden on African American history that few other scholarly fields must carry, urging us to judge our ancestors according to how well they advanced the freedom struggle. It has often infused a subtle romanticism into African American history, with Black people playing the role of humble folk heroes overcoming adversity against the odds, or "fugitives" defined by a common history of dispossession and "yearning for freedom." Most of all, it has shrunk our vision of Black life down to the few areas of Black life where federal law and social movements made a difference. There are shelves full of books about the struggle for the right to vote, to open up the workplace, schools, and military, and to challenge a violently racist criminal justice system. Overshadowed are many other parts of life that Black people might have cared about just as much but that do not fit into a story of freedom—things like marriage and divorce, old-age care, property-owning, running churches and businesses. Historians have echoed the racial justice advocates of the 1950s and 1960s, whose courthouse showdowns with hostile white officials have become canonized in films such as *Selma* and *Just Mercy*. Because African Americans were "'afreaid to go to the court house to vote,'" as one Black farmworker wrote in a letter to the NAACP, scholars have assumed that they were afraid to go to the courthouse for anything else.[8] It has been easier to imagine Black people fighting for "freedom" or "justice" or "full citizenship" than to imagine them arguing over alimony or a deed of trust.

In the freedom struggle story, Black people are seen as ordinary and heroic precisely *because* they knew so little about law. But if that is so, then why, when a mass movement against racial injustice finally took hold in the 1950s, did so many Black people put their faith in law at all? Civil rights history has left Black people disconnected from our own legal commonsense, the way we actually think about and use law in our daily lives. It has made it harder to see Black people *as people* in full.

The Holcombs used civil rights all the time. They just weren't the ones we think of today as "civil rights." They were "the ordinary rights of a freeman," as one of the Framers of the Fourteenth Amendment put it in 1866—rights of everyday use.[9]

Before the Movement is about the many ways that Black people like my ancestors have thought about and used American law over the past two centuries. It begins in the last decades of slavery, when Jackson

Holcomb and Louisa Brown were born, follows Black life through the grim decades of Jim Crow, northward to places like Chicago and South Orange, New Jersey, where Thomas and Annie Reaves Holcomb moved in 1927, and through the 1960s, when a mass social justice movement challenged America to rout white supremacy from the law. My goal is to tell a history of Black legal lives and, in so doing, to pull back a curtain on seldom-seen parts of Black life itself.

The story this book tells was not always hidden. Open up almost anything written by Black people before the 1960s, and the "hidden" history of civil rights practically crackles on the page. Here are lawyer jokes in 1827 in America's very first Black newspaper: a lawsuit between the devil and the pope would be a close call because "the pope had the most money, but the devil the most lawyers." Here is another Black newspaper in 1877 telling its readers that "signatures made with a lead pencil are good in law" just like ink, and that promissory "notes bear interest only when so stated." Here are Black college students in 1895 taking "Lessons in making out bills of material," "Rural Law and Farm Accounts," "Estimates," and "Contracts." Here is a Detroit church in 1975 putting on an all-day "Mortgage Burning and Laying of Cornerstone" celebration. Law was everywhere, and that is why Black historians before the civil rights movement used to write so much about African Americans' achievements in the world of contracts, property, and the law of associations. Many of those historians, such as Luther Porter Jackson and John Hope Franklin, worked at Black colleges. Most of them were not even academics; they worked for Black churches and newspapers. Their audience was overwhelmingly composed of other Black people, like Annie Holcomb's niece, Yolanda Reaves Baskerville, whose cherished copy of Franklin's *From Slavery to Freedom* is sitting on my shelf now.[10] Today those early Black historians are remembered vaguely for establishing African American history as an academic field but in fact a lot of what they wrote was about Black legal lives. This forgetting is more than a matter of academic credit. It is part of the history this book tells.

Still, the history related in this book is little known, and has stayed that way because much of it comes from sources that are difficult to access. The most revealing documents are not published or even held in a traditional archive. Instead, they are stored in the back rooms and basements of county courthouses. They are written in spidery handwriting on yellowing paper, trifolded and tightly packed, sometimes flaking away or chewed by mice and insects.[11] They are full of arcane legal terminology and cryptic abbreviations. And they do not identify people by race.

That was a surprise. After all, most of these old records were written in the era when even water fountains were marked "white" and "colored." But it was also a research problem: it made Black people invisible. When I started this project twenty years ago, the only way to find out the race of the people on these old documents was to look them up on the microfilmed U.S. Census, a multistep process that could take a half-hour for just one name. Around that time, however, the Mormon Church had just embarked on a massive, decades-long effort to digitize the Census and make it searchable on the internet. (Mormon theology holds that church members can baptize any ancestors who died without knowing of the faith, as far back as they can trace their family trees.) In 2005, I started writing down the names of the people on the docket books and looking them up on Ancestry.com when I got home each night. Soon, a succession of talented graduate students began helping me transcribe and look up the cases. Once I had a list of cases involving Black people, I went back to each courthouse, and read some of them. It wasn't foolproof—no historical method is. But gradually, a picture emerged of when, where, and why Black people used the courts.[12] By the end, we looked up more than fourteen thousand civil cases, from two dozen courthouses in five states and the District of Columbia, and we identified more than fifteen hundred that involved Black people. These county court records are the foundation of this book.

But they speak in fragments, and in a coded legal language seemingly designed to frustrate non-experts. In this book, I attempt to decode that language, to bring readers into Black people's lives through the prism

Interior, Office of Circuit Clerk, Cumberland County, Virginia. Back record room wall with early deed books, order books, and pull drawers containing folded case files.

of law, and show you how, again and again, Black people held up that prism to the light to see what colors it could cast. My ambition is to capture the rich spectrum of their ideas and experiences by laying these courthouse documents alongside newspapers, files from small-town law firms, Supreme Court cases, diaries, sermons, and more.

The longer I spent in the courthouse basements, the more it became clear that law mattered a great deal to African Americans, and in a different way than scholars typically tell us it did. Scholars have typically focused on what law did to Black people and their heroic efforts to resist legal oppression and change the law itself. Or they have argued that rights are hollow without economic justice—that the right to sit at a lunch counter didn't mean much if you couldn't afford lunch. Others contend that fighting for rights through the courts is a fool's errand, because rights are too inherently unstable, too narrowly constraining, to promote lasting progressive change. It is hard to disagree with these pessimistic views of law's impact on African Americans. And yet, since long before the Movement, Black people have turned to law, and to rights. This is because rights are not only symbols of the respect that a society owes to one of its own; they are also tools for asserting legal claims or duties owed by others.[13] Activists care about whether people *have* rights; most other people care about what they can *do* with rights.

When I say that law mattered, I mean that African Americans had a working knowledge of formal legal rules, theories, and concepts, and that they put that knowledge to everyday use. I mean that when white people did recognize Black people's property or contracts, it was not out of a sense of fairness or paternalist obligation, or because formal legal rules occasionally trumped white racism.[14] White people recognized Black rights because life's ordinary business could not go on if whites could not make contracts and convey property to Black people. African Americans' property and contracts had legal meaning; in a very real but very limited sense, Black lives mattered to whites. White people who sought to murder, intimidate, or cheat Black people out of their property had to contend with the interests of other whites as defined by particular legal rules, rules that were broadly understood as part of the common sense of law. And African Americans, in turn, repeatedly demonstrated that they cared deeply about law and order—not the "law and order" that today's Republicans use as a code for anti-Black policies but the law and order that Rev. Joseph H. Jackson, head of the country's biggest Black religious organization, talked about in the 1960s, the law and order that led hundreds, if not thousands of African Americans to file civil suits in county courthouses in the century after slavery's end. After all, what they suffered wasn't just overpolicing, it was also underpolicing, the problem of getting the law to redress the wrongs committed against them.[15] For African Americans, property and contract *were* civil rights. African Americans hammered out their relationships with one another and with white people within the law, not just in struggle against it. And in doing so, they helped make and remake the law.

Given its long chronological span, this book necessarily sketches certain periods more fully than others. And its structure tracks the history of Black life and Black legal thought—Black people's changing ideas about family, church, property, and contract—as much as it does turning points in the Black freedom struggle. I tell the story in four parts: the last few decades of slavery, Reconstruction, the Jim Crow era of the 1880s through the 1920s, and the subsequent forty years when battles over the scope and meaning of civil rights broke out again on the national stage.

Before the 1950s, African Americans' ideas about rights were rooted in their experience with two important legal traditions. One tradition, that of associational privileges, emphasized one's "standing in the community" and the privileges and immunities of membership according to the law of "associations," a body of law whose furthest branches touched political party and government itself. The second tradition centered on civil rights, which were the rights of private individuals in dealing with one another under the rules of common (judge-made) law. Then and now, these civil rights of property, contract, and standing were understood as part of private law, defined mostly by the states, and available—albeit unequally—to women. Black people drew from both of these traditions—associational privileges and common-law civil rights—as they navigated their lives.[16]

For most of American history, civil rights had little to do either with racial (or gender) discrimination or with federal law. Instead, civil rights simply meant rights that a court could protect. In the 1830s, politicians and judges used the term "civil rights" as a way to define what prerogatives belonged to a free people, a conceptual beacon in a storm-tossed era. Some of the most important prerogatives were not "rights" at all, but "privileges" of membership in an association, like Midway Baptist Church, or of one's status as a white person, a householder, a citizen of Virginia. During slavery, it was well-established practice in many parts of the country for slaves like my forebear Jackson Holcomb to have the privilege of owning property and making bargains even though they did not have rights. The vast majority of Americans' rights and privileges were not spelled out in the Constitution. Instead, they were defined by the states—in thousands of statutes (laws written by politicians) and accumulated court decisions (laws written by judges)—and by associations, in their by–laws and charters.

During Reconstruction, Congress wrote these assumptions into America's first national civil rights law, the Civil Rights Act of 1866. Then, in the Civil Rights Act of 1875, Congress tried to widen what civil rights meant, only to be rebuked by the Supreme Court. In the years that followed, activists never stopped fighting to widen the meaning of civil rights, yet nearly everyone agreed that, at the least, it meant something like "the rights of free people," the basic rights that leaders such as Abraham Lincoln had pointed to in the 1850s when they explained what freedom was. During Jim Crow, these were rights that people exercised not just in court but in their daily lives, though they rarely had occasion to call them "civil rights." When Annie Holcomb applied for her Social Security card, when she paid the insurance man on her doorstep each week, when she and Thomas sold land to Midway Baptist, when they wrote down instructions about how and where they wanted to be buried on that land—every time, that is, they did something that a court could protect—they were doing civil rights, exercising freedom, making it mean something more than the negation of slavery, the end of whips and chains. Civil rights were rights of everyday use.[17]

Over the decades, Black people kept using and thinking about law in countless aspects of their lives, but the *idea* of Black rights and the idea of civil rights shrank down until they were practically synonymous. A distinctive vision of Black legal life came into focus in the early 1900s, was sharpened by law professors and federal government lawyers, popularized by a 1947 presidential commission, and lifted to almost sacred status by a mass movement whose most famous figures were deeply religious Black Christians. Prodded by what Martin Luther King Jr. called "The

Negro freedom movement," Congress and the Supreme Court wrote the principles of nondiscrimination and anti–humiliation into the heart of a new, national body of civil rights law, including the Civil Rights Act of 1964, the Fair Housing Act of 1968, and *Jones v. Mayer* (1968). But by then, many activists and commentators were coming to see civil rights as weak and old–fashioned compared to the radical possibilities of human rights or grassroots democracy. In the century after emancipation, civil rights went from being the fundamental rights of free people to being the right of minorities not to be discriminated against.

In the pages that follow, I try to recover some of the ideas and the experiences that the freedom struggle narrative has obscured. I show that Black people focused on working through state and local law, not—as most histories of race in America tend to assume—on trying to mobilize the federal government. I show that lawsuits between Black people were not obstacles on the path to freedom; they were just the most visible manifestations of Black people's efforts to define who they were as individuals and as families, and who had power over whom. I show that African Americans' experience of slavery and second–class citizenship left them agonizingly aware of law's power, and grimly determined—perhaps more than most white people—to master its intricacies. And by uncovering this hidden history of Black legal lives, I tell a history of Black life more broadly. In this history, Black people—not race relations—are the center of gravity. From an elderly DC resident in 1880 bargaining for someone to take care of her, to a Mississippi tenant farmer in 1900 arguing over a lease with a powerful white landowner, to a DC resident in 1966 threatening a church members' march on their bishop's house to "fight for there rights" to keep the pastor they wanted, I try to bring to light Black people's loves and angers and loneliness, their efforts to get ahead or at least stay afloat, their mistakes and embarrassments, their fights, their ideas, their hopes and disappointments, in all their messy humanness. And I show how their legal activity helped shape legal institutions, practices, and doctrines—in short, not only that they helped make and remake American law, but *how.*

Today we think of civil rights as a special body of law that concerns minorities. When the police or an employer or a school board abuses its power, a civil rights suit is often seen as the natural, if deeply unsatisfying, remedy. That modern conception of civil rights—closely identified with our national government and concerned with principles of nondiscrimination—is only the latest chapter in a story that begins more than a hundred years before, in the fields and cabins of slaves.

A NOTE ON TERMINOLOGY

Unless I say otherwise, you can assume that the people who walk these pages were Black. By treating Blackness as the unmarked category, I aim to demonstrate through form how common it is to treat whiteness as the default.

Some historians of slavery in the United States, as well as some government agencies and educational organizations, have recently urged substituting the words "enslavement" and "enslaved person" for "slavery" and "slave," which they contend rob historical figures of any identity beyond the dehumanizing one imposed on them. Similarly, they urge substituting "enslaver" rather than "slaveowner" and "owner," which are said to obscure the violence and immorality that enslaved people suffered. I sometimes use the new terminology in this book. But often, the words "slave" and "slaveowner" and "former slave" convey exactly what I mean to say. Generally, I have followed the approach recently outlined by Tiya Miles, who uses "slave" and "slavery" when she is "referring to categories defined and imposed by southern owners of people, to societal as well as legal dictates, and to racial systems of capture," and reserves "enslaved" or "unfree" for passages where she "designate[s] a person from their perspective, the perspective of their community, or our perspective as researchers and readers." Like Miles, I also sometimes opt to preserve "the sound or rhythm in the sentence rather than performing linguistic acrobatics to avoid using the word 'slave' or 'owner.'" It is worth noting that in both Native American history, as Miles points out, and in African history, many scholars and community members are moving *toward* the words "slave" and "slavery," because they want to reject what they see as dangerous euphemisms, like "captive" and "domestic."[1]

Finally, the assertion that using certain terminology restores enslaved people to their full humanity is rooted in an understanding of the history of slavery that I do not share, and it implies a theoretical stance toward the concepts "slavery" and "freedom" that uncomfortably resembles the liberal individualism that this book critically examines. Slavery in the United States was built on the exploitation of slaves' humanity. Their humanity does not need to be restored. It should be taken as given.[2]

PART I

SLAVERY

1

The Privileges of Slavery

Why did Confederate soldiers pay my ancestor Jackson Holcomb? Answering that question requires rethinking our understanding of slavery. In the past couple of decades, scholars have emphasized the sheer brutality of life under slavery and how that brutality stemmed directly from the fact that slavery was, above all, a business. Slavery, they have shown, unleashed horrifying violence on Black people. Slaveowners drove Black people relentlessly through deadly heat and disease. Overseers whipped them in the fields, leaving inch-deep gashes in their skin that never really healed. An overseer

White traveler's drawing of the Appomattox River near Farmville. At the bottom right corner is a cloth-covered "batteau," one of many that were operated by free and enslaved African Americans in the early 1800s.

broke Harriet Tubman's skull with a two-pound iron weight and she suffered from seizures the rest of her life. White women beat, kicked, and burned the Black people who worked in their homes, and taught their daughters to do the same. Slaveowners tore families apart, selling children away from their mothers and brothers from sisters. They used rape as a weapon. They skimped on food, clothing, and shelter. From the biggest slaveholders, whose sophisticated accounting techniques and productivity experiments helped pave the way for modern business management, to the middle-class farmer renting a slave or two whenever he could afford to, slaveowners made their money from an unholy fusion of precision management and cruel violence. Profit was the point.[1]

The more scholars agree that slavery was essential to the development of capitalism, the more tempting it is to imagine slaves as inhabiting a kind of law-free zone—that slaves were brutalized because they were utterly outside the law and that the civil rights movement of the 1950s and 1960s was the culmination of a centuries-long struggle toward equal rights under the law. Yet there is a different way of understanding slavery, in all its cruelty. To grasp it requires looking at something most people today would probably call an oxymoron: the legal lives of slaves.

To even read a sentence like that might seem strange. It's difficult to imagine that slaves had anything to do with the law, other than to suffer under it. But while Jackson Holcomb didn't have rights, he and millions of other enslaved people in fact made claims of property and contract that whites respected. Whites did so because slaves' *privileges* stood upon the same widely shared understandings about law that white people's *rights* did. And one of my contentions is that we cannot understand Black legal lives during freedom without first examining Black legal lives during slavery.

By the time the soldiers got into Holcomb's boat in 1865, white southerners were used to seeing Black people own property and make contracts: these were privileges of their status as slaves. The word "privileges" doesn't sound as though it has much to do with law, but in the

1800s, it did: a privilege was a law granting "special prerogatives" or exemptions that were not available to other people in the community.[2] Privileges came with membership in a community, whether a church, a club, a town, or the United States itself. "Privileges" were sometimes interchangeable with "rights"—as in the Constitution's "Privileges and Immunities" Clause—but even slaves' privileges were defined and enforced by community norms strong enough that courts sometimes acknowledged them. Then, during the 1840s and 1850s, white northern leaders like Abraham Lincoln invented a worldview where a small bundle of prerogatives called "civil rights" marked the fundamental difference between freedom and slavery. To them, it was unthinkable that a man like Jackson Holcomb could have owned a boat, because slaves did not have civil rights. And when slavery was finally overthrown, the party of Lincoln wrote that vision into America's first civil rights act and the Fourteenth Amendment, arguably the most important amendment in our Constitution. The Republicans swept aside slavery's complicated, ambiguous world of privileges. They gave the nation a "new birth of freedom" built on one beguilingly simple principle: when it came to civil rights, the law should not discriminate by race.

Can people without rights do legal things? In the nineteenth century, they could. First, individual rights were not the only way, or even the chief way, that people did legal things. Second, even individual rights depended on legal logics and legal practices that were open to people without rights. Jackson Holcomb trusted the soldiers' promise to pay for the ferry crossing, even though he could not have sued if they didn't pay. Another slave, Joseph Bacon, who lived in coastal Georgia, understood that "legally" slaves had no right to property, but he insisted that "a master who would take property from his slaves would have a hard time." His own master, he said, "never interfered with me and my property at all."[3] Why not? Because slaves' claims rested on a common, widely shared set of understandings about property and contract.

Modern lawyers have words for this kind of thing: "trade usage," "custom," "course of dealing," "prescription," and more. All these terms are means of acknowledging that, often, law doesn't dictate rules so much as it codifies what people are already doing, blessing "community opinion"—a term I am borrowing from a loose group of early-twentieth-century legal thinkers known as the legal realists—as to what the law is.[4] In the 1850s South, "community opinion" took it for granted that slaves had certain privileges.

One example was in their work lives. There were about four million slaves in the United States in 1860. Their work generally followed one of two patterns. Along the coast of Georgia and South Carolina and in the tobacco and iron factories of Richmond, a "task system" assigned each slave a certain amount of work each day, with remaining time to use as they wished. White people knew that slaves who worked by the task felt that they were entitled to work in that system and at that level. Reporting on the South's economic system in 1856, Frederick Law Olmsted, the journalist and future designer of New York's Central Park, described task work as a "prescriptive right." A prescriptive right means a prerogative that, through open, continuous, and undisputed possession over time, has become legal. (The classic example is someone who takes a shortcut across her neighbor's yard for twenty years, and then sues when the neighbor puts up a fence.) Of course, slaves could not go to court over a prescriptive right. Indeed, one slaveowner bragged to Olmsted about doubling his slaves' customary tasks. But that could be expensive, Olmsted's white informants told him. If the slaves' "right" were infringed or "denied," the master risked a labor slowdown in the fields or an even more expensive "general stampede to the 'swamp' "—the slaves would go on strike. For centuries, since the 1660s, masters had looked at their profits from the task system and decided it wasn't worth risking all that just to show that slaves didn't have rights. Instead, they negotiated with slaves over the nature of slaves' privileges: how many square feet of hoeing customarily counted as a "task," for example, or how many acres their allotted "private fields" were supposed to be, who they were allowed to trade with, and so on. The logic of prescription lent predictability and structure to the unequal and dangerously unstable negotiations between masters and slaves over the terms of slaves' work.[5]

The second, more familiar pattern of slavery is gang labor: lines of people moving in unison down a vast field of cotton, under an overseer's whip, from sun-up to sun-down. Here, too, slaves had certain privileges, which they tried to establish as prescriptive rights: the privilege not to work for their masters on Sundays, to be paid for after-hours work, and to own and market small amounts of property. Many slave families in upcountry South Carolina had garden patches beside their cabins, which they were allowed to work during certain allotted times: usually Sundays, sometimes Saturday afternoons, and at night, if they could stand it. In Alabama the garden patches could be as big as a half-acre. In upstate New York, Sojourner Truth's enslaved parents—this was the early 1800s, when the state was gradually abolishing slavery—raised and sold tobacco, corn, and flax, though they did not get Saturdays. Many slaves, maybe even most of them, got paid incentives for "overwork" during the harvest and planting seasons. Slaveowners did not do this out of the goodness of their hearts. They did it to save money, offloading the costs of feeding and clothing their workforce onto the exhausted workers themselves. From their patches of land, slaves had to supply a significant portion of the vegetables, chickens and eggs, meat, and more that kept them alive and healthy.[6] Slaves across the South, under both task and gang systems, seized these allotments of time as "a prescriptive right."

On this foundation of overtime work, they created other prescriptive rights, of property ownership and trade. Enslaved people were key players in the South's market economy, not just as commodities and workers, but as buyers and sellers. Country storekeepers liked selling to slaves, wrote Charles Ball, who escaped slavery in Georgia, because the slaves "always pay cash," whereas poor white customers "almost always require credit." Slaves sold wood and fish to steamboat captains and portering services to steamboat passengers. Some bought wagons and mules and hauled goods. Others, like my great-great-great-uncle Jackson Holcomb, bought boats and ran ferries. White travelers could find themselves stranded on the riverbank if enslaved ferrymen decided "that the job wouldn't pay" enough. At least one slave even shipped goods by rail. Enslaved buyers and sellers crowded city markets from New Orleans to Natchez to Alexandria. In small towns they sold cakes and drinks from booths during "court week," the periodic weeklong sittings of the local circuit court.[7] Slaves' economic activities—the food growing, the fishing and foraging, the livestock-raising, the hauling, the buying and selling—were a form of superexploitation, in which slaves exhausted their precious Sundays and nighttime hours to give themselves and their families a better life than the bare-bones allowances their masters provided.

Slave hiring entailed the same offloading logic: slaveowners rented enslaved people out and then let them keep some of the money. Or the slaves hired themselves out, finding their own meals and lodging, making "their own contracts," and forking over most of

Scene on the Appomattox River in the vicinity where Jackson Holcomb lived. One of the figures in the boat is a Black man; the second may also be Black.

their earnings to their masters each month, as Frederick Douglass did when he hired as a ship-caulker in Baltimore. Slave hiring helped employers tamp down wages for free workers. Yet hiring also made slaves parties to a bargain, a bargain that had the look and logic of a contract: an agreement—written or oral—where "a party undertakes to do or not to do a particular thing."[8]

Slaveowners also used contract-like bargains to lessen another serious drag on their profits: sick and old-age care. The issue has a surprisingly modern ring to it. Slaveowners liked to pretend that they took care of slaves better than the slaves could themselves, but politicians knew better, because many of them were slaveowners themselves. They knew that many of their peers just offloaded the costs of "care" onto the public by freeing people as soon as they got too old or too disabled to work anymore—and slavery left huge numbers of Black people physically disabled every year. Partly to guard against such cost shifting, state governments all over the country put up roadblocks to manumission. In the North, state legislators required masters to get a local bureaucrat's written approval before manumitting any slave.[9] In the South, they made it illegal to set free old and disabled slaves. A few of the richer slaveowners reacted to these legislative roadblocks by taking out insurance on their slaves. Others got rid of elderly slaves by selling them off at rock-bottom prices. Or the slaveowner simply abandoned the old person in a hut, knowing that her relatives would use their precious after-work time to take care of her. Frederick Douglass's grandmother was left to die in a shack in the woods, and Moses Grandy said his mother was turned out like "an old horse." And still other slaveowners found ways to offload the business costs of healthcare and eldercare onto the slaves themselves. They made deals to let young slaves take care of their elders, or let former slaves buy their aging parents and take them home to live with them. Occasionally, slaveowners put this cost shifting into writing, making a contract with the slave's free relatives to support her.[10] Such bargains reveal that slaveowners treated disability and old-age care much the way they did food and clothing: as a business cost that they could dodge by granting slaves privileges.

Recent historians have assumed, like the abolitionists did in the nineteenth century, that the essence of slavery was "the chattel principle, the property principle," the act of treating a person as a thing. But the secret of slavery was that it had no overarching principle. It could treat a person as a thing, or as an agent of his master, or as a party to an agreement. It all depended. My point is not that hiring and old-age agreements made slaves' lives easier or that slaves could enforce them as rights. It is that contracting "'infected' the field of slavery," as the historian Hendrik Hartog puts it. It encouraged hundreds of thousands of enslaved people to think in the logic of contract, and made millions of white people used to the idea of bargaining with slaves.[11]

The privileges of slaves weren't exceptions or deviations from the law, they were part of the law. They stood in different pools of the same "community opinion" that white people's rights did, and they so closely tracked legal logic that some observers simply called them "property," "contract." Besides the fact that these practices made money for slaveowners, another key reason they were so common had to do with official law itself: slaves' property and bargains drew from the same ideas about possession, notice, and usage that underpinned the formal legal rules of property and contract. Jackson Holcomb "owned" his boat because the people around him recognized his ownership of it, not because some far-off judge said he had a "right" to it. This wasn't all that different from how working-class free people in New York and Baltimore owned their clothes,[12] or, for that matter, how Holcomb's master owned him. Property consists of public recognition. Holcomb's master had pieces of paper to back up his claim of ownership—deeds of sale, an entry on the slave register down at the courthouse—but as we will see, those pieces of paper were merely sturdier anchors for "community opinion."

When Olmsted said that slaves in task-system areas had "a prescriptive right" to the time left after a task, he was invoking a basic legal principle, still very much alive today: that community recognition can, over time, endow a claim with legal force. In property law, prescription doctrine means that a trespass can "ripen" into legal title—that, under certain circumstances, courts will legalize theft. In contract law, this principle of community recognition underlies the doctrines of "usage" and "custom": for example, in the shipping industry, "fourteen days" means fourteen working days; in the lumber trade, two packs of shingles are 1,000 even if there aren't actually 1,000 in them; and in the bagel business, a dozen is thirteen.[13] And at the heart of prescription, usage, and custom, as well as many other doctrines in contract and property law, is the concept of "notice."

Notice is one of the things that makes property property. In seventeenth-century England, buying and selling land required not only writing a deed "executing" (literally *doing*) the conveyance, but also a stylized public performance called "livery of seisin," where the seller stood in front of witnesses, recited certain words, and actually handed a twig or clod of dirt to the new owner. In the thirteen colonies, white landowners walked their boundaries with crowds of neighbors, establishing their ownership claims in public memory and creating witnesses who could testify about creeks and notched trees and other markers if there were ever a dispute. The point was to publicize this deed and fix it in people's minds, so that five, ten, or thirty years in the future, anyone who thought he had a claim to that land would know whom to sue.[14] "Notice" was especially important when people borrowed against property, because, unlike a sale, where neighbors could see the change of ownership every time the new owner walked in the door, borrowing added a part-owner who might never touch the property. It created an *invisible* interest in the property called a mortgage.

Over time, colonial leaders created a norm that property sales and mortgages should be "recorded"—written in ink on a ledger kept at the courthouse—and that any free person could look at those ledgers and get a certified copy of any conveyance they wanted.[15] To this day, these ledger books are taken very seriously because they are the backbone of the entire property system. So, while cash-strapped local officials have thrown away whole shelves-full of other kinds of county records, you can walk into the Cumberland County courthouse, catty-corner from the Exxon station, and leaf through deed books that are older than the U.S. Constitution. You can do that because "community opinion" holds the ledgers to be the definitive proof of who owns what land.

Enslaved people like Jackson Holcomb could not use the courthouse deed books to publicize their property interests, so they created "notice" through other means. They did it by displaying their possessions and securing acknowledgment from their masters and fellow slaves. The physical arrangement of the plantation was essential to this practice. Most big southern plantations clustered the slaves' cabins together in rows somewhere near where the master lived or where the overseer lived, if there was one. Slaveowners liked this layout because it kept slaves in "sight of his watchful and jealous eye." This extended to slaves' belongings. "In the rear of each cottage, surrounded by a rude fence," slaves kept "vegetable gardens, chicken coops, pig pens, rice ricks, and little store houses," all under the control of individuals and families. In cities, where enslaved people lived in attics or backlot sheds, their "huck patches" were even easier for all to monitor.[16]

When slaves visited one another, any property that was cooped, penned, or stacked became more or less public knowledge. "I was backwards and forwards every day," recalled Henrietta McLaughlin, an ex-slave from the town of Jackson, Mississippi, "lived only a door from Mrs. Lee [and] I knew what property she had. I didn't know every thing she had in her trunks and boxes, but knew what was in sight, such as provisions and bedding." As Samson Bacon, an ex-slave from the seacoast region known as the Low Country, testified: "I know it was his because every man on one place know every other man's property. . . . he can't help from knowing it. All go in his yard before his door."[17] Although their masters designed the slave quarters with their own interests in mind, slaves used the layout to their advantage as well.

Slaves' property claims were not recorded on the courthouse ledgers or on bills of sale, so as they sought to etch their claims onto community opinion, all they had was the performance of their possession. "I seen it in her possession, and her master knew it, and everyone considered it her property," said a witness in an Alabama case.[18] Testifying in the case of Prince Stevens, who had filed a compensation claim against the U.S. government for property federal troops took during the Civil War, Samson Bacon explained that he "never heard [Stevens's] master claim his horse. No sir no such thing as that, he had been riding the horse too long back & forth between there & his master's." Rights of use or possession translated over time into real claims of ownership. As another of Stevens's witnesses put it, "I know it was his because it was right there under his 'controlment' & no one else claimed it."[19] Such acts of possession did much more than affirm slaves' humanity and dignity, or set up a separate legal culture, as some recent scholarship has argued. They were acts that meant something within generally applicable theories of property. After all, except for land, few white people had deeds or bills of sale for their property, either.

In effect, by marking their personal property in public view, the slaves declared their property claims to an interpretive community that recognized acts of possession as the origin of property generally, not just for slaves. "Possession," "usage," "a sort of ownership," "moral duty": white observers did not use these words by accident and neither did slaves. They were *legal* terms, ones that everyone, including slaves, relied on.[20] Slaves owned property in every legal sense of the word except that no court would protect their ownership as a right.

That slaves participated in the same legal system as whites can be observed, too, in their ownership of property that moved—wandering animals like hogs, cows, and horses. As one white traveler wrote, one of the first things that any newcomer did when he came to the Arkansas bottomlands was to "cut his hogs' ears in some mark or other [and] turn them out to root for themselves." For example, a slave might cut "an upperbit in one ear & a crop & a hole in the other." Southern whites knew how to spot such marks because they relied on them to protect their own claims on livestock.[21] Marks were "the ordinary indications of ownership" of animals, and county clerks were supposed to keep a record book of marks and brands, just like the land deed books with their handwritten descriptions of funny-looking trees and crooked creeks and notched posts.[22]

In 1837, North Carolina's legislature decided to crack down on enslaved entrepreneurs. They passed a law commanding the county wardens of the poor to seize and sell off animals that belonged to any slave or had "any slave's mark." A slaveowner named Robert McNamara challenged the law. The hogs really belonged to him, he said, not his slaves. What did the legislature mean by the words "belong to a slave"? The state supreme court judges focused on markings. They admitted that, normally, the master had the title to the hogs his slaves possessed. But, the court said, he lost it when he let his slaves "mark them in their mark." That crossed the line into "acts of dominion and ownership," and that is what the legislature meant by the word "belong." So McNamara lost, and the hogs were forfeit. A slave could "nominally" own property, the court said later, as "long as the master keeps the actual, as well as the legal control of" it. But such fine-grained distinctions fell apart in practice, because legal ownership was grounded in "ordinary indications" that were not reserved just for free people. In neighboring South Carolina, a slave's property wasn't forfeit unless it was officially seized and condemned.[23] Some masters kept giving their slaves "a mark for their hogs"; and some slaves paid white neighbors to do the marking for them, knowing that, much like with livery of seisin, those neighbors could someday vouch for the slaves' claims of ownership by describing the marks in detail.[24] *McNamara v. Kerns* reveals how centrally important notice was to property law in general, not just for slaves.

Property's tendency to sprawl across the free/slave divide is evident as well in politicians' sporadic efforts to keep slaves from owning "illicit" property. The same 1837 law that tried to confiscate slaves' livestock also made it a crime for slaves to buy or sell "certain articles" to each other or free Black people: mostly guns, liquor, and commodities like cotton. But the legislature did not declare that it was illegal for a slave to own property. In fact, the law specifically said that it was "lawful" to do business with a slave if the slave had her master's written permission. This was revealing. If slaves could possess property, control it, enjoy it, and could get permission to lawfully buy and sell everything except guns, land, and liquor, then slaves could lawfully exercise most of the sticks in the "bundle of rights" that makes property property. That is why white people so casually bargained with slaves at Sunday markets and roadsides, why the soldiers paid Jackson Holcomb at the riverbank.[25] Slaves owned property *through* law, not in spite of law.

Similar dynamics were at work in contract law. Slaves could not make legally binding contracts but they made agreements all the time, including the ones that let them earn property. Under the hiring system prevalent in the South, slaves made bargains for their time—and some of the hired slaves, in turn, subcontracted other slaves to work for them, ostensibly acting as agents of their own masters. Once in a while, slaves even hired white people to do things for them. Some masters kept written accounts with slaves, marking credits and debits against the slaves' so-called "little crops," and they acted like probate judges when slaves died, presiding over the distribution of their property to the slaves' "heirs." Slaves tried to protect these agreements by publicizing them, much the same way they protected their claims of property. Harriet Jacobs's grandmother Molly made sure that everyone in town knew that she had an agreement with her mistress to buy herself, and that she was baking at night, after hours, to save up the purchase money. When her mistress died and the executor tried to sell Molly privately—supposedly "to spare her embarrassment"—Molly insisted on a *public* auction, trusting that the "common knowledge" of her agreement would keep the bidding down to a price she could afford. It worked: "the crowd hushed," letting Molly's mistress's sister buy her and an uncle using Molly's own money, and then quickly free her.[26] Southerners knew that slaves sometimes borrowed money from white people, and that white people borrowed money from slaves, giving a "receipt" or promissory "note." Molly's mistress once "begged" her for a $300 loan, "promising to pay her soon." Even if we discount the improbable report of an Alabama slave holding $1,000 worth of "interest-bearing notes" on loans to white neighbors, it is clear that some whites paid attention to the accounting of credit and debt with slaves, a kind of accounting that typified nearly everyone's dealings in a cash-poor economy. And it is equally clear that slaves had an interest in publicizing those accounts—in making sure people knew who owed what to whom.[27]

These payments represented the closing of bargains. That is, deals between masters and slaves were typically not swaps, paid on the spot. Rather, they were mutual promises of future performance, induced by what lawyers call "consideration"—an act, a non-act, or a return promise that motivates someone to do something, the quid in a quid pro quo. In form, logic, and purpose, these were contracts—exactly what southern appellate judges increasingly said was impossible.[28] Yet that is what Frederick Douglass, Sojourner Truth, and a surprising number of white people called them.[29] What they lacked, of course—what made them "bargains" rather than "contracts"—was that the slaves couldn't sue to enforce them.[30]

Slaves did not have standing to sue because they did not have civil rights. The classic example of slaves' contractual incapacity was when the master (or his heirs) reneged on a promise to set someone free. That person might then sue for her freedom. The "freedom suit" was the exception that proved the rule of rightlessness, because it started from the premise that the petitioner was not a slave in the first place.

Unlike freedom suits, slaves' property and bargains came into court via a path that did not depend on them having rights—through criminal prosecutions (where the goal was to restore the public peace), or by presuming that the slave was acting as an agent for his master.[31] Thus, white men were indicted for stealing from a slave, or held accountable for debts owed to slaves, or even told that they had lost their right to their slaves' possessions when they let the slaves act "as if they were their own." In such cases, the white person's rights served as a legal fiction—a very common maneuver where, in order to reach the "correct" outcome, the judge assumes something that is not actually true. So, for example, in order to prevent a white borrower from walking away without repaying $2,424 he had borrowed, the Tennessee supreme court pretended that the money belonged to the white go-between who had fronted the loan rather than the two enslaved barbers who had handed him the money to lend out. And when the Civil War came, the Confederate Congress sought to energize the southern economy by granting patents—intellectual property—to masters for their slaves' inventions.[32] The law vindicated the slave's claim by recognizing the master's right.

In this, as in so many things, the laws on the books served several sometimes contradictory ends. "The law" expressed the principle that slaves could not and should not make contracts, and "the law" also sought to promote economic growth by ignoring supposedly illegal bargains between steamboat travelers and slaves, and by admitting it was "absurd to suppose" that slaves actually carried written passes every time they went off the plantation. It wasn't *explicitly* illegal in every case for slaves to own things or make bargains. Instead, laws barred slaves from owning and bargaining for certain kinds of things, in certain ways, at certain times, and were silent on everything else. The gaps and occasional contradictions in statutes reveal a lack of political consensus. White southerners cared more about making money and preventing revolts than about keeping slaves away from contracts and property. As mentioned above, laws regulated the kinds of things slaves could own (generally no guns or hard liquor), and what they could do with it (trading without a license, or trading certain goods, like cotton). Laws put curfews on slaves' market days and pinned special trader's badges on their chests. Many of the regulations were passed during spasms of white anxiety—like just after Nat Turner's rebellion in 1831—and then, after a while, people ignored them.[33] Slaves were not supposed to own guns, but some did anyway, including an Alabamian who owned "*three guns*—one of them a valuable fowling piece of a noted London make." Grocery stores did a thriving trade with enslaved customers, and slaves made money driving taxis around Vicksburg. When people got sold away, they were given time "to gather [their] few belongings" before being chained up for the long journey. Some had money to buy tobacco and melons while they waited, distraught, in the slave pens of New Orleans and Louisville.[34] These facts do not lessen the horror of slavery, but they do challenge the notion that slaves had no dealings with the law beyond their status as slaves.

Wherever slaves made bargains and owned property, it uncovered familiar cracks in the pillars of white society. Only a quarter of white southerners owned even a single slave, and that slaveowning minority vacillated between fearing that such practices undermined "good order" and an aristocratic sense that they were too "trifling" to bother about or even that they were good for the system. Meanwhile, in a running debate reminiscent of today's arguments over "illegal aliens," the other three-quarters—their non-slaveowning white neighbors—could not agree whether slaves were stealing jobs from deserving white workingmen or providing convenient, cheap services.[35] More important is that, in *regulating* how slaves owned and traded things, the law implied that it was, in some sense, *legal* for them to own and trade things, as long as they had their master's consent. Judges sometimes pointed out this implication. As the North Carolina supreme court put it in 1845, when politicians regulated what slaves could "have" or "sell or buy," they were, in effect, recognizing a "a sort of ownership by slaves."[36]

Was it legal for slaves to own things? Southern courts did say something definitive about slaves' property rights in one particular kind of situation: when it cropped up in lawsuits between white people. In those cases, judges affirmed "a sort of ownership by slaves," "a gratuity" and "not . . . a right," grounded in custom, justified as good policy, and legally vested in the master. The idea was similar to how courts treated white married women at the time: under the legal fiction of "coverture"—a word borrowed from the French, meaning "covered"—they didn't have a *separate* legal identity but they did have *a* legal identity. It was just subsumed under the husband's. Legally speaking, slaves were covered, not annihilated. And so, like a slave's chickens and pigs, a wife's butter-and-egg money might "belong in strict law to the husband," but "usage" and common sense told that it was hers, nonetheless.[37] If the wife or slave spent money, the husband or master could not sue to get it back.[38]

After the Civil War, at least one court would acknowledge that slaves had, in fact, enjoyed something like civil rights. A white man named James Wilson bought a house-lot in Wilmington, North Carolina in 1863. An enslaved man named Jefferson James was already living there, and Wilson accepted money from him, money that Wilson considered to be rent. In 1866, Wilson apparently decided to get rid of his holdover tenant, but James refused to leave, so Wilson sued for possession. James made an audacious argument: he wasn't Wilson's tenant at all; he *owned* the property, because he had paid full value for it, long before Wilson arrived, and had possessed it for the prior fifteen years "not . . . as tenant but in his own right." The white justice of the peace refused to hear testimony from James's witnesses because they were Black. So James's lawyer tried a long-shot argument at the state supreme court: James couldn't have been Wilson's tenant because a slave could not make a contract, and now, after so many years living there undisturbed, he had a prescriptive right to it by adverse possession—the doctrine that grants legal title to someone who occupies a piece of land openly and adversely for a certain length of time. In *Wilson v. James*, the North Carolina supreme court flatly rejected this argument. If a slave could occupy his master's land "adversely," then no ex-slaveowner's land was safe. But then Justice

William Rodman conceded something important. Because a slave could not have made a contract, the fact that he had been paying rent since 1863 did not "estop" him from disputing his landlord's title in 1866. It was "too broad" to say "that a slave was incapable of making any contract," wrote Rodman. "The executed contracts of a slave were . . . *voidable*"—that is, a slave's contract was binding until a court said it wasn't.[39] In order to reject an ex-slave's property claim after slavery's end, Rodman presumed that slaves had had the right to contract back in the days of slavery.

If a slave had ever tried to sue someone for, say, taking his pig, he would have been stopped at the courthouse door for lack of standing to sue, not because it was illegal for him to own a pig. But some jurists said his master could bring the suit for him, or they treated his master as the victim of a theft, and it is easy to imagine that it was actually the slaves who injected these questions about slaves' property into cases that were, ostensibly, civil disputes between white people or criminal cases—that for example it was James Martin's slaves who told his executor about their cotton-selling arrangement with Martin before he died.[40] In daily life it was hard to see the line between "possession" and impermissible "ownership." Ownership couldn't be just the having of a thing, or else no slave could ever pick up a wheelbarrow or carry a sack of cotton. Was it "ownership" to let slaves mark pigs with their own mark? Was it a lack of permission from the master? Was it the amount of money—that $1,500 was just too much for a slave to have?[41]

It was easier to avoid these sorts of questions if you trivialized the issue. In a lawyerly hypothetical that obviously came from personal experience, Louisiana Supreme Court Judge Francois Xavier Martin wrote that whenever a stagecoach or steamboat arrived, "black boys crowd" around it, offering to carry the passengers' trunks and baggage. Of course, it was against the law to buy "anything from a slave." Yet nobody would expect a passenger to waste his time finding out "whether the boy be a slave or a free person," Martin pointed out, much less whether the slave "has his owner's permission." Everyone knew that even the most law-abiding citizen would "buy a melon, or other trifling article, without" asking for "this permit." And in fact, the conscientious citizen was justified in making these dockside deals with slaves, Martin said, because the law does not concern itself with trifles.[42] The maxim was (and is) deceptively important: the justice system *has* to ignore certain things or else it will grind to a stop. Martin was saying that the courts were not going to wade into the argument about whether a slave had the right to make deals with steamboat passengers. This approach was sometimes controversial. States kept passing laws against slaves owning hogs and doing business in town because angry white voters were effectively telling judges like Martin that making deals with slaves was not a trivial matter.

Of course, law wasn't made just by high-court judges or legislators or even by county justices of the peace, who held court in "taverns, country stores, front porches," or under a tree. Parallel and sometimes mixed up with those white-run legal institutions were Black ones: especially churches and what some people called "plantation courts," the quasi-formal tribunals for handling disputes among slaves. White observers laughed off plantation courts as harmless make-believe. In a sense, they were right to scoff: the plantation courts posed no threat to the slave system, not least because they only dealt with disputes *between* slaves. Yet slaves took the plantation courts very seriously. They often had elaborate trappings: public charges, an investigative "committee," warrants, "a law book" taken "from the white folks house," and gradated punishments. Their penalties were no joke. There was nothing funny about being forced to pick up a quart of tiny benne seeds scattered in the dirt, or being excommunicated from the only church for miles around, or forfeiting your precious after-hours earnings, much less going to hell.[43] Through their close attention to form and process, these Black-run courts answered an intensely felt need among slaves for law and order. After all, what slaves suffered wasn't just overpolicing—the slave patrols lurking in the woods, the whippings meted out by the master—it was also *underpolicing*, the fact that there were no remedies in the official courts for the wrongs committed against them.

The enslaved people who ran plantation courts frankly acknowledged that they didn't have rights, yet they were deeply invested in law-like general concepts and rules that transcended the particularity of their slave status. A Louisiana freedman named "Doc" Lewis served as "judge" at a "trial" that took place just after slavery ended and that probably drew from prewar patterns. The overseer had invited all the ex-slaves to help themselves to one pig apiece from the plantation's pen, but one elderly man, a nearsighted parson named Rev. Benjamin, mistakenly "killed the biggest hog in the pen." The overseer accused him of stealing and the matter went to the plantation court. As Lewis's son told the story later, the "whole thing resolved itself into the question, 'When does a pig become a hog?'" It wasn't so much that country people had trouble guessing the moment of swinish puberty. It was that they couldn't articulate the basis on which they made such judgments, a basis for a *legal* rule. This is the core logic of the Anglo-American system of common (judge-made) law: an insistence on using specific cases to articulate rules that will apply to all other cases where the facts are similar. The witnesses agreed that what the old man had taken was a hog but they couldn't explain why they thought so. "'I jis' knows a hog when I sees him,'" shrugged one. "'Because I seed him with these eyes,'" said another. Through skillful questions to the witnesses, "Doc" Lewis slowly teased out a workable principle on which to decide it, and gave that principle to the "jury" as the general rule they should apply in this particular case: that "As long as a pig sucks its mammy, irrespective of size or age, it is not a hog." This pig was suckling. Rev. Benjamin was acquitted.[44]

"Doc" Lewis wasn't just engaging in a judge-like ritual, or trying to protect a fellow freedman from punishment. Rather, he was *thinking like a judge.* He was searching for rules that might lead to a "just" outcome, one that would have value as precedent for other cases, while staying attuned both to what today's lawyers call "trade usage" (how people in the farm business usually classify hogs)[45] and policy considerations

"Trial of Rev. Benjamin," from J. Vance Lewis, Out of the Ditch *(1910).*

(the overseer's need for controlled order, the freedpeople's worry over an old man's welfare). The episode hints that some plantation courts were not just mimicking the trappings of the official courts, as whites mockingly assumed. Slaves and ex-slaves understood legal logic—the creative interplay between innovation and structure that constituted the common law.

Property-owning, bargaining, court week, church tribunals, and plantation courts fostered a legal culture during slavery, one that would make Emancipation a much less sharp break than historians have assumed. The capstone of that legal culture, paradoxically, was the repulsive things law did *to* slaves during slavery, things that dramatized their lack of rights. For example, slaveholders dealing in the giant New Orleans slave market complained that slaves somehow knew enough about the law of warranty and redhibition (nineteenth-century

Louisiana's version of a lemon law, providing buyers a right to a refund if the purchased item was flawed) to game the system, telling lies about sore backs and crazy fits in hopes of getting resold somewhere nearer to their families. Whatever the truth behind such complaints, slaves' experiences of slavery were clearly a brutal education in law. They knew that property rights could be divided, for example: that if a father thought his son and daughter-in-law might squander their inheritance, the father could protect his grandchildren by granting his son the possession and use of a farm and slaves but not the *title*. They knew that hiring a slave was not the same thing as owning one, and that some of the master's slaves were actually owned by his wife or her children or some other white relative. They had to have a rough grasp of wills and estates law—to know that when a slaveowner died, his slaves got "turned over" to "an administrator," and to know when an administrator was mishandling his legal duties. They had a basic grasp of mortgages: that a deed of trust conveyed powers that a crafty man could abuse, and that in some situations, being mortgaged might actually save your life. Slaves knew enough about law that, after the Civil War, whites sometimes asked their former slaves to testify as witnesses in lawsuits against other whites, because, as one man put it, "I knew more about the [white people's] affairs than any one else."[46]

More than any specific legal rules, what Black people learned from their experiences of slavery was one of Anglo-American law's most subtle, yet crucial principles: that most laws are not self-executing—that the law helps only those who help themselves, who take the trouble to learn about legal rules and then enforce them as rights. This principle flashed vividly in the law of separate estates, a branch of property law that treated a married woman as having property rights distinct from her husband's, as if she were outside the veil of coverture. Arkansan Katie Rowe learned in the most terrifying way that her grandmother Nanny belonged not to their master but to their white mistress, along with "all de chillun Nanny ever have," and that "nobody can't take 'em for a debt." Once, their master tried to do it anyway. He handed over Nanny's daughter to a white man to settle "a paper about some kind of debt," but soon another white man, named Littlejohn (probably summoned by other slaves), rode up, saw Nanny screaming in the yard, quickly sized up the situation, and took off. "He jest job de spur in his hoss and go kiting off . . . after dat white man." At a creek crossing, Littlejohn ordered the white man "to come back wid dat little nigger 'cause" the debt "paper don't kiver dat child . . . and when de man jest ride on, Mr. Littlejohn throw his big old long hoss-pistol down on him and make him come back. De man hopping mad, but he have to give over my mammy and take one de other chillun on de debt paper. Old Master allus kind of techy 'bout old Mistress having niggers he can't trade or sell."[47] It is difficult to imagine a more impressive demonstration of the legal power of a separate estate agreement—or of how any legal right utterly depended on local understanding and practical action: on whether there was anyone alert enough and tough enough to do something about it. Promissory notes, deeds of trust, separate estates, rescission, estate administration—each represented a moment when white people's exercise of civil rights cut through the bone and sinew of Black people's lives. And each made slaves keenly aware of the power of civil rights and determined to master their intricacies.

Slaves participated routinely, energetically, unequally in the world of law. The fact that they had no rights—no prerogatives that a court would protect—did not mean that they lived outside the law, because law was not just for people with rights, and because rights themselves existed in a thick network of shared understandings and symbolic acts: recording, talking, using, and showing. No judge would have protected Jackson Holcomb's ownership of the boat or enforced the soldiers' promises to pay. His only safeguard was the "usage or custom of the country"—the "sense" of the "community." But this was not categorically different from what safeguarded white people's contracts and property. In fact, seventy years after he ferried the soldiers in 1865, self-described "legal realist" law professors would use almost exactly the same words not only to describe how property and contracts worked in real life but to explain how judges decide cases—a general theory of judicial decision making. We might say that what southern law withheld from slaves wasn't just physical protection—the threat of arrest and jail for anyone who harmed them or their interests. It also withheld a clear statement of "community opinion" about the legal status of slaves' prerogatives, the "sense" of the community that actually makes bargains "contracts" and property "property."[48] By refusing to speak clearly and consistently about slaves' prerogatives, the law left them at the margins of legality, where whites could conveniently profit from them.

When freedom came in 1865, it started a new chapter in an ongoing story of Black legal life. Many if not most freedpeople had dealt with law and legal rules during slavery, and now, for the first time, they could try to enforce their claims in a court of law. Because now they had civil rights—the fundamental rights that belonged to all free men.

2

The Rights of Freedom

If slaves held privileges that looked like rights, what did free Black people have? In August 1848, sitting in their one-room office on the second floor of the Talman Building in Rochester, New York, Frederick Douglass and Martin Delany, coeditors of the *North Star* newspaper, answered that question in the grandest terms. "Whatever privileges we may enjoy, they are granted to us as a *favor,* and not a right," they wrote; we are "nothing more than *nonentities*" in "our native land." This denial of free Blacks' rights was rooted in the "scourge" of slavery. So long as "Africo-American[s]" were not "entirely free—free . . . to the full enjoyment of all those rights and privileges common to American citizens," Douglass and Delany contended, then they were "slaves."[1]

Unlike Jackson Holcomb, free Black Americans in 1848 did have certain rights. But they did not have *equal* rights. State and local laws singled them out because of their race: laws that restricted or barred them from voting and from attending school, laws that doomed most of them to grinding poverty, and laws that constantly humiliated them with petty, racist discrimination. Free Black abolitionists like Douglass and Delany began to turn their experience of unequal rights into a sweeping argument about Black freedom, full citizenship, and racial justice. America's founding creed demanded not just an end to slavery, they declared, but rights for the freed—equal rights in all spheres of life, not just the world of the "civil." In the 1850s, although mainstream Republicans including Abraham Lincoln felt it was bold enough to say that free Black people were entitled to the basic, natural rights of life, liberty, and property, the Black abolitionists' argument planted seeds that would bear fruit a century later, in the 1960s, when activists converged on the idea that second-class citizenship was no citizenship at all, but another kind of slavery.[2]

At the same time, free Black people like Douglass and Delany constantly used the basic rights Lincoln talked so much about. That is how they publicized their claims about "the Africo-American": they had employment contracts with printers and reporters, they leased an office, and they sent their newspaper to readers who had signed contracts called subscriptions. Moreover, behind the activists' rhetoric about rights was another, equally important story about the organizations they led: the law of associations. From the neighborhood church to Yale College, from the City of New York to Douglass and Delany's *North Star* newspaper—each of these entities was an "association," a group of people legally empowered to act collectively in pursuit of a common enterprise.[3] Once we realize that Black churches and activist organizations were *legal* entities, we begin to see that the very same associations that fought for "all the Rights and Immunities of Citizenship" under state and federal law were also struggling constantly with the rights of members under their own association by-laws.[4] These internal tensions over membership and its privileges would profoundly shape Black people's legal thought for the next 150 years, right down to today—tensions over whether those who sank time and money into Black churches and racial justice organizations held "privileges" in those organizations, or something more like "rights."

One marker of a civil right is whether it is justiciable—whether it is something a judge can protect. Free people of color asked local judges to protect their rights, and the most common reason they went to court was not freedom suits or trials of racial determination (where courts decided what race a person was), but rather contracts and property, the basic legal relations that made ordinary life possible for everyone. Free Black people were intricately involved in the daisy chain of IOUs that laced whites and Blacks together in the farm business, where nearly everyone was simultaneously a debtor and a creditor, signing promises on scraps of paper to cover small debts like a month's worth of flour and salt, cosigning on bonds for bigger debts, or on deeds of trust to buy land. Some free people of color hired and bought slaves on credit. When economic crises unlaced the daisy chain and everyone began calling in their own loans in order to pay off their own panicked creditors, free Black people found themselves hauled into court, their farms and cows auctioned off to richer neighbors. In court, they endured and sometimes profited from the same procedural delays and the same pattern of low-level officials discreetly "bend[ing] the law" that white litigants did.[5] Today, pundits and policymakers often tout "access to credit" as a way to solve poverty, but free Black people's quiet desperation in the nineteenth century reminds us that credit means very little on its own.[6]

Credit and debt stood atop another basic fact of Black life: free Black people had property rights, rights that were never seriously questioned before the Civil War. There had been free Black people in North America since at least the 1630s, and their numbers fluctuated over the next two centuries as whites opened and shut the two main pathways to freedom: manumission (a slaveowner voluntarily set someone free) and self-purchase (a slave paid for his own freedom or that of a loved one). There were a quarter million free Black people in the South by 1860, and they owned nearly $8.8 billion of property (in 2021 dollars)—some 60,045 acres in Virginia alone—twice as much per household as their parents had held. A few free people of color owned slaves, who sometimes were their wives and children, sometimes not. The 1860 Census counted 16,172 free Black property owners in the South (including Washington, DC), each worth an average of $1,252 ($543,000 in 2021 dollars). Very few of them got their property from guilt-ridden white fathers or benevolent emancipationists, as much recent scholarship has implied. They bought it by the sweat of their brows.[7]

Those who did not own land often owned other kinds of property, which also became essential to contractual relations because of the IOU economy. To secure a debt of $52.09, for example, Samuel Chisman, a free Black tenant farmer, put up a horse and cart, a cow, four hogs, and the crop of sweet potatoes and corn he was growing on the land of a white man named W. S. Smith. That is, he signed over these items to a person called a trustee (usually a third party but often the lender himself), who held them in trust to secure payment of the debt, more or less the way a mortgage works today. That deed was then recorded at the clerk's office in Hampton, Virginia, in Deed Book M, page 450, which is where Luther Porter Jackson, the trailblazing Black historian, found it in 1939. Some Black women signed prenuptial contracts, or stayed single, to avoid being held liable for a husband's debts, an especially terrifying possibility for those who were desperately saving up to buy their children or cousins out of slavery.[8]

Credit was just one example of how free Black people's exercise of property and contract rights embedded them in a web of legal relations with whites. The mere fact of Black landownership meant that whites would have a stake in Black rights. When Black people bought land, their rights became essential to anyone who loaned them money against it, or who bought it from them or their "successors in interest"—anyone in the "chain of title" stretching out into the future. Thus, decades after slavery ended, whites were still tracing their titles back to free people of color, testifying about how free Black women, for example, had bought land with money earned by enslaved husbands.[9] In short, the more that free Blacks bought, sold, mortgaged, and bequeathed property, the more their civil rights became essential to white people's civil rights.

Free Black people's civil rights made some of them attractive clients for white lawyers before the Civil War, even in the Deep South. Historians have tended to focus on freedom suits, but much more typical were the run-of-the-mill filings of Alexander Field, a white man appointed by the Mecklenburg County, Virginia, circuit court to handle the estate of a free Black man named William Stewart. Field reported that Stewart's relatives wanted to save their family's land from being auctioned off but were so poor that "none of them" could put up the required "security." So, he "bid it in [him]self, for $1.76 pr. Acre," in order to keep the heirs from losing their home.[10] Long before Abraham Lincoln was elected president in 1860, he was a lawyer in Sangamon County, Illinois, and he represented free Black people in at least nine civil suits, mostly against whites, ranging from divorce to debt collection. Lawyers like Field and Lincoln were neither abolitionists nor "cause lawyers"—lawyers fighting for the public good. They took Black clients either because it paid or because they thought the cases presented interesting technical questions.[11]

Some of the variation in free Black people's rights stemmed from a powerful culture of personalism—the idea that "the negro" might be dangerous but not the Negroes *you* knew. Personalism was less about friendship or even principled fairness than it was a style of economic dealing; a reluctance to play hardball against people you might need on your side someday, just as it is for modern businesspeople. When he bid on the Stewart family's land, Alexander Field was only doing what he thought was his duty as a fellow property owner and (temporary) officer of the court until he could unload these parcels and "be exonerated from the Business." What really underpinned whites' respect for free Black people's civil rights was a stronger version of what underpinned the privileges of slaves: the fact that so much private law was so closely entwined with community opinion and woven in such a way that repudiating Black rights would have unraveled their own rights. Or, put another way: it did not threaten the racial order to recognize free Black people's rights of everyday use.[12]

That racial order was strained, though, as northern states gradually transformed the basic logic of race and rights. In 1848, when Douglass and Delany said that second-class citizenship was a kind of slavery, the Anglo-American world was in the middle of a long struggle over the limits of lawful coercion in a market society, a struggle that was throwing into question all kinds of status-based rights, privileges, and duties. Traditionally, voting, serving on a jury, poor relief, and a whole range of other matters had been "privileges" of status within a particular community, not rights under the U.S. Constitution. If a citizen of Boston fell on hard times he was entitled to bread and shelter from Boston but not from Worcester, and Worcester's officials could "warn him out" if he tried to live there. Riding first-class on a railroad was a privilege reserved for "respectable" members of the traveling public. Practicing law was a privilege granted by each state to qualified state citizens of good moral character.[13] The logic of status privileges was doubly clear in the world of work. For hundreds of years, huge numbers of white English people had been routinely coerced on the basis of their status: "apprentice," "indentured servant," "wife," and "son." The "master" (or head) of a household had legal authority to "correct" (that is, beat) the people who worked for him—his "servants"—and a husband had legal authority to "correct" his wife and his son.

Since the 1770s, white men had fought to turn status privileges into "rights," available on equal terms to any free man. The Constitution's Privileges and Immunities Clause, Article IV, section 2, was central to this evolution in thinking. The clause marked an odd and momentous feature of the new nation. Americans had dual citizenship: Jackson Holcomb's master was a citizen of the United States and also a citizen of Virginia. The United States was a sovereign nation composed of states that were also, somehow, sovereign. But the clause was vaguely worded: "The Citizens of each State shall be entitled to all Privileges and Immunities of Citizens in the several States." States controlled most of the privileges anyone cared about, so which privileges and immunities did this clause guarantee across "the several States"? If a Virginia citizen moved to Manhattan, did New York have to recognize his privilege to practice law? To own a slave?

Slowly, the high courts converged on the idea that there were a few privileges and immunities that were more fundamental than the rest: "natural, inherent and inalienable rights of man," as the Supreme Court put it in 1795, beyond the power of any state to interfere with. An influential 1823 case offered a loose list: "life and liberty," "the right to acquire and possess property," "to pass through" or live in any other state, to sue and be sued, the writ of habeas corpus (a court order that forces the government to justify detaining someone), the right not to be taxed higher than other citizens of the same state, and, maybe, the right to vote. Because these rights were "general," common to citizens across the nation, they formed the nucleus of an idea of national citizenship.[14] Because rights were imagined as belonging to individuals without regard for any status relationship other than their citizenship, their smooth hard surface gradually ironed out the wrinkled fabric of status privileges, in whose folds Black people—even slaves—had long found a little room to breathe.

Where once the law had recognized a variety of statuses—indentured servant, wife, master, father, king—each attached to certain privileges, immunities, and duties, the law in the 1840s and 1850s increasingly recognized only two: freedom and slavery, with nothing in between and each defined as the opposite of the other.[15] A slave, legal experts now claimed, was a person "deprived of all civil rights," like a felon serving a life sentence. He was someone who could not enforce a promise in court, who could not sue or be sued and who could not own property or make a contract, not even one for his freedom. A slave "has no civil rights whatsoever," said the supreme court of South Carolina.[16] That was what made a slave a slave.

The flattening of status privileges into a world of rights also simplified how people thought about coercion. White workers fought to throw off the traditional status relations of labor law, known in those days as "the law of master and servant." Through strikes, marches, and constant politicking, they managed to remake the rules of work. The ideal that took shape by the 1830s was a relationship between two parties of equal legal status, bargaining freely in the marketplace. Since "every man" was "the sole owner, and master of his own goods and labour," said a meeting of white Philadelphia craftsmen in 1806, he had a right to set the price for them, and to accept or reject whatever offers came his way. It was a world defined by the principle of equal status with respect to property and contract. Every free person was his own master, with the right to sell his most basic property—his work—by getting a job, an employment contract. In this emerging world of free labor, slavery began to seem distinctive, not only because slaves were Black but because slavery was seen as the only relationship where a private person had legal authority to physically coerce another adult.[17]

Free Black people disrupted this simple picture of white freedom and Black slavery. And America's free Black population was growing: from 59,466 when the Bill of Rights was ratified in 1791, to 434,449 by the time the *North Star's* readers picked up their newspaper in 1848. Alarmed, many white people wanted to restrict rights to only certain kinds of free people. Rights, they said, were only for citizens, and free Black people were merely "denizens," or "inhabitants," who did not hold rights but rather only whatever privileges their local white community deigned to allow them. Whites pushed wave after wave of anti-Black laws that set free Blacks apart as inferior, or barred them completely. New York decided in 1821 that all white men could vote a year after moving to the state, but Black men had to wait three years and prove they owned at least $250 worth of real estate (about $168,000 in today's money). In 1860, just before the Civil War, ten northern states barred free Black people from voting at all and four others put special restrictions on them, including restrictions on testifying against white people. In schools, streetcars, railroads, and theaters, free Black people were generally segregated by law, if not barred altogether. Black people were not even allowed to settle in Indiana, Illinois, or Oregon.[18] As white labor leaders stumbled toward a world of "free labor" defined by rights of property and contract, white voters tried to stomp free Blacks' status downward until it was synonymous with slavery. No wonder Douglass and Delany said that free Black people were treated almost like slaves.

White northerners justified these restrictions by claiming free Blacks were members of a lesser race: dangerous, criminal-minded, lazy, natural paupers, a drain on the honest white taxpayer. They lapped up foully racist newspaper cartoons and they cheered minstrel shows and white-supremacist politicians who slung those stereotypes with gusto. Illinois was not going to let itself become "an asylum for all the old and decrepit and broken-down negroes," Senator Stephen A. Douglas declared, defending a law barring free Blacks from his state. Even if these laws weren't consistently enforced, they emboldened whites to harass and terrorize Black people into leaving. For example, just after Ohio's supreme court affirmed that that state's anti-Black laws were constitutional, white mobs rampaged through Black Cincinnati until half the city's Black people fled. As the historian C. Vann Woodward pointed out in 1955, in a book meant to open whites' eyes to how "strange" and changeable America's racial history had been, segregation was actually "born in the North" before the Civil War.[19]

In devising a strategy to fight the hail of anti-Black laws and anti-Black popular sentiment in the 1830s, the white abolitionists James Birney and Theodore Dwight Weld decided to focus on the narrow band of fundamental, or "civil" rights: the right to move from one state to another, to make contracts, to own property, and to sue and be sued. They thought that if white voters could be convinced to allow free Blacks "their *civil* rights," then "social rights" would "follow naturally in their wake." Birney's and Weld's civil-rights-first strategy, which they pursued at great personal risk, not only galvanized antislavery activism in the Midwest, it also forced whites to think hard about the relationship between race and rights.[20]

Thus, when the leaders of the Oregon Territory had petitioned for statehood in 1858 with a proposed constitution that said free Blacks could not settle there, testify in court, own property, or make contracts, Congress balked. Several congressmen felt that these were the most fundamental civil rights—the legal endowments that protected natural rights, the God-given "unalienable Rights" of the Declaration of Independence—and that, in taking them away, Oregon's politicians had gone too far. The Oregon dustup showed that standing up for fundamental civil rights could dovetail with a kind of least-common-denominator racial politics, and it was this combination that powered the Republican Party to the White House in 1860. As the party's leader, Abraham Lincoln, put it in 1858, one didn't have to *like* "the negro," or want to be around him, or to think he was as smart or virtuous or deserving as a white man. "But in the right to eat the bread" he earned with his own hands, he was "the equal of every living man." And some Black leaders sought to work within that basic-civil-rights framework. To refute those who claimed Black people could not take care of themselves, free Black leaders bragged about the $200,600 worth of property owned by Black Cincinnatians; to refute those who assumed free Blacks always wound up on welfare, they presented a former slave who was about to foreclose a mortgage against a white lawyer who owed her $2,000.[21] In short, free people of color turned property and contract into an argument for Black freedom.

Already in the 1840s, more radical antislavery activists and politicians were going further. By widening the definition of "slavery" to include racial discrimination against people who were not slaves, activists like Frederick Douglass and Martin Delany developed a critique of what we now call "second-class citizenship." The northern states' anti-Black laws were nothing less than "Slave Laws" written by Democratic-party minions of the "Slave Power," they said. These activists insisted that having rights did not necessarily make you free unless you had the same rights, on equal terms with everyone else. So long as Black people were not "entirely free," said Douglass and Delany in 1848—free "to the full enjoyment of all those rights and privileges common to American citizens"—then they were "slaves." Even in the North, argued the National Convention of Colored Freemen that same year, "we are not slaves to individuals, not personal slaves, yet in many respects we are the slaves of the community."[22] It was a stark assertion, one that reduced the complex experiences of African Americans like Samuel Chisman and William Stewart—not to mention those of women, Native Americans, and paupers—to a simple, abstract line between slavery (no rights) and freedom (equal rights).

The Supreme Court's decision in *Dred Scott v. Sandford* (1857) wrote this simple slavery/freedom binary into the Constitution. The case was a freedom suit by Harriet and Dred Scott, who had married around 1836, when their masters were living at Fort Snelling, near what is now St. Paul, Minnesota, and who were now enslaved in St. Louis. The Scotts (their suits now combined under Dred's name) claimed that Scott's master had inadvertently set him free by holding him as a slave in Illinois and in federal territory, two places where slavery did not legally exist. Scott lost in Missouri's supreme court in 1852. Scott and his team tried again in federal court. Under the Constitution, a federal court could only hear his case if he and his opponent were citizens of different states. So they added another claim to the lawsuit: that Scott was a citizen of Missouri. Chief Justice Roger Taney disagreed. He held that Scott could not sue in federal court because he was not a citizen, and, further, that Scott was not free because Congress never had the power to bar slavery from federal land. Slavery was national, not southern, Taney implied. Taney's opinion relied heavily on history. In particular, he said that, in 1787, when the framers wrote the Constitution, Black people "had no rights which the white man was bound to respect." *Dred Scott* may be the most notorious case in American history. It was widely blamed for helping to hasten the outbreak of the Civil War, and it has become almost synonymous with results-driven judicial activism and the way that formalistic legal reasoning can lead to fundamentally immoral outcomes.[23]

In *Dred Scott*, Taney turned legal reasoning on its head: according to him, free Black people had lacked certain rights in 1787 and that proved that they could never be citizens. In order to frame the question he wanted—are free Black people citizens?—he ignored historical evidence that free Black people had in fact voted, made contracts, owned property, and more, both before and after the Constitution was ratified. In dissent, Justice Benjamin Curtis used that very same evidence to argue that free Black people *had* been considered citizens in some of the states at various times.[24] Tightly focused on individual rights, both justices treated freedom and slavery as polar opposites. Of course, Black people's legal lives were more ambiguous than either Taney or Curtis admitted. Slaves had property and entered into agreements that were valid and binding in the eyes of their communities, but they did not have rights. By turning property and contract into abstractions, stripped of the sociality and community recognition that actually constituted them, the shining gospel of individual rights—whether preached by Black abolitionists or white judges—helped make slavery sound like the opposite of freedom.

Another reason the language of individual rights didn't really capture how Black people really lived is that many of the most important prerogatives in antebellum America were not "rights" but rather "privileges and immunities" derived from one's membership in an association. Free Black people took full advantage. They formed all kinds of associations, from religious associations (that is, independent Black churches), to mutual benefit associations (basically, insurance companies), to benevolent associations (most famously the Prince Hall Masons and the Colored Convention movement) to business associations, like Douglass and Delany's *North Star* newspaper.[25]

The law classified associations by whether they were incorporated, not by race. An unincorporated association was a web of contracts among its members. It was (and is) created through contract law rather than by a charter from the state. That means that its rights and liabilities lie in each member and reach only as far as their individual rights reach. A corporation provides a more powerful legal structure for organizing and channeling people's resources. It does this by offering three huge advantages. First, it shields its "investors" from at least some of the risks of the group's activities. Second, incorporating enables people to centralize the management of their groups—a way to move from discussion to decisive action. Last, it endows the group with "legal personality." A corporation really is a legal "person," just as Mitt Romney blurted out in 2011. That is, a corporation has civil rights, distinct from those of its members. It can hold property, make contracts, sue and be sued, admit and expel members, and make by-laws—private statutes—to govern itself.[26]

Some Black people formed business associations.[27] Black leaders thought they should form even more. There was plenty of capital in Black communities, argued Brooklyn businessman and activist John N. Still in 1852; the problem was that they were investing it in the wrong places. Instead of putting their money in white banks or pouring it into Black churches and benevolent societies, they should organize for-profit corporations and partnerships. "Why should we not have 'Building and accumulating fund associations' [for] our cooks, stewards, whalemen and others [to] profitably invest[] the[ir] hard earned monies"? he asked. Why not form " 'Protective union associations,' 'Borrowing and loaning associations,' " or any other moneymaking enterprise?[28] Stop giving away your money to white people, urged leaders like Still. Buy Black.

Both free Black northerners and southerners knew that an association's health depended partly on notice. So Black officers, like their white counterparts and much the way slaves did with their chickens and hogs, found ways to publicize their associations' legal acts. In the early 1800s, an association became a corporation by applying to the legislature for an official charter. That charter both empowered and regulated it. By the 1830s, Americans were flooding their legislatures every year with petitions for corporate charters, and some of those petitions came from Black people. In New York City, at least six Black-run associations received corporate charters between 1800 and 1850, and the South was dotted with unincorporated Black-run societies, now long forgotten, like the "Consolation Sisters," "Tobitha," and "Sisters of Usefulness."[29]

Even if they didn't shell out money for an official charter, Black-run associations were constantly putting on public performances—marches, outdoor speeches, banquets—and publishing lavishly illustrated official "histories." For example, in 1829, to celebrate "the anniversary of [its] incorporation," the New York African Society for Mutual Relief held a "procession" of invited Black "societies," whose members marched from the Mutual Relief Hall (corporate property) to the African Zion Church (also corporate property). Black associations also kept written records, suggesting that their members understood the distinctive power of writing to endow otherwise ordinary acts with legal meaning. If you joined the Daughters of Africa Society in Philadelphia, the Society would write your name on its "Order Book," and then mark down your dues payments, which entitled you to the privileges of membership. One of those was the privilege of borrowing money. In May 1822, the Society "Lent Ann Hacket a member a lo[a]n acordian [according] to 10 article of the Const[it]ution the sume of four dollars for the burial [of her] child."[30] A loan is a contract. This loan's terms were set by the Daughters of Africa Society's Constitution. If a situation arose that wasn't answered by those terms, then New York's common law of contract would fill the gap. Putting this loan contract in writing helped balance the Society's books. It would also be legal evidence if the Society ever had to sue Hacket. That is, it would be proof in a court of law not only of the loan and of Hacket's membership, but of the Society's own legal existence. Like slaves' performances of property and contract—indeed, like the deed to your house or the lien on your car—these acts of recordation put the public on "notice." Free Black people literally wrote their associations into legal existence.[31]

That made an association's name a high-stakes legal question. As many historians have shown, Black people formed associations to assert "a public racial identity," one that enabled them to critique the idea of a democracy founded on the principle of white supremacy. And so they debated about names—whether they were "African" or "Negro" or "colored" or simply "Americans." But in forming associations, Black people also made the question of Black identity fundamentally a *legal* question: a question of corporation law. By law, every corporation must have a name and that name is "essential to its corporate identity." The name identifies the collective "person" that is responsible whenever the corporation acts. It turns out that one of the leading cases in early corporate law concerned a Black-run corporation, the New-York African Society. James Varick, a prominent Black religious leader, was one of the men who had signed the treasurer's bond, which was essentially a promise to pay the Society if the treasurer did wrong. When the treasurer embezzled $800 and left town, the Society sued Varick to collect on that bond. Varick filed a demurrer (a motion to dismiss the suit before trial), arguing that the Society had used the wrong name when it sued him: they should have sued as "*The Trustees of* the New-York African Society for Mutual Relief," not "The New-York African Society for Mutual Relief." The New York supreme court overruled Varick's demurrer, holding that small variations in corporate names did not matter for the purposes of a deed: the corporation could still sue Varick in its "true name."[32] Naming controversies within free Black communities involved more than questions of cultural identity, because an association was a collective, immortal "person," empowered by law to act in the world, and it risked extinction if it was not called by its "true name."

Today, we tend to think of corporations as the epitome of private enterprise, but in the 1800s they were private and public at the same time. In adopting constitutions and by-laws, electing officers and myriad committees, Black people created what the historian Hendrik Hartog calls "technologies of public action," with grants of public resources and state-delegated powers of self-government—the power to elect or appoint officers, to accept donations, to decide who could join, to make rules for their members, to tax their members, to administer justice—and to have a judge enforce those decisions.[33] None mixed private and public more than the corporations run by Black people. Through constant organizing to feed and clothe the poor, Black-run associations provided the safety net that white-run governments withheld. And just by existing, they represented a challenge to the white supremacist assumption that Blacks were too primitive to govern themselves. Black people used associations to power their political activism, most famously in the Colored National Conventions, where, from the 1830s to the 1860s, thousands of Black delegates from around the North and Canada gathered annually to discuss issues of shared concern, from the struggle to abolish slavery, to voting rights, to anti-Black racism, to labor. They were the forerunners of the racial justice organizations we know today. Even their for-profit businesses inevitably had a public mission, too: to uplift the race.[34] As a result, few other Americans felt the tension between private interest and public duty as keenly as did the Black people who led associations.

A corporation had civil rights but its members had only privileges. Some of the thorniest problems that associations faced, regardless of race, were about the prerequisites and privileges of membership, including membership in the one kind of association that Black people and white people *did* join together: a church. Southern churches were remarkably integrated compared to today—in part because whites were firmly in charge.[35] But white leaders could not exclude or even completely subordinate Black Christians within churches because those Black people were members with certain privileges and immunities that were spelled out in church by-laws and constitutions.

Cumberland Baptist Church, in southern Virginia, was probably typical. In the 1850s, nearly two-thirds of Cumberland's members were slaves. Jackson Holcomb was most likely one of them. In a leather-bound book where they kept their meeting minutes, the white leaders proudly wrote that their church had its own "constitution, or code of by-laws." When "colored members" joined, they were "baptized" and "received into full fellowship," "their names entered upon the record." Like white members, they had to attend services or give a valid excuse. When they left the church, they got letters of dismission, a standard document any Baptist needed in order to join a new church.[36]

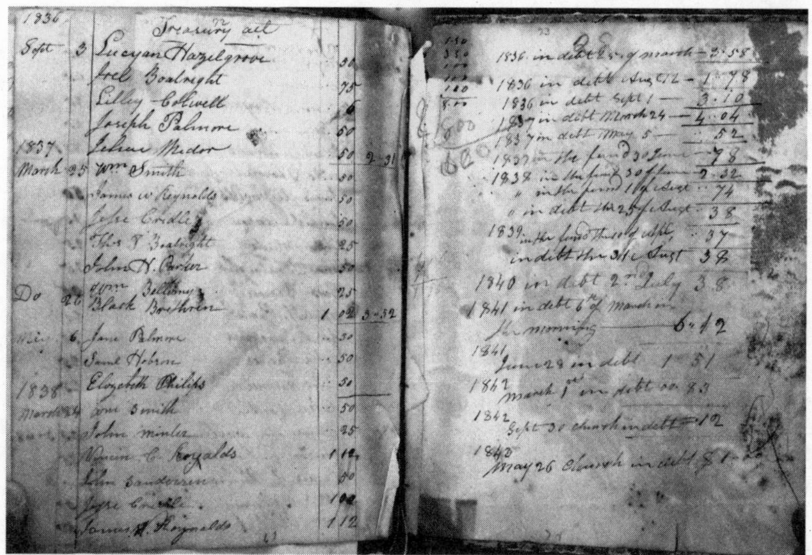

The "Treasury Account" in the Cumberland Baptist Church Minute Book, 1836–1856. The entries for contributions from "Black Brethren" in 1837 totaled more than any single donation from a white member that year.

Cumberland Baptist also required its enslaved members to donate money. It "tax[ed]" its members "according to [their] ability" to pay, not whether they were free. In fact, donations from "Black Brethren" like Jackson Holcomb helped keep many of the South's "white" churches afloat. So, for example, every Sunday morning, the Black members of Richmond's First Baptist Church filed out past "Deacons at each door" and put money into a hat to pay the white minister. This kind of theatrical collection sent a tricky double message. It underlined status hierarchies: white men paid the most because they were better than everyone else. But it was also a regular, public reminder that the church needed the slaves' money, too.[37]

The white people who ran majority-Black churches justified these money demands by pointing to "the privileges" that the "coloured members" enjoyed. "All the members of a church have equal rights," wrote one Baptist leader. Cumberland Baptist's white officers claimed that at their church, "taxation and representation" were based on "the true principle of republican government." But of course that wasn't actually true. Enslaved people, free white women, and children were not allowed to vote on the most important things: matters of "discipline and government." True, the white men were supposed "to consult the[ir] wishes."[38] But they didn't have to, because within the church, women, slaves, and children had only privileges, not rights.

And yet the line between privileges and rights kept blurring, precisely because churches and other kinds of associations held sway over such broad swaths of people's lives—because they *governed.* Looking back, it seems obvious that the idea of Christian fellowship—that all church members were equal in Christ's eyes—contradicted slavery's basic precept that Black people were lower beings. What is less obvious is that that contradiction had legal implications. This was first because it slowly fragmented the church along racial lines. Over time, a pattern developed of holding prayer meetings for Black members separate from the main Sunday service, and these prayer meetings evolved into distinct Black congregations, nominally controlled by the main church's white leadership but often in a separate building and collecting their own money. Second, the contradiction between slavery and Christian fellowship had legal implications because churches were, in a very real sense, public institutions. Southern churches typically ran a parallel legal system, judging not just theological issues but also "civil disagreements between neighbors," the kinds of things a county court normally handled. What should a congregation do when a member begged for the right to remarry after her spouse had been sold away? Or said she had been sexually assaulted by another slave? Or by her master? White church leaders listened to these petitions, not because slaves had civil rights but because they were members with privileges—because their relations with one another affected "the peace of the congregation." This was the same logic that justified secular courts prosecuting slaves—and occasionally whites—for hurting or killing other slaves: killing a slave injured "the public peace." At a time when evangelizing among

Blacks seemed crucial to the future of American Christianity, when many churches depended on donations from Black people, southern churches had a stake in vindicating Black people's privileges as church members. Not only that, but because nearly two-thirds of the Black people who answered God's call were women, they had a particular stake in the question of Black *women's* privileges.[39]

But privileges were not rights. And in mixed-race churches all across the country, white officers in the 1780s denigrated Black members' privileges, whether those members were enslaved or free and no matter how respectable they were. White church officers poured separate communion cups for the "Africans" and shunted them to specially built upstairs galleries. They seized control of side-buildings and budgets that Black members had been quietly running for years with little oversight. Black church members bitterly resented the crackdown. After one Virginia church decided to put up a "partition 'to divide the white's and blacks,'" it faced a backlash from its enslaved members and agreed to have "a pass way cut through" the partition. At Cumberland Baptist, the enslaved members were allowed to use the church building for themselves one day a week, and even on their one day they had to put up with white people gawking when they started shouting and fainting from the Holy Spirit. African Americans pointed out that their subordination in church contradicted the gospels' emphasis on equality and the white preachers who had been promising that there were no masters or mistresses or overseers in God's heavenly kingdom.[40] No one listened.

And then the dam broke. In 1787, on the first Sunday morning after Philadelphia's St. George's Methodist Episcopal Church started sending its "coloured" members to the low-status upstairs gallery, four Black men defiantly went to their usual seats downstairs. Amid "scuffling and low talking," two white church leaders went into the pews and pulled them up off their knees. When the prayer had ended, recalled Richard Allen, one of the four men, "we all went out of the church in a body." The pattern repeated itself in both northern and southern churches: after months or years of fruitlessly remonstrating through church procedures against their loss of privileges, Black members finally threw up their hands and left. An even bigger exodus would come after the Civil War, but these early-nineteenth-century walkouts, which subtracted as many as four-fifths of members in a given mixed-race church, shook those churches like earthquakes. On a single day in 1817, 4,376 Black people left Bethel Methodist Episcopal Church of Charleston. From Boston to Philadelphia to Savannah and even smaller towns like Charles City and Petersburg, Virginia, Black people set up their own churches, empowered by the same kinds of state-issued charters that backed Yale College and the New York African Society. The very first Black-owned corporations in the United States, in fact, were a pair of Black churches in Philadelphia, each incorporated by one of the men who led the 1787 walkout from St. George's: St. Thomas African Episcopal Church, incorporated by Absalom Jones, and Bethel A. M. E. Church, incorporated in 1796 by Richard Allen.[41]

Whether they were religious, like Bethel, or political, like the Colored National Conventions, associations gave Black people a way to exercise civil rights of property and contract, to define the privileges of membership in those collectivities, and to govern themselves. The South's mixed-race, white-run churches had long depended partly on offerings from slaves and free Blacks. Now Black people started diverting those offerings to Black churches. In the 1840s and 1850s, Black Baptists in the Upper South went on a building boom, financed by flocks of new members, who came up with creative new ways of fundraising, such as "public concerts" by church choirs. The choirs, along with church auxiliaries like Sunday schools and "missionary societies for the poor," gave beleaguered people a way of massing the "small sums" earned from slaves' "patches and pigs & poultry" into something bigger.[42] After all, a white-owned corporation and a Black-owned corporation held equal rights under the law, even as their members did not.

But independence only shifted the problem of members' rights; it did not solve it. The more that Black-run associations defined their mission in terms of a struggle for freedom, racial justice, and equality, the more glaring became the antidemocratic features that shielded injustice within them. Relentless white racism prodded Black associations to argue that inequality was wrong only when it came to race, not when it came to sex or class or age.

The problem lurked in the very roots of Black associations, their reason for existing. Early Black independent churches often began by walking away from white-run biracial churches' racist practices, and the Colored Conventions framed their agenda around the "privileges" of membership in the broader society. The leaders of Black churches and conventions attacked racial exclusion in the place where it cut deepest: in the vast, quasi-public world of "church privileges and . . . steam boats," railroads, and colleges—roughly the same world that modern civil rights law targets today. They argued that, under their state-granted corporate charters, these places of public accommodation owed a duty to serve the *whole* public, not just white people. Frederick Douglass repeatedly invoked the common-law doctrine of comportment, arguing that he had a "right" to eat dinner with whites at the same hotel table, so long as he "deported" himself "as a gentleman."[43]

Yet Black churches and the Colored Convention movement applied a different logic to govern their own affairs. Black churches barred women from most leadership positions and from voting on church decisions. Likewise, voting membership in the Colored Conventions was not open to all colored people. It was a "privilege" that cost fifty cents a year. Moreover, the Conventions argued for years over how to choose the voting delegates who, supposedly, represented the many different Black communities that made up "our people," and over how to guard the rights of Convention members against its leaders. In 1834, delegates representing Philadelphia accused New York's delegates of "packing the convention" against them—manipulating the membership rolls to outvote them. The very same organizations that fought for "all the Rights and Immunities of Citizenship" under state and federal law struggled constantly with the rights of members under the organizations' own laws.[44] These internal tensions over membership and its privileges—tensions over whether membership in Black churches and racial justice organizations conferred "privileges," subject to control by leaders, or something more like "rights," which a court might enforce—would deeply shape Black legal thought over the next 150 years.

One vivid example of this tension appeared at Friendship, a little Eastern Shore log church where a free Black landowner named Perry Hinson "held undisputed sway as self-appointed pastor in charge" because the church stood on his own land, with no oversight—no board of trustees or stewards or quarterly conference. When others aspired to preach as he had done, he would lock everyone out and demand, "Who is the head of this church?" Surrounded as they were by watchful white slaveowners, it is easy to imagine the calculation that enslaved worshipers made in their heads as they talked ambitious young people down from the pulpit: "humor 'Unc.' Perry" so that we can keep going to church. It was, after all, the only Black-run church for miles around. Black churches would confront this problem again and again in the decades to come: when the church property legally belonged to its founders, they sometimes acted as if they owned the church itself.[45]

Some of the Black churches founded before the Civil War avoided the Uncle Perry problem by incorporating. But that created a different problem. Precisely because it put control into the hands of laypeople, incorporation promoted the very kinds of dissent that had evolved into the mass walkouts from the white-run biracial churches in the first place. Within a few years of winning its freedom from the white church, Philadelphia's Bethel A. M. E. broke in two, touching off a fresh volley of lawsuits between now-rival Black churches. Boston's African Baptist Church in the 1820s was riven by "dissension so serious that members ostracized one another, nailed pew doors shut, and took one another to court."[46]

These church fights had a sharp gender dimension because church rules withheld so many privileges from women. Black ministers repeatedly steamrollered church majorities led by Black women. In 1848, for example, Rev. Daniel Payne persuaded the members of Baltimore's Bethel A.M.E. to make a huge donation to another local church. He boasted later that only five of the trustees objected, but the opposition was probably much more than five because Bethel didn't let women members vote. Payne's power to bend church rules to his will—to use his status in the church corporation to drown out members' common-law property rights—was so frustrating to many members that they lost faith in the church's ability to govern itself, and took the law into their own hands. In the middle of the Thursday night church trial where Payne was about have his opponents kicked out for good, two women went up to the altar with a bag of nails and clubbed Payne down. Then they hit one of the male secretaries and left him bleeding on the floor.[47]

Throughout the 1800s, prodded by women who refused to be quiet, African Americans repeatedly debated "the woman question": what women could be and do in their churches, activist societies, and fraternal orders.[48] For hundreds of thousands of Black churchgoers, that debate over Black churches' sexist governance starkly highlighted the difference between rights and privileges.

At the beginning of the Civil War, there were just under half a million free Black people living in this country, whom the states and federal government treated as second-class citizens, their rights subject to the whims of each state's white voters. When the war ended and the slaves were freed, there were nine times as many free Black people, and their rights and citizenship were uncertain. Black activist organizations around the country banded together in the winter of 1866 to send a delegation to Washington, DC, headed by Frederick Douglass, to lobby for "full rights" and "equality before the law" for "the colored people of the United States."[49] Later that year, Congress passed this country's first national law of citizenship, the Civil Rights Act of 1866. It was the first time Congress had ever spelled out who was a citizen and what citizenship entailed. It laid the foundation of modern civil rights law.

The Act guaranteed racial equality in "civil rights" to all citizens. U.S. citizens "of every race and color" would "have the same right, in every

State and Territory . . . to make and enforce contracts, to sue, be parties, and give evidence, to inherit, purchase, lease, sell, hold, and convey real and personal property," and to have the same benefits and penalties under state law that "white citizens" had. This one provision emphatically renounced the *Dred Scott* doctrine—which had deemed all Black people "so far inferior, that they had no rights which the white man was bound to respect"—along with the countless anti-Black laws on the books from Oregon to Virginia. On April 9, 1866, the moment the Civil Rights Act went into effect over President Andrew Johnson's veto, Black people all over the country rejoiced. In Hampton, Virginia, they held a torchlight parade. In Cleveland, a Black minister told his listeners to take home a copy of the Act and tell their friends and neighbors what it said. At Mount Olivet Baptist Church in Chicago, speakers called the Act "a new *magna carta* to all persons dwelling beneath the folds of the fire-cleansed and blood baptized flag of our country."[50]

Did this mean Black people could now vote? Marry white people? What did Congress mean by "civil rights"? For an answer, the Act's advocates in Congress pointed to the source of their authority to pass the Act: section two of the Thirteenth Amendment, ratified four months earlier, which had made slavery unconstitutional. The real intent of the Thirteenth Amendment "was to make him the opposite of a slave, to make him a freeman," they said. Not surprisingly for a bunch of privileged white men who had never had much contact with actual slaves, the congressmen's notion of slavery was highly idealized and it centered on the absence of civil rights. A slave was a person who "had no rights," said Senator Jacob Howard, of Michigan: no "right to become a husband or father in the eyes of the law," no right to own property, no right to "the bread he earned and ate . . . he was nothing but a chattel, subject to the will of his owner." In short, civil rights were the rights that slaves had been denied. So the Civil Rights Act, argued its sponsors, would do more than just end unpaid "personal service" to a master. It would "establish Equality before the law" with respect to "the ordinary rights of a freeman": "the privilege to go and come when they please, to buy and sell when they please, to make contracts and enforce contracts."[51] Nine years earlier, Chief Justice Taney had ruled that Black people's lack of rights proved that Dred and Harriet Scott were not citizens. Now, "civil rights" would be the definitive, everyday proof that they *were* citizens.

Ironically, in redefining "civil rights" as the rights that marked someone as not a slave, the Civil Rights Act of 1866 crowned a long-term shift in law and political discourse that made it unthinkable that slaves could ever have owned property or made contracts. And yet slaves across the South had done just that. These practices were so widely recognized that, as we saw earlier, the U.S. government itself would later pay ex-slaves compensation for the things its armies "foraged" from them during the war, retrospectively deciding that it had been property all along and thus silently refuting the Act's presumption that only free people can own property.[52]

After two hundred years of furtive struggle over whether it was legal or wise, millions of southern whites had gotten used to buying and selling goods and services with slaves and free Black people. The only difficulty had been whether slaves had *rights* to do those things, and even there the courts and legislatures had never consistently said no. Of all the changes that emancipation brought, Black civil rights may have been the least radical one of all. During Reconstruction, even as whites fought to deny Black people the right to vote, to hold office, to sit beside them in a theater or train, and more, almost nobody denied that Black people had contract and property rights. Indeed, white people's own rights increasingly depended on it.

PART II

RECONSTRUCTION

3

Does Color Still Matter?

Dedicating the national cemetery at Gettysburg in November 1863, President Lincoln expressed hope that the Civil War would give America "a new birth of freedom." But in July 1865, when reporter P. Houston Murray ventured south for a leading Black newspaper, the war was over, Lincoln had been murdered, and the war's end seemed to be igniting a reign of lawless terror. What good is "the right to sue, testify, and plead in courts, if rebels . . . make and administer the law?" lamented Murray. What good is "the right to own, buy, and sell property, if virulent prejudice bars us from all the avenues of industry?" The message was clear: "Colored men cannot have justice in Mississippi," he warned. *"Slavery is not dead."* Generations of scholars have echoed Murray's anguished lament: they have started from the proposition that southern whites "could not 'conceive of the negro having any rights at all.' " The era known as Reconstruction, the twenty or so years when freedpeople and a Republican Congress set southern state governments on a remarkably progressive path away from the lawlessness of 1865, ended in a white counterrevolution. Beginning in the 1870s and accelerating through the 1880s and 1890s, white businessmen, politicians, and landowners joined forces to wreck this great experiment in multiracial democracy, locking the schoolhouse gate and the voting box, and making law an alien, hostile force in Black life for generations, until racial justice activists arrived in the 1940s, '50s, and '60s. As W. E.

B. Du Bois wrote, looking back from 1935, "the slave went free; stood a brief moment in the sun; then moved back toward slavery."[1]

Yet in 1889, in downtown Charlottesville, near where a bronze statue of Robert E. Lee would in 2017 attract a horde of khaki-clad white supremacists, a very different scene unfolded. A Black man named Robert Scott sat in the law office of one of Robert E. Lee's ex-soldiers, "Colonel" R. T. W. Duke, to discuss a real estate lawsuit his niece had brought against him. Houston Murray wasn't wrong to wonder what "rebels" would do to Black rights. But looking closer, it is clear that even as "rebel" court officials and lawyers like the "Colonel" used state power to humiliate and oppress Black people, they also helped former slaves turn the privileges of slavery into rights. They did not do it because they believed in Black equality, or because the federal government made them do it. They did it because they took it for granted that ex-slaves had the right to own a house or hire a lawyer like the "Colonel." This consensus about "civil rights" emerged among white southerners very quickly after the Civil War because everybody knew that before the war slaves had had property and made bargains. At the same time, Black people now seized hold of the possibilities of law, going to court in greater and greater numbers, forming opinions about the legal process and about the lawyers they hired, and airing those opinions in public and private. Black civil rights may have been born in the halls of Congress, but they came of age on roads and front porches and court squares all across the country.

What did it mean, in a legal sense, to say that "slavery is not dead"? Slavery was not a stand-alone set of laws that one could simply pluck off the bookshelves. It was tightly woven into many different areas of American law. Slavery was property law. It was contract law. It was wills and estates, commercial law, insurance law. It was hopelessly tangled up with all of these and more. Even today, slavery cases are being cited as "good law"—valid precedents—in a huge variety of different legal fields.

If abolishing slavery means rooting slavery cases out of the law books, then the only way truly to abolish slavery would have been to rewrite the laws of nearly every state of the Union. Congress would have had to tear down and rebuild "the entire domain of civil rights," as Justice Samuel Miller put it in *The Slaughter-House Cases* of 1873, the very first major opinion on the Reconstruction Amendments. Instead, Congress took a shortcut: it made Black people citizens and then wrote the principle of equality into national law as a set of constraints on how states could treat their citizens. The Civil Rights Act of 1866 was explicitly racial: it guaranteed to all citizens the fundamental rights that white citizens had. Republicans in Congress assumed that, once the legal disabilities of slavery were gone, the legal implications of Black freedom would get worked out in and around places like Albemarle County Courthouse, where Robert Scott plotted with his lawyer against his niece.[2] During Reconstruction, the problem of civil rights had as much to do with *what rights were* as with who could exercise them.

Already by 1873, when Justice Miller's *Slaughter-House* opinion wrote his states-rights beliefs into the Constitution, drastically weakening the newly passed Thirteenth and Fourteenth Amendments' liberatory potential, Black people were actively participating in the South's county and state courts, amplifying and extending a pattern set during slavery. In my sample of trial courts in Virginia and Mississippi, Black people filed 12 percent of the civil suits in 1872 (when they made up 56 percent of the population in those select counties), and 15 percent of them in 1882. It was Black people's everyday use of the ordinary tools of contract and property law that largely determined what it meant that slavery had ended and what was inside the "domain of civil rights."[3] Black civil rights were forged *within* southern law, not against it.

This story has been veiled precisely because almost none of those 805 cases identified anybody's race. That poses a practical problem. How can you tell what Black people did in local courts if you can't tell who was Black? But in 1872 it was also a big change in the everyday operation of law. Before the Civil War, court records in the South had routinely (though haphazardly) identified people as "negro" or "slave." They had done so because those words were legal statuses, with specific legal implications. After the war, court officials essentially stopped marking their records by race in any systematic way.[4] You can read a hundred pages of testimony or a thousand pages of a docket—or open up a law school casebook, for that matter—and not know that some of the people named in them were Black. You would not know, in other words, that Black people's lawsuits helped make American law.

The four decades after emancipation were the formative era of modern contract law, and in this formative era, leading law professors, judges, and legal commentators cited Black people's cases as precedents across a wide range of areas: the doctrine of fraud, accord and satisfaction, the parol evidence rule, the meaning of the word "deed," duress, mistake, breach, insurance, implied contracts, delivery of gifts, landlord and tenant, inadequacy of consideration, failure of consideration, the statute of frauds, and more. Black people's cases appeared even more frequently as secondary, indirect citations; lawyers and judges borrowed rules and theories from these cases to apply in cases involving only white people and corporations. They almost never mentioned that Black people were parties to these suits, silently "passing" them into legal doctrine. In doing so, they stripped away facts that were not only vital to the parties, but also were "material"—that is, made a difference to the outcome of the case. Stripping out racial facts influenced the legal doctrines these cases established, enabling some doctrines to sweep wider than they otherwise would have, hemming others in, and shaping how lawyers and judges understood them.[5]

Legal professionals were perfectly free to do this. The new federal laws—the Civil Rights Act of 1866, the Fourteenth Amendment's Equal Protection Clause, the Ku Klux Klan Act of 1871—seemed to say that no state could create separate bodies of contract law for people of different races, but Congress never said that judges had to *ignore* race. Ever since, legal professionals have been making up their own minds, case by case, about when race matters in contracts. In the late 1800s, during the same years when public law increasingly segregated people by race, the decisions lawyers, judges, and law professors made about race marking in private law helped consolidate "Contracts" as a distinct, coherent body of law.

The starting presumption was that in contract law race had no legal meaning of its own. To borrow a term from chemistry, we might call race a "doctrinal catalyst of opportunity." Like the trace of platinum in a car's catalytic converter scrubbing out poisonous exhaust particles, race became material only when bound to a particular rule or category, catalyzing arguments that legal professionals wanted to advance. Treating race as a doctrinal catalyst of opportunity discouraged lawyers and judges from considering it as a matter of structural inequality and instead tempted them to invoke race opportunistically, depending on which position seemed likelier to help them win the case. For example, in the *Slaughter-House Cases,* Justice Miller insisted that the Civil War was fought over "African slavery" and that "the one pervading purpose" of the three Reconstruction amendments—the Thirteenth, Fourteenth, and Fifteenth amendments—was "the freedom of the slave race, the security . . . of that freedom, and the protection of the newly-made" free citizens from their former masters. By contrast, the lawyers for the ex-Confederate butchers who had filed the suit—they were challenging a new Louisiana law that, to protect the public health, consolidated all of New Orleans' livestock slaughtering at one place—talked about everything *except* race. Rehearsing well-worn themes of white grievance politics, they gave the justices a potted history of oppressed white people, from ancient Romans to medieval French peasants. The point was to show that the slaughterhouse regulation imposed a kind of slavery on small businessmen.[6]

Hundreds of facts get presented in the course of any case, and judges and lawyers are constantly deciding which of those are "material facts"—facts that would make a difference to the outcome of the case and that a judge can therefore weigh in her decision. The *Slaughter-House Cases* showed that lawyers and judges could widen or narrow the scope of a constitutional provision by manipulating the materiality of race. Smart lawyers figured out that they could do the same thing in private law too. Consider the 1916 case *Southern Express Co. v. Byers*, where the United States Supreme Court barred contract damages for mental anguish as a matter of federal law. John Byers, a Black North Carolinian, sued the Southern Express railroad for failing to deliver "a silver gray casket, robe, gloves, [and] hose" in time to bury his wife, who had died suddenly while "visiting her mother" in South Carolina. The question was what his damages should be under his contract with the railroad. Southern Express argued that all it owed him was either the cost of the casket or $50, the maximum spelled out in the fine print of the bill of lading he had signed. The jury disagreed and awarded Byers another $200 for "mental anguish." A divided North Carolina supreme court upheld that verdict, relying on another recent case that also happened to feature a Black plaintiff. At the time, courts all over the country were wrestling with similar questions, and many of these mental anguish cases explicitly stood on racial facts.[7]

Did it matter to the Buncombe County jury or to the North Carolina supreme court that this case was about the wounded feelings of a Black man? Was it a "material fact"? Byers's lawyer must have thought so because he made sure to get it into the record. The first sentence of Byers's testimony read: "That he was about 50 years of age; that he was not a slavery darkey, but was born right after the war." The rest of the testimony—and the legal question at issue—was about Byers's anguish. His lawyer aimed to show that he "suffered in mind and body" when he "got down there and found that the casket was not . . . there." "I was hardly able to attend to anything on account of the loss of my wife," Byers testified, "I was kinder broke down."[8]

Writing for the U.S. Supreme Court, Justice James McReynolds had to decide how much a Black man's feelings were worth. McReynolds was one of the most virulently racist people ever to sit on the Court. He frequently used racist language in other contexts. Yet in *Byers*, he did not say a single word about race. He wiped race from this contract case for the same reason he declared race immaterial in criminal and voting rights cases, and for the same reason that Byers and his lawyers tried to put race into the record: because it suited his doctrinal goals. By dismissing John Byers's anguish without mentioning his race, McReynolds was able to lay down a broad principle: that "mental suffering" was "too vague for legal redress" through contract damages when it was not connected to any "injury" "to person, property, health, or reputation." If he had talked about Byers's race, it would have limited his holding to cases with similar facts—to *Black* shippers rather than shippers in general, much the way Justice Miller had narrowed the scope of the Thirteenth Amendment to "African slavery," rejecting the white butchers' complaints of regulatory "slavery."[9] Ignoring Byers's race enabled McReynolds' pro-business holding in *Byers* to frustrate not just Black plaintiffs but any plaintiff seeking contract damages for mental anguish. Justice Miller highlighted race and Justice McReynolds suppressed it, but each Justice's choice illustrates how opportunistically race has been treated in law.

P. Houston Murray warned that "Colored men cannot have justice," yet the trial dockets, deed books, lawyers' papers, and newspapers show that "colored" men and women were using law more than ever before. It seems like a contradiction until we remember how nineteenth-century white Americans thought about rights. By the 1860s, Americans tended to imagine rights as existing in three different categories, each fuzzy around the edges but strongly felt: civil rights (granted by government to secure the natural rights of life, liberty, and the pursuit of happiness), political rights (voting and other privileges of making decisions for the public good), and social rights (friendship, neighborliness, and other personal relationships, which government had no business poking into).[10] For things that fell in the category of "social rights," color still mattered, and the legal documents relating to those still required people to specify race. For example, to enforce longstanding bans on interracial sex and interracial marriage, many states told county clerks and ministers to start marking race on people's marriage certificates,

Marriage License

Virginia County of Cumberland **to-wit:**

To Any Person Licensed to Celebrate Marriages:

You are hereby authorized to join together in the Holy State of Matrimony, according to the rites and ceremonies of your Church or religious denomination, and the laws of the Commonwealth of Virginia,

Eugene Smith Jackson Reaves and Ethel E. Jones

Given under my hand, as Clerk of Circuit *Court of* Cumberland *County (or City) this* 19 *day of* Dec., 1925 Lewis Crawley, *Clerk.*

Marriage Certificate

To be annexed to the License, required by Section 5074 of the Code of Virginia, 1919, as amended by Act of February 14, 1920.

VIRGINIA: In the Clerk's Office of the Circuit *Court for the County (or City) of* Cumberland

Date of Marriage Dec. 30 1925 *Place of Marriage* Cumberland, Co.

(FULL NAMES OF PARTIES)

Eugene Smith Jackson Reaves *and* Ethel Elizabeth Jones

Age of Husband 23 years; Condition (single, widowed or divorced) single

Age of Wife 21 years; Condition (single, widowed or divorced) "

Race (White or Colored) Col.

Husband's Place of Birth Cumberland, Co Mailing Address (PRESENT) Farmville, Va.

Wife's Place of Birth Cumberland, Co. Mailing Address Guinea mills, Va.

Names of Parents: Husband Willie Reaves and Mary Reaves

Wife Eddie Jones and Eliza Jones

Occupation of Husband Farmer

Given under my hand this 19th day of December, 1925.

Lewis Crawley, Clerk.

Certificate of Time and Place of Marriage

I, Rev John Miles, a Minister of the Baptist Church, or religious order of that name, do certify that on the 20 day of Dec, 1925, at [illegible], Virginia, under authority of the above License, I joined together in the Holy State of Matrimony the persons named and described therein. I qualified and gave bond according to law authorizing me to celebrate the rites of marriage in the County (or City) of [illegible], State of Virginia.

Given under my hand this 20 day of Dec, 1924.

Rev John Miles

(Person who performs ceremony sign here.)

The Minister or other person celebrating a marriage is required, within thirty (30) days thereafter, to return the License and Certificate of the Clerk and his certificate of the time and place at which the marriage was celebrated to the Clerk who issued the License; failure to comply with these requirements of the law makes the Minister or other person celebrating the marriage liable to a fine of not less than ten nor more than twenty dollars for each offense (see Section 5074 of the Code of Virginia, as amended by Act approved February 14, 1920, Acts 1920, chapter 28, pages 36 and 37).

State of Virginia,

County of Cumberland, to-wit:

I, Imogene W. Tunstall, Clerk of the Circuit Court of the County of Cumberland, the same being a Court of record having a seal, do hereby certify that the foregoing is a true copy of the marriage record of Eugene Smith Jackson Reaves and Ethel E. Jones, which is of record in my said office in Marriage Register No. 2 page 14

In testimony whereof, I have hereto set my hand and annexed the seal of the said Court, this 28 day of January, 1972.

Imogene W. Tunstall, Clerk,

By: Betty R. Halter, Deputy, Clerk

Marriage License of Eugene Smith Jackson Reaves and Ethel Elizabeth Jones, 1925, Cumberland Co., Va., copy in possession of their son, the late Osborne Reaves, LTC (ret.), Newport News, Va. Notice that there is only one blank for "color." Since it was illegal to marry someone of a different race, there was no legal reason to print a blank for each spouse.

and told county registrars, judges, and lawyers to mark it on divorce decrees and filings. If state bureaucrats like Walter Plecker, founding registrar of Virginia's State Bureau of Vital Statistics, were the managers of the "legal factory" that produced and reproduced racial categories like "white" and "colored," then the county courthouse was the factory floor.[11] And in the process, these bureaucratic practices were also sharpening the overarching categories that organized the law, slotting marriage (which was literally a contract, a civil right) into the category of "social rights," where states were free to discriminate by race.

The persistence of this three-part vision of rights helps explain, for example, why there are "white" and "colored" marriage registers but not deed books, probate books, civil and criminal dockets, or corporate registries. Anti-"miscegenation" laws made race legally relevant for the marriage registers, but for the others race didn't generate legally meaningful categories anymore.[12] Zoning and restrictive covenants made no sense in the countryside, where most Black people lived. In corporation law, the big distinction was between "domestic" and "foreign" (out-of-state) corporations, not "colored" and "white" ones. Race was not even mentioned in the chapters of the Mississippi Code—that state's compiled statutes—on wills and testaments, land, conveyances, or even landlord and tenant. In Cumberland County, Virginia, Jackson Holcomb appeared in the "colored" section of the voter roll. Yet between 1883 and 1918, he and his relatives mortgaged, sold, or bought land twelve times, and only three of those deeds mentioned the word "colored."[13] In many courthouses today, a wall full of nonsegregated deed books and corporation registers is one shelf away from stacks of "white" and "colored" marriage registers.

Because the materiality of race was slippery, lawyers and their clients had to think carefully about how it might get used. In some cases involving Blacks, no one brought it up on the record. In others, the lawyers argued about whether it was proper to put race in. And in still others, racial facts got in via a direct question (as in Byers), or by stipulation. Lawyers strategically disclosed race in the trial record, knowing that chancellors and appeals court judges could not see or hear the people testifying, and would have to rely on a transcript of the trial. The cues could be obvious: "Were you ever a slave?" Or they could be subtle, as when one lawyer addressed a witness as "Uncle Albert" instead of "Mr. Southall," or when another lawyer slyly wrapped his client's petition in a page torn from the "Colored" section of the city's poll tax list. Sometimes lawyers had to bend over backwards to get racial facts into the trial record. "You all are a colored family are you not?" queried one lawyer. "That is what they tell me," the witness retorted sarcastically. "Of course I am colored."[14] The point is not that these people were racially ambiguous (a topic that has attracted a great deal of scholarly attention over the years); it is that lawyers were deploying race tactically to enlighten judges who were not in the room to see it for themselves.

The almost-but-not-quite end of race marking in local legal records reflected a far-reaching realignment of the connections between race and rights. This realignment has hidden huge swaths of the story of Black civil rights. Proslavery ideologues like Taney had used civil and political rights to try and make Blackness synonymous with slavery, arguing that Black people's lack of rights at the Founding proved that "the slave races" could never be citizens.[15] Now, beginning with the Civil Rights Act of 1866, federal law had broken that connection between slavery and race, and, moreover, had explicitly barred states from attaching any legal significance to race in the category of civil rights. And it was civil rights that local courts overwhelmingly dealt with. The fact that race no longer explicitly defined people's civil rights didn't mean that African Americans would get justice, but it did mean that those who wished to use race as a legal weapon in matters of property and contract might have to explain why race mattered, one case at a time.

Thus, it was Black people's interactions with local officials, not Congress or the Supreme Court, that determined whether slavery really was dead and defined what "civil rights" would become. Low-level officeholders "dealt with 'the practical rights of the people,'" said an Alabama white lawyer—that is, their "business and lives." From coroner, police chief, and policeman to board of supervisors, levee board, and county clerk, these low-level offices not only controlled the levers of local policing but were also the hub of the county's administration and record-keeping, and its public face—the only government officials most people would ever deal with. And white officeholders seemed to recognize that in a world where everyone was free, Black people were entitled to the rights of everyday use.[16]

State and county officials seem to have worked out a set of understandings about when race mattered to the apartheid state they were building. For example, just as Justice McReynolds wrote *Byers* without mentioning that Byers was Black, state politicians wrote the legal framework for convict-leasing, one of the most brutal systems of race exploitation in human history, without using the words "colored" or "Negro" even once. But they could not write their ban on interracial marriage without those words. The logic glints as clearly from law dictionaries as it does from Eugene and Ethel Reaves's marriage license. For decades, "color" had meant one of two things to lawyers: it was either a technicality of the pleading process or an aspect of "personal relations" that proved someone was a slave. In 1883, the editors of the country's leading law dictionary dropped the second meaning. By 1897, there was a new entry for "colored man." This meant "one of the negro race," and "there is no legal technical signification to this phrase which the courts are bound judicially to know." That was a big assertion. "Judicial notice" is a special version of the "notice" concept that underpins property. It means that "facts of universal notoriety" don't have to be proved in court. In 1905, you did not need to prove that whiskey will get a person drunk, that the third of August 1890 was a Sunday, that an average man was less than six feet tall, that vaccination prevents smallpox at negligible risk, or that the United States fought a civil war from 1861 to 1865. But if you wanted to argue that your client's rights were infringed because she was Black, then you first had to prove that she was Black. Here, in America's best legal dictionary, we can see the spirit of the age: a formalist fantasy of law as a quiet, velvet-curtained chamber where wise judges could work without being distracted by extraneous concerns from the outside world. This is what Justice John Marshall Harlan meant when he wrote, in a less famous part of his dissent in *Plessy,* the separate-but-equal case (discussed later, in Chapter 7), that the Constitution did not "permit any public authority to know the race of" people claiming civil rights.[17]

During his lifetime, Harlan was nicknamed "The Great Dissenter," and today he is rightly famous for his dissenting opinions in *Plessy, The Civil Rights Cases,* and other cases involving discrimination against the poor and racial minorities. But when he wrote that "our Constitution is color-blind," he did not mean that *he* was color-blind, much less that there was no such thing as race. He meant that the Constitution required government to treat citizens equally "in respect of civil rights." Harlan's disagreement with the *Plessy* majority was that he thought the right not to be excluded from a train was a civil right and they thought it was a social right. Homer Plessy had a ticket—a contract with the East Louisiana Railway. Harlan believed that Louisiana's segregation law treated Plessy the way Taney had treated Dred Scott: like a slave who had no civil rights. But when presented with a law that discriminated with respect to "social rights"—one that punished adultery more harshly when it was interracial—Harlan voted to uphold the law.[18] The reason Jackson Holcomb was able to buy land in 1883, the reason the courthouse deed books and court dockets feature so many names that turn out to belong to Black people—indeed, the reason those names weren't marked as "colored" in the first place—is that white lawyers, judges, and county clerks imagined race and rights much the same way Harlan did: race inevitably factored into "social" rights but not "civil" rights.

Cases like *Plessy* are landmarks in the history of legal thought and legal theory, but until recently, books about the history of legal thought tended to assume that the thinking and theorizing was done by white people like Justice Harlan and lawyer Albion Tourgée, while Black people like Homer

Plessy supplied the facts—taking action, resisting oppression, giving testimony of the wrongs committed against them.[19] It wasn't until the 1990s, for example, that law professors began taking seriously the Plessy team's innovative ideas about "property in whiteness" and "public rights," and the former slaves and former free Black activists who helped invent those ideas.[20] Yet, the things Black people said and wrote about law in newspapers, church pulpits, and other Black-run institutions amount to a history of Black legal *thought,* one that flourished alongside and wove itself into the more familiar legal intellectual history penned by and about whites.

Before the war, most Black people had learned about law from watching white people. After the Civil War, Black people were more and more likely to learn law through direct experience and through Black-controlled institutions, especially newspapers, churches, and fraternal associations, or through the grassroots networks of farmers, schoolteachers, barbers, shopkeepers, and ministers who helped working-class Black women fill out federal pension applications.[21] These Black-run networks and institutions taught thousands, if not millions, of African Americans about what "rights" meant—or could mean—for their lives as free people. They had no systematic program of legal education. Instead, they did it through myriad small lessons embedded in their preaching, reporting, and editorials.

In fact, they had been doing it for at least forty years already. Black newspapers had always had a lot to say about law, and most of what they said concerned the rights of everyday use: personal-injury suits (such as "an aged colored woman [who] was run over by a street car"), slander suits (such as a Black lawyer's suit against a Philadelphia Black minister), and the legal successes and wranglings of Black religious associations—that is, churches. When Black newspapers did cover discrimination suits, they often emphasized the damage awards that Black plaintiffs were winning, suggesting that Black people thought racial discrimination was not just a matter of collective dignity but also a tangible injury, like a streetcar accident or a slanderous sermon.[22] They were full of practical legal advice, too. The *Christian Recorder,* based in Philadelphia, published a "table" of "simple rules of law" for farmers to "cut out" and hang on the wall:

> Signatures made with a lead pencil are good in law . . .
> The act[s] of one partner bind all the others . . .
> Principals are bound by the acts of their agents. Agents are responsible to their employers . . .
> Contracts or notes made on Sunday are void . . .
> Notes bear interest only when so stated. It is not necessary to put into a note the words "for value received."
> All contracts and agreements should be made in writing and in proper form, that is . . . to express the intention of the parties, and nothing more.

The point, of course, was the same one the future Supreme Court Justice Oliver Wendell Holmes would make in his famous 1897 speech at Boston University Law School, a speech widely treated as a landmark in the history of legal theory. The point was that law is everywhere in daily life, and the wisest people try to stay out of court by knowing something about law.[23]

Black newspapers eagerly encouraged this allergy to lawsuits, just as their white counterparts did. Editors loved to publish horror stories about foolish men who "died in poverty" after blowing a fortune on lawsuits over "an old saddle" or a twenty-five-cent butcher bill. Indeed, *Freedom's Journal,* America's first Black newspaper, had published these kinds of stories back in the 1820s. Alongside serious news about elections and the sacred cause of abolition, it ran corny lawyer jokes, a yarn about a French donkey put on trial for sacrilege, and a £1,000 lawsuit over a turtle.[24]

Black newspapers also held strong opinions about when a Black person *should* contemplate going to court. Beginning with the first issue of *Freedom's Journal* in 1827, editors cast Black citizenship as a moral issue, yearning for the day when "the law [would be] based upon right."[25] That message about the difference between formal "law" and moral "right" cut two ways. On the one hand, it said that "Justice is a perfect farce" in cases between whites and Blacks, that the entire justice system was designed to "hurl [Black people] off to the chain gang." On the other hand, the editors' moral critique of the justice system came with a pragmatic corollary: that a Black person could get a fair hearing if he had some "prominent white man" on his side, or if he brought the right kind of suit, or if his opponent was Black, or if the judge was friendly and local opinion not too hostile. The same informality and personalism that unleashed harsh justice *on* Black people, Black newspapers implied, could work *for* Black people.[26]

In other words, nineteenth-century Black newspapers invited readers to use their civil rights. They warned readers of two very different risks in exercising those rights: one risk was the bias they would face if they tangled with a white person, and the other was simply the expense and fearsome technical rules that everyone associated with courts and lawyers. Law's complexity could empower as well as harm, Black newspapers told their readers. The key was to be able to guess—to prophecy, as Judge Holmes would later put it—how others might react to your legal claim.[27] And in order to prophecy, you had to know something about law.

Churches and newspapers taught freedpeople what rights could be, but it was lawyers who shaped what rights *were*, through their choices about which clients to represent and which kinds of legal matters they handled. Once I identified who the Black litigants were on the docket books in Virginia and Mississippi, I realized that almost every single one of their lawyers was white. White lawyers had been the architects of slavery and they had just spearheaded a civil war to preserve slavery. What good would rights do for Blacks now if "rebels . . . make and administer the law?" Houston Murray had wondered in the violent summer of 1865. It is difficult to peer so far back into the past to see how Black clients and white lawyers dealt with and thought about one another, because lawyers usually do not leave their papers behind. But some did. And these rare collections of lawyer papers give us a glimpse of Black rights being made on the ground, so to speak.

The Charlottesville law firm Duke & Duke was founded by former slaveowner and ex-Confederate lieutenant colonel R. T. W. Duke (1822–1898). After the Union army captured Richmond on April 3, 1865, and just before the main Confederate army surrendered at Appomattox Courthouse, Duke retreated westward with his battalion and he was captured just a few miles from where Jackson Holcomb was running his boat. A few years later, Duke went to Congress as a conservative Democrat, notably opposing the Fourteenth Amendment and promoting the myth of the "Lost Cause," the myth that the South had not fought to protect slavery but rather to protect freedom and states' rights against northern aggression, and that slavery itself had been a gentle school for civilizing "the African." For the rest of his life, people in Charlottesville called him "Colonel." His son, R. T. W. Junior (Tom, or "Judge," 1853–1926), helped found a Sons of Confederate Veterans chapter and got it named after the "Colonel." Grandson Eskridge (1893–1959) carried the firm through the 1950s. Through the years, Duke & Duke was a small partnership with a typically diverse practice—mostly real estate, debt collection, and probate work at the beginning, later adding property management, loans and bonds, and insurance.[28] Nothing in these men's past hints that they were especially friendly to Black people or that they ever doubted the rightness of white supremacy.

Tom Duke's first case, just after passing the bar in 1874, was "to defend a negro accused of breaking in a corn house." He threw himself into the case, he wrote later in his self-published memoirs; he was "intensely interested" in it. "Made a speech which was much complimented & [the] darkey was acquitted." Why did Tom Duke work so hard on behalf of a Black client, much less brag about it in his memoirs? For one thing, it fit his rebel bona fides: his client's accuser was the disgraced Commissary-General of the Confederate Army, whose failure to fix the army's supply-chain logistics made him a scapegoat for the Lost Cause. Apparently Duke also felt there wasn't much "evidence against the negro." Or maybe it was just because he was fresh out of law school and eager to shine.[29] Whatever Tom's feelings about the case, this was just the first of many Black clients his family's firm would represent over the next eighty years. In a time and place where racial justice lawyering was unthinkable, white lawyers like Duke & Duke routinely took on Black clients for money, for reputation, and occasionally for intellectual challenge.

In 1872, just before Tom passed the bar, the firm (then called Duke & Jones) handled the estate of Jane West, a wealthy mixed-race woman who died in 1869, and a real estate transaction for Jane's adopted son John, who would eventually become one of the richest men in Charlottesville and a steady client of the Dukes. During a five-year period in the 1880s, the Duke firm handled legal matters for at least five more Black Charlottesvillians. These were mostly routine things—winding up an estate or buying a farm, with an occasional courtroom trial, including one that resulted in a woman recovering $1,000 from the C&O Railroad in what was probably a tort suit for the death of her husband. Tom Duke took at least one Black client's case to the Virginia supreme court: the case described at the start of this chapter, Robert Scott's inheritance dispute with his niece. If there was anything special about Duke & Duke, it was that they sometimes argued before the state supreme court, not that they had Black clients. Plenty of white southern lawyers did in those days.[30]

Indeed, some white lawyers during Reconstruction went out looking for Black clients. Richmond attorney William Beveridge handed out little advertising pamphlets that mixed legal advice with notes about his "liberal" terms on fees and late hours ("to give working people a chance to see me without" taking time off from work). Beveridge, who trained one of the first Black lawyers to practice in Richmond, may have been unusually open to the idea of Blacks as professional peers, but his willingness to take working-class people as *clients,* probably including Black people, was quite typical of white lawyers in the Reconstruction South. Consider Robert Harvey Thompson, a white lawyer in Brookhaven, Mississippi. Here are the cases that walked into his office during the week of January 1, 1871, his first week in practice: a white man who wanted to "bust" his father's will, a white woman seeking a divorce, two white men who wanted him to write a deed to convey a little piece of land, "an old negro man" who wanted to sue a white woman "to recover a pot" he had entrusted to her before the war for safekeeping, and a white man suing another white man for killing his ox.[31] Thompson remembered the "old negro man" precisely because he was just another client.

Nineteen years later, Thompson played a key role in nullifying Black voting rights.[32] He evidently did not see any contradiction between helping a Black man sue a white woman and taking away that man's right to vote. And that is because voting and suing were different kinds of rights. Men like Ellis Gray Loring (who argued on behalf of the Black plaintiffs in *Roberts v. City of Boston,* an important school segregation case from the Massachusetts supreme court) and Albion Tourgée (who would later argue on behalf of Homer Plessy) represented Black people because they believed in the cause of protecting Black rights against racially discriminatory laws, and they believed they could help vindicate those rights at the highest courts in the land. Today they would be called "cause lawyers." But most lawyers were not like Albion Tourgée and most cases were not like *Plessy.*

Although the rise of the cause lawyer was still a long way off, lawyering itself was starting to change in ways that would eventually open the doors to a wider range of claims by Black people. But those same changes slammed shut the doors of opportunity for Black lawyers.

Ever since Macon Bolling Allen was granted a Maine law license in 1844, there had been a tiny cadre of Black lawyers. After the war, their numbers grew. At the same time, a series of technical changes in many states' rules of fees and costs made it easier for poor and working-class plaintiffs to get into court. This opened up litigation possibilities to a huge number of potential clients: people who needed help collecting debts, dealing with land titles or inheritance and, increasingly, suing over accidents.[33] Partly in reaction to this tide of new working-class litigants, many of whom were Black, white lawyers began to organize and to think of themselves as professionals, with a shared identity that they forged partly through racial exclusion. They set up trade organizations called "bar associations" to promote their interests. They founded trade journals and published snide, racist little stories in them. Have you heard the one about the "negro justice of the peace" who weighed the evidence by seating the witnesses on an actual scale? Or the old "contraband" (a slur referring to freedpeople) who didn't know how to be sworn in as a witness? Elite white lawyers disdained workaday lawyers both for their low-class clientele and for how they served that clientele. The legal elite denounced contingency fees—where the client paid the lawyer out of the hoped-for settlement money rather than up front—because it attracted "sordid huckster[s]" who clogged the courts with "groundless and vexatious" suits lodged by silly people, "a whole variety cast show full of Dutch comedians, song-and-dance men, negro eccentricities and the like." Poking fun at the "justice shops" and the people they served was a way for the "new high priests" of the law to chalk out the boundaries of their fragile new profession and keep it for themselves.[34] It combined casual racism with guild elitism.

Of course, a lawyer could laugh at stories about Black clients and still take their money. Why else would the very first meeting of the all-white Alabama bar association in 1879 denounce "shysters" for hiring people to "rope" in "negro" clients? Why else would Black lawyers take out ads in Black newspapers warning against smooth-talking, "sharp practic[ing]" *white* lawyers?[35] The point was never to wall off Black people from hiring lawyers—it was to control the competition for their business.

Op-eds and court dockets can only reveal so much about Black people's dealings with lawyers. More revealing is what happened in the rare instances when a Black client sued a white lawyer, or vice versa. If read carefully, such cases can function as what legal anthropologists call a "case of trouble" within the lawyer-client relationship itself, bringing out things that usually went unsaid. One "trouble case" was *Pinn v. Fall,* where, in 1881, three members of a Black family from Warrenton,

Virginia—James, Julia, and Betsy Pinn—sued Frank Fall, a white Washington lawyer, for fraud. The year before, the Pinns' eighteen-year-old cousin Sandy had been convicted, along with two others, of murdering a white Washington grocery clerk, and sentenced to death. His lawyers sought clemency but seemed to be getting nowhere. Soon after the conviction, the Pinns said, Frank Fall showed up on their doorstep, claiming that their sister Alice had sent him on the fifty-mile trip from DC to save their nephew's life. All they had to do was mortgage their farm to pay him $500. They signed five $100 promissory notes and a deed of trust to secure those notes, and they were thrilled when, months later, President Rutherford Hayes commuted Sandy's sentence to life in prison. But they refused to pay Fall because, they felt, he hadn't really done anything in the case. In fact, they now knew that he *couldn't* have done anything because, by the time he showed up in Warrenton, it was an open secret in Washington that the president was going to commute Sandy's sentence.[36] So they asked the Fauquier County Circuit Court to cancel Fall's deed on their family home.

Had the Pinns made a binding contract with Fall, and had Fall upheld his end of the deal such that he could take their home by enforcing the deeds they had signed? Sandy's original lawyers, Charles Smith and Thomas F. Miller, gave testimony helpful to the Pinns, describing Fall as an upstart from "the poorest class of lawyers" in town, a young novice whom Smith had taken into his office almost as an act of charity, and who had turned around and schemed to steal his mentor's client. Fall's big idea—collecting signatures on a clemency petition to the president—had actually done more harm than good. According to Smith and Miller, it was their good lawyering and networking that saved Sandy's life. Fall "had nothing whatever to do with it."[37]

Frank Fall told a different story. In his telling, Sandy's mother, Alice Pinn, came to *him,* begging him to take her son's case, and wrote ahead to her relatives in Warrenton that he was coming to see them. To keep Sandy's case alive, Fall got up "a petition from many influential and tax paying citizens," and met twice with President Hayes on Sandy's behalf.

His colleagues could criticize his tactics all they wanted but the Pinns had hired him to represent Sandy and he had done his job. Fall had no doubt that he was the one who saved Sandy.[38]

Unfortunately for Fall, nobody else could vouch that he was at those meetings with the president. In the end, all he had, apart from his own memory, was some testimony from his "office boy." So perhaps it isn't surprising that the Pinns won.

What is surprising about this case is also deceptively simple: all of these white lawyers took it for granted that Black people had civil rights. Indeed, some of them had staked their careers on that assumption. Alice Pinn described Fall as a slick talker who "came to my house . . . one night" making big promises. "Mr Fall told me that he would do for me more for nothing than Mr Smith and Mr Miller [had] done for money," she testified. But Fall wasn't unique. Smith was normally a patent lawyer, so why did he take this criminal case? For that matter, why did he agree to "join up" with Fall if he thought Fall was "so incompetent as a lawyer"? Because he needed the money. Fall "offered . . . to advertise the business in the papers," Smith confessed, "pay all of the office rent, furnish an office and pay me a certain sum," all in return "for the use of my name." Whatever arrangement these two white lawyers had—whether it was merely an "association," as Smith called it, or a real partnership, as Fall insisted it was—they saw this Black family's case as a meal ticket, not a crusade.[39]

Details of the case also hint at how Black clients viewed law and the white lawyers who worked for them after the Civil War. What did the Pinns do while their lawyers squabbled? First, they followed cousin Sandy's trial avidly in the newspapers and asked around DC what their lawyers were up to. That is how they became convinced that Fall was a cheat. Out in Warrenton, James Pinn stayed in touch with the lawyer who had written up the deed that was supposed to cover Fall's fee. That lawyer's informal advice at a critical moment may have given them the confidence to sue Fall in the first place. Second, the Pinns acted on what they thought they knew, in ways that raised tensions between their lawyers but probably also helped save Sandy's life. Alice Pinn planted herself in lawyer Smith's office day after day, keeping tabs on the case and discreetly complaining about him to his "colored" "office boy," Edward Pinckney. As Miller and Smith dawdled along, recalled Pinckney, Alice Pinn would come to the office and "magnify Mr. Fall, and run the other gentlemen down, and set down and cry, and all that sort of thing, and I would Sympathize, and talk with her." Pinckney heard Smith promise that "if she would give him one hundred dollars he would put Sandy on the pavement," and yet, Pinckney archly observed, "he had not done it." And although Fall claimed the petition was his idea, it was actually Alice Pinn who trudged all over town to gather the signatures.[40] Desperate over her son, Alice Pinn tried everything she could think of to make sure these smooth-talking bargain-basement white lawyers did their jobs properly.

To understand how the Pinns thought about law, we might ask the same question Judge James Keith faced in deciding whether to cancel the deeds on the Pinns' home: who saved Sandy's life? One answer, voiced by his mother and some of the lawyers, was that it was Sandy's "good character" and the "white friends" who vouched for that character. Another answer was his lawyers' "influence." Betsy Pinn recalled Fall telling her on his visit to Warrenton that he had to "hurry back" to "use his influence with some man" back in Washington (that is, President Hayes). This view portrayed law as a world of "influence" and personal networks, where the lawyer won by knowing the right people and how to talk to them. Yet another possible answer was that Sandy just got lucky because President Hayes was worried about his "unjustified . . . reputation" for capital punishment,[41] and thought it looked "too brutal . . . to hang three men on one gallows." The Pinns paid careful attention to legal rules; they had to. But, like the Black newspapers of that era, the transcript of *Pinn v. Fall* is also pervaded by the assumption that law is a matter of influence, and that legal outcomes mostly depend on whom you know.[42] Black people during Reconstruction were wary, even cynical, about what law could do for them. But they did not assume that "colored men cannot have justice."

Reconstruction was an era of vast promise and horrifying violence, when the federal courts increasingly waded into matters of public importance, when the major political parties openly debated whether to appeal to America's newly enfranchised Black voters or suppress them, when southern landowners, freedpeople, and northern entrepreneurs laid the foundations of an economy without slavery, and when the legal system was finally thrown open to everyone, at least on paper. African Americans made sure that their access to law was more than a paper promise. They could not do it in all areas of the law, but in growing numbers, across the country, Black people during Reconstruction vastly expanded their use of the courts, and aired out their opinions about the legal process and about lawyers. Some hired white lawyers to work for them. Others hired Black lawyers, nurturing a new class of Black legal professionals, whose workaday efforts would soon plant seeds for a fragile Black middle class. White lawyers, for their part, seem to have accepted African Americans as clients, or even to have gone looking for them. To the lawyers, Black clients were just part of the job. But to the clients, access to the law was often a life-changing experience. To us, looking back a century and a half into a world where slavery had just ended, these relationships between Black clients and their lawyers suggest the beginnings of something remarkable and new. In slavery, Black people had held certain privileges, rooted in shared ideas of contract and property. Now, in the early days of freedom, those same legal ideas began to ground a vision of civil *rights*.

4

From the Ruins of Slavery

In August 1875, four longtime Black members of the mixed-race, white-run Cumberland (Virginia) Baptist Church—Charles Palmore, Page Pryor, Maurice Brown, and Archer Harris—recorded a deed at the county courthouse. The deed said that they had purchased two acres of land along the Guinea Road "for . . . a Colored Baptist Church to be called Midway Baptist." They were its first trustees. A new building soon went up. Eight years later, Jackson Holcomb, whose family would become lifelong members of Midway, bought their hundred acres nearby.[1]

A couple of counties away, in Danville, Virginia, a white mob fired on a defenseless crowd of people who were demanding the arrest of a white vigilante. Four Black people died, along with a white man who was hit accidentally. The Danville massacre of 1883 was part of a drawn-out white-supremacist coup that ended the Reconstruction experiment in multiracial democracy in Virginia and across the South.[2] From one perspective, Reconstruction's anti-Black violence looks like an epidemic of lawlessness. It seems obvious that "colored men cannot have justice in Mississippi," as P. Houston Murray's "hard-working colored man" lamented in 1865. But Murray's desperate informant spoke of injustice, not lawlessness. Anti-Black violence was often law-bound, not lawless. It was fueled by white greed and grievance yet was conditioned by the rules of property and contract. Although it might be easy to whip up a lynch mob by yelling that a Black man ought not own a nice farm or horse, that argument made no sense in a court of law, because it was not illegal for Blacks to own nice farms or horses. And that mattered.

The rise of Black property-owners like the Holcombs and Midway Baptist is one of the most remarkable and least understood phenomena in American history. Stretching from Reconstruction to the nadir of Jim Crow, it has not gotten much attention from historians and popular culture, which have usually cast rural Black people as sharecroppers and wage workers[3] and have focused on criminal justice, segregation, and racial violence like the Danville massacre. This chapter tells how a small but determined diaspora of Black landowners began to step out from the ruins of slavery, with almost no help from the federal government or southern whites. It is the story of how former slaves, southern whites, and white northern politicians and legal experts argued over the basic rules of contract and property. Those rules had always been shaped, unequally, by the interplay among these different groups' common sense about what "the law" was. But now that background common sense seemed to be shifting.

For the South's four million freedpeople, it would take backbreaking effort and fierce unity to realize the dream of landownership. Precious few of them had a kindly white father to inherit from. And only a few hundred of them would ever actually get the legendary "forty acres and a mule" promised by General William T. Sherman's wartime order to temporarily parcel out the vast plantations of absent white traitors to Black farmers. Nobody was giving away land to Black people. On the contrary, when the traitors came back, their land restored by a vindictive white president, they saw Black people as a source of cheap, landless labor.[4] But sometimes, short of cash and long on debts, they looked at a Black person and saw something else: a potential buyer.

Like most people today, most people in 1870 didn't have enough saved up to pay all at once. Unlike today, there was no such thing as a bank-issued, government-backed, thirty-year mortgage. Though a few Black farmers got loans from Black-owned banks or took advantage of "savings departments" at the newly founded Black colleges, most of them bought the same way that cash-poor Americans had always made big purchases: by financing through the seller. That is, they paid part of the money down and "borrowed" the rest, not from a bank but from the person selling them the land. There were two main types of seller financing: the purchase-money mortgage and the deed of trust. Under a mortgage, the buyer got to move in right away and also got the property's legal title, while the seller kept a lien for himself until the price was fully paid. A deed of trust worked almost the same way, except that the title would be held by a third-party trustee. In either case, the buyer would pay off the purchase price over a few years. Five years after the Civil War ended, 4.8 percent of the South's Black families, or about 43,000, owned real estate.[5] Over the next fifteen years, as whites sold land to Blacks on credit, that figure steadily rose.

It is fairly easy to see why whites might sell property to Blacks. Sometimes they just needed the money. But why would they respect Blacks' rights to buy and own? There were two reasons, broadly speaking. First, whites were already used to seeing slaves have property, and it was not a very big step from the idea that slaves could have property to the notion that ex-slaves could have property *rights*. Second, the formal rules of property law itself demanded some amount of respect for Black rights. Property law is conservative. Whole new fields of law have risen since the 1800s—torts, for example. Others have been radically transformed—the law of master and servant is now called "employment law." And contracts can be customized in all sorts of ways. But property remains stubbornly standardized around a few forms of ownership that have barely changed for two hundred years.[6] So it would have been very hard for judges to invent a law of property for whites and another for Blacks. In practice, what this meant is that owning land put Black people into the "chain of title."

The chain of title is crucial in property law. At one end is a land transaction—perhaps at an office building or a kitchen table. There is a stack of papers to sign. The real estate agents make small talk; the title company rep keeps the pages turning, hurriedly explaining what they mean. Everyone pretends not to look at their watches. And then the deed is copied onto one of the ledgers at the courthouse. The ceremony of signatures, solemn attestations, stamps, and seals serves to fix the deed in the public's mind, much as handing over twigs had done in Shakespeare's time and acts of possession had done in the slave quarters. Made of paper rather than metal, the chain of title is a series of written entries on courthouse ledgers. It anchors the property rights of all future owners by assuring buyers and lenders that they are getting good titles. Once Black people became free, and especially since they could now own land and not just pigs and chickens, the property system's emphasis on transparency and continuity meant that there were legal consequences to cheating, murdering, or intimidating Black landowners, even if the criminal justice system refused to act. When whites broke the law to seize Black property, they broke the chain of title that anchored other people's property.

In other words, property is fragile. It exists because people believe it exists. When I say I own my car, I am not describing my legal relationship to the car; I'm saying something about my legal relations with other people *about* the car—the dealer who sold it to me, my neighbors who see me park it, the police who stop me on the highway, the strangers who see me driving it. In other words, property is fundamentally social. It is a set of legal relations between people about a thing. These living, breathing legal relations are what written chains of title purport to capture and hold still on paper. As the legal theorist Carol Rose puts it, you "cannot have property all alone." White southerners' understanding of the community-ness of individual property made it common sense to respect Black property.[7] This backdrop—the still-fresh memory of property ownership by slaves, the new federal civil rights law, and property's inherent conservatism and community-ness—meant that, generally speaking, there would be no "law of Negro property" to govern the swelling ranks of "Negro" property owners.

Whites had more leeway to write their racial preferences into contracts, but there, too, they faced constraints. Federal anti-discrimination laws (like the Civil Rights Act of 1866) meant that writing explicitly racist terms into a contract entailed some risk that a judge might throw out the whole contract if it ever wound up in court. And at the conceptual level, a contract is inherently social, too. It is a promise backed by the threat of force. A contract serves "evidentiary, cautionary, channeling and deterrent policies," not only for the parties to the contract but also for others who are not parties but who might have an interest in it, such as future buyers and lenders. That is, it provides people with tools to create trustworthy evidence that can be relied upon in bargaining: pieces of paper, but also witnesses to handshakes and spoken words. The rules and rituals of contract, the fancy legalese like "consideration" and "whereof" and "party of the first part," all warn people away from making rash decisions and they put people on notice when they are about to slide from "just talking" into a legally binding obligation.[8] In other words, even though state law did not prohibit people from putting racist language into contracts, white people's embeddedness in webs of IOUs—the fact that they needed to be able to rely on Black people's promises—discouraged them from doing so. And, of course, they didn't need to. They had plenty of other ways to stay on top.

In order to understand how so many Black people managed to become landowners—and why the federal government didn't do more to help them—we have to plunge into the turbulent history of nineteenth-century white political thought. Specifically, we need to examine how elite white lawyers and judges thought about slavery and freedom.

The Republicans became the party of freedom by convincing voters that freedom was the polar opposite of slavery, and that the bright line between them was a certain set of fundamental, "civil" rights that "all men" were entitled to. Drawing that bright line, in turn, required distorting the realities of both freedom and slavery. In the 1850s, antislavery politicians took the vast array of practices that made up the slave system—the horrific violence, including sexual violence and family separation, the task and gang systems, the hiring and trading and bargaining and property ownership—and boiled them down to one essential idea: "the chattel principle." All of slavery's cruelties, they insisted, flowed from this principle of treating a person like a thing, deprived of fundamental rights. First formulated by escaped slaves in the 1840s, this antislavery ideology of "the chattel principle" eventually was absorbed into the Republican Party's winning argument that southern slaveholders were a mortal threat to a nation dedicated to personal liberty. Today, though the Texas board of education and the editor of the 1619 Project fiercely disagree about so much else in American history, they both assume that there is a sharp chasm between slavery and freedom and that, standing like a guardrail along the cliff's edge of freedom, are certain "unalienable rights."[9]

But although jurists and activists in the mid-1800s were converging on the idea that slavery and freedom were absolute opposites, with civil rights the bright boundary between, more and more white people nevertheless felt that it was money, not civil rights, that made a person free. America was becoming divided between a few rich families and "a permanent factory population" living in bondage, they said. White union leaders in northern cities echoed southern proslavery propagandists like George Fitzhugh: there was nothing liberating about a contract to work sixteen hours a day in a Massachusetts cotton mill. The white working man was just "a slave without a master," they complained, forced by rich capitalists to either "work or starve."[10] In short, as the nation lurched toward civil war, competing factions of white people treated "slavery" as a conceptual tool to hammer out their vision of what America should and should not be.

The Republican Party won the White House in 1860 largely because its leaders told a compelling story about why the sixteen-hour-a-day factory worker—driven off the family farm by mortgage-lenders, fertilizer suppliers, and the whipsawing of a globalized commodities market—was still, fundamentally, a free man. And it won by deflecting northern voters' rampant racism—vividly on display in minstrel shows and the barrage of anti-Black laws we saw earlier—onto what Republicans contemptuously called "the Slave Power," the southern plot to dominate the national government, overturn the will of the founding fathers, and spread slavery everywhere, from New Hampshire to Oregon.[11] By rallying around the principle of "free soil"—the idea that the North had to be kept clean from the stain of slavery—the party managed to be both antislavery and anti-Black. "Free soil, free labor, free men" was a successful campaign slogan because it demonized slaveholders *and* their slaves as a threat to the American way of life. During the Civil War, Republicans came to believe that emancipation would prove, once and for all, that there was no coercion in the free market.[12] So, close on the heels of the Union army, and under the auspices of the new Bureau of Refugees, Freedmen, and Abandoned Lands (commonly known as the "Freedmen's Bureau"), northern entrepreneurs fanned out across the South to remake its economy in the image of the North.[13] Four million newly freed Black people[14] would prove to the world that Fitzhugh was wrong—that a white workingman was not "a slave without a master"—by going back to work the cotton fields, this time for money.[15]

But Republican officials, economists, and jurists were surprised to discover that freedpeople did not think that signing a contract made them free. Freedpeople wanted to know what was *in* the contract, because they understood, perhaps better than the white people who filled the *New York Times* with editorials about "Free Labor Experiments in Louisiana" and "What Shall Be Done With the Emancipated Slaves," that a contract was *binding*, and that there was no obvious difference between the bondage of contract and the bondage of slavery, between the coercion of a sheriff and the coercion of a master. For example, here are the terms of the contract that a white man, William R. Baskervill, and a Black woman named Rosa—one of fifty-five "negroes formerly his slaves"—signed on June 7,

1865: from that day through Christmas, "the negroes" agreed to do all the work they had been doing "heretofore," to be "obedient" to William R., and to keep their children "in their proper places." In return, William R. agreed to pay them one quarter of the crops, the same rations of "meal and meat as heretofore," minus any corn their nonworking relatives ate. Anyone who quit would forfeit his entire payment, even if he quit on Christmas Eve. Rosa did not sign this contract because she forgot to bargain, or because she didn't know how a contract worked. It was because she had no other options. All over the South, former slaves like her desperately tried to strengthen their bargaining positions by widening their options. Instead of working for wages raising the big cash crops that fueled the U.S. economy—cotton, tobacco, sugar—they raised their own food, hunted, fished, worked at skilled trades like blacksmithing, did odd jobs, and, whenever they could, they sent their children to school in hopes of a life better than a quarter-share of corn. This was just hard-nosed market behavior. But to northern whites, who assumed it was up to them to decide "What Shall Be Done with the Emancipated Slaves," it looked like "loafing," and that justified, in the words of the Bureau's commissioner, Oliver O. Howard, "a little wholesome constraint."[16]

It may seem strange that the men who once led the fight against slavery and anti-Black laws in the pre–Civil War North would then turn the Fourteenth Amendment—enacted to protect newly freed Black people—into a shield for big business. But it isn't so strange when we remember what "freedom" meant to many of those nineteenth-century Republicans: it meant the bare fact of not being a slave, the freedom to sell one's own labor. This concept of freedom—what the historian William Nelson calls "the jurisprudence of antislavery"—pervaded a distinctive and highly influential style of legal reasoning known as "legal formalism." Instead of starting with the facts of the case before them, legal formalists started from some very abstract, very general "first principle" and then, ignoring all context, policy considerations, and personalities, reasoned downward to decide the case, as if they were solving an elegant geometry puzzle. The first principle these judges invoked more than any other—the one they used to batter down health and safety laws, unions, taxes, and more—was "freedom of contract," and it came directly from their (flawed) understanding of what slavery had been. Republican judges blithely refused to see that there was anything coercive about Rosa Baskervill bargaining with her former master, or a white family accepting starvation wages to strip tobacco leaves for fifteen hours a day in a dank New York tenement. They refused to see it because, for them, voluntariness was the opposite of coercion, and the epitome of coercion was a Georgia overseer.[17]

These Republican judges strongly believed that the best way to banish the overseer's whip was to protect the civil rights of property and contract, whether from southern rebels, government bureaucrats, or labor unions. Anything that violated a man's "sacred" right to freely sign a labor contract was intolerable, wrote Supreme Court Justice Stephen Field in his influential 1873 dissent in *The Slaughter-House Cases,* because it set up a "slavery of white men." A law requiring iron factories to pay workers in cash at regular intervals? That, said the supreme court of Pennsylvania, pinned "the badge of slavery" onto both the worker and his boss. A union on strike for better pay? No different than a Chinese gang or a slaveowner. By the 1890s, judges were using the antislavery ideal of "freedom of contract" to strike down health and safety regulations and the federal income tax, and to enjoin strikes. Labor leaders fought their bosses using the same idea, even the same language. Workers " 'do not *consent*' " when they sign contracts, warned one union leader; faced with starvation, "they submit but they do not agree." And that lack of real agreement between worker and employer over the terms of work made white men the "slaves" of their employers.[18] In short, the ghost of slavery haunted America's rise to global power. Instead of paying attention to what Black people were actually saying and doing with contracts, white judges, labor leaders, and academics used their own imagined ideas of "slavery" and "the negro" as mental shortcuts to work out their vision of a modern industrial economy.

This formalistic, antislavery reasoning about coercion enabled judges to assume that, once the South's four million ex-slaves had the right of contract, the invisible hand of the free market would simply wash away the region's vast racial inequalities. In an abstract sense, freedpeople like Rosa Baskervill were indeed free and equal bargainers. But in real life, they were so poor and so cut off from alternatives that only magical thinking could imagine that they were free, self-willed individuals voluntarily choosing to shackle themselves to white men like William R. Baskervill. The Freedmen's Bureau supplied that magical thinking. Echoing almost verbatim the rhetoric of antislavery Republicans before the war, the Bureau announced in 1865 that freedpeople would have to "enter into *free and voluntary contracts* with employers of their own choice" or else be arrested for vagrancy. Then Bureau officials undermined the freedpeople's bargaining position by making it impossible *not* to sign on with men like William R.—by taking away any alternatives that might distort the smooth workings of the free market: collective bargaining, strikes, land redistribution, better jobs in towns. Freedmen's Bureau agents were already acting as substitute judges while the regular county courts were out of commission. They assumed that former slaveowners—rich in land and equipment, well armed, and still in control of the state legislatures—would rebuild the region's economy by negotiating mutually beneficial agreements with the freedpeople. Republicans applied the same logic to the North, too. Beginning in the 1860s, northern states arrested thousands of jobless white men and sentenced them to "enforced labor" in the penitentiary. In 1877, Republican leaders would send soldiers to violently suppress a vast, continent-spanning, multiracial labor protest that united steelworkers, railroaders, coal miners, and others. And in the aftermath of that "Great Strike" of 1877, Republican leaders would build giant new military bases within striking distance of big cities like Chicago, so that the Army could protect the railroads and meatpacking factories from their own workers. In short, the Republicans enforced their vision of freedom against workers of all races, at the point of a gun. And yet despite all of that, they did not think they were coercing anyone, because in their minds, coercion had been abolished along with slavery.[19]

Today it seems strange to say that a free person can be forced to work. But it made perfect sense to the Republicans of the 1860s. Forced labor was unfree only if it discriminated on account of race, as the infamous Black Codes did. The Codes were a spate of southern state laws enacted in spring 1865 to spell out the legal rights and duties of the freedpeople. The Codes granted all African Americans the rights to acquire, own, and sell property and to make contracts, but they did not grant the same rights that whites had. For example, every Black person *had* to sign on with some white employer—a year-long contract, and if he quit before the end of the year, he forfeited all his pay and could be arrested on sight by any white person. The Codes granted Black people the right to testify in court but only against other Black people. And so on. The Republicans contended that by discriminating in "civil" rights on "account of color," the Black Codes had resurrected slavery. "Liberty and slavery are opposite terms," said Senator Lyman Trumbull during the floor debate over the Civil Rights Act of 1866, and civil rights "draw the precise line . . . where freedom ceases and slavery begins."[20] Congress enshrined this formalist anti-discrimination principle in the Civil Rights Act of 1866 and in the Fourteenth Amendment's Equal Protection Clause.

The Republicans' anti-discrimination principle carefully targeted only those kinds of coercion that treated people differently "on account of color." It was never meant to disturb the background constraints on the choices that are available to us, constraints that seem natural because they are embedded in the taken-for-granted rules of property and contract. But in the modern free market economy that the Republicans of the 1860s did so much to create, coercion does not look like a plantation overseer. No one stands over us with a whip or a gun. After all, even Rosa Baskervill made a choice when she literally agreed to work like a slave for six months for a quarter-share of corn, much as today's home health aides "choose" to work sixty hours a week cleaning and bathing and feeding elderly people for minimum wage. This fundamental fact of life in a free society is what one legal theorist would later call "the baseline problem."[21] And although the baseline problem affects everyone, it hits hardest for people who are not white. The Civil Rights Act of 1866 and especially the Fourteenth Amendment are among the most important laws in American history, but their focus on racially unequal treatment has always made it difficult to challenge problematic rules that do not discriminate by race. Indeed, it has helped make those rules seem like simple justice.

The judges in the South's local courthouses had to apply Congress's new anti-discrimination principle to actual cases under *state* law, the arena that overwhelmingly defined Black people's experiences with contract and that contained so many invisible forms of coercion. And as the judges did so, they developed a theory of civil rights that took account of racial inequality without violating the principle of nondiscrimination. In the process, they began to embed racial ideas into contract law itself.

Contract law grants ordinary people an extraordinary power: the power to make laws for themselves. When two people make a contract they can decide for themselves what their obligations are going to be under the contract, and a court will enforce those obligations. Of course, it is hard to believe that someone would agree to borrow $200 at 1,000 percent interest, or to work six months for a quarter-share of corn, unless she was lied to or had no alternative. But should a judge have the power to modify or cancel such grossly unfair contracts? In 1865, the Freedmen's Bureau answered: yes. They borrowed from the law of "equity," a collection of doctrines that are supposed to enable judges to provide a remedy whenever the "common law" can't resolve the dispute fairly and with justice. Thus, if one party had taken advantage of the other's "ignorance" or had gotten them to sign an "unfair and unjust" contract by hiding or misrepresenting key facts, Bureau officials could nullify the contract. By mediating contracts between "the ignorant freedmen and governing [white] race," the Bureau would save America's economy from shipwreck.[22]

But for judges and legal theorists, this equitable theory of Black civil rights prompted troubling questions about courts in general, far beyond cases involving freedpeople. For centuries, equitable remedies had been seen as dangerous because they enabled unelected judges to freelance, to act like tyrants, imposing their personal values—"politicians in robes," as people say today. Bureau officers justified using equitable remedies in the occupied South by arguing that freedpeople were categorically different from other kinds of contracting parties—not because they were Black, but because they were "wards . . . *under the guardianship of the Nation*." By treating freedpeople as "wards . . . of the Nation," antislavery judges reassured skeptics that they were not going to use equity law as an excuse to freelance over white people's rights. They also set a pattern that long outlasted the short-lived Freedmen's Bureau: race would open a door into the law of equity, but only in exceptional circumstances and only by treating Black people as incapable. The wardship idea provided a way to align the Republican Party's free-market-oriented insistence on equal civil rights with the reality that white and Black southerners did not come to the free market as equals, while still preserving the idea that judges were constrained by the rule of law. Wardship would soon be picked up by white southern judges and lawyers, who turned the vulnerable, "ignorant negro" stereotype into a defensive weapon for Black clients, and by the 1960s it would be absorbed into the efforts of legal liberals to make "poverty law" an engine of social reform.[23] But its most immediate impact was to open a door for Black people to get into court against whites.

Black people's new civil rights were put to the test when whites cheated them out of property or violently abrogated their contracts. Contracts are legally binding private agreements. In 1866, they were almost always drafted by nonlawyers, which meant that often the terms were ambiguous and confusing. Many contracts were not written at all and relied on other forms of public knowledge that were not that different from what had secured slaves' property and bargains.[24] Sorting out contract disputes was the bread and butter of county circuit judges.

The most common type of contract they dealt with was work contracts. What should a judge do when people disagreed about what kinds of work were part of the contract and what kinds were outside it—when an ex-slaveowner's "interpretation of the contract" "extort[ed]" so much extra work that it looked like slavery? When a freedwoman refused to "wash[] extra clothes" or cook or work on Saturdays or during "lay-by" time, was that a breach of contract that forfeited her share of the crop? What if a girl's father made a verbal deal for her, and then, before it was put in writing, she signed a written agreement with someone else? What if two men agreed to rent a farm on shares, one of them left for a higher-paying job, promising to find a substitute, and then the sub didn't show up? In construing labor contracts, judges in the Reconstruction-era South looked less to their personal sense of justice or to free-labor ideology than to the things that any county judge would weigh: to the actual words on the paper, to custom (or "usage"), and to what modern lawyers would call course-of-dealing.[25] In other words, they *judged.*

It was here, in local courts across the South, that people fought over the economic resources that shaped so much of their lives. The baseline rules of property law and contract law gave huge advantages to those who already had land and capital. For example, some white bosses ducked paying Black workers by hiding behind a maze of procedural rules. The workers could sue, but because they had no savings, they might starve before they recovered any money. Even when employers paid them on time, the standard labor contract essentially made freedpeople unwilling creditors to their employers for eleven months every year. Rosa Baskervill went to work each day but William Baskervill didn't have to pay her until Christmas. None of these practices were against federal law, because they did not discriminate on account of race.[26] And so, even though we know from newspapers and other sources that disputes over such contracts were very common, they rarely show up in my sample of local court records from 1872: out of 447 cases, only nineteen involved a Black plaintiff suing a white defendant.

To see what Black people did with contract and property during Reconstruction, we have to look at pretrial motions—the various procedural rules one can use to delay or dismiss or speed up a lawsuit *before* it goes to trial. Consider *Holland v. Holland* (1882), from eastern Virginia, in which Robert Holland was buying a farm in installments from a white man named Joel Holland (who may have been his old master). No matter how much Robert paid, Joel said he still owed more. Eventually he decided to switch creditors: he would borrow money from someone else and pay off Joel. Joel refused. He sued Robert for allegedly selling off the timber from the property before it was legally his. Robert hired a lawyer, who filed a "demurrer," the formal objection that says, essentially, "so what?" (That is, even if the plaintiff is right about the facts, those facts don't add up to a legal claim and the case should be thrown out.) Robert's demurrer said that it was Joel who came and talked him into buying the land. Joel wanted Robert and his family "to stay in the neighborhood so that he could get [their] services when he needed them," an arrangement many former slaveowners sought out in those early years of freedom. In cases like this, the pretrial proceedings typically became an argument about the history of the debt. Robert showed the court receipts showing not only the money he had paid Joel but also all the ditching, picking, washing, and cooking that his family had done for Joel since 1875, work that should have almost paid off the whole debt by now. He demurred that he had "offered time and again to pay whatever any sensible white man would say he justly and lawfully owed" if Joel would just hand over the deed. In the end, two months after filing it, Joel dropped his timber suit against Robert. In all likelihood, Robert's gamble—hiring a lawyer and fighting Joel with a pretrial objection—paid off. It did not erase his debt. But it probably bought him time to line up a new creditor, and a court-appointed commissioner to pin down what he really owed. And that was all he had asked for.[27]

Defending against a white man's lawsuit was one thing. Suing him was something else altogether. *Robertson v. Wright,* from nearby Amelia County, wasn't about the balance of the payments (as it was in *Holland*) but rather what *kind* of contract two men had made with each other. In the spring of 1866, a white man named James Wright, acting on behalf of his brother-in-law H. V. Thompson, sold to a Black man, John Robertson, a farm called "Peachland," for $1,500, due in two payments. They signed a paper that looked like a standard contract for selling land: it used the words "sale" and "sells." But it also had a twist: it said that once Robertson made the first payment in June 1866, the two men would swap deeds: Wright would give Robertson a deed to the land and Robertson would give Wright a deed of trust to secure his second payment, due a year later. And it said that Wright waived the "rent" "as a part of this sale."[28] Was this a sale contract or a lease? Had Wright sold the land to Robertson or just rented it? The words on the paper were ambiguous, and Wright exploited that ambiguity.

On New Year's Day 1867, Wright went to a justice of the peace and swore out a "distress warrant," saying that Robertson had failed to make his first $500 payment. Constable William A. Godsey seized Robertson's work animals, crops, and tools and prepared to auction them off. Wright now claimed that the payments Robertson had been making to that point were just *rent,* not installment payments toward a purchase. Robertson insisted he'd been *buying* the land all along. But as badly as he wanted to recover the equity he had paid toward the land purchase, his most urgent problem was to get back his things. He stepped up a staircase of legal actions, each more confrontational than the last. First, he offered to post bond until the local circuit court could sort out their dispute. Constable Godsey refused. Now Robertson got a different justice of the peace to write out a "notice" demanding that Godsey "surrender" the work animals, crops, and tools back to him, warning that he was going to post $700 bond and swear out his own writ, to prove in court that the seizure was unlawful. He signed it with his X mark.[29]

A few days later, on the morning of January 12, 1867, things came to a head: Robertson's written "notice and demand" was served on constable Godsey in front of Robertson's house, just as he was about to start the auction. Godsey barrelled onward, telling him "he would not wait a second for Robertson" to post bond and "would not give a damn" if he did post it. Robertson then said "that he forbid and protested against the sale as illegal and would hold Mr Godsey responsible to him for the damage sustained." The words sound almost as if he lifted them from one of the everyman's law handbooks that justices of the peace carried around in those days. He swore that "he would run the law to the last." And three weeks later, Robertson sued seven people—Wright, Thompson, and the five men who bought up his things at the auction—for an injunction (a court order to block the delivery of his things) and "specific performance" (to force Wright and Thompson to accept his money and complete the sale).[30]

It is difficult to know what happened in the end. Clearly, at least two local officials did things that hurt Robertson: Thomas E. Whitworth, the justice of the peace who issued the distress warrant to seize Robertson's things, and Godsey, the constable who seized his things. And the court dissolved its injunction in October.[31] By 1871, the two sides had apparently reached some settlement out of court. If we are keeping score, it looks as though Robertson lost.

Yet Robertson did get an injunction—a powerful remedy that judges did not issue lightly—on the strength of a complaint notarized by another white justice of the peace. He also secured cooperation from both white and Black men at every step of the way, including from his opponent's lawyer. Someone wrote the "notice and demand" to Godsey for him. Somehow he knew that he had to "protest," using certain words, just before the constable started the auction. His protest tracked the language of the statute on protesting a distress warrant.[32] A local Black landowner cosigned his injunction bond. Three Black men and at least four whites testified for him in front of various justices of the peace, including Whitworth (the one who had issued the distress warrant), and John Jeter, a white farmer who, as one of the buyers at Godsey's auction, was technically one of Robertson's opponents. Before the auction, when Robertson confronted constable Godsey at his office, he brought along another white man, and the papers "were read" out loud by a white lawyer named F. R. Farrar "and several others." Farrar himself said at the time that Robertson should have had a lawyer, since he, Farrar, was working "for the other side."[33]

The most telling detail is that nobody ever denied that Wright and Thompson (the actual landowner) had been talking with Robertson about selling him land, much less that a Black man could make a contract to buy land. Even Wright admitted that Thompson had been trying to sell this land for a while and that he had suggested that Robertson "could no doubt get it if he would pay" what old man Thompson was asking. Indeed, the white men's defense was essentially that those conversations were just talk—talk that had never amounted to a contract. ("Defense" means a claim that a contract should not be enforced.) As law students everywhere know (and knew), discerning when mere talk crosses the line to a binding "offer" and "acceptance" was (and is) a problem endemic to contract law generally, and the fact that Robertson was Black meant everything but determined nothing. The white men casually assumed that Robertson had the right to own land, to make a contract to buy land, and to sue white men over that contract. In fact, four of the men who snapped up his property at the auction were Black.[34]

Perhaps the clearest test of Black people's new civil rights came when whites cheated or terrorized them out of their property. To fight such racist plundering, Black people and their lawyers had to persuade judges to see race. This was tricky, because although the legal system certainly was not color-blind, it did not contain a separate "Negro law of contract." The strategy they devised helped etch racial thinking into contract law.

During Reconstruction, Black people and their lawyers began to hone two explicitly racial arguments to get out of bad contracts: the "ignorant negro," and the "intelligent white man." Prefigured in Chief Justice John Marshall's idea of Native Americans as "domestic dependent nations," and in the Freedmen's Bureau judges' idea that freedpeople were "wards of the nation," each argument drew from older English doctrines: mistake, fraud, duress, incapacity, and unconscionability. These equity doctrines had been fashioned centuries earlier to protect the interests of specially vulnerable categories of people, such as women, children, and sailors at sea. Now they became loopholes in the rigid antislavery freedom-of-contract ideal, a means to sidestep the baseline problem without questioning either the free market or white supremacy. Indeed, they were perfectly pitched to harmonize with—and sometimes reverse white people's interest in—the era's reigning sex and race stereotypes.[35] A judge could cancel a "hard" bargain that took advantage of a "foolish and unlettered" person, a "child," or an "ignorant and superstitious negro," because "the parties were not on an equal footing." As we will see, the "ignorant negro" was freely used by Black people who were clearly not ignorant. It spread through America's legal system in the 1860s and 1870s.[36]

The flip side of Black ignorance was not just white shrewdness but white power, power that put Black people under "duress." A duress defense argues that one of the parties to the contract shouldn't be bound to his promise because his promise was coerced. Few whites thought it was wrong to coerce Black people. But theoretically it could jeopardize their contracts with Black people. As whites threatened and bullied Black people to sign binding contracts in an era when contracts were thought to express the free will of the parties, the result was to blur the line between legitimate "inducement" and illegal "coercion"—a line that ran through the heart of contract law itself. In *Talley v. Robinson's Assignee,* a case from Cumberland County, where Jackson Holcomb lived, a free Black man named John Robinson was violently harassed in 1864 into selling his 143-acre farm to a white man named

William Talley for about half what it was worth. Robinson signed a sale contract. But he never handed over the deed. In 1867, Talley sued Robinson for specific performance—that is, to make Robinson go through with the deal and deed over the farm. Robinson asked Cumberland County Judge H. H. Marshall to rescind the contract instead, saying "it was extorted from him." A white mob had threatened to shoot him on sight if he did not leave the county, and "this flustered me so that I did not understand the right of the contract." Talley shrugged. He had nothing to do with the mob, so Robinson was still bound. Judge Marshall sided with Robinson, citing the basic rule that people were not legally bound to bargains made under duress. "Lawless violence" had forced this bargain on Robinson, Marshall decided, and Talley knew about it at the time.[37]

On appeal, the Virginia supreme court overturned Marshall's decision by rewriting the law of duress. "Undoubtedly, a great outrage was perpetrated by certain persons upon Robinson," wrote Justice Richard Moncure, but since Talley wasn't actually in the mob, Robinson was stuck with the contract. It was formalistic reasoning, willfully ignoring the realities on the ground, especially the fact that Talley *knew* about the violence and had profited from it.

And yet Moncure's formalism took account of other on-the-ground realities: the realities of how property was owned in the nineteenth-century United States. Robinson was a propertied "free man of color" when he made his bargain in 1864, and as surely as his property put a target on his back, it also made him part of a web of legal relations, one that local whites had a stake in maintaining. After all, the mob didn't just take Robinson's land, they made him sign a "warranty deed," which meant that Robinson promised to defend Talley's title if anyone questioned it. Anything that undermined one property title would necessarily destabilize any interests tied to that property: mortgage interests, ownership interests, tenancy interests. When lots of property titles were insecure, people couldn't sell land or rent it out or even mortgage it to raise cash. Sloppy land titles in Kentucky were the main reason Abraham

Lincoln's family moved to Indiana when he was a boy; they helped cause the 2008 financial crisis by making it impossible to determine which banks held mortgages on which homes.[38] If the mob had simply killed Robinson or driven him away, there would have been no deed at the Cumberland courthouse showing that the next person who moved in—or borrowed against it, or bought it—actually had the right to do so.

In short, Talley's purchase was an attempt to create "notice," the thing that made property property. It offered a way to rein in the mob's lawlessness and thus preserve everyone's property rights, albeit at Robinson's expense. The agreement looked like any other real estate contract. It listed the chain of owners leading down to Robinson. It transferred to Talley a debt that Robinson had been paying off to one of the previous owners, a white widow named Betsy Anderson. Anderson now got her money from Talley, and gave him a receipt for it. Talley got Robinson's "general warranty," witnessed by two other men, to protect his rights in the land, as well as a federal government seal once he got the agreement tax-stamped a few years later. Much of the violence Black people suffered during Reconstruction was just this sort of by-the-book plundering: rather than simply take a Black person's horses or land, whites used brutal whippings and threats to coerce him to sign a contract of sale or a lease.[39] Practically speaking, these were just legal niceties—Robinson was still out of luck—but in such niceties vibrated the consistent principle that African Americans now had civil rights as state citizens, not just citizens of the United States. Whites could certainly trample those rights but, unlike during slavery, someone would have to tidy up the legal mess that left behind.

It was unusual for Black people to go up against whites in court. Rosa Baskervill never sued William R. My ancestor Jackson Holcomb never sued anyone, as far as I can tell. Yet even if they weren't frequent, cases involving Black litigants began filtering up to the high courts, and those cases started to influence legal doctrine. That influence was apparent not just in federal and constitutional law but also in the state-level, private-law rules of property and contract and association—the paradigmatic "civil rights" of the nineteenth century. Within a few years of the *Talley* decision, handed down in 1872, other state supreme courts were citing it in contract disputes between white people. In *Fairbanks v. Snow,* a Massachusetts case from 1887, future U.S. Supreme Court justice Oliver Wendell Holmes began developing the *Talley* rule into a general theory about voluntariness and coercion in contract, one that became enormously influential in the twentieth century. In *Southern Express Co. v. Byers,* where the jury awarded the grief-stricken John Byers $200 damages for "mental anguish," the United States Supreme Court barred contract damages for mental anguish as a matter of federal law—an issue that is once again before the Court today. In *Union Mutual v. Wilkinson* (1871), a former slave sued his late wife's insurance company for its refusal to pay on a $2,000 life insurance policy because on her application form she had given some inaccurate information about her and her mother's health during slavery. The *Wilkinson* doctrine quickly became the leading case on an important issue in insurance law and on the doctrine of "equitable estoppel." Yet these influential decisions almost never mentioned race. White judges, lawyers, and law professors began to cite and discuss contract and property cases involving Black litigants without mentioning that they were Black. They "passed" Black people's cases silently into the mainstream of private law just as light-skinned African Americans like Homer Plessy were "passing," sometimes unwillingly, into the "white race."[40]

For a few years in the late 1860s, former slaves, white southerners, and northern-born judges worked out how to translate the privileges of slavery into rights of everyday use. Over the next two decades, millions of Black people made work contracts and eked out a living, subtly but decisively shaping the jurisprudence that remade the legal world of the South. Tens of thousands of them, far more than we usually think, saved up enough to buy land. From landowners to tenant farmers to sharecroppers to tradespeople, they entered directly into the practices and institutions of southern law, recording deeds, signing contracts, testifying, forming associations, and occasionally suing. During the roughly twenty years after the end of the Civil War—an era that witnessed momentous changes in the Constitution—their cases helped shape contract law, and, as we will see, the law of religious associations. But that was not the only impact of their legal activity. It also put enormous pressure on their families—and on the very idea of "family" itself.

5

Do for Love

After the Civil War, Eliza Brown, who had grown up enslaved in eastern Maryland, moved with some of her relatives across the Chesapeake Bay to Washington, DC. By 1880, after years of washing and ironing other people's clothes, she owned a house in the city's Southwest quarter. She had "got too old to work" and was renting out rooms to help make ends meet. She could not read or write, so for years she relied on other people to arrange loans and write out receipts.[1]

Brown had also become estranged from her family. She told people she had no relations, except for "a niece who lived some where in Baltimore" who had "never done any thing for her." Once, back on the plantation, she had had a husband and at least one daughter. But that daughter—never named in any of the testimony—was sold away from her. There is no evidence that she ever remarried or had any more children. That is, no more *biological* children. For she, like many other Americans, had her own ideas about who her family was, about whom she "owned" as kin.[2]

Brown's dearest friend was Maria Herbert, who lived across the street. The two women, both raised in slavery, were so close that witnesses described them as being like "sisters." Other neighbors sent their children over to Brown's house to visit or help out, but Herbert's daughter Henrietta was special. Brown "thought as much of [Henrietta] as if it was her own child," a witness said later; these three women "were just the same as one family, almost." When Maria Herbert lay dying in 1879, Brown took care of her. After Henrietta married and gave up her job as a live-in servant to keep house for her husband, she still spent a lot of her time and money looking after her mom's old friend, Mrs. Brown. According to Henrietta and several other witnesses, Brown frequently said that she was going to leave her property to Henrietta. But there was no will.[3]

One day in the fall of 1880, Eliza Brown decided to see a lawyer about her property. She picked a white lawyer her old friend Maria Herbert used to work for—James Saville—and she took Henrietta with her to his office. As Henrietta later recalled, Brown told Saville that Henrietta "had always been kind to her, and always, from a child, I had done for her—always waited on her—and that for ten or eleven years since I had been married, I always gave her money to pay her taxes." Brown told the lawyer she "wanted me to have the house at her death," but she wanted him "to fix it so that" she could keep living there. And she didn't want to make a will, even though that would have been the obvious choice. So Saville had Brown sign a "pocket deed": a deed conveying her house to Henrietta, which he promised to keep safe and not to put on record or give to Henrietta until after Brown died.[4]

Five years later, in the winter of 1885, Eliza Brown died, making forty-year-old Henrietta (Herbert) Jefferson the owner of a valuable piece of real estate in the nation's capital.[5] Or was she?

That spring, a Baltimore woman named Euphemia Stewart hired a lawyer to settle her late aunt Eliza's estate. When her lawyer found the deed to Henrietta Jefferson, she sued. Stewart brought several witnesses to testify that Brown "always owned" "Phemie" and the other siblings as "her nephews and nieces," that "she always wanted them to have . . . the property," and that "she had no one else to leave it to."[6]

Phemie's argument was simple: Henrietta Jefferson had tricked a helpless old lady into signing away her property to a stranger. Whatever Eliza Brown signed in lawyer Saville's office that autumn day in 1880 was a fraud, because she could not read or write and therefore had no idea what she was doing, and because by then she "was not of sound mind" and was "incapable" of making any legally binding decisions. Phemie Stewart and her lawyers brought witnesses who testified that Brown had raved about "the Devil and the ghostres and witches" in her last years. And as proof of Henrietta's bad intentions, Phemie (through her lawyers) insinuated that Henrietta had been suspiciously "careful to keep [the] deed off the record until after" Brown died, "a period of nearly five years."[7]

In February 1887, the court dismissed Euphemia Stewart's lawsuit without comment and charged the legal costs to her.[8] Henrietta had won. Along the way, Phemie's marriage broke down and her husband divorced her in the same DC court.[9]

Although the case dragged on for two years, long enough for Phemie to switch lawyers and the court to replace its chancery examiner, it was not a very hard one for a judge. The fact that Henrietta could show a signed, notarized deed from Eliza Brown trumped all the testimony about who was "really" kin to the dead woman. The only serious threat to her claim was the testimony about Brown's alleged insanity, which apparently did not convince the court. Forgotten for nearly 140 years, *Stewart v. Jefferson* provides a precious glimpse of one of the most intimate aspects of Black life at a moment of profound transformation.

Before the Civil War, a half-million free Black people had staggered under the burden of caring for their loved ones without a social safety net. After 1865, millions more Black people suddenly faced those same wrenching decisions, decisions that, more than ever before, pushed them to think about law. Who would keep a roof over their head when bad luck or hard times or just plain old age set in? What did a husband owe his wife or a child her parent? What *was* a family in the first place? Seared by generations of racist stereotypes about Black family life—some of it promulgated from the highest reaches of the federal government and academia—modern scholars have tended to write about "the Black family" in cultural terms, and as a refuge from white oppression.[10]

But the end of slavery meant that Black people also had to think of family as a legal category, something that granted rights over children and land and even a spouse's muscles. Black people demanded that courts enforce those rights—not just against whites but against other Black people. At the same time, African Americans began to argue over land. They argued because land embodied evolving ideas about the duties and privileges of being part of a family, and because getting it usually took tremendous hard work that only a family could mobilize.[11] Their lawsuits forced judges, insurance companies, and government bureaucrats to confront what slavery had done to Black people's genealogies. By the early 1900s, Black people's divorce and inheritance suits were helping to expand legal theories of "the family," grounding it in work as much as in blood or marriage or love, and conditioning family membership on people's willingness, as Eliza Brown said, to "do for" each other.[12] Becoming citizens, with civil rights under state law, did not solve inequalities between Black men and women or between Black parents and children. But it did change how Black people negotiated about power and resources, both with white people and with one another. It began to push Black people's ideas of family from the sphere of privileges to the sphere of rights. This was one of the little-known consequences of freedom.

On June 5, 1866, about a year after she had been freed from slavery, Chery Williams sent a letter through the Tennessee Freedmen's Bureau, with a note asking someone to read it to her husband, Hardy Williams. "My dear husband," she wrote. "I am so glad to know that you are yet a live but why do you not come have you forgoten me and your children"? Have "you forgoten the last word you ever said" when you joined the Army, that "if the lord would spare you that you would come" back? Now the war was over and Hardy was back, but not with her. "You was mine when you left and you are yet mine I shall always claim you and love you," Williams went on. "I can do more for you and wait on you better now than ever." But "I have the rite to your love and protection," Williams warned, and "if you don't come I will compell you to come." "I will have you confined."[13]

In slavery, Williams had had no right to see her husband, only a privilege bestowed by their masters. Now, as a free woman, she arguably did have that right, a right that a court could enforce. But no master was preventing Hardy Williams from coming back to her and their children. He was living right nearby, without them. Emancipation shook millions of intimate relationships like the Williams's. It put legal force behind duties and privileges that had always been held at a master's sufferance. It enabled Black men and women to think of themselves as having rights in one another and in their children, rights that carried the threat of force, as Chery Williams warned—not only against white people but against their own loved ones. And it pushed them to think of divorce, rather than separation, as the only way to renegotiate or end those marital rights and duties.[14] Emancipation pushed them to think about law.

Divorce was one of the most common reasons anyone, of any race, went to a court during Reconstruction. Although it isn't always easy to tell what a case is about from its docket entry, 127 of the 1,067 identifiable civil cases I sampled in the years 1872 and 1882 were divorces, and divorces made up the single most common reason Black people filed suit in those two years. For decades, Black activists like Frederick Douglass and Martin Delany had said that one of slavery's most grievous wrongs was that it deprived people of the right to marry and to claim loved ones as their own. Now that slavery was ended, some said that "the Marriage Covenant" was "the foundation of all our rights."[15] Why, then, did so many Black people go through the hassle and expense of filing for divorce?

One reason was that freedom did not just give Black people the right to be a family; it completely rewrote the rights and duties of family. During slavery, Black people had not been allowed to exercise the rights that free people exercised over their families, or to perform the duties that free people owed to their families. Chery Williams had had to serve her master, not her husband, a legal reality the historian Tera Hunter has memorably dubbed "the third flesh." After slavery ended, many ex-slaveowners took that right to the service of married women like Chery Williams, along with that of their children and other relatives, and reassigned it to the husband. Work contracts for families, for "squads" (a scaled-down version of the old plantation gang), and, by the 1880s, for sharecropping—these were all compromises between planters, who no longer had the right to whip slaves or the money to pay overseers but who still thought Black people wouldn't work unless a white man supervised them, and Black people, who rejected gang work as a relic of slavery. Each Black head of household became the legal equivalent of an overseer, contractually bound to keep his wife and children in line.[16]

The fifty-five X-mark signatures on the Baskervill contract, for example, actually represented ninety people, because many of the men signed for themselves plus one or more relatives: "London for Lucretia," "Gilbert for Sallie," "Essex + 2 chargeable" (meaning that at payout time, William R. Baskervill would subtract two children's worth of food rations from Essex's quarter-share of the crop). These men signed their wives and children onto this work contract, binding them to "work diligently" and "conduct themselves . . . respectful[ly]," but the women signed only for other women, or for children, or just for themselves, like Rosa Baskervill. This was because the state of Virginia, like every other state in the union, did not allow a wife to bind her husband to a contract. Such sex-based inequality in the baseline rules of contract sparked arguments in the mid-1860s, as wives refused to "ratify" the contracts their husbands made for them. The problem had no clear-cut legal answer. Freedmen's Bureau officers usually decided that husbands needed to get their wives' consent before signing them on. But the officers also thought that a wife needed her husband's consent before she took a job for herself. And under the case law of most states, most contracts for farm work covered all able-bodied household members, just as the Baskervill contract did.[17]

Subjugated by law, many Black women fought back through law. Just as a middle-class white woman might get divorced to keep her husband's creditors from seizing the property she had scrimped and saved up for, poorer Black women filed complaints at the Freedmen's Bureau arguing that state law "entitled" them to their children and demanding that the children be "deliver[ed]" up from ex-wives, ex-husbands, and white farmers alike. Black couples argued about the "expence and trouble" of caring for infants and sick relatives. They complained about being deprived of children old enough to be "worth something." They bought land with their children's earnings.[18] In short, divorce petitions were just one of many ways that Black women tried to use the law to control the terms of work, not only against white people but against other Black people. Divorce was like a declaration of marital bankruptcy, enlisting a judge to oversee the orderly disposition of the family's biggest assets: each other.

Paradoxically, another reason Black people divorced during Reconstruction is that many of them hadn't actually chosen to be married in the first place. The law had not recognized marriages between slaves. Now that those slaves were free, southern legislators panicked at the prospect of raising taxes to support out-of-wedlock Black children. Or worse: emancipation could wreck the real estate business by snarling up thousands of title chains. All across the South, politicians rushed to solve the problem of slave marriage with a fiat declaration: if you were living as man and wife on a certain date in 1866, you were legally married and subject to all the rights and duties that came with marriage.[19] They assumed that African Americans would not work without coercion, and if they could not be whipped to work, the threat of a bigamy charge would do just as well. Judges then interpreted the statutes to make slavery-time unions legally binding on all "colored" couples, even on those who had been free before the war and could have gotten married if they had wanted to. These laws caught many Black people by surprise, setting off waves of lawsuits about everything that slave marriages touched, from inheritance to child custody to old-age care—and especially divorce.[20]

Those waves washed across dramatically lowered barriers because the divorce process itself was getting simpler and easier. In 1800, in every state, getting divorced had required a special bill from the state legislature. By 1865, a county circuit judge could do it. Local lawyers, who had been figuring out how to make divorce quicker and cheaper for whites—fill-in-the-blank petitions and promises to pay court costs—simply tacked on boilerplate language for Black divorce seekers. Black divorce was more than a consequence of white legislators forcing marriage on former slaves. It was an attempt by African Americans to find legal solutions to painful problems and it quickly took its place alongside white divorce as a permanent feature of American life. Legally, no one had the right to divorce. It was a privilege bestowed by judges.[21] But former slaves quickly came to see divorce as one of the quintessential exercises of civil rights. And over the next two generations, their children and grandchildren would gradually help transform both the law and the popular culture of divorce from a privilege to something like a right.

Another common reason former slaves went to court was inheritance. As slaves, Black people had had the privilege of inheriting and passing down property, but not the right. Once those privileges became rights, they could take their inheritance disputes to court. Ex-slaves sued one another over inheritance as early as 1866, not just in the South but wherever slaves and their descendants went: California, Nebraska, Illinois, Massachusetts, Ohio, Florida, and New Jersey.[22] In order to bring these lawsuits, they had to translate their ideas of family into terms a judge could recognize.

There are generally two things that can happen to your property when you die, depending on whether or not you have made a will. If you have made a will, your executor (the person you named to carry out the terms of your will after you are gone) is supposed to file a probate petition at the county courthouse to prove the will is valid, and then, under a judge's supervision, he or she will take charge of paying your debts and carrying out your instructions for what's left. If you have not made a will, then you are "intestate," and a judge appoints someone to "administer" your property according to your state's rules of intestacy.

For freedpeople in the late 1800s, this interaction was usually routine. For example, an elderly Black woman, Maria Parker, signed an X mark to a simple will in 1866; six years later, one of her beneficiaries, Jane Gill, filed the will with the county clerk to put it on record. A good will anticipates future problems and finds ways around them. But it isn't always clear what rights the testator (the person who made the will) actually had in the property, such as with the flawed land titles discussed earlier, or John Robertson's not-quite-paid-off land purchase. For freedpeople, there was also the question of whether the relatives could even be tracked down. Maria Parker's will left her clothes to her sister but "if they cannot be given to my sister, as I suppose to be the case," then they should go to Jane Gill; to her son William she bequeathed "Whatever interest" in her house and land legally "belong[s] to me,"[23] suggesting that Parker wasn't totally sure what kind of interest she owned in it. Because "owning property" is not a straightforward proposition, even a simple will like Parker's probably required long, careful conversation with the man who wrote it for her.

Sometimes Black people went to court over inheritance rights. One widely publicized type of inheritance dispute tested what should happen when a white slaveowner left property to his "shadow" family. As the legal scholar Adrienne Davis has shown, state supreme court judges solved the "contradictions of the antebellum sexual economy" by casting Black inheritance as a white master's act of charity, not a Black person's right.[24] In the trial courts, however, there was not much talk of masters' charity because in the vast majority of inheritance cases involving Black people, the bequest came from other Black people.

Inheritance suits always dredge up family history, but Black people's inheritance suits often became seminars on the history of the Black family. It was one thing for state legislatures in the late 1860s to declare that cohabiting Black people were legally married. It was something else entirely to wave a magic gavel over two *slaves.* And that is what judges were asked to do in cases where an enslaved parent died without making a will. Intestacy suits forced courts to figure out whether slave marriages had been legal *during slavery.*[25]

The question wasn't entirely new. It had come up occasionally before the war, as people claimed inheritances from parents who had married as slaves and later become free. In dealing with these rare oddities, the antebellum courts had laid down two competing doctrines that would have sweeping implications after slavery. One doctrine, set out by the Louisiana supreme court in *Girod v. Lewis* (1819), said that slaves' "civil rights" to make contracts and inherit from their parents had always been "dormant," waiting for freedom to awaken them. The idea of sleeping rights was not as surprising as it may seem. Lawyers were used to thinking that a white woman's legal rights went under the "wing . . . or cover" of a husband, as the English jurist William Blackstone famously put it, and then peeped out again when the husband died.[26] By the 1860s, the sleeping-rights concept had been quietly eroding for decades, sanded down by thousands of wealthy couples' separate maintenance agreements and more recently by state statutes called "married women's property acts."

The other doctrine, set out in a North Carolina case called *Howard v. Howard* (1858), held that slave marriages were void from the start, not dormant; that emancipation did not "magic[ally]" make them valid; and that their children were illegitimate.[27] Joel Bishop, author of America's leading treatise on the law of marriage, summarized these two theories for the 1864 edition in a new chapter titled "The Impediment of Slavery."[28] In short, before the Civil War, southern judges had started using slave marriage to puzzle out the relationship between freedom and civil rights. Their solutions, expressed in the competing doctrines of dormancy and voidness, set the legal rules freedpeople would face in the 1860s and 1870s as they planned their families' futures. Although free Black people had been passing down property to their loved ones since the early 1600s, this first wave of inheritances after emancipation represented by far the biggest generational transfer of Black wealth in American history up until then—an epochal moment, now forgotten.

Most inheritances went uncontested, just as they did among white people. But when Black people sued over an inheritance, one of their best weapons was the fact that slaves could not legally marry. Over and over, Black people and their lawyers argued that their opponents could not inherit because their parents "were never married"—that children "born . . . of a slave marriage" were "not born in lawful wedlock" and therefore "had no heritable blood." Not all Black people involved in such lawsuits used this argument, but those who did fought tenaciously against these "illegal heir[s]" who "came in and tried to take the land" that rightly belonged to them, a defense that ignored the slave auctions and forced separations that had rendered those heirs "illegal" in the first place.[29] State legislatures had given a snap answer to the question, "Who counts as married?" and then state judges slowly worked out the implications of that answer. These litigants were asking, in effect, "Who counts as one of the family?"

Most judges decided to construe the marriage-by-fiat laws very broadly, rejecting Black litigants' claim that their opponents had "no heritable blood." They ruled that these laws retroactively ratified slave marriages—that, although slaves had held no "civil rights," their rights to marry and inherit had always been there, dormant.[30] But although white judges—stewed in racist stereotypes about Black people's supposedly lax morals and ravenous sexual urges—enjoyed lecturing Black men about family responsibility, the dormancy doctrine only raised more questions for judges in inheritance cases. If slaves' rights had just been dormant, then which marriage was the legal one? Which set of children or nieces or brother should get the farm?

Judges soon hit on a lasting solution, one that had worked for white people since the American Revolution: they would infer marriage from the couple's behavior. If a Black couple who had been together during slavery *acted* married after emancipation, when they had the legal capacity to make contracts—if they had "done for" each other, as Henrietta Jefferson had done for Eliza Brown—then there was no need to prove an official ceremony. Their slave marriage was retroactively valid from the day they jumped the broom, and their children were legitimate. But if either parent ever did something to repudiate the marriage—live with someone else, tell people they weren't married—then it was retroactively void and their children were bastards. Federal pension agents wound up applying a similar standard to the widows of Union soldiers, including white soldiers, whose marriages were also hard to document.[31] Ironically, this repudiation doctrine made the status and rights of free people dependent on the agency of their enslaved forebears. It forced litigants and lawyers to hunt for clues of willful intent in the personal histories of people who legally had no will of their own—whether a Missouri man taken to California ever talked "about coming back here" to get "her and his boys back," or whether a Virginia couple ever lived together, whether anyone "called [them] 'Father' and 'Mother,'" whether the father sent the son "clothes money and provisions, at Christmas" when the son was in prison.[32] Most of all, it invited people to keep coming to court with stories about the behavior and intentions and reputations of slaves from long ago.

For decades after slavery officially ended, a dwindling but still sizeable number of Black people found themselves having to prove kin relationships with relatives who had been swept away by slavery and war. "I dont know the names of the others," admitted a witness in a Washington, DC, case. "They were way down in Maryland. They were slaves and didn't come here until after the war. How could I know . . . whether they were married or not," the witness went on. "It was hard telling about people's marrying in them days, I tell you." Another man bluntly admitted that he did not even know whether his brothers and sisters were still alive, "because they were sold from me before the war [when I was] young."[33]

In order to prove their kinship ties (and hence get their inheritance),

Black people had to turn those gut-wrenching histories of loss into lists of "successors" that a judge would accept. They brought witnesses to testify about long-ago marriages, childbirths, and the like. They told what they knew to court-appointed commissioners, who wrote reports for the judges saying, for example, that the plaintiff had "three brothers and a sister who were taken to the South and sold some time in the forties (1840's) and have never been heard of since, and another brother who became insane & left here some 10 or 15 years ago." A New Jerseyan named Porter Dobbins brought witnesses to testify about Mary and "Uncle Dick," the parents of his great-uncle, John White. As slaves in Maryland, Mary and Uncle Dick had talked and acted like a married couple, said the witnesses, and had "lived upright, moral and irreproachable lives" to the day they died. Why should a judge believe such testimony, when, after all, Uncle Dick had been "sold to Georgia" and never heard from again? Because the testimony was so detailed. "I seen him [Uncle Dick] when [he] was led out in the barn," testified one of Dobbins' witnesses. "Seen him in the chain gang, seen the man leading him along to the Georgia train." John White's mother Mary had "bid him good-by, you know, that is all she could do. He stopped along and bid them all good-bye. They all cried, and I was little, too. I cried."[34] Such heartrending testimony served a specific legal purpose: the more tears shed, the more monogamous and "upright" Mary and Dick's relationship appeared, making it an "irreproachable" fact that Porter Dobbins really was John White's grandnephew and ought to inherit his property.

Because Black people now had civil rights, Black lives mattered to white people, too, at least sometimes. Whites who wanted to buy land sometimes found that they had "to work to locate the heirs" of long-dead Black landowners, heirs whose rights could not safely be ignored. W. M. Edwards wound up embroiled in a lawsuit after he bought land from a Mississippi Black family without asking enough questions about their patriarch's other slave wife and child. "Well I *thought* they were giving me the facts," Edwards insisted later. "I had leased the place" already for a few years "and had often talked with" them and they "did not ever mention" those other names. In another example, when a Washington, DC, real estate agent, William Main, resold a parcel of land he had bought from the heirs of an ex-slave named Henry A. Jackson, he found himself facing a lawsuit from Jackson's children by a hitherto-unknown slave wife back in West Virginia. The suit was "blackmail," Main sputtered. His purchase was as "straight as a string, gentlemen." But he had to answer the suit, a white businessman caught in the middle of what was, essentially, a Black family quarrel.[35] Even as white popular culture brimmed with poisonous stereotypes of Black family life—the "Mammy" devoted to serving "her" white family, the Black rapist leering at virtuous white women, the Black Jezebel seducing helpless white men—white lawyers and judges and other local officials took real Black families quite seriously, investigating their family trees, identifying and notifying heirs of their rights. They did not do this out of pity or a sense of duty toward faithful old "servants." They did it because the rules of property law demanded it. White-owned businesses and individuals had a stake in the orderly resolution of Black inheritance because Black landowners were links in the chain of title that anchored *everyone's* property rights.[36]

There were other, subtler ideas tugging on the law of property, too, ideas rooted in the privileges of association. In the 1860s and 1870s, many people of different backgrounds thought land was more than a commodity or even a civil right—they thought it was a "propriety," imbued with intense personal, social, and political meaning. In places where enslaved people had weathered the hurricane of the interstate slave trade—which in the generation before the Civil War had ripped hundreds of thousands of people away from their homes—freedpeople now tended to claim the particular parcels of land that had come to mean "home." "Never was there a people . . . more attached to familiar places," one Union officer had reported in February 1862. The idea of land as a "propriety" played out at mass meetings where freedpeople declared they had "a right to the land," grounded in their own forced labor and that of their ancestors. It stirred freedpeople to go on strike all across the South Carolina Low Country and the Louisiana cane fields. Thousands of ex-slaves, clutching a gun in one hand and a "Sherman warrant" in the other, told reporters they would rather "die where they stood" than give up their claims to the forty-acre parcels that Union troops had put into their possession after their treasonous owners had fled. And although President Andrew Johnson restored nearly all those lands to the traitors, many former slaves merely began saving up to buy their "familiar places," as well as new proprieties. All this left America's fast-growing Black landowners with a knot of ideas about landownership.[37]

In popular speech, these ideas are often called "heir property," or "family land." In legal terms, family land is a "tenancy in common," a form of ownership where each owner has a right, not to a physical piece of the land, but rather a fractional interest in the whole, undivided parcel. Each can cash out at any time, but when one co-owner dies, his interest goes to his children, not to the other co-owners. Because few freedpeople made written wills, much of the land they acquired during Reconstruction became tenancies in common, "fractionating" as it passed from a father to five children to eighteen grandchildren, until it legally belonged to a large and complicated tangle of kin, whose rights were founded on descent from what one man called the "old Founders," the "Fathers and Mothers [who] cleared those Swamps and Marshes."[38] These landowning families each became something like an association—a family corporation—whose members were expected to act in the corporate interest, and who held certain privileges and duties within it, according to their status. Like the shareholders of a business or the members of a religious corporation, families did not always agree. The rise of family land, owned by corporation-like Black families, is another example of the rich and sometimes surprising story of Black life that emerges from looking closely at law.

Black landowners laid down two principles about family land in the early months of freedom. What I call the "founders principle" reckoned land privileges by relation to the person who acquired the land. Like the debate over slave marriage, this principle essentially put ancestry in the spotlight, and thus made land privileges a matter of proving genealogy. The "conduct principle" said that those who acted like family *were* family, and those who acted like strangers were *not* family, no matter who their biological parents were. If the "founders" principle made family land a debate about ancestry, the "conduct" principle politicized ancestry itself. The interplay between these principles produced what we might call an "ancestral politics of family land," one that wove in and around the official rules about tenancy in common.

Like most things in family life, the ancestral politics of family land are almost invisible from the outside, especially from the distance of a century, but sometimes they flashed into view on the records of the county court. Sometimes the spark came when someone used a farm or a house to secure old-age care for herself. Ellen Henson "was determined" to cut out her relatives because "th[ey] had never done anything for her; never came to see her." Instead, she decided to leave her property—two Washington, DC, house-lots—to her "best friend," a Baltimore steamboat steward named Richard Hill, for his "many years" of "kind and attentive" care after her husband's death. Once word got out, "she was very much bothered by persons running there trying to persuade her not to will it over to him," especially "the members and trustees of the Israel Methodist Church," who told "her she had done wrong by giving her property to Mr. Hill and that the first thing she knew she would be out in the street."[39] Here we have an African American woman who leaves property to a nonrelative, and then has to fight her estranged relatives *and her church* to keep her word.

Precisely because ancestry was so often political, and because people can change their minds about bequests until the minute they die, there were risks for anyone who agreed to "do for" an older person in expectation of an inheritance. Eliza Brown's niece, Euphemia Stewart, used to help her aunt, "but they fell out" a "long time ago," so badly that some of the neighbors were not even sure whether "Phemie" was really her niece. And in the end, as we saw earlier, Brown left her property to Henrietta Jefferson. But while Brown was alive, Henrietta and her husband had worried that Brown might cut them off too, in spite of all they had done for her. "My husband told me not to give her any more money, until I had something to show for it," Henrietta said later, "because if she was to drop off, I would not have any thing to show for the money I gave her"—nothing in writing that would bind Brown to her promise, nothing but words. Indeed, before she offered Henrietta her property in exchange for old-age care, Brown had already approached Henrietta's cousin, James Bowser, with the same offer. "I am all alone here in this house," James recalled her saying. "I have a lot of tenants here, and they aint very good tenants. If you and your wife will come over and live with me, and take care of me, until my death, I will give you the house and lot." Bowser was intrigued but his wife flat-out rejected it. She "would do everything she could for Aunt Eliza," Bowser remembered. But "she did not want anything to do with *heired* property" because "Aunt Eliza's heirs might come and give trouble."[40] That is, the kind of trouble Eliza's niece Phemie gave when she took Henrietta Jefferson to court.

The wariness that the Jeffersons and the Bowsers showed toward "heired property" suggests that would-be heirs, Black or white, had to worry not just that the older person might change her mind but that her blood relatives—like Euphemia Stewart—could dispute whatever promises she made. Using property to leverage help from friends and neighbors was an effective strategy but it also subjected Black-owned property to a wider set of claims from people like Henrietta Jefferson, who could legitimately say they were family, even if they were not "heirs." Like many whites, African Americans pursued a vision of kinship as conduct, a vision that sustained and drew strength from both civil rights of property and from the idea that a family was, for some purposes, a kind of membership corporation.

This turned courts into stages for the remaking of Black families. As they talked with lawyers and gave depositions, Black people did much more than describe their family trees; they *rewrote* them. Ann Middleton testified that Eliza Brown always referred to Euphemia and her siblings as "her nephews and nieces—always owned them to me." In another case, Jacob Bell knew that John Booth was the son of Sam Sumby because "Sam Sumby claimed him as his child" over the "~~twenty~~ thirty years" they all worked together at a corkyard. By the same token, violating family rules could turn blood kin into strangers. In *Richardson v. Richardson,* an 1868 case heard by an Army court in South Carolina, a Union veteran named Lot Richardson found himself lopped off the family tree after he tried to claim his share of a sixty-acre parcel that his late father had bought from a northern businessman in the closing days of the war. His relatives began, as one witness put it, to make "a fuss among the people." They said things at church. They loud-talked it in each other's yards. They even said that he had murdered his father through magic. One of the neighbors testified: "Lot was respected by all the people, but since this report got out the people mistreat him & suspect him." Relatives and neighbors not only moved to "keep [Lot] out of the Land," but also started denying "that he . . . is one of the family" at all. No one accused him of taking more than his share. The problem was that he had sued to divide the land, land that "the whole family" had been working as a single, undivided unit.[41] Much as state courts used the repudiation doctrine to decide cases of inheritance from enslaved couples, this Low Country family corporation decided that Lot had repudiated his connection to them. Lot's conduct proved that he was a stranger. Being someone's son or niece was something that had to be created and maintained over time by "doing for" one's relatives. It rested on "community opinion," even more than property and contract did. Courtroom testimony about kinship ties did not simply prove facts about kinship. It actively shaped those "facts."[42]

Historians in recent decades have often portrayed Black people's economic, political, and social lives as guided by a communal ethos that repudiated the liberal individualism of capitalist America, an ethos founded on the resilience of "the Black family." In some ways, lawsuits around family land did tap into a powerful alternate tradition, not just in Black culture but in Anglo-American property law, a tradition that viewed land as the "propriety" of a family whose claims reached far into the future. This tradition blossomed in nostalgic songs and movies and it survived in certain niches scattered around the laws of most states: homestead exemptions (protecting the family home from creditors) and married women's property acts (protecting a daughter's inheritance from her husband's creditors). But the idea that Black people had a communal ethos reflects the politics of the 1960s more than it does the state of Black legal thought in the 1860s. In the years after the Civil War, family land was political, not cultural, and a dissenter like Lot Richardson was not betraying the freedom struggle: he was cashing out his stake in a family corporation that was blocking him from pursuing his interests as he saw them. Some families' holdings would last for many decades, aided by white judges who, well into the 1900s, often protected family land from people like Richardson.[43] A century later, family land would become the centerpiece of a movement for economic justice. But for that to happen, it first had to be stripped of the intraracial, intrafamily concerns that had brought it to life—the complex, often painful decisions that people like Lot Richardson and Eliza Brown had made about who was family and what it meant to *be* family. In the meantime, tensions about belonging and collective identity were also spreading in another, more public kind of Black association: the church.

6

Who Is the Church?

A group of trustees of a fast-growing church went to the main civil court of the nation's capital on September 28, 1867, and sued their pastor. Speaking on behalf of the congregation, Joseph Alexander and his fellow trustees charged that Albert Bouldin was treating Third Colored Baptist Church as his personal property. He had blended his own savings with monies from the collection plate, they said, and then refused to let anyone see the finance books. He had gotten the deed to their new building recorded in his own name instead of in the name of the church and its trustees, the way church property was supposed to be held. He had orchestrated the expulsion of a woman for having a child out of wedlock "without [also] turning . . . out" the man who made her pregnant. He had spitefully withheld Christian pardons and insulted his own parishioners. When some of the trustees had objected to what he was doing, he had expelled them, along with two hundred members, arbitrarily and without a church trial. And then he had "gone to Law with his Brethren"—sued them in a secular court. Bouldin and his allies claimed it was all the trustees' and deacons' fault: they were the ones who "drove *us* out of the church . . . broke open the windows," and took away the keys. The trustees asked the judge for possession of the church property, to appoint an outside auditor to go over the books, and for an injunction that would bar Bouldin from interfering anymore. Bouldin vehemently refused even to talk about stepping down: he said he had been "heare Preaching when they came" and had mortgaged his own personal property to have the church built. The case eventually went to the U.S. Supreme Court.[1]

In *Bouldin v. Alexander* (1872), the Court had to decide whether it could decide. That is, it had to explain what kinds of church disputes a secular court could settle without violating the Establishment Clause of the First Amendment, which says that government cannot promote any particular faith or create a theocracy—a country ruled by God through priests. Everyone knew that church members had rights, but were they the kind a secular court could enforce? In rendering its decision, the Court set an important and lasting precedent in American law, extending and modifying a principle it had laid down just a few months earlier in a case involving white Presbyterians: that majorities in congregational churches had certain rights that a court could protect, such as contract, property, and particular kinds of due process. These were "temporalities"—things of this world rather than the next—or, as the Georgia supreme court had put it in another prominent case that also involved a Black church, their "civil rights."[2]

In the decades after emancipation, Black people seized the powers of the law of associations to found hundreds of new churches, businesses, colleges, fraternities, and even Black towns, and they solidified their gains by filing incorporation papers under state law. For generations, historians have marveled at this "remarkable 'thickening' of African American civic and associational life" during Reconstruction, without exploring the legalities that made it possible.[3] It is easy to forget that an association is a *legal* entity, empowered by the state to own property, make contracts, discipline members, choose leaders, and more. The history of Black-owned associations shows that Black people were not alienated from law or ignorant of law; they were deeply invested in law and thought about it often.

Today we think of Black churches and businesses and colleges as sites of pride and collective empowerment and as places where Black people could seek the justice they could not get in white-run courts. But Rev.

Bouldin's saga suggests we ought to turn that idea around: Black people have also "gone to Law" when they felt they could not get justice from their "brethren." To do that, they had to translate their concerns—which were often intensely personal and spiritual—into temporalities, the categories that secular courts recognized as civil rights. White judges and legislators repeatedly intervened in Black church affairs, not to assert white domination but because Black religious people asked them to. Black people's efforts to translate, navigate, and police the boundary between the sacred and the civil not only helped modernize the private law of religion; by the 1950s it would also help transform the public meaning of civil rights, slowly confining it within the sanctified terms of the Black freedom struggle. That modern vision not only covered up a vibrant history of Black legal engagement and Black legal thought but also obscured a rich internal history of Black life, of how Black people related to one another through associations. The argument about whether and how to pursue civil rights *through* "the Negro church" grew out of a century of debate about what rights Christians held *in* their churches.

Black people founded all kinds of different associations after the Civil War: mutual benefit associations like the Good Samaritan Daughters and the Daughters of Zion, the Port Gibson school association, and quasi-public ones like the Good Will Fire Company of Natchez, Mississippi. In Tennessee, a group of Black people formed a "Real Estate and Homestead Association" to promote migration to Kansas, and incorporated a Black town there, the Singleton Colony. A handful of Black people, all prominent in business or politics, formed for-profit business associations. To block the segregation laws that were once again spreading across the country, a group of French-speaking Black New Orleanians established a Citizens' Committee for the Annulment of Act. No. 111, Commonly Known as the Separate Car Law, and soon engineered a test case in the name of one of its members, a light-skinned shoemaker named Homére Plessy. To mobilize the untapped power of Black voters, other African Americans founded political associations, like the Equal Rights League of Wilmington, North Carolina, the Union Monitor Club of Norfolk, Virginia, and myriad chapters of the Union League (a New York corporation). Expanding the free Black northerners' Colored Conventions of the 1840s and 1850s to the south and west,[4] African Americans used associations to nationalize their political activism, paving the way for what would eventually become the National Association for the Advancement of Colored People (NAACP). And, of course, they founded religious associations—like Third Colored Baptist Church.

Some of these associations secured state charters and incorporated themselves. In the year 1882, just in the state of Texas, at least nine Black-run associations filed incorporation papers, from Wiley College to the Colored Farmers' Association of Texas to the Colored Men's Land and Commercial Joint Stock Association. Hungry for investors and members, these Black-run corporations advertised their valuable corporate powers. One Louisiana charity got the local Black newspaper to reprint the whole text of its corporate filings. And just as the New York African Society for Mutual Relief had thrown itself a corporate birthday parade in 1829 through lower Manhattan, Virginia's United Order of True Reformers celebrated the twenty-fifth anniversary of the granting of its corporate charter by commissioning itself a birthday book: a lavishly illustrated self-congratulatory company history, full of reprinted by-laws, constitutions, lists of corporate officers, board meeting minutes, and bygone corporate lawsuits.[5]

Most Black-run associations probably didn't bother incorporating. After all, an unincorporated association held many of the same powers as a corporation, including control over membership and internal affairs, the power to bind members with by-laws, the power to own property and make contracts, and the power to sue and be sued. But there were drawbacks to staying unincorporated. One was that it left the members more exposed to harsh market forces and authoritarian leaders.

Many Black people bought their life insurance from fraternal lodges like the Black Elks and Odd Fellows; the lodges, in turn, borrowed to finance building projects and other investments, just as State Farm and Prudential do today. But an unincorporated Odd Fellows lodge didn't have to keep a capital reserve or meet stringent state insurance rules that were designed for bigger and richer companies (like State Farm). If the lodge's business sagged, its creditors would have to get their money back from its members, because there was no corporation to sue. And most of the lodge's "creditors" were its own members—people who had paid their dues and were counting on its benefits. Staying unincorporated was cheap and flexible, and it helped keep white politicians' noses out of Black people's business. But was that worth sacrificing the right to hold someone accountable when things went wrong? There were rarely easy answers to the incorporation question.[6]

Property rights, too, raised tough questions for Black-owned associations. Church members who gave money to pay off the mortgage objected when the church's leaders spent it on something else.[7] Deeds to church land and buildings typically had a "dedication" clause saying that they were owned by trustees "for the use of" some specifically named "religious society," so naturally people got upset when pastors like Rev. Bouldin or national-level denominations tried to write *their* names into those property deeds. Recall that when Charles Palmore and three other men left Cumberland Baptist in 1875, they recorded a deed in the name of "a Colored Baptist Church to be called Midway Baptist." If one of those four men had tried to open a saloon in the back of Midway Baptist, or invited white preachers to the pulpit, or started doing faith healings in the aisle, then any other Midway member could have shown that dedication clause to Judge Joel Flood of the Cumberland County Circuit Court and gotten it stopped. They would have argued that a saloon does not belong in a "church"; that white preachers do not belong in a "Colored" church; and that faith healing is not "Baptist." Black rights during Reconstruction meant much more than racial justice, more than federal protection from white violence and discrimination. They also meant state laws that regulated power and discrimination among Black people.

In our era, we think of associations as either public (like the Corporation of the City of New York) or private (like Exxon or Google). But in the 1800s, millions of Americans pursued public goals through organizations now typically seen as "private"—clubs, fire brigades, corporations, churches, and unions—while things we now view as public, such as political parties, were seen, in some respects, as clubs. (Indeed, in the 1860s and 1870s, the word "disfranchisement" still referred primarily to the rights of corporate investors, not the voting rights of citizens.) The Mutual Benefit Building and Loan Association was founded to help "the colored people of Newark" become homeowners. The Belle Ville Farmers Association, organized in 1867 to buy land and set up an all-Black "colony" in coastal Georgia, had a president and general agent, a sheriff and deputy, a fence viewer, road master, market inspector, and janitor, freely mixing what we might today call public and private functions. But Black associations fused public and private purposes longer and more consistently. Many of them owed their existence to white racism; they were formed after white-run associations rejected them.[8]

For Black-run associations, then, racial exclusion layered on yet another dimension of public-ness, even beyond the public functions that white-run associations carried. They owed something to more than just the shareholders or members of the association. After all, not every Black person in America belonged to the Belle Ville Farmers Association. Yet they did not have a duty to the public at large, because that would have implied a duty to the *white* public too. And so, Black-run associations developed a distinctive discourse as they sometimes struggled to reconcile business imperatives—the sheer need to stay financially afloat—with a vague but powerfully-felt duty to "the Negro race."[9]

The United Order of True Reformers is a good example. The True Reformers were the "colored" auxiliary of a white anti-whiskey activist

The Saints of Christ Grocery, circa 1900. Incorporated in Pennsylvania in 1895, the Church of God-Saints of Christ, which ran this store, illustrates how Black-run associations often mixed business with broader duties to "the race" or to God. Few other Americans felt the tension between private interest and public duty as keenly as did the Black people who led associations.

group called the Good Templars. In the 1870s, an enterprising former slave named William W. Browne decided to turn the True Reformers' Alabama branch into a Black insurance company. Browne's "Mutual Benefit and Relief Plan" made each member a "stockholder" in the True Reformers corporation. The Plan also created "a separate fund" in each chapter (or "Fountain"), diverted part of members' dues and fees into those funds, and issued each member a "certificate or policy" guaranteeing a certain "benefit" to be paid at death. The Plan appointed trustees to hold the growing pile of money (in trust for the policy-holding members), along with secretaries and treasurers to keep account of it, and required each of these officers to sign a bond against malfeasance. A few years later, the True Reformers refined the mutual benefit plan by dividing the membership into age-stratified "classes" paying different premiums, and eventually started requiring prospective members to get a doctor's exam before they could sign up for benefits. If "money is power," as Browne insisted,[10] then Black power in the waning days of Reconstruction grew in large part from the details of corporation law. Browne borrowed the corporate form of a white temperance organization, endowed it with the moral indignation of racial discrimination, and used it to weld together a clutter of tiny benevolent societies into one big enterprise operating "upon a plain business basis." But it was not always easy to reconcile "plain business" with the corporation's duty to "the race."

William Browne left Alabama because of racism. Yet, to the mixed group of women and men who had been running the True Reformers of Virginia, his arrival in 1880 as Grand Worthy Master was something like a hostile takeover. Disgusted by the male leaders' machinations, one of the women delegates to a pivotal meeting demanded that the Grand Fountain refund the money her local chapter had paid in. Another picked up the meeting's official journal ledger from the Grand Worthy Master's table and started back to her seat. Browne "hurried" after her, wrestled the ledger out of her hands, and orchestrated a vote to "cut off all the rebellious factions" for good—by filing a charter of incorporation. Four years later, Browne got himself elected leader for life.[11]

For decades the leaders of Black benevolent associations like the True Reformers repeatedly fought over money and how to use that money, over what authority the main organization had over its chapters, and over who had the right to vote in the meetings where these decisions were made. They fought their own members, refusing to pay benefits or cancelling memberships for violations of some term of the insurance contract. Disputes erupted after associations ran short of money to pay claims, as scores of them did during the economic depressions of the 1890s, 1920s, and 1930s.[12] Far from trying to protect a zone of Black autonomy against a hostile legal system, they repeatedly asked white judges to intervene in these fights, filing lawsuits and countersuits against one another.

Racist attacks from rival white-run associations papered over these internal divisions, encouraging members and leaders to close ranks against a common foe. From 1904 to 1929, white fraternal orders tried to destroy the biggest Black fraternal orders. They sued to stop Black orders from using their own names, insignia, regalia, and even handshakes, on the grounds that the Black orders were stealing their business—that a customer might mistakenly buy an insurance policy from, say, the Improved Benevolent and Protective Order of Elks of the World (Black) instead of the Benevolent and Protective Order of Elks (white). Leaders of the major Black orders decided to fight. By then, they had years of experience being sued by their own members. And they took advantage of their organizations' corporate structures to organize a coordinated nationwide defense. In 1912, in *Creswill v. Grand Lodge Knights of Pythias of Georgia,* the U.S. Supreme Court decided in favor of the Black Pythians, and by 1929, the rest of the Black fraternal orders had won their cases against the white orders.[13]

But there were consequences. Although the cases were decided on fairly narrow, technical grounds, the experience nevertheless galvanized some leaders to think of themselves as litigating for "the race," for the "rights of colored citizens," and against "prejudice." This was their mission, these leaders contended, and the mission justified not only the high-profile court cases against white rivals but also the elaborate parades, the expensive building projects, and their own authority as leaders.[14]

Not everyone swallowed that rhetoric. It was expensive to wage an all-out, nationwide court battle, and some members rebelled when the national leaders raised members' "taxes" and started diverting money from the insurance benefits members thought they had been paying for. John Mitchell Jr., a newspaper editor who headed the Pythians' Virginia lodge, scoffed that the national lodge's expensive Supreme Court victory over the whites was practically worthless. Mitchell soon sued the national leaders for "an unwarranted, unlawful, tyrannical exercise of autocratic power," "misappropriation of funds," and "gross mismanagement." Another state lodge warned that thousands of Pythians were quitting because national leaders were chasing big, showy, money-losing building projects instead of paying "death claims" and "operating expenses." Members complained about "steam-roller elections," where insiders manipulated meeting dates and parliamentary rules to get incumbents reelected. When the Pythians' leader announced in 1927 "that he was unalterably opposed" to holding the annual meeting anywhere "in the South as long as segregation, jim crowism, discrimination and disfranchisement obtained" there, critics openly mocked him. The real reason, they muttered, was that the next meeting was scheduled for Dallas and he was worried that a popular Texan rival would beat him for reelection. By the 1910s, a wide range of Black people were trying to vindicate "the rights and privileges of" "fraternal citizenship" against their own leaders.[15]

National leaders steered those claims on "fraternal citizenship" toward claims to American citizenship. From the 1910s to the 1950s, the leaders of America's biggest Black-run fraternal associations converged on the twin ideas that civil rights meant equal rights under federal law and that Black people had to be taught about rights. The Elks ran an annual "oratorical contest for students" on "The Negro and the Constitution." Leaders of all the major Black fraternal orders urged their members to support the NAACP's campaigns for "full Constitutional rights" and against lynching and "prejudice." The Black Elks' top leaders boasted in 1954 that they had traveled "into every state in order to make the people civil rights conscious." Everywhere they went, the two leaders told their audiences that civil rights meant school desegregation, voting, and an end to all forms of "discrimination on account of race and color." Silent on other forms of discrimination—such as gender—and willfully ignoring decades of agitation by Black people to assert their "rights and privileges" against autocrats like William Browne, Black leaders declared that "the people" had to be taught that "freedom, like peace, is indivisible." But of course, freedom was not so simple.[16]

The blossoming of Black associations in the Jim Crow era laid professional and conceptual groundwork for modern civil rights. The associations generated tremendous amounts of law: not only widely cited cases like *Creswill* but also corporate charters, amended constitutions and by-laws, "legislation," official histories, deeds, contracts, and blank standard forms. The associations also created internal Black-run legal institutions: a "Register of Deeds" for the association, a "Law Department" headed by a "Supreme Attorney," whose job it was "to worry for you." They familiarized millions of Black people with basic principles of contract law and the law of associations. They nurtured a generation of Black lawyers who were heavily networked, skilled at complex litigation, and conscious that they were helping to make law across a wide range of doctrinal areas.[17] And Black associations fostered a distinctive discourse about the purpose of associations and the privileges and rights of their members. By the 1950s, when the modern civil rights movement began, the question was coming into focus sharper than ever: what is a Black corporation for?

The law of associations profoundly shaped the South's politics, for better and for worse. Much of the vicious political violence of Reconstruction was committed by people acting as members of associations: rifle clubs, militias, and the Democratic Party. White Democrats organized to rig elections, and when they could not rig them, they simply shot their opponents. So African Americans organized themselves as if for war: they got up before dawn on election day and walked "in a solid column" of up to 450 men. Some carried flags. Some wore homemade uniforms. When they arrived at the polling place, they lined up shoulder to shoulder, protecting each voter as he stepped up to the ballot box holding his color-marked ticket (there was no secret ballot then). In an era when Black voting literally required "a military operation," the association provided not only a practical mechanism for mobilizing political violence, but also a *legal* form to make it legitimate: the "militia," the "rifle club," and more. Fifty Black men drilling in a field during the lead-up to the 1876 election were just fifty Black men walking around with guns, but a charter made them "an incorporated body," with powers delegated by the South Carolina legislature. If the whites who shot them lacked a charter of their own, those whites became "rioters"—criminals. Because states delegated to militias many of the powers and duties that today belong to police and the National Guard, it is no surprise that Black people so insistently asked their governors for charters. After all, "one man's mob is another man's militia," and the difference was often a corporate charter from the state.[18]

With or without charters, Black people also used unions—labor associations—to better their lives. From levee workers in Memphis and Mobile and longshoremen in port cities like New Orleans and Savannah to lumberyard workers in Washington, DC, African American workers organized themselves into unions, many of which came together in a national federation called the Colored National Labor Union. It was harder for women to associate because their jobs—as cooks, maids, and laundry workers—were scattered across thousands of homes. Some managed to pull it off: for example, a group called the Ladies of Labor in Galveston, a short-lived "protective association" in Atlanta in 1879, and a stronger one in 1881 called the Washerwomen's Association of Atlanta. The Atlanta group gathered data showing that they were being systematically underpaid and then set up "a schedule of prices" to "protect their rights." For years, white southerners had been manipulating licensing laws to keep Black people from becoming draymen, grocers, barbers, hucksters, oystermen, or laundresses—that is, from doing anything but pick cotton for white people. So, when Atlanta's city council threatened to require a new, expensive license, the Washerwomen's Association decided to engage in some manipulation of their own. They creatively reinterpreted it as "a protection, so we can control the [prices and rules of] washing for the city." That is, they decided that this *license* ("an official permit to . . . carry on a business or trade") was really going to be a *franchise* (a "special privilege conferred by government"). Things never got that far because the city council quietly dropped its licensing proposal.[19] But the episode illustrates the Black workers' lively engagement with the law of associations, licensing, and franchising, at a time when all three were very much in flux.

Black labor unions looked different in the countryside, where labor contracts were tangled up in the law of landlord-and-tenant. Consider the squad-labor system that flourished for a few years in the late 1860s before the tenant-farming system of Jim Crow, and that helped plant the seeds of large-scale southern Black property ownership. The squad was, in effect, an unincorporated association. Squads bargained collectively with plantation owners, signed work contracts, and sometimes built their own supply storehouses. Perhaps even more strictly than other associations, squads expelled members who didn't pull their weight. Whites did not necessarily discourage Black-run unions unless they spread "dangerous" ideas, such as claiming the power to vet their members' work contracts, or holding themselves "not . . . accountable to the Freedmen's Bureau, or any white man."[20]

Some rural Black people tried to vault into landownership by setting up rotating credit associations, a kind of peer-to-peer lending the World Bank would later call "the poor man's bank." In formalizing the affiliations of kinship and neighborhood in this way, African Americans essentially took the corporate form that was helping them establish churches and life insurance companies and used it as a land-buying tool.[21]

Joining an association meant accepting certain legal duties and risks that were distinct from people's rights as individuals, and so some groups chose to *dissociate* after getting their land. One of the best examples of the legal risks that came with association was a Mississippi venture called Bear Camp. In February 1878, nine Black families bought a 963-acre plantation together. They financed the purchase, as well as their operations (plows, mules, feed, food, and the like), by signing deeds of trust to the Vicksburg merchant firm Halpin, Bonham & Co., using the land as collateral. In 1882, when they fell behind on their payments, Halpin had the land auctioned on the county courthouse steps, bought it up, and quickly resold it for more than twice the auction price. The nine family heads hired a lawyer and sued. Their strongest argument was that a joint promissory note could not swallow up their homestead exemption (a state law meant to protect wives and children by shielding a certain amount of a debtor's property from creditors). In order to claim that homestead exemption, they had to prove that they were tenants in common (individuals owning undivided shares of the whole property) and *not* a Black corporation ("a single entity" jointly liable for its debts). With such large sums of money in play (about $4 million in 2021 dollars just for the land), the Bear Camp case produced a "vast amount" of testimony.[22]

The families insisted that there never was any such thing as "the 'Bear Camp Colony,'" not even a "secret . . . understanding" uniting them. They were just neighbors who helped one another out. Each family had built its own houses and stables, hired its own workers, shipped its own cotton, and borrowed its own money. Peter Hamilton, who was identified as "President" on the colony's founding "agreement," merely "acted as foreman in buying the place," said one witness. "He was no more than any of us," said another. "We gave [him] no authority." By contrast, witnesses for the Halpin firm insisted that the buyers "were known generally as the Bear Camp Colony," "a sort of communistic company" that would hold the land "in common until it was paid for." The Mississippi supreme court sided with Halpin. Citing documents that specified proportional returns on each family's contribution, and references to Peter Hamilton as "President" of the "Bear Camp Colony," the court ruled that Bear Camp was "a partnership in . . . one common venture," and that the plantation was one of its assets, "liable for its debts, just as any other asset of a partnership." The auction sale stood. The Black families lost their land.[23] Historians have long celebrated Black collectivities, including land-buying ventures like this one, as examples of cultural resistance, episodes in the long struggle for freedom. But organizing carried legal implications, not just cultural or political ones, and, like Rev. Bouldin's church and Lot Richardson's land, it sometimes pitted their civil rights as individuals against their privileges and duties as members of associations.

Nowhere did the tension between rights and privileges appear more starkly than in churches. After the Civil War, Black churches across the South seized civil rights to pursue independence from whites; those declarations of independence provoked white-dominated courts and religious denominations to set strict limits on when courts could intervene in church affairs, extending and clarifying a doctrinal trend that had been set, to that point, by white church suits.

The debates that racked Black churches during Reconstruction reverberated well into the 1960s. As notorious as the Jim Crow era was for creating an American apartheid, these were also the years when American religious institutions and theologies transformed, when legal theorists and judges were wrestling with key innovations in contract and property law, and when more African Americans were using the courts than ever before. By the 1890s, when Black people had lost the right to vote and so much else, African Americans were putting property and contract—the paradigmatic civil rights of the nineteenth century—to everyday use. But did they have civil rights in church—rights that a court could protect? It was a difficult question. A church such as Third Colored was a group of people who believed in Christ, a piece of property, duly recorded in cloth-bound ledgers at the county courthouse, and a sacred place, set apart from the world of the civil—all at the same time. And while any state citizen had civil rights, privileges within religious associations depended on one's status—member or nonmember, deacon, minister, or bishop. Linking privileges to status tended to concentrate power in the hands of church leaders, who were nearly all men, and who did not necessarily respect the rights of church members, who were mostly women.[24] In the early 1900s, as some Black churches amassed huge memberships and property, and as Black denominations became national corporations, legal doctrines that had been developed in the mid-1800s—in part from Black church cases—enabled Black male leaders to amass extraordinary authority. By the 1950s, as we will see, national religious leaders, such as Joseph H. Jackson and Martin Luther King Jr., would disagree about the role Black churches should play in the fight for American democracy yet embraced the antidemocratic possibilities enabled by judges' willingness to defer when it came to the internal affairs of their own churches.

Legally, a church was (and is) a "religious society": a private association organized under state law for a religious purpose. Like a business association (such as Exxon) or a fraternal association (say, the True Reformers), a religious association enables people to exercise civil rights of property and contract through a corporate "person" that lives forever. The price for eternal life is that the church must hand over those civil rights to a third party: trustees, chosen by the members, who sign contracts and hold church property in trust for the benefit of the members. The creation of a corporate person means that state power will always play a role in church affairs, and it empowers the parishioners by making clear that, ultimately, church government answers to them.[25]

Thus, in August 1875, when Charles Palmore, Page Pryor, Maurice Brown, and Archer Harris, those four Black members of the white-run Cumberland Baptist Church, went to the county courthouse and recorded their purchase, as trustees, of two acres along Guinea Road "for the purpose of erecting a Colored Baptist Church to be called Midway Baptist," they acquired several important rights and protections on behalf of their brethren: rights of property and contract; standing to sue and be sued as a collective rather than individually; and, eventually, tax-exemptions.[26] That is, founding a church and running it was an exercise of civil rights. Importantly, the standard legal theories and doctrines that applied to associations also assigned those rights *within* the newly independent Midway church, specifying the relative legal powers of the minister, church officers, and congregation. Defined under state law, not federal law, these civil rights affected both churches' internal governance and their dealings with white outsiders.

When slavery ended in 1865, the white-run biracial churches had to confront a big problem. We saw earlier that, during slavery, most of them had depended partly on donations from "Black Brethren" who could not vote or lead in church affairs.[27] We also saw that by the late 1850s the tension between Black people's contributions to the church and their threadbare privileges as church members was beginning to manifest itself physically, as one church after another segregated the pews and built add-ons "for the colored members." White church leaders had always trimmed the principle of Christian equality to the white supremacist dictates of state law, but after 1865, when state law recognized Black civil rights outside church, white leaders refused to accord their "Black Brethren" equal status or privileges inside the church.[28] The result was a religious exodus. Midway Baptist was one of hundreds, if not thousands, of Black congregations that seceded from white-run churches during Reconstruction.

The exodus flowed through channels carved by changes in the law of religion. Beginning back in the 1840s, as America's major denominations splintered over the slavery question, state supreme courts had gradually fashioned rules for what courts could do in church suits without violating the fundamental freedom of worship. Generally, they had refused to hear cases involving purely ecclesiastical matters. By putting a "veil" between worldly matters (like property) and spiritual ones (like whether baptism required full immersion or just a sprinkle of water), judges had tried to give themselves a carefully limited power to intervene in church affairs. In a pair of cases just after the Civil War, the U.S. Supreme Court tried to synthesize those ideas into a definitive doctrine: *Watson v. Jones* (an 1871 case involving white Presbyterians) and *Bouldin v. Alexander* (the 1872 case that began this chapter). In these twin cases, the Court held that judges should generally defer to the denomination, enforcing whatever decision its own rules or highest governing body dictated.

This "polity-deference" doctrine, whose basic outlines still govern today, treats religious organizations as something like sovereign entities, free to control their internal affairs—even undemocratically—and to have the state enforce that control. And yet, the Court hastened to add, deference did not tie judges' hands. No court could "decide who *ought* to be members of the church," the Court insisted in 1872, after Rev. Bouldin expelled his opponents and stacked his trustee board, but a court could interpret Third Colored Baptist's own rules to decide "whether the . . . expulsion *was* the act of the church" or not. By 1875, when Charles Palmore and his three fellow members filed their deed at the Cumberland County courthouse, the deference doctrine had raised the stakes of determining who "the church" was—a delicate question in churches such as Cumberland Baptist, where two-thirds of the members were freedpeople but all the church officers were white. And indeed, state judges, who were not bound by *Watson* or *Bouldin,* often refused to defer, and instead waded into church cases, grimly determined to stop wayward churchmembers or ministers from taking property held under a trust dedicated to one faith and converting it to a different faith. "The guarantee of religious freedom," one court warned in 1870, "does not guarantee the freedom to steal churches."[29]

From the 1840s to the 1870s, the deference doctrine and its exceptions sketched religious bodies' relationship to the nascent domain of civil rights. In their rulings, the judges mapped out two roads for the Black exodus. One was for Black Christians to quit, take church property with them, and record it in the name of a Black-led entity such as the African Methodist Episcopal denomination (A. M. E.). The other was for them to stay put and change the church itself by outvoting their white brethren. In hierarchical denominations such as the Presbyterians and Methodists, where property was held in trust by a board of trustees for the denomination, it briefly seemed possible in the mid-1860s that African Americans could take Methodist buildings and real estate into the A.M.E. After all, back in 1845, the South's white Methodists had themselves grabbed hundreds of church properties when they quit the national Methodist denomination—a proslavery "Great Secession" that had splintered Methodism into the "Northern" and "Southern Methodists" we know today.[30] And white Methodists knew perfectly well that the Black Methodists had helped pay for those properties out of their meager earnings during slavery.

In January 1865, a few weeks after General William T. Sherman's March to the Sea shredded the Confederate army, Sherman and Secretary of War Edwin Stanton met with a delegation of Black religious leaders in the newly liberated city of Savannah. This meeting has been viewed by historians as a key moment when African Americans laid out their vision of what freedom meant to them. It is even more famous as the genesis of Sherman's "forty acres and a mule" field order number 15. But, in fact, the officers of Savannah's Black churches wanted something more specific and immediate: they were seeking the upper hand in a years-long fight over church properties. One by one, each minister told the gathered federal officials that his church wasn't held in trust by whites for the use of its "colored members," but rather that his church *belonged* to its "colored members." Indeed, seven months earlier, the AME had already authorized a delegation to ask Secretary Stanton for an order granting them "possession of all . . . church property now held by" or "built for the use of" Black Methodists across the whole South. And two months after that, top bishops had come down from New York to plant the flag of African Methodism in Savannah, touring around with reporters in tow, preaching guest sermons, and lingering theatrically over relics of slavery like a bill of sale found in a desk drawer.[31]

But southern judges were not about to let freedpeople "steal churches." The now all-white Southern Methodists sued Jacob Godfrey, one of the "colored" delegates to that fateful meeting with Stanton and Sherman, and they won. The "instant" Black Methodists "associated themselves with the African Methodist Episcopal Church," the Georgia supreme court said in 1871 in *Godfrey v. Walker*, they broke their connection to "*our* churches" and "surrendered all legal right" to the properties. This decision willfully ignored the Great Secession of 1845 and the fact that the money to build the two buildings being used by the Black members had actually come from the Black members themselves. These white judges' tendentious decision against Jacob Godfrey and his co-worshipers ended a thirty-year-long argument over who "the Methodist Church" really was. Black members did not have "civil rights" to those church buildings, the court held, only the privileges of their status in the white-run denomination. In effect, Reconstruction-era judges stripped Black believers of their rights by defining them out of the faith.[32]

Black civil rights posed a more serious threat to white people's control in a "congregational" denomination such as the Baptists, where the property belonged to the congregation, not the denomination. During slavery, the polity-deference principle had enabled the white leaders of Cumberland Baptist to welcome slaves as members without worrying about being outnumbered two to one by slaves or about accepting donations from the "Black Brethren" or even letting them have the building for themselves once a week. All they had needed to do was make sure that the legal titles to the semi-autonomous Black churches stayed vested in white people. But in a string of cases that culminated in Rev. Bouldin's fight at Third Colored Baptist, the Supreme Court decided that when a Baptist church split, the majority of the members *was* the church—so long as they could convince the judge that they had stayed true "to the organization and to the doctrines"—and a court would enforce the majority's claims to church property as a civil right.[33] Because Black people now had civil rights under state law—rights that even the infamous Black Codes clearly contemplated—the *Bouldin* rule threatened white people's control over mixed-race congregational churches across the South.

So, Cumberland's white minority decided to keep the Black majority from exercising those rights in church affairs. In 1866, the white leaders granted the Black members "permission to withdraw" and join another church, permission to create "a Baptist church of Cold members" in Cumberland's old Meeting House, and letters of dismission, that is, letters that Baptists normally presented when they asked to join a new church, showing that one had left one's old church as a member in good standing. So far, Cumberland was still one church, even though its white and Black members were meeting separately. In 1872, the white leaders got a crucial provision inserted into the deed to the main "Jenkins" meetinghouse: an express trust dedicating it "for the use

A photo from 1976 shows Midway Baptist Church in Cumberland County, Virginia. The church was founded in 1874 by Black members of a white-run Baptist church in the same county.

and benefit of the . . . white members only." It was like an early version of the racially restrictive covenants of the 1930s and 1940s: it tied future owners' hands so that the property would never go to Black people. And finally, in October 1874, citing "the unsettled social status of the races in this country," Cumberland's white members voted to stop accepting any more Black people.[34] Less than a year later, Charles Palmore put the deed to Midway Colored Baptist on record.

Emancipation is often said to have been a turning point in the history of Black religion, the moment when "the invisible institution" became visible, when slaves no longer had to listen to white men preach obedience to their earthly masters, when they no longer had to steal away to "hush arbors" in the woods to pray to a God of hope and of liberation, when "the Black church" became the nucleus of Black community life and the heart of the freedom struggle.[35] It was all those things, and more. But a key reason emancipation marked such a turning point in

Black religious life had to do with civil rights. Black civil rights threatened white control of southern churches, and whites reacted by writing whiteness into the church property and into the churches' own rules. In turn, the name "*Colored* . . . Midway Baptist" created an implied trust for Black members, protecting them against any white people who might try to take over. Black people had many reasons to quit Cumberland Baptist, and the deference doctrine encouraged them to *record* their declaration of independence at the county clerk's office—to grasp the ordinary tools of property law to write their new church into existence.

Fighting to become independent from whites exposed a lurking tension between Black people's civil rights and their privileges as church members. Once Black worshipers won their independence from whites, that tension between rights and privileges began to disturb Black churches from the inside. Such reckonings had convulsed free Black churches since the 1790s; just a few years after Philadelphia's Bethel A. M. E. used its corporate charter to break free from its white overseers, it found itself embroiled in lawsuits and walkouts by its own members. After the death of "Unc" Perry Hinson, the free Black landowner who, as we saw in Chapter 2, had run Friendship Church for years as his personal fief, some members thought it was "time to set the house in order morally, and spiritually." They called in members "to face charges and complaints" regarding all "kinds of irregular living," such as adultery, stealing, and alcoholism. They took special aim at "the evil[]" of informal slave marriage. "Dear old Friendship now became the Ecclesiastical Court House, as well as the Church," wrote one of its members later, a parallel legal system in a log-cabin church, where some Black people sat in judgment over others.[36]

Now that Black people had churches of their own, they could adjudicate the privileges that people held by virtue of their membership. But what happened when the members tried to turn their privileges into civil rights—when they went seeking justice at the county courthouse?

The courts gave their answer in cases like *Bouldin v. Alexander.* Black churches came up with answers of their own.

Back in 1855, African Methodist Episcopal church leaders had decided that members could "justifiabl[y]" go to court if they were summonsed, and could sue one another over debt or "serious injury." The next year, it had set up an internal court system, with bishops acting as judges over cases "when our Discipline is silent on [a] matter of law." And over the next fifty years, the AME had self-consciously styled those "rulings and decisions"—on everything from how to report Children's Day Money to whether to count chickens as part of the preacher's salary—as "the established laws of the Church," a body of "Methodistic jurisprudence." The Baptists, whose congregational structure made governance a more local affair, also aspired to create a "constitution and doctrine" suitable for "a gospel church." In short, from the last decades of slavery through Reconstruction, the leaders and members of America's major Black denominations sought to establish what we might call "church constitutionalism"—a legal culture that demarcated what kinds of disputes could go to secular courts and what belonged in church courts applying their faith's "jurisprudence" as derived from written constitutions and books of religious doctrine. Conceived during the mid-1800s to protect the fragile autonomy of newly independent Black religious institutions, church constitutionalism by the 1890s arguably also seemed to carefully set limits on that autonomy by explaining when it was appropriate for secular courts to intervene, and to protect church members against ministers' "arbitrary" authority. It is no surprise, then, that Black people argued about their rights *within* their churches.[37]

By the end of Reconstruction, both church leaders and secular judges, each for their own reasons, had established standards for deciding when the privileges of membership in a religious association, such as a church, became civil rights—things a judge could step in and protect. Getting a judge to listen meant showing that you, and not your opponents, were the true keepers of the faith.

How could a court figure that out? When was a Baptist not a Baptist?

That, said leading experts, was a "difficult and delicate" question, but, clearly, courts sometimes had to "investigate . . . fine points of [religious] doctrine" to determine who the church was. In the 1890s, a generation after the exodus from the white-run denominations, Black religion began a forty-year period of theological ferment. This was the era that witnessed the explosive rise of the Church of God in Christ and other Holiness-Pentecostal churches, the emergence of Father Divine, two schisms within the huge Baptist denomination and, eventually, the founding of the Nation of Islam. Law guided that religious ferment, because often the road to a new faith was paved with lawsuits.

The deference doctrine—the doctrine that judges should generally defer to a church's internal rules and tribunals—now smuggled the intricate mysteries of faith into the courtroom, where they arose again and again as a debate over those "fine points" of theology.[38] When churches and mosques split over religious orthodoxy, judges often ignored the deference doctrine, waded in and awarded the property to the faction they deemed the true believers, sometimes based on nothing more than the judges' own religious common sense.[39] Those property determinations, in turn, often redrew the boundaries of faith. In 1899, for example, the Mt. Helm Baptist Church, just outside Jackson, Mississippi, was engulfed in controversy because its pastor, C. P. Jones, was doing faith healings and ritual foot washing in the sanctuary. Jones's opponents sued to bar him from the pulpit. The opponents pointed out that the original deed from the Helm family specifically dedicated the land for Baptist worship, the opponents said, and Baptists did not do faith healings. And they won. The Mississippi supreme court simply declared that obviously no true Baptist believed in such things. But that was only obvious if one ignored strong evidence that many Black Baptists, including most of the Mt. Helm congregation, thought those practices were perfectly consistent with being a good Baptist. Stripped of their church home and legally defined out of the faith, Jones and his losing faction now fanned out across the South as apostles of a new faith called "Holiness." The pattern was common. State courts and legislatures profoundly shaped the rise of "the Black church" during Jim Crow, not because of a white supremacist impulse for social control but because Black religious people appealed to them.[40]

During Reconstruction, African Americans seized the chance to turn things that had once been privileges, held at the sufferance of a master, into rights that a court could protect. They acquired thousands of acres of land, negotiated contracts, and drew on what they knew about law from the days of slavery to navigate the world of property and contract in their daily lives. They became valuable clients for white lawyers and the lifeline for a fledgling Black legal profession. As they entered more fully into the world of law, they began to use it not only to unify—to express solidarity in the face of unpredictable white behavior—but also to disunite, to argue, and to rewrite their relationships with one another. They got married and they divorced through law. They formed churches through law and then broke them up through law. They used law to turn friends into family and family into strangers. In the process, they helped remake the law. But as Reconstruction was dismantled in the 1890s, the rights of everyday use seemed to hang in the balance.

PART III

THE JIM CROW ERA

7

"Goat Sense"

Beginning in the 1880s, southern politicians set up a system of apartheid. It went by different names—"separate but equal," "segregation," and "the color line." The one that stuck, "Jim Crow," came from an old blackface minstrel show in which a white New Yorker smeared charcoal on his face, went up on a stage, and told racist jokes. Jim Crow was the era when nearly every southern state took away Black people's right to vote, cordoned off public space by race, and perverted the criminal justice system into a tool of social control that punished Blacks' tiniest infractions against whites but turned its back when whites raped and murdered Blacks.

Again and again, the Supreme Court was asked to decide whether the Constitution barred the states from doing these things. *Plessy v. Ferguson* (1896), which held that a state could mandate segregation, is the most famous of these cases, but it was actually something of an afterthought at the time. The Court had already laid out its thinking thirteen years earlier, in *The Civil Rights Cases*, a quintet of cases lodged by African Americans who had each been barred because of their race from a "public accommodation"—a privately owned place that was open to the public. In his opinion for the Court, Justice Joseph Bradley, a mainstream Lincoln Republican who said he loved "the Anglo-Saxon, Anglo-American race" as much as he hated slavery, rebuked the Black plaintiffs by harking back to the three-part definition of rights that had won Republicans the presidency in 1860. Everyone was entitled to civil rights—"the essential rights of life, liberty and property"—but not political rights or social rights.[1] As it had for Abraham Lincoln and other Republicans, dividing rights in this way allowed Bradley to simplify the world into two stark opposites—freedom and slavery—divided by a line called "civil rights." Slavery meant both forced labor and being deprived of civil rights: the "fundamental" rights of property and contract, to sue and testify in court, to move without a master's restraint, and the right not to suffer harsher punishments for crimes. The Court had to answer two questions in *The Civil Rights Cases*: which rights were "fundamental," and what could be done when white southerners took away those fundamental rights. Bradley answered the first question bluntly: "It would be running the slavery argument into the ground" to say that a cabdriver or theater owner was violating a fundamental right when he chose not to welcome someone into his taxicab or theater. After all, Bradley went on, there had been "thousands of free colored people" in the days of slavery, and "no one, at that time, thought that" discriminating against them made them anything less than "freemen," because theaters and cabs were about *social* rights.[2] Bradley was just as emphatic about the second question: Congress could not protect people's "social rights" with a nationwide law. It could only counteract "state action." If Black people were wronged by anything other than an explicitly racist state law or government official, Bradley insisted, they must go to their local courthouse and sue. Bradley's formulation, known to constitutional lawyers ever since as "state action doctrine," cut off the simplest and best paths for protecting Black rights. State action doctrine is why so many of today's civil rights laws are written around the Commerce Clause and not the Fourteenth Amendment, as if the reason segregation is bad is because it affects the price of gas.

By contrast, Justice John Marshall Harlan's dissent revived the Black abolitionists' idea that denying *any* fundamental rights on the basis of race was tantamount to slavery. Although free Black people had enjoyed civil rights, the northern states had indeed treated them as less than citizens, Harlan argued, discriminating against them no matter how neatly they dressed or how decently they behaved. Those pre–Civil War Black Codes in the North had reduced them to what one white abolitionist lawyer had called "civil slavery," what the Colored Conventions of the 1840s had called "slaves of the community," what today we call "second-class citizens." And now, Harlan warned, the Court was inviting whites to do it all over again. Horrified by the *Civil Rights Cases,* Black activist groups redoubled their efforts to push northern states to address civil slavery, getting laws passed in eighteen states banning racial discrimination in public accommodations.[3] Harlan and Bradley agreed that freedom was the opposite of slavery. They just disagreed about what rights it took to call yourself free, and whether the federal government could do anything to protect you.

A generation later, in 1912, the "legal bureau" of the newly founded NAACP laid down "a general policy." From then on, it would turn down "cases which do not specially involve the Negro question but come to you simply because a Negro is involved." For example, the legal bureau received a letter from a widow who was facing foreclosure on her home. The NAACP could not help with "these purely civil and personal matters" of property, explained W. E. B. Du Bois, editor of the NAACP's official magazine. It had to save its precious legal resources for cases "involving discrimination and injustice because of race or color," cases that would set precedents for "the rights of colored people as a whole."[4] So in 1925, when another homeowner, Ossian Sweet, was prosecuted for shooting into a white mob that was attacking his home, the NAACP spoke out loud and clear. "If in Detroit the Negro is not upheld in the right to defend his home," it warned in a press release, "then no decent Negro home anywhere in the United States will be safe." The Ossian Sweet case fit neatly into the NAACP's stated priorities, a list that looks painfully familiar in 2023: voting, criminal justice, lynching, mob and police violence, wage discrimination, and humiliation in public spaces.[5]

The problem was that those were not the only cases they got. Black people kept pestering the NAACP for help on all kinds of legal issues, from murder cases to abusive railroad conductors to the widow staring at foreclosure. But the NAACP stood firm. As "painful" as it was, the legal bureau had "to rule out" these cases of "injustice to individuals" who happened to be Black.[6] The idea was self-reinforcing. Once Black rights were defined in terms of anti-discrimination, then, almost by definition, cases involving property or contract, or other Black people, became "purely civil and personal." Both the Ossian Sweet case and the anonymous widow's case were about property, but the NAACP picked the Ossian Sweet case because it was also about race. If Sweet's white neighbors had shown up waving foreclosure papers rather than throwing rocks, one wonders whether the NAACP would have taken his case either.

In defining Black rights as anti-discrimination public law and focusing on precedent-setting "big" cases, the NAACP was bridging forward from the Black abolitionists' fight against "civil slavery"—a concept that still strongly resonated with Black religious leaders and activists in the early 1900s—to the struggle of activists in the 1960s against "second-class citizenship."[7] In doing so, it ceded the vast ground of private law—the only kind of law most Black people thought about very often—to local lawyers, most of whom were white and uninterested in racial justice. It overlooked a vibrant discussion among Black newspaper editors and small businesspeople and lawyers, one that creatively attacked discrimination on railroads and restaurants in the language of contract and property and that sometimes borrowed arguments typically used by big business corporations.[8] The NAACP thus defied its own members' eagerness to embrace the kinds of rights that Jim Crow afforded them, the rights the widow was asking Du Bois about—the rights of everyday use.

In many parts of the country today, the criminal justice system is designed to control and exploit working-class people of color with harsh fines and prison sentences, and to keep them from voting. It reminds even well-off people of color that the state can crush them at any moment, if a white person happens to feel uncomfortable. The blueprint for this system was drawn in the era of Jim Crow. For that reason, generations of scholars have mocked Justice Bradley for assuming that Black people could exercise their civil rights by going to the county courthouse.[9] If Reconstruction had cracked open the doors of justice, the thinking goes, surely Jim Crow slammed them shut again.

But the evidence from county courthouses suggests that Black people went to the trial courts during Jim Crow even more than during Reconstruction. From filing an average of 8 percent of the civil suits in my 1872 sample slice (taken from the docket books of select counties in five states and DC), the percentage of Black civil plaintiffs rose to 11 percent in 1892, and 17 percent in 1902, where it leveled off for the next twenty years. They were less likely to sue than whites, but not drastically less. Relative to their share of the population, Black people were plaintiffs in 12 percent of the civil suits I sampled in select Mississippi counties for 1872, when 62 percent of those counties' population was Black; by 1902, when Blacks were 72 percent of the counties' population, they filed 36 percent of the civil suits. Sometimes they were *overrepresented*, especially when they were a tiny fraction of the population. For example, Blacks were plaintiffs in 13 percent of the 113 civil suits in my sampled Illinois counties for 1892, when they were only 2 percent of the people in those counties.

Black people used their local courts for all kinds of things, much as white people did. As noted earlier, they sued for divorce. They sued Black-owned insurance companies and white ones, too. Black-owned insurers sued Black policyholders.[10] Black people sued over car accidents, railroad accidents, workplace accidents, farms, unpaid rent, and personal property.[11] They swore out writs to get "satisfaction" from white neighbors who assaulted them, from town officials who damaged their property, and to hush up a daughter's out-of-wedlock pregnancy. They used private law in more routine, nonadversarial ways, too: they sold easements on their land; made wills and got them probated; had cars towed off their property; sorted out homebuilding contracts, drunk-driving charges, and landlord-tenant disputes;[12] and bought, sold, and gifted land.

Even as white local officials cut them off from formal schooling, Black people stayed up to date on contract law (which was significantly changing in those years) because they dealt with it all the time: when a wife ran a farm in her own name in order to avoid her husband's debts; when they sold butter, eggs, chickens, and other wares to richer white women on credit (carefully balancing the accounts each winter); when they organized associations to set regular pay scales and hours for their work; and when they ran their own financial institutions, churches, colleges, and bar associations.[13] Black tenant farmers took pride in having what one of them, an Alabamian named Nate Shaw, called "goat-sense"—the common sense that God gave a goat, as the saying goes—the "rough-and-ready" legal knowledge, ideas, and assumptions that most grown-ups possessed, to varying degrees.[14] Shaw knew, for example, that each party to a joint note is liable for the others' debt, that a husband's mortgage did not cover household goods unless his wife signed too, and that a renter at the end of his lease had the "right" and "privilege" to take "anything that aint tied down." That "goat sense" was refined through daily experience and discussed in churches, schools, and Black-owned newspapers.[15]

With few exceptions, Black people's legal activity did not challenge white supremacy in any substantive way. Black people routinely had contract dealings with white people, but most of their lawsuits were against other Black people—only 8 percent of the cases in my Jim Crow sample crossed the color line. Nor did African Americans' lawsuits challenge white supremacy in any symbolic sense because there was nothing unusual about a Black person going to court, not even in Mississippi. Yet African Americans clearly cared about private law. Indeed, even in the worst years of segregation, prominent African Americans expressed a wary faith in contract and property as levers to "uplift the race." "When we own railroad stock we can have the Jim

Crow car taken from the road," the A. M. E. Church Review predicted. "Buy land. . . . Be a free holder, and no powers on earth can keep you down," preached a leading minister.[16]

Black elites were just as active in the world of law as working-class Black people. They were the ones who filed the race-discrimination suits that became cases like *Plessy,* and their lawsuits against abusive policemen and railroad staff helped forge the brand-new field of tort law. They did turn up their noses at some kinds of lawsuits, but that was only because they felt "neighborhood and church disputes," divorces, and personal-injury suits were a waste of time and money, and because such lawsuits aired people's dirty laundry to the world. By contrast, if the railroad ran over your best sow, Black leaders seemed to say, or if someone slandered you, or if you had a rent dispute—well then, by all means, go ahead and sue somebody.[17]

In fact, elite African Americans *had to* exercise civil rights, because the organizations they led—the Negro Business Leagues, Black colleges, fraternal orders and churches, the NAACP—were associations, which existed "only in contemplation of law," and because their members and officers held legally enforceable rights within those associations.[18] For example, most of the fraternal orders sold mutual life insurance. Taking out a policy created both a contract right (the right to a certain payout at death) and a set of associational privileges (like getting to vote for the board of directors). Thus, disputes over insurance invariably involved questions about the privileges of association membership and common-law contract rights. Although Black business leaders certainly cared about the anti-discrimination principle that racial justice activists were focusing on, their success also rested on the law of property, contracts, and business associations—what today we call corporate law.

In short, the obstacles to Black people using their civil rights during Jim Crow were not always as simple as the "white" and "colored" signs that were going up over the water fountains. White hostility raised high barriers around the local courts: the clubbiness of the local lawyers, judges, and clerks who ran the courthouse, the imperatives of making money and cutting costs, and the substantive legal rules that favored the haves over the have-nots. Certain legal rules made it easier for landowners than for tenants and sharecroppers to hire lawyers, get into court, and withstand pretrial motions. A landowning family like the Pinns, whom we met in Chapter 3, could hire a lawyer to keep their young cousin Sandy off the gallows by mortgaging their land. A tenant who got thrown off his land in the middle of his lease (like Ben Houston, whom we will meet in Chapter 8) had strong grounds to sue (breach of contract, forcible entry, and detainer), and he too could pay a lawyer by borrowing against his growing crop out in the field. But a sharecropper had very little to entice a lawyer: the grounds for suing were probably narrower, and the money needed for a lawyer and court fees was tied up in the crop, which legally belonged to the landlord until it got harvested in October.[19] As a consequence, not many sharecropper cases reached the courts. Because so many structural constraints worked against Black people being able to file a lawsuit, the cases on the county courthouse dockets are only the tip of the iceberg of Black people's legal grievances.

Tort lawsuits could attract decent lawyers because unlike a contract case, where the most you could get was usually whatever amount was in the contract, a tort could bring punitive damages. (A crime is an act that hurts the public: for example, *State of Minnesota v. Derek Chauvin.* A tort is an act, or a failure to act, that hurts a private person: for example, *Schaffer, as Trustee for the Next of Kin of George P. Floyd, Jr., Deceased v. Derek Chauvin, Tou Thao, Thomas Lane, J. Alexander Kueng, and the City of Minneapolis.*) Before the civil rights movement, winning a tort suit showed the world that Black people's lives had value, that whites might have to pay for what they did. Even in the worst years of Jim Crow, Black passengers won damages from railroads for insulting conduct, breach of contract, assault, and failing to protect passengers' basic safety. That recognition of whites' legal liability to African Americans also appears in records of pretrial negotiations, luckily preserved by a handful of law firms. In Charlottesville, white lawyer Eskridge Duke (grandson of the "Colonel") helped Moses Fleming win $106 and court costs after a 1937 car crash with Charles Garth, a middle-aged white man from a notoriously violent family. Indeed, in pretrial negotiations Duke matter-of-factly suggested Garth should pay not only for Fleming's banged-up car but also for Fleming's commuting costs while the car was in the shop.[20]

A tort suit was an awkward tool for Black freedom because it only acknowledged that Black people's lives had *monetary* value. And not everyone was worth the same amount. The lawyer for Martin Luther King Sr., father of the Nobel laureate and a famous minister in his own right, who was hurt in a taxi on his way to the airport, told him that "the sky will be the limit on the value of the injury and the loss of future earning capacity." For Alice Freeman, who tore her knee ligaments falling into an unlit and unmarked ditch in Clarksdale, Mississippi, the limit was just $200.[21] Suing one's boss was a dismal prospect, too. Black people usually got the lowest-paid jobs on any work site, and when those jobs killed them, the prospective damages weren't big enough to attract the kind of skilled and effective lawyer who could take on a powerful wrongdoer. Working "up the case of an ignorant negro or white mill boy or farm boy" took so much "time and expense" that many such people could not "get an attorney to help them." The mother of the great racial justice activist Fannie Lou Hamer was blinded by a flying splinter in 1939, but she knew that no lawyer could make money representing a woman who earned only $1.25 a day. When Hamer herself found out that a white doctor had sterilized her without telling her, she never even contemplated suing. "At that time? Me? Getting a white lawyer to go against a white doctor?" she later recalled. "I would have been . . . screwing tacks in my own casket."[22]

Then there were procedural traps. In accident cases, big companies and landlords put a lot of pressure on Black workers to sign away their rights, sending agents to hustle blank release forms out to the shacks where Black workers lived. If Hamer's mother had stuck to it and sued for her lost eyesight, the landlord could have asked the judge to make her post bond—proof that she could cover the court costs if she lost. Bond demands pressured plaintiffs into dropping their cases. If a Black plaintiff made it to trial, the judge's instructions to the jury could wreck even a strong case. Even the few Black workers who actually got to trial probably did not win much, if only because courts pegged the damages to the victim's earnings before the injury, and Martin Luther King's father earned a lot more than Fannie Lou Hamer's mother did. It wasn't just the companies pressuring working-class victims to back off. Their lawyers and even their own relatives often coaxed them to be realistic and take the settlement, fearing they'd get nothing if they went to trial and lost.[23] Tort suits could not protect African Americans from the violent aspects of America's booming industrial economy.

In the South, the more serious obstacle to suing white people was that they might just kill you. Violence lurked behind every step of interracial disputes, and it shaped what happened with lawsuits. In southeast Arkansas in 1919, the mere rumor that sixty-eight Black people were planning to sue their landlord for an accounting—a court order to open the ledgers in which he had cheated them out of their share of the cotton crop each year—brought down a weeklong massacre.[24]

The Black-versus-white lawsuits in the county ledgers are the ones that surmounted such obstacles. In most of the cases, the plaintiff and defendant were of the same race. Only 18 percent of the 372 Black plaintiffs in my sample of the Jim Crow decades were suing a white person or business, much lower than the 32 percent of the Black defendants who got sued by a white person or business. Because there are far fewer Black-on-white suits than we would expect from their shares of the county populations, it seems clear that African Americans had a lot more grievances against whites than they took to court.[25]

What explains the few litigants who did make it past all those obstacles? Four other factors came into play: the kind of legal claim it was, Black litigants' connections with local whites (and the social standing of their white opponents), their ability to summon up "good facts" and fit them to legal rules, and the behavior of white local officials, especially county clerks.

One thing seems clear enough: if you were going to sue a white person, you needed some friendly white people on your side, or at least not lined up against you. Friendly white people helped Black litigants survive pretrial motions to dismiss their cases. White people sometimes "stood security" for Black litigants—that is, they signed bonds pledging their property to secure the court costs (much the way the Pinn family signed a deed to secure lawyer Fall's fee). White people also helped with the informal talks that often preceded any lawsuit, talks aimed at heading off both violence and lawsuits. In 1918, Barney Wicks got a white man to write an olive-branch letter to his landlord apologizing for "the way things turned out" and asking permission "to send some

The law office of J. W. T. Falkner on court square in Oxford, Miss., ca. 1961. The office was probably occupied by the son of the Falkner who represented Jessie and George Reno.

Falkner's opposing counsel in Reno v. Steinbeck had his office just off court square, at least by 1961.

one for his little household plunder and chickens." Sometimes it was whites who tipped off Blacks to their legal danger in the first place. It helped if the white opponent had enemies, or an unsavory reputation, say, as a predatory lender, someone infamous for being "in the business of lending money to negros." Successful Black litigants also tended to have help from local white officials and lawyers. When the county clerk told George Reno that someone else was paying the property tax on his and his wife's land, Reno asked the clerk, "What would you do?" and that is how, in November 1915, the Renos ended up in the office of local attorney John Falkner.[26]

Indeed, even more directly than lawyers, county officials were the people who decided what civil rights actually meant in daily life: sheriffs, justices of the peace, clerks, special masters, and notaries. These were the men who seized and sold off your property when you defaulted on a loan, the men (and a growing number of women) who recorded your tax payments each year, who kept track of every mortgage and sale and tax payment on every house and building in the county in heavy leather-bound books—the pen-and-ink foundation of American property rights. Thomas Holcomb's neighbor and brother-in-law George Smith never hired a lawyer, as far as I know, but every year he paid his property taxes over the counter at the Cumberland county clerk's office. In the rural places like Cumberland, with their rough roads and spread-out population, justices of the peace had to "bring justice to every man's back door," and local officials held in their hands what one white lawyer called "the practical rights of the people." This is why, when the white supremacists bulldozed their way back into power across the South in the 1890s, they fired all the low-level Black officeholders, right down to the courthouse janitor. Thomas Holcomb's generation would spend their lives in a world where the law was not only written by white men but also administered and enforced by white men, who doled out judgeships and clerkships to one another in a tightly knit courthouse ring.[27]

Low-level officials had a great deal of discretion, and they used that power against Black people across many areas of law. Most obviously, they made "Negro law" a separate and unequal part of America's criminal justice system, a tool, as Du Bois put it, "for enforcing caste rather than securing justice." In areas where federal law seemed clearly to forbid racial discrimination, southern states essentially delegated Jim Crow to local officials. They nullified Black rights through superficially color-blind statutes that required, for example, that voters pass a literacy test, or that jurors have "good intelligence, sound judgment, and fair character," and trusted county registrars to turn the right people away. Unlike deed books, land-tax books *were* divided by race, and county boards and clerks colluded to make Black landowners pay more than their fair share of taxes, forcing them to subsidize schools and hospitals they weren't allowed to use.[28] Not surprisingly, some county officials acted like "blood-sucking" "leeches," treating "the slum or 'nigger quarters'" as a hunting ground for fines and fees, balancing the county budget with "costs . . . extracted from the negroes['] . . . little peccadillos," and snapping up land for themselves.[29] The roots of Ferguson, Missouri–style "predatory policing" run deep.

Still, local officials' greed did not map neatly onto the imperatives of white supremacy, nor could those officials consistently ignore formal legal rules. Divorces, partitions, estates, and guardianship matters, which filled up more than half of chancery dockets, presented no obvious means to uphold white supremacy because such cases almost always featured people of the same race. Suits to collect money, which made up at least two-thirds of the typical justice of the peace's docket in Mississippi, and a similar fraction in Chicago, helped white creditors plunder Black communities, but they also hounded white debtors, who complained that J.P. and county courts were nothing but "legalized collection agencies," and who joked bitterly that "J.P." really stood for "judgment for the plaintiff." Conversely, as we will see, the fact that states streamlined the procedures for probate, mortgages, divorce, and commercial law was probably also a response to poor plaintiffs—many of whom were Black—who needed a quick, cheap divorce or letters of administration or an accident settlement.

For all these reasons, when white officials bent the rules, they often did so in ways that integrated Black people into the system as second-class citizens rather than shutting them out entirely. "Picture" the justice of the peace "in his office on a hot August day," said the *Mississippi Law Journal* in 1935. He hunches over a cheap desk in the sweltering front room of a lawyer's office, "laboriously . . . writing a legal looking document" in broken, misspelled English "while a negro man and a negro woman" sit watching. "Rufe, I swear to you, I have got the hardest job here I ever undertook," he complains to a "lawyer friend" walking by. "I am just giving these here negroes a divorce." Hold on, the lawyer remonstrates, I thought J.P.s "had no jurisdiction to grant divorces. To this the justice of the peace replied: 'The hell I haint. I married 'em and now I'm gwine to divorce 'em.' The divorce was granted," and soon the husband used it to defend himself from a bigamy charge down in Hattiesburg.[30]

Marion Post Wolcott, "Group of men killing time during dinner hour in sheriff's office. Granville County Courthouse on court day in county seat. Oxford, North Carolina," Nov. 1939.

That vignette wasn't just a figment of elite white people's imaginations; J.P.s themselves expressed the same willingness to put human needs over legal niceties. In 1925, after arresting a white man for desertion and nonsupport, a New Jersey constable tried to do some impromptu marital counseling while driving the estranged spouses to their hearing. Why didn't the man "cut out this foolishness and go back and live with his wife?" the constable needled; "there are children involved here." (It didn't work.) In North Carolina, the legal code was cleverly designed to give J.P.s like Roger T. Stevenson the discretion to "disfranchise the nigger" without running afoul of the Fifteenth Amendment, but it also gave him the discretion to help Black people exercise other rights. He offered quick, cheap marriage ceremonies, used his jail to sober up abusive husbands, stopped "cases from goin' to [the more expensive circuit] court," badgered squabbling couples and neighbors to "kiss and make up," and treated peace warrants as a license to dole out fatherly advice. To a Black woman who had gotten a warrant against her husband and then begged Stevenson to let him out of jail, Stevenson replied, "What for? You want him to beat you up again?" But he then did as she asked. The point is not that Stevenson was a racial liberal. He was not. It is that in order to protect their vision of a well-ordered society, low-level functionaries often used their extraordinary power over people's lives to extend to Black people the same rule-bound personalism that they did to white people. White J.P.s granted them the limited privileges of their community status as "negroes" as well as its sharp disabilities.[31] That status personalism worked *through* Black civil rights, not in tension with them.

It was a similar story with clerks and notaries. Clerks kept circuit courts' written records. Since circuit judges held three- or four-week sessions at a given county courthouse only a few times a year, clerks carried on much of a circuit court's business on their own, on so-called rule days. For example, a clerk was usually the one who decided whether to make the plaintiff post bond for the court costs (fifty cents for each witness summonsed, twenty-five cents for the clerk to write the case on the docket, and so on), and who decided what kind of bond was acceptable. The structure of the court system made it harder for poor people to sue rich people or companies than it was for them to sue other poor people or to file "friendly" suits (that is, suits that both sides expected to go uncontested) like partition or divorce. The case numbers reflect the unfairness of a system where a defendant could stop a poor plaintiff in his tracks simply by filing a request for a bond against costs.[32] But the system also encouraged low-level officials to think of people—including Black people—as potential fee-paying customers.[33]

A sizeable fraction of civil litigants had no lawyer. Instead, for their basic legal needs—filing petitions, taking affidavits—they relied on notaries, clerks, and what I call "quasi-lawyers." To understand how this worked, we must remember that court officials are not supposed to give out legal advice, only "information." But the line between "legal information" and "legal advice" is often very hard to see. In 1900, notaries and clerks didn't just "authenticate" legal documents, they also explained them—something that was essential for people who could not read or write. Sometimes they outright gave people legal advice.[34] They really just wanted to keep the court running smoothly, but in coming up with creative fee arrangements, granting quick decrees on routine matters, and explaining legal documents, white county clerks helped Black people exercise their rights.

The tactics people used to surmount the barrier of fees and costs reveal still more about white lawyers' and court officials' attitudes toward Black rights. Letting poor people file as paupers interrupted a stream of money. In the Deep South, lawyers figured out one way to re-route the stream: they had the person sign over part of his next crop settlement. The fact that lawyers often wrote in handwritten guarantees of clients' court costs suggest that certain kinds of cases brought by African Americans (like divorce) had become routine, that small-town lawyers were coming up with approaches for working with Black clients on fees and costs, and that they were confident they could make money from them. White lawyers did not put themselves on the hook for legal fees because they were committed to Black rights. They did it because this was how general-practice lawyers made a living in the Jim Crow South. Handle a small partition suit and you might get appointed trustee for the sale. Handle a divorce well and the husband might ask you to draw up his will down the road.[35] White lawyers simply took it for granted that Blacks had the right to file a lawsuit, at least against other Blacks.

The only Black people who were in a position to pursue difficult cases were property owners and those whose suits might win them a lot of money. They typically had either a farm or some animals to mortgage (like the Pinn family), or they were suing for enough to make a contingency contract (where the lawyer took the case in return for a percentage of any damage award or settlement) look attractive. But it was risky to bet the farm on a suit whose outcome was uncertain. It was probably a last resort.[36] Both the criminal *and* civil justice systems posed grave dangers to middle-class Black families.

At the same time, the contingency system subtly aligned the interests of white lawyers and their clients, including Black clients. "I dont know what kind of case he has [or] the value of the land" at issue, wrote one lawyer as he invited the Greenwood, Mississippi, firm Gwin & Mounger to join him on a Black inheritance case, but "I think I can manage the negro so we can make some money out of the estate if his case is easy to win." Gwin & Mounger made a similar calculation about a white woman who wanted to divorce her doctor husband. The firm's fee was "contingent upon our recovering something," so the partners needed to find out "just what mortgages, or claims there are against the [client's] property," and even to guess whether the unhappy couple might patch things up midway through and leave their lawyers holding the bag.[37] That was the trade-off from the lawyer's perspective—time spent versus the size of the fee—and most of it was educated guesswork. Lawyers calculated such trade-offs every day, and even though they sometimes lost money on Black people's cases, they kept taking them, right alongside their debt-collecting for big planters and businesses. Black people's cases were part of the ebb and flow of small-town court business: suits over "mules and jerseys [cows] and fat hogs," a cycle of chasing fees from clients who were sharecroppers, doctors, and small farmers,[38] their race unmarked in the ledgers except in suits touching "social rights," like divorce.

Black people lived their legal lives in particular places: a lawyer's office, a kitchen, a roadside, a field, a justice of the peace's office, the county courthouse. The courthouse was usually in the center of the county's main town, with a lawn and a Confederate statue standing sentry out front. Courthouse square was still the main public space in most counties, and even in the South it was relatively open to African Americans unless they were doing something crazy, like trying to practice law or register to vote. In some towns, Black boardinghouse owners like Jessie Reno, of Oxford, Mississippi, made money serving the people who came into town for court sessions, much as Solomon Northup's wife, Anne, had done a generation earlier in upstate New York before he was kidnapped into slavery.[39]

The courthouse square widened a gap between two kinds of litigants: "repeat players" and "one-shotters."[40] The repeat players came to court all the time and acted accordingly. They built relationships with the judges, the clerks, the deputy clerks, and the regular lawyers. They knew the eatinghouses and stores around the square. They weren't necessarily rich but they were overwhelmingly white—often small businessmen—and their lawsuits were disproportionately about collecting debts. The one-shotters were more racially diverse. They only cared about the case that had brought them to town that day, and they did not expect to be back anytime soon. Although there certainly was a handful of African American repeat players—John Robinson, the free Black man we saw in Chapter 4 accusing a white mob of coercing him into selling his farm, was party to as many as a dozen other cases over the years in and around Cumberland County—Black people were overwhelmingly one-shotters. The subtle and not-so-subtle disadvantages that daily courthouse practice piled onto one-shot court users handicapped Black people more directly and consistently than any racist act perpetrated by court officials. It meant that a disproportionate number of Black people experienced their local court as a debt-collection agency.

The structure of the bar—the local lawyers' guild—widened the gap between one-shotters and repeat players. This was less of a problem in big cities like Chicago, where nearly every one of the fifty-two plaintiffs in my sample from the Jim Crow era who had a lawyer had a different lawyer. But out in the countryside, whether in the South or the North, Black litigants faced a local bar and local court that was dominated by a small group of white insiders. More than one-seventh of my sample's 241 Jim Crow–era civil cases for Coahoma County, Mississippi, were handled by one firm: Maynard and Fitzgerald, of Clarksdale. Either that firm or somebody from the Cutrer clan, a wealthy white family, represented more than a quarter of the plaintiffs. The courthouse square made visible these invisible interpersonal networks that dominated counties. Law offices lined the four streets that framed the square, each one a short walk not only to the courthouse but also to most of the county's other law firms, stores, and elected officials. Stenographers and title searchers would have bustled back and forth from office to courthouse to look up deeds and cases, joshing and making small talk while they banged down the heavy tomes and slid their fingers expertly down the pages. That close proximity of the circuit clerk's office in the courthouse and the law offices around courthouse square probably kept small-town lawyering a close-knit, back-slapping fraternity.[41]

Professional and family ties knit white lawyers and white court officials even tighter together. Half of Coahoma County's law firms were in

Albemarle County Courthouse, Charlottesville, Virginia, circa 1930.

just one building in downtown Clarksdale. Several of the county's lawyers were related. They lived in the same neighborhoods and belonged to the same fraternities. These insiders got to know one another fairly well from their daily encounters in and around courthouse square. Lawyers' memoirs make clear that that familiarity oiled the law's machinery with foreknowledge of what the other side might do, and smoothed their behavior toward one another. Since the leading attorneys in these towns tended to cycle from private practice to circuit clerk or judge or state senator and then back again, they were keenly aware that the opposing lawyer in today's divorce suit might very well be the judge a few years from now, or even their law partner. Even in Chicago, where there were more lawyers to choose from, insiders had a leg up, as collection agencies bought up unpaid bills from small grocers and plumbers and landladies—at a deep discount—and used their courthouse connections to move them down the conveyor belt to judgment faster than any plumber could.[42] In short, North and South, the justice system in the countryside and small towns was run by a courthouse ring, one that simultaneously gave repeat players an advantage over one-shotters, kept African Americans from voting, *and* helped them exercise their civil rights.

The lawyers in the courthouse ring squared off against one another every day, including on behalf of Black clients. From today's perspective, these white men don't look like civil-rights lawyers. They did not specialize in Black cases or express any particular concern for Black rights. Coahoma County's top five lawyers represented 41 percent of the county's white plaintiffs and 45 percent of its Black plaintiffs. They took clients whose stories made legal and business sense—for the "haul," as one lawyer put it. Several of them, like R. T. W. Duke, were prominent Democrats or former slaveowners. John W. Cutrer, owner of the biggest mansion in Clarksdale and for decades the patriarch of one of Coahoma County's richest families, was president of the powerful levee board, delegate to the 1890 constitutional convention that disfranchised Mississippi's Black voters, and a perennial player at the Coahoma County

Marion Post Wolcott, "In front of the Courthouse on Saturday afternoon, Lexington, Holmes County, Mississippi Delta, Mississippi." Nov. 1939.

courthouse. Once he actually killed a man for insinuating that he had Black ancestry.[43] But when he took a client, he put his insiders' network to work. And that is probably why people hired men like him: he could give a one-shot client the advantages of a repeat player in a cozy legal system that rewarded repeat players.

Sharecroppers did not have much choice but to deal with white lawyer-patriarchs like Cutrer or Leroy Percy. Percy fashioned an almost symbiotic relationship between his law practice and his plantation business, moving "negro" laborers on and off his lands almost as he pleased, making deals with other white businessmen to "take up" their debts, and telling his overseers to "rough" up anyone who tried to organize the workers for a fair shake. And yet the lawyer-patriarchs of the Deep South found that even they could not always control what Black tenants did with their limited rights. When a Black man swore out a writ against his plantation managers for false arrest the local judge refused to let Percy and his cronies quietly "arrange" things. With his own workers, Percy found that neither fines nor high-profile arrests could "stop the lawing among the tenants on the place."[44]

Unlike Percy, who argued cases at the Mississippi supreme court, or Cutrer, who took some cases all the way to the U.S. Supreme Court, most lawyers never went any higher than the county circuit court. Of course, they usually weren't in court at all, because most of what lawyers did was office work—low-cost, simple, time-consuming tasks that rarely required appearing in a courtroom. Indeed, even the term "office work" doesn't quite capture what ordinary lawyers did because so much of it happened somewhere other than an office. "I drew the deed on my way to school Monday morning," explained N. B. Clark, a "colored lawyer" in Newport News, Virginia, whose main job was schoolteaching, "and I passed by his house and gave it to him, and he acknowledged it [there] in his house." A lawyer would get hired to write a will, took down "rough instructions" from the client, and turned it into a "rough draft." Once the finished version was ready, they (or the client herself) would get someone to put her name on as a witness, usually whoever happened to be nearby. "Lulu, I want you to sign this form," called out one Black Chicagoan to her coworker in the next-door office on the way back from lunch. Sometimes lawyers had to take turkeys or molasses as payment.[45]

In other words, civil rights were forged not just in courtrooms and lawyers' offices, but through everyday use on a thousand porches and streets. This was especially true for wills and contracts, which nonlawyers can write for themselves. Addison Day, a Black undertaker in Washington, ran a side business as a notary public, mostly notarizing deeds of trust, mortgage-like documents commonly used to borrow money. He had so many customers that he started keeping a notary seal handy so that people could get their loans right away; they made their X marks on their way to work and hurried "right off." Or consider how Philadelphian Retta Lum described her mother's dealings with a man named John White, who was also Black. One day, Lum's mother sent her to

Camden, New Jersey, on an errand "to Commissioner Jones' house" and "to collect" from White "a little bill he owed Mamma" related to the Keystone Society (a fraternal order they both belonged to). White was busy when Lum came in. She asked what he was doing "and he said, 'I am making out a will.' " Later that day, White got two of his gambling buddies to sign as witnesses to his will while sitting on his front stoop, possibly on their way to play "policy" (a kind of illegal lottery). When one of them said he couldn't write, White replied, "You can mark, can't you?" Law journals could laugh all they wanted about the wills and contracts that laypeople like John White and Retta Lum's mother wrote up for themselves, about the silliness that came from letting every ignorant layman be "his own draughtsman." But all kinds of people did this, not just African Americans. Self-drafted contracts and wills—written or oral expressions of civil rights—were the bread and butter of most law firms, and cases involving them were fast becoming classics in law school classrooms.[46]

What tamed this unruly world of self-taught private law was the humble, fill-in-the-blank paper form. Many of the legal acts that constituted civil rights were becoming routinized and standardized in the late 1800s, and this had subtle but important implications for both Black people's civil rights and for lawyers' practices. A good example is Mariah Dennis's petition to probate her late husband's will in 1912. Her husband's main asset was a life insurance policy from the "Colored" Masons. Her lawyer, Lewis J. Winston, one of the last Black lawyers in Mississippi and a fellow Mason, sent a form letter to A. W. Pegues, the Masonic official in charge of Dennis's policy.[47] The letter's fill-in-the-blank format saved Winston valuable time. It gave technical legal instructions in plain English, ensuring that Pegues would bring exactly the right items in exactly the right format to the courthouse, and ask the circuit clerk exactly the right question. Standardized forms offered obvious advantages for clients. They were convenient and affordable, and they shifted a lot of legal work into the category of "legal information" at a time when state bar associations were banning clerks and nonlawyers from

Greenville, Miss.......................191......

Hon. A. W. Pegues........
Abbeville.............Miss,

Dear Sir:—

Enclosed find Petition, Affidavit, Will and Decree in the case of..........
......John Dennis..........deceased.

Please take Mariah Dennis..........................
at once, to the Chancery Clerk of your County and have her sign and swear to the petition asking for the probation of the will of John Dennis..........

At the same time you go ~~to~~ take witness the Chancery Clerk and sign and swear to the affidavit as a witness to the said will.

You need not take all three of the witnesses as ONE witness under the law is sufficient to have the Will probated. I only want the Will probated. I do not want Letters Testamentary.

Have the Clerk send me at once, a certified copy of the probated will, to 712 Washington Ave, Greenville, Miss. Give all the papers in this case, including this letter to you, to the Chancery Clerk, so as he can see what it is I want.

If Mrs. Dennis.................................
has not the money with which to pay the Clerk for probating the Will and sending me a copy of same, have the clerk send his bill with the certified copy of the probated Will, to me and I will remit his fees.

KINDLY GIVE THIS IMMEDIATE ATTENTION.

Fraternally,
L. J. Winston
Attorney.

African American lawyer L. J. Winston's fill-in-the-blank form for insurance clients.

giving "legal advice." Forms kept the white circuit clerks happy because they got to plow through their dockets faster. The combination of standard forms and informal small-town lawyering did not in itself put Black rights on a lower plane than whites' rights, because this was how everybody did deeds and insurance and wills and divorces.

That combination did, however, tend to give an advantage to the repeat players, who were overwhelmingly white. Black litigants, most of whom were one-off clients, stood before their lawyers as supplicants, "beg[g]ing for information" about their cases, waiting for the settlement money they expected any day now from "my case against my step father" and "the clame of my Wife Policy." White lawyers sometimes went behind the backs of their one-shot Black clients, talking with the other side's lawyers and settling whenever they saw fit. The lawyers for Washingtonian Barbara Scott, who was embroiled in a lawsuit over her late husband's will, decided that her case was "hopeless" and made a deal with the other side's lawyers. When they told her about it, Scott "refused to listen to any offer of compromise and denounced the whole thing as a swindle on her," and fired them. People like Barbara Scott often got precious little from exercising their right to sue, and sharecroppers got even less, because their lawyers could secure their fees from any settlement before the sharecroppers saw a dime.[48]

Yet Black rights mattered even in such one-sided relationships, because lawyers still had to think *through* clients even when they were going behind their backs. It could not have been otherwise. Not only did some Black clients speak up—Barbara Scott's lawyers knew exactly what she wanted because she told them, vociferously—but the law said that the lawyers *needed* their clients' assent. Under Canon 15 of the Code of Professional Ethics, the only person who could approve the lawyers' settlement offer was Barbara Scott. Only the parents of the "young Negro boy" injured at work could accept the insurance company's settlement offer—and, their lawyer wrote, they would settle for "not a cent less" than $1,200.[49] Once a client signed on with a lawyer, they owed certain duties to each other. And, as we will see, Black people, including Thomas Holcomb, would keep pushing white lawyers to live up to their professional duties, right through the 1960s.

African Americans understood the basic principles of legal

representation, and took precautions when hiring lawyers. After a white railroad conductor maimed his son, Harrison Smith made careful inquiries, asking around "who the railroad lawyer was so he would not get mixed up with him." Smith knew that the railroad company's lawyer would try to get him to sign a "release," a fine-print contract that waived his son's right to sue in return for a piddling settlement check. Not until he was sure that he was talking with Samuel Gwin, a white lawyer who wasn't connected to the railroad, did Smith even let on that he "had a claim against . . . the railroad." As Smith left to check on Gwin's references, Gwin warned him "not to talk about the case" to any railroad lawyers. Clearly, Smith knew better than to do that. As worried and angry as he must have been about his son's sprained ankle and torn face, Smith understood that a lawsuit would be a "business" proposition.[50] As much as white lawyers tried to mold or override their clients' expressed wishes, both professional duty and self-interest as well as Black people's understanding of their rights and duties as clients enabled the inherently unequal relations between Black clients and white lawyers to be more than a one-way street.

Because lawyers *represented* clients, they acted as translators between the law on the books and popular ideas about law. Experienced lawyers knew that people came to them with their own, sometimes wrongheaded, assumptions about what "the law" was. For example, some people assumed that they could remarry as soon as they filed for divorce and that the final decree was just a "technical[ity]." Others overestimated what the decree could do for them. "Is it not lawful for a husband to at least pay rent for a wife," a Philadelphian asked lawyer Raymond Alexander, "when he just walk[s] off for . . . another [woman]?" Can't he be arrested for not paying alimony, or for "rearing a family" as someone else's "illegal husband"? Mary Bacon thought she had a right to quit her husband not only because he forced her to have "unnatural sex" but also as a matter of religious conscience—he "was not . . . 'clean' "—that is, not sanctified.[51] People were often wrong in their assumptions about what the law was and what it could do, yet it was usually those mistaken assumptions that prompted them to go see a lawyer in the first place.

And so, lawyers listened and translated laypeople's ideas of law, ideas that scholars sometimes mistook for pure ignorance. A Black farmer named Dilsey Chambliss told the pioneering Black sociologist E. Franklin Frazier in 1931 that she needed a "scrip" to get divorced, and that a divorce had to be obtained from the same place where the marriage occurred. To Frazier, this seemed like a perfect example of rural Black people's ignorance and alienation from the legal system. But in fact, Chambliss's error was that she was thinking too narrowly and legalistically. Working people like her were familiar with scrips. White employers often paid workers in "scrip," a paper substitute for money, and the similar-sounding "script" also came up a lot in property conveyances (it was the original document when a conveyance was signed in duplicate). Chambliss seems to have assumed that a script served a similar function for divorce. She could not write, so she "got a man to write it" for her husband, suggesting that she thought a written agreement was more binding than an oral one—an intuition that most Americans still hold today, regardless of their race.[52] What is more, it isn't at all clear that the average white person knew much more about Mississippi's divorce statute than Chambliss did. Consider this note that was written, either as a favor or for a few pennies, by J. M. Huffstickler, a white Mississippian, to the circuit clerk of his county in 1903:

> Dear Friend. This. Will Be Handed. you. By a Colard. Man. he wants to marry. he. has a Living Wife But She is Wandering all over the Cruntry. he Will [tell the details]. You can Explain to. him What to Do. in. the. Case. If you Will, you Oblige me_

At least Huffstickler knew enough to defer to someone else. The "Colard Man" had already gotten bad advice from a justice of the peace, who was *supposed* to know something about the law.[53] It was exactly this mix of assuming and wondering what "the law" was that brought most people to the lawyer's doorstep in the first place, and that actually *was* the law to most intents and purposes. Just as during slavery certain practices became "prescriptive rights" by virtue of long and broad acceptance, "the sense of the community" during Jim Crow could turn principles like the divorce "script," or remarrying before the divorce was finalized,

Dorothea Lange, "Cow Hollow farmer, Came from Oklahoma." Wife is cosigner with her husband on chattel mortgage. She signs with an "X."

into part of "the practical rights of the people": potent locally, yet liable to evaporate if taken outside that community.

At a time when legal knowledge circulated widely but not always reliably, lawyers found it was good business to behave a little bit like teachers, correcting mistaken assumptions and explaining how the legal process worked. For example, in a divorce suit lawyers knew that it was faster and cheaper for everyone if the defendant just signed and mailed back the required "process" (or summons) rather than having a sheriff go out to serve it in person. But a court "process" is a scary-looking piece of paper, one that any normal person—such as your soon-to-be ex-husband—might stuff in a drawer and try to forget. To avoid wasting time chasing down defendants, lawyers tried to make the "process" less terrifying. The white lawyer John Simms sent along a cover letter to his new (white) client's husband. In the letter, he explained who he was (a lawyer, disinterested), explained what a summons was and how it worked, and walked the husband through, telling him exactly where and how to sign his name and which copies to keep. Although it seems to "require[] that you appear here," Simms reassured the man, you don't actually have "to be personally present, because this is only a formal way of giving you notice of the pending suit. It means that on that date I will file in the clerk's office of the court the pleadings (called a bill in equity), setting forth the grounds on which your wife is asking for divorce." He wasn't trying to sort out who was telling the truth, Simms told the man, just doing his job. The husband could fight his wife in court, Simms seemed to say, but if the marriage was really over, it would be simpler to sign the thing and be done with it.[54]

In short, the lawyer-client relationship involved questions of power and control that were distinct from questions prompted by, say, the landlord-sharecropper relationship. One of its distinguishing qualities was that it often centered on a kind of knowledge that was not off-limits to Black people, knowledge that powerful segments of white society *wanted* them to have.

As much as they took it for granted that Black people had certain rights under law, during Jim Crow whites became downright hostile to the idea that Black people had a right to *practice* law. This hostility went hand in hand with a transformation in the legal profession itself. For more than two hundred years, the way a person qualified to practice law wasn't by going to law school; it was by apprenticing with an established lawyer. Once he passed an oral examination by the local judge, the young man (and it was always a man) was admitted to "the bar." During Reconstruction, this system had given aspiring Black lawyers a small opening, as some white lawyers willingly trained Black people and got them admitted to the bar. Black lawyers had hung out their shingles not only in northern cities like Chicago but all over the South; some of them had even had white clients. This angered white lawyers. Instead of competing with Black lawyers, Jewish lawyers, and women lawyers, the elite white lawyers decided to drive them out. They organized the "best" lawyers of each town and state into a "bar association," empowered by the state to act as gatekeeper to the profession. No longer could you qualify by apprenticing, you had to go to an accredited law school and take a "bar exam." Any "liberal-minded white lawyer" who dared to train a Black apprentice got frozen out on courthouse square. The Supreme Court cheered on this white-collar pogrom by deciding that there was no constitutional right to practice law, and that states were free to exclude whomever they wished. Looking back from the perspective of 1930, Irvin Mollison, a Mississippian who spent his legal career in Chicago and New York, knew exactly why he did not get the chance in Mississippi that his father had gotten during Reconstruction: "The Democrats overthrew the carpet bag government" and ran the state's Black lawyers out of the profession.[55]

White lawyers did it mostly to stamp out business rivals, but they hid their greed under platitudes about professionalism. The white lawyers who ran the trade journals, law reviews, and "bench and bar" biographies spooned racist rhetoric into their new "legal ethics" and newly tightened standards of "merit." White law journals urged judges to keep out "the colored lawyer who hangs around the police court" looking for clients. Court was no place for the "negro lawyer," a character dumb enough to defend his client from a bigamy charge by claiming that, because the man had three wives and not two, the man was only guilty of "trigonometry." Of course, the ridiculous images of Black incompetence in courts and law offices betrayed what was really driving the nasty rhetoric: Black customers *were* in those places and many white lawyers wanted their business. Elite lawyers and judges showed their cards when they mocked legal ignorance in *white* people too.[56] What was the silliest lawsuit they'd ever handled, the law journals asked their readers—the Iowa farmer who sued over a twenty-one-cent debt, or the seventy-five-cent lawsuit by "an old Colored trash hauler" in Kansas? The smug chortling targeted small-time white lawyers who took these "Five and Dime Claims" almost as much as at their supposedly foolish Black clients. The real problem with Black lawyers wasn't just that they were Black, but also that they were not professionals. The "pretentious negro" with his big words and "scanty knowledge" was an example of the bad old days of legal education before the new law schools were founded.[57] With one hand, the white legal fraternity chalked out its new professional boundary against outsiders, while with the other, they carved in the color line. Making fun of the "colored attorney" was part of a broad push to take law out of the hands of laypeople.

It worked. Elite white lawyers drove Black people almost completely out of the legal profession. The few Black lawyers in the South who hung on tended to be in cities, or in niche practices in small towns. In the North, solo practitioners eked out a living from an all-Black, working-class clientele, forming their own Black bar associations and trying to imagine what future "the Negro lawyer" might be able to weave from the migrants stepping off the trains from Georgia and Mississippi. These survivors did not practice "civil rights lawyering" in the modern sense of anti-discrimination any more than white lawyers did. But there was an important difference: unlike their white colleagues, Black lawyers' experience of racism in the legal profession prodded them to think of "the ordinary business of practicing law" as being in itself an example of the "progress" of their race.[58] Those who later rose to fame as "civil rights lawyers" did so by building on the material and intellectual foundations of the Jim Crow era of Black lawyering, when being a Black lawyer meant doing exactly the kinds of "ordinary" private law this book explores.

Being relegated to bread-and-butter neighborhood practice meant that Black lawyers missed out on the glittering opportunities that emerged in the early 1900s with the rise of the first modern megafirms. These law firms, like New York's Cravath, Swaine, & Moore or Sullivan & Cromwell, built up a prestigious, high-paying clientele by specializing in certain areas of law—corporate regulation, for example, and complex trusts—and by tapping the top law schools for bright young men called "associates" to handle the extra work. Cravath's pipeline ran to Harvard and Yale and Columbia, not Howard Law School or Central Tennessee College. Indeed, Cravath did not hire Black people at all. The megafirms' insistence on hiring from a handful of nearly all-white law schools ensured that the country's Black lawyers stayed stuck in general practice. Black lawyers during Jim Crow were solo practitioners who handled "all kinds of legal business," most of which "rarely required an appearance in court": collecting debts, pension payments, and bounties, renting out houses and lands, drawing up wills, negotiating payment schedules for people behind on their bills, and personal injury work. Such "legal business" paid so little that it was hard for lawyers to make a living unless they could juggle dozens of clients at a time. Not only that, but many Black people didn't expect "to pay for . . . legal advice." They "looked upon me," recalled one Black lawyer, "as their racial friend and acting as a friend who just happened to know law." It is no wonder that many Black lawyers (or their spouses) kept side jobs farming or schoolteaching or running a boardinghouse.[59]

It was a vicious circle. The take-all-comers generalism that kept non-elite lawyers afloat was the very thing that made them embarrassing relics in the eyes of the new legal elite. Nothing was more horrifying to the snobs at Boston's *Green Bag*—"An Entertaining Magazine" for legal insiders—than lawyers "hang[ing] around the police court" to drum up clients, or advertising "good meals and lunches . . . at all hours, cheap for cash." To make matters worse for Black lawyers, middle-class Black people and Black churches and businesses started turning to white lawyers because they worried "that a lawyer of their race could not get a square deal in the courts."[60]

What Black lawyers yearned for was either a career-making criminal case, or to be appointed receiver for a bankrupt business, or, best of all, to be hired by a large church or fraternal order. Black lawyers saw churches and fraternal orders as their professional lifeboat—not just because they had deeper pockets than most individual clients but because they were repeat players who bought legal services all the time and knew what they were worth. Here was one area where Black lawyers actually had a leg up on their white rivals, who couldn't join these associations even if they were smart enough not to turn up their noses at the Black fraternal orders with their "high-sounding names." The successful turn-of-the-century Black lawyer was ecumenical—he joined the Elks, the Pythians, the Masons, the Odd Fellows, and the Woodmen, and he was also a trustee of his church, his many memberships rendering him a kind of convenient in-house counsel for several Black associations at once. The feeling was mutual. Black associations needed good lawyers just as much as Black lawyers needed good clients. The reason the leaders of Baltimore's Union Baptist church lobbied in the 1880s for Black lawyers to be admitted to the Maryland state bar was not just because they cared about the principle of equality, but also because they wanted to hire those Black lawyers. There may be no better symbol of that mutual need than the fact that, to celebrate the first Black person admitted to the Maryland bar, the church gifted him "a set of law books."[61]

Elite white lawyers drove Black people out of the profession, but they could not stop Black people from practicing law. This was because the legal profession still sometimes blurred the line between lawyer and nonlawyer, and because legal institutions (like courthouses), legal forms (like contracts), and legal knowledge (like what it took to get a divorce) were still relatively open to nonprofessionals. This openness was essential to how most people thought about law. We can see this in an 1897 foreclosure case from southwest Illinois. In 1885, a white man named Adam Karr foreclosed on Charles, Mary, and Eliza Freeman, three Black siblings who had mortgaged their shares of a seventy-five-acre farm they had inherited from their father back in 1857.[62] Karr drafted a decree for the judge to sign, a common time-saver in those days. But through sloppiness or fraud, that draft decree foreclosed on *all* the land, including the interests of several relatives who had nothing to do with the mortgage. Those relatives sued in 1892 to void the mortgage, carve out Karr's rightful share, and make Karr cough up the seven years of rent money he had collected from the wrongly seized lands.

The key question for the courts was how that flawed mortgage deed had been written—specifically whether, in writing up a draft decree and taking it to the county clerk's office to be made official, Karr's lawyer had broken an implicit understanding that he would first run it by the Freemans' lawyer, Alonzo S. Wilderman. The flaw in the deed was the kind of mistake that a harried or bored lawyer might make, the kind that Wilderman would easily have caught if he'd had the chance to skim it. But was Wilderman really the Freemans' lawyer? Karr's lawyer said no, of course. And Charles Freeman, the only one of the Freemans who testified, said nothing about hiring a lawyer. That left Wilderman himself as the key witness. And Wilderman equivocated. "Well, now," he testified at the trial, "I was spoken to by a number of these colored people," "mostly some of the younger ones," who were fighting Karr's foreclosure suit. Yet he hemmed and hawed on the crucial question. "I could not say that I felt that I was employed in this case at all," he testified. "I looked after it, but what I was doing was mostly . . . consult[ing] a great many colored women . . . to find who were the heirs"—some of whom were three hundred miles away in Chicago—"and get them arranged" into "a great long pencil statement," a roadmap for Karr's lawyer "to get the [foreclosure] bill in shape" for the judge to sign off on. Wilderman filed no pleadings for the Freemans, "never asked for any fee," and didn't even remember whether he asked to "see the [draft] decree before it was finally passed on." The only thing he was sure of, it seemed, was that he never thought of himself as "really employed as" the Freemans' attorney.[63] So, it seems, Karr should have won.

Instead, he lost. Both the county court and the Illinois supreme court held that Wilderman was indeed the Freemans' lawyer, and canceled the mortgage Karr held against them. The two courts did this without any written evidence of a contract between Wilderman and the Freemans and over Wilderman's own denials.[64] *Karr v. Freeman* was a sign of how far "office work"—the low-prestige stuff that went on in bank offices and rented storefronts and front stoops—was becoming recognized as lawyering by the 1890s. We can also read the Illinois supreme court's opinion as simply acknowledging the reality that ordinary people faced when confronted with serious legal choices. How could you find out your rights if you could not afford to hire a lawyer? The answer for the Freemans was the same one that occurred to millions of other Americans: you went to someone you figured would know something about the law, and you asked him.

If most people were seeking someone *knowledgeable* before seeking someone *professional*, there was room for nonprofessionals to play a role in the legal process. The most important thing an initial consultation did for prospective litigants was that it helped them figure out whether their problem was a legal problem, or just a problem. And although bar-qualified Black lawyers were scarce, some of the non- or quasi-professionals who featured in these all-important preliminary conversations were Black. Mary Woodson, who lived out toward the Blue Ridge mountains of western Virginia, hired a white lawyer to keep her white relatives from snatching away everything her slave-owning father had promised her before he died, but the first person she consulted was a "Mr. Oliver, out here, this lawyer, this colored man. I was talking to him about what the old 'Boss' had promised me and that he had died" without a will. "He told me he thought if I seeked into the law, that I was entitled to my labor." Before Felix Brown hired one of Clarksdale's top lawyers to sue a white landowner for fraud, he consulted Sam Jennings, a fellow Black tenant farmer, who "told me that he had studdied law for himself and that he knew what law was and that he could tell me how to work it." And rather than just take white lawyers' word for it, Black clients would sometimes leave the office saying diffidently, as James Saville ruefully recalled Eliza Brown telling him, that they "would think over the matter, and consult Brother Some one, whom I suppose was a preacher." Black litigants nearly always hired a white lawyer, but some of them got their first legal advice from a Black person with goat sense.[65]

This pattern may help us understand what happened to Black lawyers after 1900, when whites chased them out of the legal profession. While the number of full-time, professional Black lawyers fell—only a handful of the Jim Crow–era cases in my sample featured a Black lawyer—the number of Black people who did law on the side, after hours, may not have fallen at all. The white judge who would not tolerate a Black lawyer in his courtroom had no problem "discussing the most complicated cases" with the "negro barber, who shaved him."[66] That barber joined church leaders and newspapers and associations and other ordinary people in fostering a vibrant discourse about law.

As cause lawyers slowly refined the Black abolitionists' idea of "second-class citizenship" into a legal campaign focused exclusively on cases involving "Negro rights," the far more numerous bread-and-butter lawyers handled almost any kind of case that might make them money, and the quasi-lawyers helped people imagine what the law could do for them. But what did any American, lawyer or not, have in mind when they thought about "the law"?

8

The Shadow of the Law

In the winter of 1903, Ben Houston, a Black tenant farmer, went and sued two of the most powerful white men in Coahoma County, Mississippi: Albert G. Hartgrove and Oliver M. Ellis. He sued them for "forcible entry," claiming that, just before Christmas in 1902, Ellis had "violently tak[en] . . . possession" of his land. The land was Houston's because he had a lease for it—a contract to possess and use it for a certain term of years. Houston contended that Hartgrove had made two mistakes in drawing up this lease: its description of the land and its boundaries was wrong, and it was incorrectly dated 1899, when Hartgrove may not have had the right to rent it out. Hartgrove had then

Interior of Coahoma County Courthouse storage area.

re-rented the land to Ellis, Houston alleged, violating the terms of his lease with Houston. Houston asked the local circuit judge for an injunction against Ellis's forcible entry, to correct his flawed lease with Hartgrove, and to enforce that corrected lease against Ellis as a trespasser.[1]

Standing at the riverside back in 1865, my enslaved ancestor Jackson Holcomb couldn't have sued if the soldiers had left without paying because he didn't have the right to make contracts. Thirty-eight years later, Ben Houston had that right. What difference did that make? Could white people disregard their contracts with Black people and trample on Black people's property rights whenever they felt like it? In the end, Houston lost badly, for reasons the court did not explain.[2] But before that happened, a judge granted him an injunction against Ellis, rejected a motion to dissolve that injunction, and allowed Houston to go to trial, presiding over a hundred pages worth of testimony from fifteen witnesses, testimony that made Ellis look like either a liar or a fool.

I found Ben Houston's case in September 2011, in a file box in the back room of the clerk's office at the Coahoma County courthouse in Clarksdale, Mississippi. I had been there the year before, to copy down my usual sample from the big, cloth-bound docket books. On that visit, I had been glad to see that, in addition to the dockets, there was a whole room-full of gray file boxes in neat rows on the shelves. Inside the boxes, I knew, were the old court papers that told the stories behind the bare-bones names and dates of the dockets. But I had learned the hard way that there were always gaps in those papers—sometimes big gaps. Whole decades, even centuries, could be lost in a flood, or burned, or chewed by vermin, or tossed when the county needed shelf space. As I returned to the courthouse, carrying a list of cases I had identified from the docket sample as involving Black people, and fortified with helpful tips from the chancery clerk, Ed Peacock, and deputy clerk (now clerk), Carolyn Parham, I wasn't sure whether the court papers for those cases had survived. I sat down and opened a box.

As usual, most of the folders were thin, holding just a few scraps of paper but no testimony. Occasionally I would look up additional names mentioned in the files in the Census only to find that the case didn't involve Black people after all. Midmorning on my second or third day I was working through the boxes when I saw a folder with a stack of testimony—more than a hundred pages' worth. It was confusing at first: something about a lease. I had seen plenty of lease disputes, and most of them involved only white people. Then on page nine, one of the lawyers asked: "Ben, you are a colored man, I believe?" And the plaintiff answered: "Yes, sir." I spent the rest of the day reading *Ben Houston v. O. M. Ellis*. Ms. Parham had mentioned that a few blocks away there was a blues club and a restaurant called Madidi's, owned by Morgan Freeman, and I was looking forward to going because, before his long and distinguished Hollywood career, Freeman had once played Easy Reader, a character on *The Electric Company,* a children's television show I used to watch. When the courthouse closed at five, I treated myself to an early dinner at Madidi's. I thought about Easy Reader.[3]

Run-of-the-mill cases like *Houston v. Ellis* have mostly been ignored by scholars. They do not show up in legal databases and they are too silted over with esoteric legal language for most historians to approach. Yet such cases reveal a hidden world of civil rights in the Jim Crow era, a world that went far beyond white lawlessness and Black alienation from law. As rich and powerful as he was, Ellis took great care to follow "the law." And Houston fought back through the law. Race haunted every step of these men's confrontation, but again and again each man spoke and acted with one eye on the county courthouse.

Seventy years before Ben Houston's case, a traveling French aristocrat named Alexis de Tocqueville observed that Americans' ideas about rights flourished in what he called "the shadow of the law." Today, scholars use Tocqueville's metaphor to conceptualize how formal legal rules written by far-off judges and legislators actually play out on the ground. The rules, these scholars say, give each of us a kind of endowment, like bargaining chips, based on what we might get if we had a dispute that wound up in court. The rules on the books never fit the facts on the ground perfectly, so we can never be certain about what the outcome would be. And most people are not lawyers. So, for special problems, like buying a house or settling a parent's estate, we hire a lawyer. But most of the time, we live according to our intuitions about law, or more precisely, our intuitions about what a judge would do if our problem wound up in court.[4]

If reading old court papers lets us peer behind the docket books, the "shadow of law" concept allows us to see the world that created those old court papers, a world that extended far beyond the courthouse. Even disputes that did not wind up in court—and Black people rarely took whites to court—were full of legal ideas and assumptions. Black people relied on their own goat sense to try to make good deals and avoid trouble, and to set up "good facts" in case a problem ever became a lawsuit. Law mattered, not as some kind of symbol ("the law") but as specific rules ("possession," "forcible," "notice"). It mattered not because Black people were legal experts, but because a working knowledge of law was part of being an adult.[5] A generation after slavery's end, as the South sank into the abyss of voter suppression, segregation, and political terrorism, Black people exercised civil rights in a thousand daily interactions, in the shadow of law.

The main task for Houston and his lawyers was to prove that Ellis had taken the land "forcibly"—that, contrary to what Ellis claimed, Houston did not really leave "of his own free will." It was easy to show that Ellis and the other white men had been carrying guns and that they moved Houston's things out of the house. But was that forcible entry? Land disputes can get violent in a hurry, especially when someone is losing the roof over his head. So state law discourages both landlords and tenants from taking the law into their own hands by making it easy to take possession of land legally. State law makes it easy for landlords to oust tenants, and gives ousted occupants a way to get back in, through a lawsuit called "unlawful entry and detainer." Even if the tenant has broken some provision in the lease, as Hartgrove claimed Houston had, he might still get the land back, plus damages, if he is put out by "intimidation, fraud," or, in the words of the leading case on the subject (where the plaintiff also happened to be Black): "more force than is reasonably necessary."[6] And to get such a case in front of a jury, the tenant just has to prove that the other person had entered against his will. These were the rules that mattered, not only to Ben Houston's lawsuit, but during the events that led up to his lawsuit. At each step in his confrontation with Ellis, through his words and his deeds, Houston tried to put himself on the right side of the law, as best he could guess how a judge might see the law.

The first time the two men talked about the land was in December 1901, when Ellis came and told Houston he had to move. "Not if my papers is right," Houston replied, and he walked Ellis over to his house to "show him the second contract," his six-year lease from the Hartgroves. Houston told Ellis "several times" that he "wasnt going till he was dispossessed." Ellis saw that he wasn't getting anywhere, so he left. Just before Christmas 1902, Ellis came back. This time he had a shotgun, a Winchester rifle, and two other white men on horseback. Ellis "didnt make any threats," Houston recalled. Instead, in the middle of a field, in front of "a right smart of people," the two men talked about property law. Specifically, they talked about two things: whether Ellis had a right to dispossess Houston—to put him out of the property—and what it took to dispossess someone legally. " 'Ben, I came down this morning to dispossess you'," Houston remembered him saying, "and I says to him, 'All right, Mr. Ellis, but . . . I think that's mighty hard.' " Houston went on: "I told him . . . that the land was mine and I thought that I had rights to it." Ellis said that his lawyers had assured him that the place was his. Houston recalled that Ellis then spoke carefully: "I hate to put a man out, but you wont go out and I have it to do I see." Houston nodded. "No, sir; I'm not going out of there." Ellis turned to face his men. "Boys, we'll go down there and put him out," he said, and started riding down to Houston's house. Then, Houston said, Ellis hesitated and turned around to float one last idea: "If you will put your [own] things out, I will testify in court that I dispossessed you." Houston politely refused, and Ellis's men went on down to the house. Ellis felt confident, buoyed by his guns and his lawyers' assurances. But Houston had talked with a lawyer, too: John Cutrer, one of the bigwigs on courthouse square, and when he told Ellis what Cutrer thought his rights were under the lease, Ellis lost his temper: "God damn him," he said, cursing out the powerful white lawyer. Then Ellis composed himself and asked Houston what to take out of the house. "Well, anything, Mr. Ellis; it doesn't make any difference," Houston answered. So Ellis and Johnson "took out some of my things": a jug, "two trunks and all of the chairs." Meanwhile, Houston saddled his mule. But before he headed into town, there was one last technicality to dicker over. Houston insisted that Ellis move *all* the things out of his house, but Ellis's men declined. "We have put enough out to dispossess you," Houston remembered them saying, "it was not necessary to put them all out." And so they stopped.[7]

What was a court to make of all this? What should *we* make of it? Most obviously, Ellis and his men had committed an act of racial intimidation. But it wouldn't do Houston much good to argue that point, because Mississippi had no law against racial intimidation, and the federal government wasn't coming to the rescue. What stands out is that both Houston and Ellis had a working knowledge of leases and of the law of unlawful entry and detainer. Ellis was not there to steal Houston's land. He was there to take possession of land he had leased, without the expensive hassle of an ejectment suit. Houston was there to be *dispossessed* of the land he had leased so that he could assert his rights against a trespasser. Each man behaved according to his commonsense knowledge of property law, stiffened by conversations with lawyers and quasi-lawyers, at a time when the law on the books gave no clear answers to the questions at issue. Houston had consulted one of the most prominent lawyers in the county, but even John Cutrer could only have guessed what a lawsuit might yield because in 1903 experts disagreed about several of the key issues in the standoff: whether a landlord could "forcibly . . . expel a tenant" overstaying his lease, what counted as "force," and whether a tenant even had to prove that force was used.[8]

By refusing to leave—or, really, by telling Ellis publicly in front of all those people that he would have to dispossess him—Houston took advantage of the fact that he, not Ellis, was actually in possession of the land. Both men knew that if Ellis used "force, fraud, or stealth," or if Houston objected out loud, on the spot, Ellis's lawful eviction might turn into an unlawful entry, meaning he could be thrown out himself and compelled to pay damages.[9] The guns were real, and Houston was extremely wary of them, but he also knew they were part of the show. You evicted someone by going to that person's land and taking things out of his house—maybe not all of them, just his household things. You didn't need to move the things off the property. The front yard would do. You didn't even need the person to leave. Ellis and his men knew all of this. So did Houston. Houston rode off to see a lawyer, not to save his skin. He said later that he felt "powerless at that time" but also that he "really thought I might have been doing wrong and I would rather come to law and get justice,—if there was any for me." He wanted to make sure that his eviction happened by the book, to preserve his legal rights as Hartgrove's tenant. His wife, Priscilla, agreed. She didn't try to stop Ellis and his men because "I thought they knowed what they was doing."[10] Ellis and Houston each had a lease but they also knew that that paper might be interpreted in light of its context—conversations before and after it had been signed, things said and done at the moment of eviction. Ellis and Houston were staging a choreographed public performance of dispossession and protest, a pair of arguments made through law-saturated words and acts, each man trying to persuade "community opinion"—a county judge, their neighbors, and future trading partners—to recognize his claim to the land as a right.

The shadow was not a specter. It was cast by legal rules that had teeth. White people lynched Black people more than ever during Jim Crow, yet it still took effort to make lynchers more than squatters, to turn mere possession into ownership. One infuriating and remarkable example was the 1894 lynching of a man named Isom McGee. His traumatized widow and daughters fled Louisiana, leaving behind a ninety-one-acre farm. The land was sold and resold. In 1919, Gulf Oil Corporation hit an oil gusher on the land and when the company lawyers arrived at the courthouse to write up a lease, they found a break in the chain of title: there was no deed from Isom McGee on the ledger books. So Gulf launched a nationwide search for McGee's heirs. It located McGee's surviving daughter, Lillie Gussie Taylor. Her signature on a new deed repaired the chain of title, and she then hired the company to sell oil leases for her. A parade of expensive lawsuits ensued, involving high-powered lawyers and machinations on the state supreme court and creating a decades-long headache for Gulf Oil. This was the same problem that prompted Abraham Lincoln's family to quit Kentucky, the problem William Talley tried to head off in 1867 by suing John Robinson for specific performance, as described in Chapter 4. The McGees' case underscores the continuing power of a general logic. If white people acted as if Black people had no property rights, they jeopardized not only their land but anyone to whom they sold or mortgaged or leased or gave that land: merchants, neighbors, banks, grandchildren. As a lawyer in another case put it, when it came to land, many people had a stake in guarding "colored people" from anything "that would affect the title."[11] Two generations of Black land buying, selling, mortgaging, and inheriting were now casting a long shadow across the public knowledge that underpinned landownership.

This reality could be seen in the fact that, in an era when farmers still typically called a tract of land by the name of one of its previous owners, Black landowners' names became a shorthand like anyone else's, a handy reference in casual conversation and written onto courthouse deeds alongside technical descriptions of quarter, range, and township. Nate Shaw bought "the Pollard place," named after an "old colored man by the name of Amos Pollard." Jackson Holcomb bought parcels of "the old R. S. Garnette tract," named after Robert S. Garnett, a wealthy former slaveowner. And as late as 1960, white people in Cumberland

County were still getting baptized at "Talley's (or Rob[in]son's) pond," seemingly unable to decide whether to honor the free Black man who had once owned it or the white man who had coerced it from him in 1864.[12] Law's shadow didn't just spread outward from the law-books into daily life, it spilled back into the law-books, writing and rewriting the public meaning of what "the law" was.

Nowhere did the shadow of the law matter more than in the realm of credit. Like Ben Houston, Nate Shaw was a tenant farmer: he rented the land he farmed and the house he lived in. Tenant farmers relied on a steady flow of credit to buy the things that kept their business (the farm) running. Shaw borrowed his money using a pair of legal agreements called a "promissory note," a written promise to pay a certain sum of money on a certain date (or dates), and a "deed of trust," the mortgage-like document that secures the note with collateral, as we saw in Chapter 4. Today, the collateral (or security) typically covers only the asset you are buying. If you default on a car loan, GMAC takes the car; if you default on a mortgage, Citibank takes the house. You negotiate over the interest rate or points, not the collateral.

Farm credit in 1900 was different: Shaw had to negotiate over the collateral too. What those twin papers really did was allocate risk in the frighteningly risky business of farming. By seizing control and oversight of the credit process, a white landlord and his network of white merchants were able to shift the risk onto tenants, dictate where tenants shopped, and inflate the prices tenants paid. Shaw tried to keep the whites who loaned him money from "saddl[ing] everything"—they wanted "that paper [to] cover[] everything you got: your mules, wagon, all your tools and your cows and hogs." Just as the white man with the hoss-pistol rode back to fetch Katie Rowe's mother because the "debt paper" didn't "cover" her, Shaw kept an eagle eye not only on his note (the interest rate) but also on his deed of trust (the debt paper), because if the crop failed or if prices fell, the deed of trust showed which of Shaw's assets could be sold to pay off his debt. All the notorious abuses—the infamous peonage laws, which criminalized the nonpayment of certain debts, the landlords who made people sign a note for $1,250 but actually handed over only $1,000, or who charged 35 percent interest for a week-long loan, secured by the borrowers' "household effects," meaning that the borrower could lose everything—all of it stood atop this fundamental struggle over credit, waged through the civil rights of property and contract.[13]

The note and the deed of trust were the battleground of Black legal life, the place where a family's fortunes rose or fell. The problem for people like Nate Shaw wasn't ignorance or fear of getting tangled up in the law. He dealt with legal matters all the time, and he knew a bad loan when he saw one. He took bad loans because there were no good ones. And he tried to protect himself, first, by attempting to keep as much of his property off the deed of trust as possible.[14] And second, by shifting his debts around, asking one person after another to "take up" the note for him, the same way that people today juggle credit cards, looking for a lower interest rate or a way to stretch out their payments. That hunt for decent credit was one of the things that propelled Black people toward southern cities like Richmond or Memphis, then north to Chicago and Cleveland and Syracuse. Predatory lending would follow the Great Migration north, disguised as payday loans and contract-selling furniture stores, and so would the migrants' coping strategies.

"Friendship business amongst the white folks," is what Shaw called the predatory lending he faced in Alabama, "just a way of controllin the nigger." It was a spider's web, spun to control and profit from Black farmers, but the web touched whites, too, and could chafe them if anybody tugged too hard on its filaments. One year, 1919, Shaw managed to pay off his debt to his white landlord, Lemuel Tucker, and swore that he would sooner "live off the fat of my gut" "than to tie myself up" with Tucker again. Suddenly, he found his credit cut off. To his horror, Tucker had "run to every guano dealer there was in Apafalya—he knowed em all—and told em not to let me have no guano."[15] After years of single-minded toil, Shaw and his family were staring at financial ruin.

Nate Shaw, pseudonym of Ned Cobb, with his wife Viola, and their son, Andrew, in 1907.

All the dealers fell into line, except one: Charlie Black. Black, it seems, had a grudge against Tucker, too: "Mr. Black wasn't goin to let Mr. Tucker bar me from gettin guano after the way Mr. Tucker done treated *him.*" For the past several years, Shaw had owed Black $100 (about $7,750 today), unable to pay because Tucker kept forcing Shaw to borrow from him and then taking all his cotton money. When Shaw told Black that Tucker had blocked him from access to fertilizer, Black finally snapped. "He looked at me, said, 'The hell they won't. Goddamnit. . . . They can't do you that way." He verbally guaranteed to supply Shaw "all the damn guano I wanted." And when Lemuel Tucker realized Shaw had found a willing dealer, he caved, and unblocked Shaw's usual supplier. In breaking up the white "friendship business," Black helped Shaw get out from under Tucker's note, which was the only thing keeping Black from getting his $100 back.[16] Like Ben Houston, these three men were exquisitely aware of their respective legal endowments—the bargaining chips granted by the baseline rules of contract law—and how to use those chips to get what they wanted without tumbling into a risky, costly lawsuit.

One reason the law cast such a long shadow in the Jim Crow South was because it was an "anxious," modernizing place. The "New South" had fast-growing cities like Atlanta and industrial-scale, heavily mechanized industries like logging and mining. It was proud of its flagship universities in Tuscaloosa and Chapel Hill (or at least its white residents were proud). Its farmers—far from the self-reliant homesteaders we see on television—increasingly got their medicine from New York and their shoes from the Sears catalogue. Fueling the region's economic growth were national and international banks, which sold credit to merchants—chain stores like Belk, country stores, landlords like Albert Hartgrove—who, in turn, sold goods on credit to everyone else. Many Black people who rented land and ran credit bills with whites were themselves landlords, subleasing and lending to other Black farmers. O. M. Ellis didn't just deprive Ben Houston of a place to live, he also prevented Houston from getting laborers and tenants to help work his other leased lands.[17] Everyone knew that the main anchors of the financial system were somewhere far-off, like Atlanta or New York. But from a farmer's or janitor's perspective, credit was essentially local: a carefully tended network of relationships with people he knew and dealt with frequently. And here is a crucial thing: those dealings were still typically conducted without any lawyers.

To credit literally means "to believe," and every credit transaction is, at bottom, one person putting his faith in another that he will be repaid. What channels that faith and puts the power of the state behind its enforcement are those twin legal acts: the deed and the promissory note. A promissory note is not just a written promise to pay a certain sum of money on a certain date. It is an asset, one that can be bought and sold. In the Jim Crow South, as they had done before the Civil War, ordinary people used promissory notes like money: instead of paying cash for your flour and guano, you took a note that someone else had written out to you (that is, someone's February promise to pay you $100 in May) and you "endorsed" it over to a shopkeeper who could then collect the $100 in May. Usually that endorsee would take it at a discount, so that you got only $95 worth of groceries or $95 taken off your debt, which meant you were effectively paying a 20 percent interest rate. The resulting daisy chain of IOUs represented—and worsened—the region's economic inequality, grinding millions of Black people into poverty. But there was another dimension to the Jim Crow credit economy: it required whites to recognize Black people's legal personhood.[18] This point is simple, but easy to overlook. A contract is only binding if both parties know what they are doing and enter into it of their own free will—if the words "I accept," or "I promise to pay" mean something *legally*. The fact that Black people were now putting their X marks to notes and deeds was both a sign of how vulnerable they were in the New South, and a signal that the rights revolution that had begun during Reconstruction was now fully mature. The South's small population of free African Americans had signed deeds and notes back in the days of slavery, but by the early 1900s Black people's capacities and understanding mattered more than ever to white people.

As a result, the law was full of rules that spelled out how voluntary an assent had to be and how much knowledge and understanding—in essence, how much goat sense—a person needed for a court to say he was legally bound by his promise. For example, the "duty to read" was a set of rules that generally made it hard for people to get out of contracts by saying they hadn't understood what they signed. But the duty to read also constrained those who wrote deeds and read them aloud: those literate people owed a "confidence" to anyone who did not understand technical legal language. So if the person offering the contract lied about what was in it, or hid important provisions in the "fine print," then "the minds of the parties did not meet" and he shouldn't expect a judge to enforce it. The duty-to-read rules also listed precautions illiterate people should take before signing, as well as guidelines for how they should sign. Testimony in trial courts and other documents suggests that these official rules, and their underlying assumptions about knowledge and understanding, were more than a figment of law professors' imagination—that adults, including Black people, generally knew that "it was illegal to force a man to sign a note without readin it to him, tellin him what he's signin," that a person should say "whether she understood" what she was about to sign, and that a binding signature could be made by "touch[ing] the pen."[19] In fact, it is likely that the judges and treatise writers derived their rules about the duty to read in part from what they knew about how people actually made deals.

Many if not most Black people had a great deal of goat sense, but it was not always in their interest to admit it in court. Sometimes it was better to emphasize their weakness and ignorance and throw themselves on the mercy of the court.[20] The wardship idea—the idea that ex-slaves were under the guardianship of the nation—had emerged in late-1860s Freedmen's Bureau courts as a way of reconciling the Republicans' insistence on equal civil rights with the reality that white and Black southerners did not come to the free market as equals, while preserving the idea that judges were constrained by law. Now Jim Crow–era southern lawyers and judges developed the wardship idea into a full-blown legal strategy for contract cases: the "ignorant negro" defense.

The stereotype of the "ignorant negro" affirmed white supremacy. But while white demagogues could justify lynching and disfranchisement by warning that "armed millions of ignorant negroes" were attacking "the proud, bleeding . . . Anglo-Saxon race of the South," a contract case required more than stereotypes. Precisely because the "ignorant-negro" defense denigrated Black people's intelligence, it required them and their lawyers to adopt a subjective, "meeting of the minds" approach, emphasizing the distinctive qualities of particular people in order to deny that the minds had truly met. The lawyers explained away X marks and spidery signatures by playing up their clients' ignorance and illiteracy. Meanwhile, those seeking to enforce contracts needed to prove that their opponents had signed those contracts freely and knowingly. They needed to show that illiterate signers were smart enough and informed enough to know what they were doing. So they insisted that they had gone out of their way to get "some able and reputable lawyer to draw up the . . . papers" and that the other party *had* heard these documents read to him so "that there could be no misunderstanding as to what he was signing." They pulled courtroom stunts to try and show that their opponents were faking ignorance.[21] Edgar Webster, the white lawyer for a white Mississippi druggist named W. A. Stinebeck, vainly attempted to pin down a man named George Reno to the deed by which he and his wife had signed their home over to Stinebeck, a deed the Renos were suing to cancel.

Q Can you read?
A Yes sir a little bit.
Q Read that out to the Court. (Hands him paper.)
A I cant see it without my glasses.
Q . . . (Hands him glasses.) . . . All right, start down there and read that.

Reno slowly read out the first lines of his own lawsuit against Stinebeck.

A "To the Honorable J. G. Mc Gowen Chancellor of the Third Chancery Court . . . Your Complainants George Reno and Wife, Jessie Reno resident"

Reno stopped. "What is that?" he wondered, innocently. "Citizens," Webster prodded. "Citizens of Lafayette County," Reno continued, until Webster cut him short. Everyone in the courtroom could see that George Reno could read. Now the question was: could he *understand* what he was reading? "What is that you have in your hand there?" demanded Webster. Reno spotted the trap. "Well sir, Mr. Webster," Reno demurred, "I am no lawyer sir." Webster pressed on. "You signed that didn't you?" Isn't that your handwriting? "Looks like mine," Reno admitted. What about Jessie's mark, can you "read that . . . to the Court?" Again, Reno shrugged. The courtroom was too dim and he'd left his glasses at home. Webster was ready.

Q Here try these glasses George.
A That makes it worse, I cant see with them.
Q Well here is another pair, try these. Can you see?
A Yes sir.

And on it went.

A ". . . cash in hand paid me we hereby began — "
Q Spell it?
A "B a r g a i n"
Q Bargain, go on?
A "Bargain, sell and convey . . ."

When Reno finished they were right back where they started.

Q What is that you have just read?
A I cant tell you.
Q Anything in there that you dont understand?
A Yes sir.
Q What?
A All of it pretty much.

Reno freely admitted that he knew "what it means to sell," and he admitted that he had signed his X mark to the paper he had just read in open court. The "ignorant negro," as he played the character, was a tricked man, not a stupid man. His defense was that he thought the paper was "security" for a loan—not a deed of sale but a deed of trust, the mortgage-like agreement that people signed all the time for short-term money needs. Confronted with stories of "ignorant negroes" up against "well informed" white men, white people and their lawyers bent over backward to say how smart those "negroes" were. Oliver M. Ellis praised Ben Houston to the skies as "away above the ordinary nigger; about as sharp a nigger as I ever met; he has been so dog gone sharp that I have not been able to keep up with him."[22] The point was not that *Black people* were smart—an assertion that would have contradicted white supremacy—it was that *this* Black man was smart enough to have protected himself in this particular contract.

The "ignorant negro" defense treated race opportunistically. Its genius was that it enabled Black people and their lawyers to wring a tactical advantage from the ideology of white supremacy without challenging that ideology or accusing whites of wrongdoing. Indeed, many Black litigants and witnesses went out of their way to avoid even implying bad faith on the part of their white opponents. Like Captain Renault in the movie *Casablanca*, Ben Houston said he was shocked, *shocked*, that Ellis "would knowingly and designedly" defraud him. This defense worked wonders on southern juries and judges during the late nineteenth and early twentieth centuries. In case after case, courts sided with African Americans who presented themselves as "poor, hard-working, humble" people, "ignorant negro[es], unacquainted with the formalities and usages of law." These tactics spread fast enough that by 1890, the "shrewd, designing white man" defrauding "an illiterate and confiding negro" had already become stock characters in a "pathetic[]" drama "set forth in the [lawyers'] pleadings."[23] In the Jim Crow South, where contractual dealings with Black people were an ordinary feature of daily life, legal professionals could neither reject nor fully embrace the "objective theory" that has become the underpinning of most contract law today: the idea that a contract means what a reasonable person of ordinary knowledge would think it means.

Thus, the "ignorant negro" was an essential part of contract law, not a separate body of law. It worked because it extended the principles of capacity and assent that arguably defined what a contract was (and was not). White people claimed ignorance, fraud, and duress, too, albeit without the supercharging racial marker.[24] Courts' treatment of African Americans was a subset of the tensions between idiosyncratic personality and general categories that permeated contract law in general. It was one thing to be "afraid to make contracts" with a person who seemed mentally unstable or drunk, but life's ordinary business could not go on if you could not make contracts with Black people. White people needed to be able to treat African Americans as competent, reasonable people, just as they sometimes needed to pretend that the rules of contract law were crystal-clear and that a scrawled-out IOU perfectly mirrored those rules. They needed Black people to have a working legal knowledge, to be coparticipants in the "community opinion" that turned otherwise ordinary behavior, like touching a pen, or putting some chairs outside a house, into legally binding acts. Judges and lawyers used the "ignorant negro" trope because it allowed them to get results in cases involving Black people without disturbing either the majesty of contract law or the principle of white supremacy.[25] In the early-twentieth-century United States, civil rights were vindicated in courts, but they were made and remade through everyday use, in the shadow of the law.

Every day, Black people used their legal commonsense, their intuitions about how a judge might apply a legal rule, about what it took to make a binding contract, about the difference between a lawful and an unlawful eviction, about promissory notes and deeds of trust, and more. Black people drew from the same pool of legal ideas and assumptions that white people did, and they had more incentive to pay close attention to those ideas and assumptions. They stood at a disadvantage, of course. But not because they were ignorant of the law or scared of the law, and not even primarily because white officials cheated or intimidated them out of their rights. Rather, they stood at a disadvantage because under the ordinary rules of property and contract—the fundamental "rights of free men" that Republicans had enshrined in the Civil Rights Act of 1866 and the Fourteenth Amendment—people on one side of the table started with a bigger pile of bargaining chips. Landlords had more of them than renters, creditors more than borrowers.

It was here, in the shadow of the law, that Black people built on the legacy of Reconstruction, grabbing hold of civil rights to make a life for themselves and in doing so, subtly reshaping those rights. In the late 1860s and 1870s they had worked to influence how the privileges of slavery would translate into the world of rights, in part by gradually acquiring land, the one kind of property that slaves had never been able to own. In the 1890s and early 1900s, as segregation hardened and Black landowning climbed to new heights, people across America, both Black and white, had to figure out how to translate private property rights back into status-based privileges. In an era when whites were obsessed with "keeping the Negro in his place," what was the place of a Black landowner?[26]

9

"Be my social security"

By 1908, my great-great-great uncle and aunt, Jackson and Louisa Holcomb, owned 279 acres of land in Cumberland County, Virginia, all of it bought from whites with earnings from tobacco farming. Every year, they would load their crop onto a wagon and take it about ten miles south for sale in Farmville. Their biggest break came when they received a tip from a local white man that Jackson's old boss, Robert Garnett, was about to go broke and sell off land under pressure. The Holcombs weren't alone. Since Reconstruction, Black homeowner-

Jackson, Teresa, and Louisa Holcomb are shown in this undated photograph. Jackson and Louisa Holcomb joined Midway Baptist Church probably around 1883. They, their children, and their grandchildren donated to the church even as many of them moved away and joined other churches.

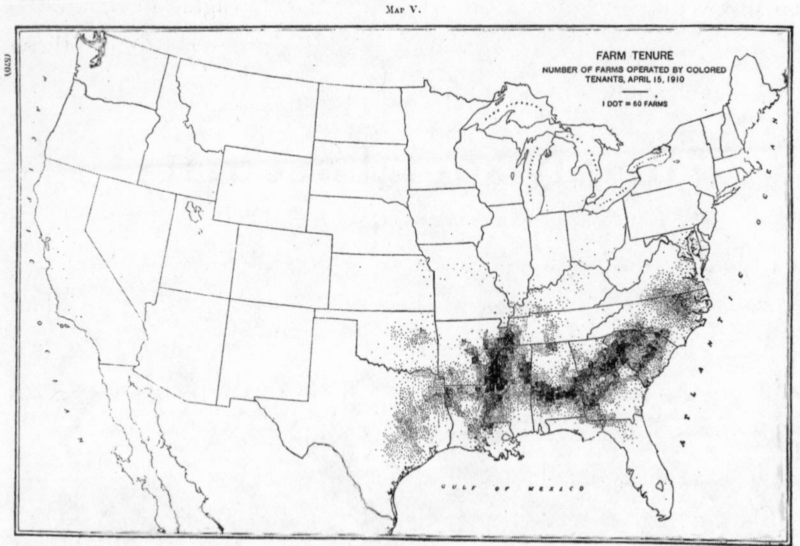

This map of Black tenant farming reflects our usual image of southern Black life during Jim Crow. Black sharecroppers and tenant farmers clustered in the Cotton Belt and Delta.

ship had climbed rapidly: from about 43,000 Black families in 1870 to some 506,590 in 1910—nearly one in four Black families nationwide. America's 218,972 Black farm-owners owned more land than ever before or since: more than fifteen million acres, practically all of it in the South. Between their land, livestock, and equipment, Black farmers owned more than $1.1 billion worth of farm property, roughly $208 billion in 2021 dollars. To be sure, Black-owned land and homes were generally less valuable and smaller than those owned by whites. But these were only part of the story. Soon, Black business districts sprang up in nearly "every Southern city" to sell homes, sewing machines, dressers, carpets, books, washstands, funeral policies, and more to the farmers, maids, and laborers who were joining America's consumer economy in ever greater numbers.[1]

During these years whites also lynched more Black people than at any other time in American history. From 34 victims in 1882, lynchings rose sharply over the next decade, to 106 in 1892, spiked again in 1908, then gradually, haltingly, trended downward through the 1920s. One of those lynchings happened in downtown Farmville, on Main Street near the brick warehouses where the Holcombs sold their tobacco crops. It seems obvious why lynching and Black landownership peaked during the same few decades: Black landownership represented a threat to white supremacy. From the destruction of Rosewood, Florida, to the burning of Tulsa's fabled Black Wall Street, lynchers often targeted successful Black farmers and businesspeople.[2] It seems equally obvious what land represented for African Americans: a refuge from racist oppression, a source of communal pride and identity, and proof that they could be capable citizens at a time when most whites doubted it.

But the story of Black landownership had always been more than a story of race relations. Since the 1860s, if not before, land had held two kinds of meaning for African Americans, as it did for white people. It was a commodity to buy and sell. It was also a "propriety," something that

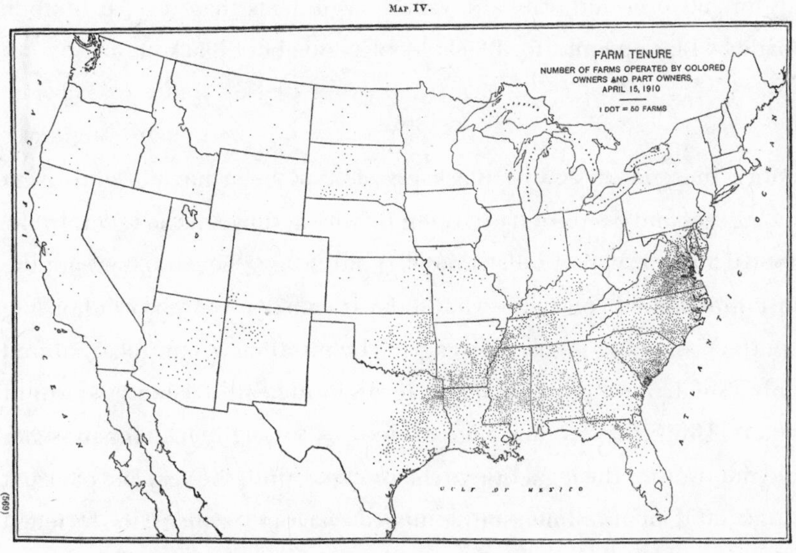

The map of Black landownership looks more widely distributed, but ownership was still heaviest in majority-Black counties like Virginia and coastal South Carolina.

anchored and expressed who they were.[3] Now, as Jim Crow solidified, new patterns of thought and action regarding land emerged, patterns that would shape the contours of Black life down through the 1960s. The idea of land as propriety increasingly emboldened people to assert rights over land they didn't actually own. The rise of Black landowning prompted white people to experiment with residential segregation—something they had never seriously considered before—and with new legal devices to exploit Black buyers, such as the installment-purchase contract. The rise of Black landownership also forced painful adaptations among Black people. Disputes over "family land" (or "heir property") fanned into flames larger struggles among African Americans over what a "good family" looked like and what "the race" could become. And in much the same way that whites asserted a right not to have Black people as neighbors, the idea of land as a propriety led some African Americans to assert what they felt was their right to keep out obnoxious or disreputable neighbors of any race. Hidden beneath the overarching narrative of the Black freedom struggle are the traces of long-forgotten arguments over authority and values, arguments that were, at bottom, made by Black people, for Black people, and about Black people.

Since the end of slavery, Black people had been buying land using mortgages and deeds of trust, often financing through the seller. In the 1880s, a third type of seller-financed purchasing began to spread: the installment land contract—what today is called a "rent-to-own housing contract" or "poor man's mortgage." The installment contract required only a small down payment but its terms were heavily skewed in favor of sellers. Unlike with a mortgage or deed of trust, the installment-seller did not transfer the legal title to the property until the very last payment came in.[4] If an installment-buyer missed even one payment, she forfeited all the equity her payments had built up, along with whatever "improvements" she had made on the land. That is, missing a payment turned her from a "purchaser in possession" into a mere "tenant," a renter, who could be put out in a summary proceeding, with no foreclosure judge to tote up her credits and debits. By the 1920s, the installment land contract was moving into cities as a form of predatory lending, a transaction designed not to sell homes but to harvest interest.[5]

But just as earlier judges had softened the crystalline edges of mortgage law, some judges now questioned the harshest features of the installment land contract. They said that when an installment-buyer defaulted, the seller could not have his cake and eat it, too—that he was not allowed both to rescind the sale deed and to keep the buyer's payments. Instead, he had to give back the amount the buyer had paid to that point, plus the value of any "improvements" the buyer had made to the land, minus a reasonable rent for the time the buyer had lived there. "Improvements" could add up to a lot of money. Buyers built fences, fixed up houses, planted trees, filled gullies, dug drainage ditches, and cleared out huge amounts of scrub brush and trees. Moreover, said the Georgia supreme court, the seller couldn't disguise usury or an illegal penalty provision just by calling it "rent."[6]

Black people used their working legal knowledge to assert their interpretations of what were, in effect, highly ambiguous contracts. Even as they handed over money that sellers called "rent," buyers pointed to terms like "land contract" on the paper they had signed, and insisted that the lands "belonged to them" and warned sellers that their so-called rent payments should go to paying down the mortgage. Sometimes they brought along people to witness these payments, and to underscore that these were purchase payments, not rent. Both buyers and tenants had one advantage: they actually lived on the land in question. And possession mattered a lot under the law. Because judges often interpreted contracts in light of "trade usage"—that is, the usual practices within a given economic field—or the parties' own "acts and conduct," possession opened paths for Black people to assert the rights of a buyer by acting like one. In short, Black people's understandings of the bargains they made—more precisely, what they *said* they understood about their bargains—carried potential legal power, because it is common for judges to construe what a contract really says by looking to how the parties understood it when they made it and how the broader community understands similar contracts.[7]

Much the way that a slave acting as if he owned a boat could persuade people to pay him for ferry service, and a pair of white New Yorkers acting married could persuade a judge that they were entitled to be treated as married, and white lumber dealers acting as if two packs of shingles contained a thousand shingles even if they actually only contained 625, these doctrines—"usage" and "course of dealing"—opened small windows for Black people in Jim Crow America to fight for their homes through contract law.[8] The problem was that, when interpreting ambiguous contract terms, judges tended to follow the understandings held by the most powerful members of the trading communities—white businessmen and rich farmers like William R. Baskervill, introduced in Chapter 5, the consummate repeat players, whose names appear again and again on the courthouse docket books.[9] And if Rosa Baskervill had managed to convince a judge of her interpretation of some ambiguous term, William Baskervill could simply write his preferred understanding into next year's contract. So, when they got a decent contract, Black people did everything they could to preserve their rights under those terms.

Nate Shaw's land-buying story is especially illuminating. Around 1928, Shaw, introduced in Chapter 7, made a deal to buy the nearby "Pollard place" in Tallapoosa County, Alabama, taking over a mortgage from a "young white man" who "couldn't handle" the payments. The price was $1,600, to be paid at about $120 per year, an amount Shaw expected to earn from the Pollard place and other land he was renting. Soon, the seller, a white man named Lester Watson, began trying to get Shaw to sign a mortgage and promissory note covering not just the Pollard place but all the rest of Shaw's property—nearly $2,000 worth of tools, "mules, hogs, cows, wagons, [and] two automobiles." It was the usual trick and it didn't work on Shaw. But once Shaw started buying supplies from Watson, Shaw began hearing from his neighbors that Watson was "goin to take all you got," even though Shaw's mortgage clearly stated that it only covered the Pollard place. Shaw shrugged: "Well, there's a law for that and the law obliges the likes of him as well as me. I aint goin to hide. When he starts, it's goin to be trouble." Shaw was as good as his word. Many of his neighbors were indebted to Watson, too. They understood Watson's predatory lending as a threat to them all, and for months, they had been warily engaging with white activists who were trying to organize the region's tenant farmers into an interracial Southern Tenant Farmers Union. In 1932, one of those neighbors defaulted on his debt to Watson, and the sheriff and his deputies came to seize that neighbor's property. Shaw and his Black neighbors confronted the officers. The officers opened fire. Shaw and his neighbors shot back but were badly outgunned. Those who survived were arrested and hauled to jail, bleeding.[10]

Historians have presented Shaw's resistance as a story of Black labor activism, a short-lived flicker of hope for an interracial southern labor movement that might have changed history. And it was. But the way Shaw told the story, it was also an argument about mortgage law. Into his bloodstained jail cell came "four big white men from Apafalya": the local banker, a powerful white neighbor of Shaw's, the landlord Shaw worked for as a teenager, and Watson, "the main man that was goin to take what I had." They put a paper in front of him to sign. Shaw wanted to know "what sort of paper" it was. They shrugged. "O, it don't amount to nothin, just a paper." Shaw couldn't read but he wasn't fooled. He guessed it was a mortgage—that Watson was aiming to pull all Shaw's unmortgaged property under a note.[11] And he told them so. The white men hemmed and hawed but they did not lie or "dispute my word." Not even the sheriff. After a while the "big white men" gave up and walked to the cell door.

Just then, out from the doorway jumped "the High Sheriff Kurt Beall," the "bad fellow" who had just shot Shaw and two other men in the gun battle at his neighbor's farm. Shaw remembered what happened next: Beall "run up to me and looked me right dead in the face, squallin like a panther," trying to make Shaw say the words he had refused to sign his name to. "Aint he got a mortgage on that stuff? Aint he . . . ?" Shaw answered him coolly: "No." Beall kept squalling: "Well, you just as well to let him [Watson] have it. I'm goin down there and get all you got . . . and put it before the courthouse to sell." Now Shaw shrugged: "You go ahead and do it if you think you can come out of there, go on." That set Beall off. "O, he jumped just as high—he was a heavy-built man, kind of pot-bellied, he'd a weight fully two hundred pounds—he jumped just as high as he could jump and stomped on the floor and hollered, 'Get back in jail you sonofabitch.' That was the end of it. Them white men cleared out of there . . . never said 'umph.'" Shaw's family kept their "mules, wagon, corn and stuff," and that is how they stayed afloat during the long years Shaw was in prison.[12] Why didn't the "four big white men" lie about what was on the "paper"? Because, out of all the defenses a person could use to get out of a bad contract—duress, unconscionability, incapacity, illegality—the easiest and most powerful defense of all was to prove that the other person had lied about what was on the paper.[13] Killing Shaw would have created other problems. Even if they did not think Shaw would actually file a lawsuit, these white men seemed to presume that he was still a person with civil rights and a basic grasp of how those rights worked.

Black people's working understanding of contract law was put to the test when, beginning in the 1890s, as more and more Black people migrated to the South's burgeoning cities, white-owned real-estate companies began refining some of the same tactics that white farmer-merchants like Lester Watson used in the countryside. In Nashville, a white-owned company called Bransford Realty manipulated the terms of installment-purchase contracts to do what a recent Supreme Court case said they couldn't: both rescind the sale and keep the payments—to have their cake and eat it too. The company's strategy spilled out in a spate of lawsuits in the 1910s, some of them lodged by Black people. One Black man, James Higdon, charged in an unreported 1914 decision that Bransford Realty's standard contract was "a subterfuge."

It *looked* like a sale in some ways. But the contract also said that if the Higdons missed even one payment, Bransford Realty could summarily throw them out with a simple court filing and keep all the money they had paid, under the fiction that they had, at the last minute, chosen not to buy.[14] Whereas men like Watson had tried to trick Black land-buyers like Nate Shaw into signing away their property rights, Bransford Realty figured out how to incorporate it right in the purchase contract itself.

Exploitative installment-purchase contracts kept spreading.[15] But Black buyers' lawsuits generated court decisions that limited what sellers could do to buyers of any race. A year after the Higdons beat the Bransford company in Tennessee's mid-level appeals court, another Nashville family took Bransford Realty to the Tennessee supreme court and won. In *Beaden v. Bransford Realty Co.* (1921), the court cancelled a pair of contracts that today might be described as predatory lending. Under the first contract, Mary and Fred Beaden, described as "a negro of average intelligence for one of his race," purportedly agreed to pay $283 down and $1,042 in ninety-four monthly installments, plus taxes, insurance, and repairs, for an "option" to buy a house. Missing a payment signified that they had "elected" not to buy, and automatically forfeited the house and all their equity, as "damages" for breaking the contract. The Beadens lived in the house for three and half years and paid in $706. Then Mary Beaden died, leaving six young children. Fred took extra jobs but fell behind on the payments. Bransford Realty threatened to have the sheriff throw him out if he did not sign a second contract, under which he agreed to give the title back to Bransford Realty in return for $5 of moving expenses. Fred Beaden signed it. Then he got a lawyer and sued.

Citing their unreported *Higdon* decision, the court held that Bransford Realty could not use the subterfuge of an "option" contract to bypass the foreclosure process. From the buyer-borrower's perspective, this was good news. Foreclosure was dismal but it was better than being dispossessed and losing all one's payments. The court also held that the contract itself was unconscionable. No reasonable person would knowingly agree to forfeit more than $300 worth of equity in exchange for $5.[16] Decisions like these took the "wardship" idea that had long shielded women, children, sailors, and freedpeople from some of the harsh effects of the marketplace, and carried it into the city, dressed in the garb of the "ignorant negro."

By the 1940s, installment-sellers would figure out how to soothe the judges' worry about shockingly inadequate bargains. Yet buyers kept disputing the nature of their contractual relationship when they fell behind in their payments, insisting that the money they paid was purchase-money, not rent.[17] Black litigants' "unconscionability" cases in the Jim Crow South became part of contract doctrine, cited by prominent scholars in places like the *Yale Law Journal*, and were a harbinger of what would someday become "the law of the poor," a major development in cause-lawyering but one that would end up on the margins of American law. In the 1960s, activists in Chicago would launch widely publicized protests and public-interest lawsuits in an attempt to harness the courts' traditional concern for especially vulnerable classes of people onto a newly muscular federal civil rights regime targeting racial discrimination. But the activists, along with the judges who heard their lawsuits in the 1960s, didn't know about what early migrants like the Beadens had done in southern cities, and what farm-buyers like Nate Shaw had done in the southern countryside. Those activists and judges did not realize that they were building on a long history of Black struggle over the uses and misuses of contract.

Fred and Mary Beaden were part of another, even bigger phenomenon. Between 1900 and 2000, something like 28.6 million people of all races left the southern countryside. The migrants changed American religion, seeding Pentecostal storefront churches and evangelical megachurches. They upended American politics, igniting the white backlash conservatism that put Ronald Reagan and Donald Trump in the White House, and galvanizing the working-class Black voters who put Barack Obama and Joe Biden there. And they transformed American culture, inventing white Nashville as the home of "country music," Black Chicago as the home of the blues, and Atlanta, New York, and Los Angeles as hip-hop meccas. The Black part of the exodus, nearly eight million strong, is known as the Great Migration (though it is often divided into two main waves and has reversed direction since the 1970s). Most of them went to cities, whose white leaders funneled them into the poorest parts of town, there to suffer in overcrowded apartments from disease, crime, abusive police, and the malign neglect of those in power. The Great Migration has become almost synonymous with Black urbanization. The Smithsonian once put on a whole exhibition called "From Field to Factory," and Stevie Wonder wrote a song called "Living for the City," imagining the perspective of a young migrant. Yet the migrants stayed connected to the South, not only culturally but also legally: through marriage, inheritance, and associations. Moreover, not everybody moved to a city. Thomas and Annie Holcomb moved from the Farmville, Virginia, area to South Orange, New Jersey, a suburb of Newark. So had half the congregation of their new church, it seemed. By 2000, more than one of every three African Americans lived in the suburbs: almost twelve million people.[18]

In reaction to the Black migration to cities and suburbs, white people designed another tactic, a kind of homeowners' counterpart to Bransford Realty's predatory sales contracts: residential segregation. Already in 1940, most of the town's Black people lived within a few blocks of the Holcombs' apartment at 113 South Orange Avenue, and today, most American cities and suburbs are deeply segregated. But it took a great deal of work to make that happen, because it turned out to be harder to segregate a neighborhood than a railroad. Unlike the law of common carriers, which could stretch itself around a principle like "separate but equal," the law of property is pretty conservative, even old-fashioned. Generally speaking, property law frowns on rules that constrain *who* can own and use property, as opposed to what owners and occupants can *do* with it. The builders of American apartheid had to surmount this basic legal hostility toward constraints aimed at the personal characteristics of owners. White politicians passed racially targeted nuisance laws, but judges quickly pointed out that a nuisance was a noxious *activity,* like operating a slaughterhouse or a brothel, not a noxious *person.* White politicians passed racially targeted zoning laws, which barred people from living outside their designated "colored" or "white" zone, and the courts struck those down, too. The problem with zoning, said the U.S. Supreme Court in *Buchanan v. Warley* (1917), was not that it violated the Equal Protection Clause—most zoning laws carefully followed the separate-but-equal formula laid out in *Plessy*—but that it violated the Due Process Clause. That is, the government could tell a white-owned railroad company how to run its trains, but it could not tell a white homeowner what to do with his house.[19]

Where the politicians failed at changing property law, white supremacist realtors and homeowners instead figured out how to exploit it: the racially restrictive covenant. There are many different kinds of restrictive covenants, but generally speaking, a restrictive covenant is a bargain between property owners to restrict how a piece of land can be used. What makes a restrictive covenant different from other contracts is that it binds not only the person who signed the original contract but also everyone who acquires the land in the future. Historically, American judges have tended not to let present owners tie the hands of future owners very much. The practice clogs up the free market. It smells like musty European feudalism. It's un-American. But in the 1920s, American courts started letting property owners do just that. Some of these 1920s-era innovations are still flourishing today: the setback (a building's walls can't go right up to the property line), the homeowner association (or "HOA"), which made possible the condominiums and other planned communities that now dot the country, and intellectual property (discussed in Chapter 13).[20] Racially restrictive covenants flourished for only about thirty years, from the 1920s, after the Court barred explicitly racist zoning, to 1948, when the Court declared them unenforceable in *Shelley v. Kraemer.* But they profoundly shaped our country because those were the thirty years when the basic geography of modern American cities and suburbs was cemented.

Racially restrictive covenants were vulnerable to legal attack in ways that the other kinds of covenants were not, and to get them past judges, lawyers and realtors had to make a series of adjustments that wound up gnawing them from the inside, like doctrinal dry rot. All these covenants put constraints on something that was fundamental to most people's notion of property: the right to sell (or "alienate"). Judges thought it might be reasonable to constrain how a parcel of land could be *used*—no slaughterhouses on Fifth Avenue, for example. But racially restrictive covenants put constraints on *who* can own. To soothe judges' skepticism toward covenants restricting "ownership," developers covered up the "who" with a "how." They wrote deeds that said instead that houses couldn't be "used" or "occupied" by nonwhites. So, for example, the first deed in the chain of title to my house just outside Berkeley, California, contains a 1916 covenant that if it is ever used for anything but a single-family home, or is sold or rented to anyone of "African or Asiatic descent," then the property will automatically revert to the seller, the North End Land Company. To sidestep the Rule Against Perpetuities (a market-promoting doctrine meant to prevent people from tying up land forever, like on Downton Abbey), the 1916 sellers set the covenant to expire in 1930, trusting that whoever bought it next would not sell to someone like me or my Taiwanese-American spouse.[21]

Then there was the odd-sounding doctrine of "horizontal privity." Requiring covenants to have horizontal privity is supposed to put future buyers on notice (the same concept that underpinned slaves' ownership of property) that there is a binding restriction on the house they are about to buy. Unlike a leaky roof, a covenant isn't obvious to a homebuyer. It's a few lines in the paperwork at the closing, copied from a deed book at the county courthouse. We only found out about ours because the title company happened to send us a pdf of it. Horizontal privity requires that the people who made the original contract (the one containing the restrictive covenant) have to do it as part of a lease or sale of the property. The idea is that leases and sales are big enough transactions that they will normally get recorded on the deed books, where future homebuyers will be likely to notice that they are about to make a binding promise never to do certain things. In the case of our house, the promise was never to sell to "colored" people. Because of the horizontal privity rule, racially restrictive covenants spread more easily in suburbs, where whole neighborhoods were being built and deeded at the same time, than in cities, where most of the housing was already built by the time the covenants arrived. It is no accident that the 1916 covenant on my house was written by the company that developed the entire neighborhood, or that nearly all South Orange's Black people lived within a few blocks of my great-great aunt and uncle's. In new subdivisions, it was easy to prove horizontal privity because everyone had bought from the same seller.[22]

The cleverness of racially restrictive covenants shows how shaky they were, how vulnerable to legal attacks based on standard property rules. Their real power lurked in the shadow of the law: the message they sent to white neighbors and potential buyers. Even after 1948, when the Supreme Court held that courts could not enforce racially restrictive covenants, many white realtors—and the giant federal homeowners' insurance agency that made possible the modern real estate industry—kept acting as if it were "against the law" to sell to Black or Asian Americans, steering them away from neighborhoods like mine. By then, the covenants had done their damage. They had helped draw the map of the modern American city and suburb, a map that "redlining" and federal highway planners would cement in place.[23] But the short, turbulent history of racially restrictive covenants suggests how tricky it was to enlist property law into the cause of white supremacy.

During the same years that whites tried to segregate property, some Black landowners moved to impose their own restrictions on property. Some of them sought to keep out people they felt were undesirable.

Others strove to keep family land in the family. All of them desperately sought more control over the labor power that made landownership possible—labor that, more often than not, came from their own relatives. At times, Black adults, especially men, skirted the edges of familial authority, treating children and wives as if they not only belonged *in* the family, but also belonged *to* the family.[24]

Black landowners relied on intestacy to protect family land. This was simpler and cheaper than zoning or restrictive covenants, but even shakier. Family land is a form of landownership called a "tenancy in common," as we've seen, and a tenancy in common ties its owners' hands. None of them can mortgage or sell it without permission from the other co-owners, unless it is "partitioned"—divided up—by a judge. A partition "in kind" divvies up the actual land. A partition by sale divvies up the land's cash value, by selling it. A significant fraction of the cases in my sample involving African Americans were partition cases. Although tenancy in common was widespread among people of all races and had deep roots in American legal culture, it held particular significance for racial minorities who, in the decades after the Civil War, were disproportionately blocked from other ways of building wealth and from formal politics.[25]

The creation of "family land" (or "heir property") through the tenancy in common was the legal instantiation of a particular type of kinship politics, one that sought to maximize the strengths of a collectivity while minimizing frictions among its members, and that did not center on, or even involve, white people. At its heart was a tension between two ways of thinking about landownership: as an individual common-law right and as a privilege of membership in a family.[26] In theory, family land was an inalienable corporate estate that belonged to all the descendants of the "old head," a genealogy that, for Black people, often traced back to the days of Reconstruction—Jackson Holcomb's 1883 purchase, for example. In practice, nearly every element of that theory—"family," "inalienable," "descent," "property"—was contested or in flux.

Consider another moment from Nate Shaw's life. After his father-in-law died, his mother-in-law, Molly Ramsey, put Shaw in charge of her family's assets. Their chief asset was "a little piece of land that they [had] quickly bought . . . not too long after the [Confederate] surrender." Now that the "old man" was dead, whites started asking to buy it, but Shaw's wife Hannah Ramsey and her siblings couldn't agree what to do. Some of them, as Shaw recalled, "jumped up and wanted to sell the place to get their part out of it. My wife kicked against it—she didn't want to sell her mammy and daddy's home place." The Ramseys "kept a naggin and a naggin bout sellin it," Shaw said. "So I studied a way to keep any of em from sellin." He arranged to have the land partitioned "in kind," that is, he "had it counted off" into equal ten-acre parcels, each with a separate deed—and worth a lot less money. "I knowed that would hitch a knot rope—didn't nobody want to buy just a piece of the property."[27] And it did. Shaw's knot-rope stratagem preserved the Ramseys' land by discouraging prospective buyers, whereas as we saw in Chapter 5, Lot Richardson's demand for a separate parcel threatened to break up the Richardsons' family land, perhaps because Richardson asked for a partition-and-sale rather than a partition in kind, or because there was stronger demand for Low Country land in 1868.

There are three things to pay attention to in Shaw's story. First is that white prospective buyers seem to have assumed that they would pursue their interests by exploiting the rules of contract and property, not by breaking them. Second, Shaw's mother-in-law put *him* in charge and not her daughter: men had rights that women didn't. The third noteworthy thing about Shaw's story is how he manipulated property law to mediate between two rival visions of landownership: an individualist vision and a collective one centered on a "home place." Hannah Ramsay thought that her family land had to be protected from *her own family members.* Shaw manipulated the law of intestacy to get what his wife wanted—to hold onto the home place—without violating her siblings' statutory right to sell.[28] The freedom struggle narrative hides these essential parts of Black life.

There is no way to know how much of the land owned by African Americans was family land. Almost two-thirds of Black landowners in 1930 had been on their land for ten years or longer, though the data behind this figure are incomplete. Black sociologists at the time reported that many Black landowners worked ceaselessly to keep land "in the family," that they took pride in those who were still living on it some seventy years after their newly freed grandparents had acquired it, that they lamented land that "got away from" the family, either through neglect or ignorance or poverty, and that they cheered their kinsmen's efforts to buy it back. At its apex, Black family land expanded to the scale of small settlements. If the Bear Camp venture (discussed in Chapter 6) had lasted beyond Reconstruction, it might have ended up becoming something like Archertown, a cluster of some twenty "closely knit" farming families in eastern North Carolina, who traced their history back to a single, land-acquiring founder. Similarly, nearby Mooretown "grew out of a family of five brothers, former slaves" who managed to acquire most of "the old plantation" from their former master, John W. Moore, and to keep it undivided for decades.[29]

It was Black settlements like these that have helped lead modern scholars to portray Black people as communitarian, rejecting the dominant white ethos of market individualism. Obviously that portrait leaves out the long history of Black entrepreneurship. But even more important, the Black-communitarian image turns family land—a practice that expressed Black people's ideas of wealth and power and identity—into a drama about cultural values. Both Mooretown and Archertown were riddled with inequalities. Not everyone had the same privileges within these family associations. Privileges to farm and live on family land belonged to those who could trace their ancestry back to the founders—the "old head[s]"; those who could not trace their ancestry back so far had to work as tenants or laborers. Senior kinsmen—those who ranked higher in the genealogical reckoning—bossed their younger relatives' labor. Black people's "ancestor pride," the genealogies they told to sociologists and recorded in "quavering handwriting" in family Bibles—these should be seen less as statements of fact than as unofficial corporate charters, political documents that rubbed out alternative genealogies and rival claims to privileges within the family association.[30]

Sometimes Black people were able to enlist judges into their kinship politics. At a time when few African Americans had marriage licenses and few people of any race had birth certificates, courts often looked to testimony about behavior: acting like an aunt or a father could prove that you were one. The District of Columbia court enforced Eliza Brown's promise to Henrietta Jefferson in 1887. It did so again in 1912, this time explaining that Brown and her best friend's daughter were like "mother and daughter, although there was no blood relationship between them." Likewise, in a 1903 case, the Illinois supreme court looked at a middle-aged, unmarried pair of migrants from the South who had cooperated, off and on, for years, hustling for a living in Chicago, and decided that they were a "family."[31] The question of slave ancestry was fading by this point, but kinship was still not a given for Black migrants. African Americans made and remade family in hopes of securing a decent old age. Then they used rules of intestacy, wills, and deeds of trust to put the force of law behind their decisions about who and what was "family."

In 1904, when Nate Shaw was nineteen, his father, Hayes Shaw, hired him out to work. "Truthful to God," Nate said later, "I got one suit of clothes out of my labor that year . . . and my daddy collectin' the balance of it. Well, that was just like slavery to me." The people in Shaw's world asserted powerful claims over members of their families—to "work em," "hire them out," even "turn [them] over" to someone else. And although Shaw chafed at his father's "bossin," no one seriously questioned the old man's right to dispose of his children, not even Shaw. Indeed, what bothered Shaw was simply that he "thought [he] was a little too old to be treated that way."[32]

John Henry Martin, born in 1907 and raised near Chapel Hill, North Carolina, had a similar story. "I never will forget what happened when I reached twenty-one years old," recalled Martin, decades later. "We was sittin at the breakfast table. My daddy turned 'round and kept a-lookin at me. He said, 'Well, John Henry, you is a free man this mornin.' I said, 'Yessuh.' He said, 'Now, John Henry, I can't make you stay here, so what do you want to do, do you want to stay here or get out?' I said, 'I want to stay here.' He said, 'Well, now John Henry, there's a field down yonder, and I'm gonna give you that for your 'bacco patch.' I said, 'Yessuh.' And he kept a-lookin at me, and he finally told me, said, 'Now John Henry, if you stay here, you will have to work and I'm gonna be the boss!' I told him, 'Yessuh.'" "He'd work you to death!" Martin said of his father, "he was a kind man—'til you done somethin wrong."[33]

What did it mean for a Black man to tell his son that he was "a free man"? What expectations and assumptions did that son's wife and children make when they worked themselves to the bone to pay off the farm he bought in *his* name with *their* labor? As Shaw observed years later about a different problem, "all God's dangers aint a white man."[34]

It is no surprise that the family was a place of authority and inequality in 1904 or 1928. In different ways and measures, it had also been so for slaves and for whites in the centuries before. Law had set up the household model of authority and made it the basis for modern labor law. Children were not literally their parents' property but only in the sense that parents could not sell them to someone else. Abraham Lincoln once said his father treated him like "a slave," and as late as the 1910s, in many states, children legally owed "service" to their parents until age twenty-one. During Jim Crow, as "family law" finally emerged as a specialized area of law, and as courts reimagined the middle-class family as a sphere of love and affection, purified of crass economic considerations, African Americans tried to put their civil rights to work within their families. They tried to turn the privileges of a wife or husband or father into legal rights that a court would enforce. Many men tried to preserve the old patriarchal ideal and found that the law was on their side. Others attempted to transform that ideal. In debates about old-age care, inheritance, marriage and divorce, and family labor, Black people struggled to define the proper relationship between the civil rights of individuals and the privileges of membership in a collective.

Nate Shaw's and John Henry Martin's fathers were able to exert "strict discipline" over their families because the laws of Alabama and North Carolina granted men a property right in their wives' and children's labor. Though Black people may not have spoken of their children and spouses as "assets" or "cheap labor" the way white observers sometimes claimed they did, the basic laws of "domestic relations" and of share-tenant contracts intensified Black patriarchy by delegating monitoring and labor discipline to the head of household. As W. E. B. Du Bois observed, writing about one striving family of Black Georgia farmers, "The father is head, and what he says is law."[35] Another Black Georgian remembered that her father used to get help for the family farm just as rich whites did: he would go "to the courthouse . . . and listen[] to trials," bail out young Black men for "seventy-five or fifty dollars," and bring them home as "guaranteed" labor. Unlike some of the whites, at least he paid them "the same as the [hired] boys." Another ex-slave recalled a "free-born" Black man who "sold [probably apprenticed] his five boys" to pay off debts—"sold 'em to the highest bidder right yonder front of the post office for cash." One of the buyers was another free Black man.[36]

When Ike Dunson's eighteen-year-old son Willie went off without permission to work as a laborer on the Illinois Central Railroad, Dunson sent word to have him sent back home, and successfully sued the railroad for $149, earnings that Willie should have brought home but instead had frittered away. When Benjamin Mays, who would later become Martin Luther King Jr.'s mentor, refused to come home from college to work on the family farm, his father threatened to "send the sheriff to get him."[37] Only a few Black farmers used the courts to round up captive labor, but just as Hayes Shaw did with his son Nate, many Black parents asserted a right—a right that judges routinely upheld—to dispose of their children's labor, to "take[] whatever I need," to "boss" them, "work em," and "hire them out." And children like Shaw, born in the late 1800s, grew up haunted by memories of their parents' and grandparents' relentless discipline. Such "strict discipline" cannot be attributed solely to fears of white violence should a child stray too far—a Jim Crow-era version of "the talk"—or to the damage inflicted by slavery. It was driven also by the imperatives of family labor, ratified by laws that "entitled" parents—especially men—to "possess" children and their "labor and earnings."[38] Men like Hayes Shaw pursued one civil right, property, by exploiting another, the right to control one's dependents.

What Black families achieved during Jim Crow was astounding: from the fifteen million acres of land and $1.1 billion worth of farm property to the tuition they paid to Black churches, colleges, and more. But stories like Shaw's and Martin's suggest that this era of widespread Black landownership stood in large part on legally sanctioned hierarchy and subordination within families—a legalized patriarchy. And Black men imposed that patriarchy not by avoiding law but by exploiting it.

Younger Black people and women of all ages resented this legalized patriarchy, along with the patriarchs who loved to boast, like self-made men everywhere, that "nobody has give me land." Wives argued with husbands over control of household property and the labor that made it, or extracted their husband's "consent for [them] to run [their] own business" and get paid for their own labor and their children's. Children extracted promises from older people that someday the family land would be theirs.[39] But it was hard for women to take advantage of their rights as individuals and even harder for children, because law still defined their legal identities in relation to men. They had certain privileges but very few rights. Whether they appeared in court for divorce, partition, or on charges of breaking the peace, Black people's disputes laid bare the rival traditions of Black legal thought—civil rights individualism and associational privileges—two ways of defining the privileges and duties of family members.

Old age was one of the things that dragged these tensions out into the open. Now that African Americans had civil rights under state law and were free to keep the money they earned, what norms or rules would govern their duties toward the older, sicker members of their families and communities? White people have been telling racist lies about "the Black family" since the days of slavery, and rebutting those lies has produced countless books, television shows, and movies showcasing its resilience, pride, and strength. However well-intentioned, the image of the resilient Black family has hidden crucial parts of Black history. Indeed, when it comes to eldercare and crisis care, it has hurt actual Black people by making it seem as though they don't need outside help as much as whites. In the early 1900s, Black people were some of the most mobile people in America, and that made it hard to know who your family really was, or who would take care of you when you got old or sick.[40] These were devastating worries, and again and again African Americans tried to cope with them by turning to law. One of the consequences of Black freedom, then, was to push Black people's ideas about aging from the sphere of privileges to the sphere of rights.

Black people coped with getting old by bargaining for care, much as white people did. Getting old was hard work for everyone. Dying was even harder. Amid the heartache, somebody still had to empty the dying person's bedpans, change and wash his soiled sheets, sponge his dry mouth, cook his food and spoon-feed him, sit by his bedside, knead the pain from his cramping leg muscles, and deal with the funeral arrangements. As with white people, the people who did this work were usually family. Indeed, it was Black women who did the lion's share of the actual work of eldercare among Black people—the "washing," "nursing" and "board" that softened the indignities of getting old and eased the journey toward death. But nobody could afford to work for free, not even when it was for family. At a time when one funeral casket could put a poor tenant farmer "in the hole all the rest of the year payin[g]," it is not surprising that someone would want back the $2 he paid out "for digging his mother grave," or want compensation "for boarding . . . and taking care of [her brother] in his last illness." So Black people—far-flung and often poor—turned to contracts.[41]

Two generations earlier, when sisters were sold away from brothers and the deadly cotton fields left so many motherless children, enslaved African Americans had substituted nonblood for blood kin, passed down property, and did everything they could to plan for a precarious old age, all without legal rights. Now, their free children and grandchildren began to think that their own children could, as one childless woman put it, "Be my social security."[42] They leveraged property—whether it was a farm, a house, or the payout from a life insurance policy—to mobilize help from relatives and other people. Promising a younger person, as Eliza Brown did for Henrietta Jefferson, that "someday all this will be yours," was a middle-class strategy of warding off the threat that their children might abandon them in their old age, of coping with a world built on free labor.[43] Black people tried to hold onto the privileges and duties of membership in a collectivity—a family, a community—by lashing them to the civil rights of property and contract.

There were grave risks for those on both sides of these bargains, risks that people perceived and negotiated in the shadow of the law. Young people worried that they wouldn't actually get the promised property in the end. Maybe it would be seized for the older person's debts. Or the older person might suddenly give it to someone else if he thought the young person hadn't "behave[d] himself . . . like a son ought to." Or the older person might be offended when the young person asked him to put the promise in writing.[44] For their part, old people worried that if they gave the property without any strings attached, they would wind up "deserted" and helpless. "I have several cousins but they seldom come to see me until they think that I am going to die," said a Nashville woman. "They find out that I am getting along fine" and then they leave. She went on: "I want to get some lady to take this place over and try to sell it but you know Black folks won't do nothing unless you give them the deeds and then they will throw you out." Before the advent of social security and company pensions, when "care was private and familial" and yet "no one had to stay home," writes the historian Hendrik Hartog, referring to middle-class white people, "growing old was a terrifying prospect."[45] When African Americans faced that terror, they could not appeal to the resilience of the Black family or the solidarity of the Black community. They turned to law. They made verbal promises, kept track of expenses. Sometimes they took each other to court.

Legally, the question was often deceptively simple: had the older person actually given the land to the younger one, or merely talked about doing so? But in practice nothing about such cases was simple. Sometimes there was something in writing. Younger people liked the deed of trust because it made the older person hand over legal title to the property right away (albeit to a third party). Older people liked the deed of trust because it let them stay in their homes, knowing that the property would revert back to them if they outlived their caregiver.[46] But typically there was nothing in writing (contracts don't have to be in writing), and when things went wrong, the older people insisted that it was all "just talk," not a binding contract, and that their adult children were only tenants. The children and their spouses typically argued that these agreements *were* contracts that a court should enforce: a promise of land in exchange for a lifetime of care. Why else would people like Jennei and Mace Clements, middle-aged themselves, have left their own perfectly good farm to come live with Mace's father and sink "practically . . . all of [their] earnings" into it? They had come, Jennei testified, because Mace's father had begged them to, had told them it was "crazy" for Mace to be "working for white folks and getting [only] half what he made, when [he] could be on his own place and getting all he made." Those words, she argued, amounted to a promise that became legally binding on her father-in-law when they moved in with him.[47]

Bargaining for sick- and old-age care stretched the meaning of family itself. The relentless hunt for decent work, and the diseases that ravaged their neighborhoods, forced Black people to improvise the family ties they needed, just the way Charles Ball had done in 1805 when he was sold away from his family. Like Eliza Brown and her best friend Maria Herbert, who joined kinsmen and neighbors in moving from Maryland's eastern shore to Washington, DC, the Black people who moved into towns and cities in the late nineteenth and early twentieth century remade family itself. They took childhood friendships formed on a faraway plantation and turned them into something like family as they nursed each other through sickness and helped each other make a living. Priscilla Warren said that after her friend Chaney Jackson's daughter died, Jackson "said she would like to die with me, so I went there and brought her home to my house." Other people leaned on fellow church members, blurring the difference between "brothers in the church" and "brothers by mother." Still others looked to neighbors. Eliza Brown often convinced neighborhood kids to run errands to "get such little things as she needed." Because Brown could not read or write, she had to rely on others to collect rent money and write receipts for her. Old age could be cruel. "Sometimes she would lay and suffer for want of attention," recalled one of Brown's neighbors, perhaps precisely because she had to rely on the whole Black community: "Anybody and everybody took care of her—the neighbors all around there." Once, when she was angry at a tenant, she started "holl[er]ing out in the street, and the people were all laughing."[48] No wonder someone like her, at the mercy of neighbors and kindly tenants, would crave something like a family, even if she had to make it herself.

As the Great Migration began to take thousands of Black people out of the countryside and out of the South, questions spread about what it took to be "family" and what the rights and privileges of family were. Some migrants accused their relatives back home of having misled them about family-owned property. Others used lawsuits to turn the privileges of family membership into individual civil rights. Fannie Brown Crossen filed a partition suit in Mecklenburg County circuit court to cut the knot rope—to have her family's forty-five acres sold so that she could take her share in cash, and to deduct money from two of her siblings' shares of the estate to make up for several years they had been living on the land rent-free. Her brothers and sisters hired a lawyer. "Who made Fannie Crossen Administrator?" demanded her brother Albert. "We didn't." If the court did appoint her, demanded her sister Mabel, "why didn't she tend to the farm?" And if she just wanted money, why didn't she let the rest of the family buy out her interest? "None of them, the rest of us, want to sell. Our mother and father are burried there," Albert insisted. The reason he and his wife were living in the family house rent-free, he said, was because the relatives living in Baltimore and Paterson, New Jersey, had asked them "to stay there and see after the place." Likewise, their mother had given Mabel "the home place," the main one-acre parcel, "so she could stay there and wait on her while she was living," and after their mother died, it was Mabel who dealt with their tenants and took care of the taxes. Nobody had ever asked Mabel and Albert for rent, Albert testified, so angry that he could barely even speak his sister Fannie's name. "Nobody but that one right there."[49]

Fannie Brown Crossen lived in the town of South Hill, Virginia, only six miles from "the home place." Such tensions could get worse if family members lived far away. In 1967, when a community-health organizer came to talk with poor Black Mississippians, a local woman stood up and said that the community's biggest problem wasn't children's health—the issue the Student Nonviolent Coordinating Committee (SNCC) activists had emphasized in their fundraising pamphlets. It was "old people" who "are being neglected" because their "families are in Chicago and St. Louis and Detroit."[50] Even when the Chicago relatives sent money for taxes and eldercare, that sometimes piled more burdens onto family relationships that were already stretched by distance and the ordinary tensions that arise in any family.

Who should take charge of aging parents and family land—the relative up North who sent money home to keep them afloat, or the ones who lived right there and dealt with them firsthand? Who should reap the value of "improvements" made on family land? The conflict was not between "legal" and "cultural" values, because property law itself recognized many of the kinds of ownership claims that people made on family land. Rather, it was between two distinct kinds of claims: those based on individual civil rights and those based on a person's status within a family corporation, a status that flowed not just from one's blood but from one's conduct, and that granted a claim to the propriety—the family land.

In the cash-poor southern countryside, as we saw in Chapter 5, few things brought the conflict between civil rights and corporate privileges out into the open faster than a funeral. Death, like taxes, was inevitable. Divorce was not. But divorce provoked similar conflicts even as the divorce process and its meaning continued to change.[51]

10

The Preacher's Wife

On a cold winter afternoon in 1886, a Washington minister named Edward Freeman and a group of witnesses met at his lawyer's office to take testimony in his petition to divorce his wife, Lucy. Over the following few hours, and at another session in the winter, Freeman and his witnesses unfolded his story to a court-appointed examiner. The Freemans had gotten married in 1861, at the First Colored Baptist Church of Fredericksburg, Virginia. The next year, they moved to DC. Edward was ordained as a minister in about 1875. Since he did not have a church of his own, he had "to go from place to place" as a circuit preacher. Their marriage fell apart sometime around 1881 when, Edward claimed, Lucy "deserted" him. In his testimony to the examiner, Edward accused her of adultery, citing the male boarders she took in while he was away preaching. He claimed that when he objected to having boarders, she put his belongings in the alley next to their home and told him to get out. Nevertheless, Edward told the court, he still wanted to stay married, if only to keep his preaching career. As a fellow minister testified, "he knew he could not . . . stand before the people and be honest and square without living with his wife as a minister ought." But Lucy let it be known that she would "not have anything to do with him," even if it got her "turned out of the church," and that if Edward tried to come back home she would have him arrested. So here he was. In June 1886, the court granted his divorce.[1] Lucy never filed an answer with the court.

During Reconstruction, as we've seen, Black people had turned to divorce as one of the rights of freedom. They had used it to mend the fabric of families torn by slavery, to get out from under blanket retroactive marriage laws, and to fight the sweeping powers that labor contracts of the mid-1860s granted to husbands over their wives' and children's labor. At the dawn of Jim Crow, when Edward Freeman filed his suit, divorce was still one of the paradigmatic civil rights for African Americans, the most common reason a Black person filed a lawsuit. Indeed, it was still one of the most common reasons anyone in the country went to court. But now, as the children and grandchildren of slaves came of age, divorce began to be swept up in powerful new currents in American life: the beginnings of what would become the Great Migration, a racist popular culture that devoured Black women for fun and profit, and a mass movement for racial justice.

From the 1880s through the 1960s, Black people poured out their family stories in court. No longer were these stories about spouses lost to the ravages of the slave trade, or about cohabiting couples who never considered themselves married, or about husbands who signed their wives onto work contracts. More and more, Black people talked about patterns of life after Reconstruction: about moving to the city, a house on 9th Street, a satchel full of clothes, earnings from boarders or from preaching, the cost of raising little Hattie, John, and Israel. For Black women, whose rights to property and contract were so much more tenuous than men's, divorce beckoned as a means to assert their identity as individuals with rights of their own. But divorce was painful. Increasingly, it also seemed shameful, especially from the perspective of a growing Black elite, who discouraged it in the name of "uplifting the race," and from leaders of the fast-growing independent Black churches, many of whom discouraged it as unchristian. The divorce laws of the early 1900s were stiff shoes that pinched everyone's feet, but their demand for "innocent" victims of adultery meant that a Black woman involved in a divorce suit had to sit in a roomful of people and listen while a man she used to love voiced a hideous stereotype. That is why Lucy Freeman chose to lose by default. Rather than fight Edward in court, she stayed silent, hoping that his accusations would quietly sink into the file cabinets of the District of Columbia. He would get the last word, but then she would be free.

To some people, it was scandalous that the Freemans could get divorced at all. Much as they would in the 1970s, pundits and politicians in the late nineteenth and early twentieth centuries thought America's rising divorce rate—it quintupled from 29 divorces per 100,000 people in 1870 to 154 in 1926—was a national emergency and that it was all the fault of "liberal[s]" and Black people, who, they claimed, without a shred of evidence, were "more addicted to divorce than southern whites." What America needed, the pundits declared, was to get back to good Christian values and make it harder to end a marriage. At the county courthouses, divorce cases really were taking up a sizeable proportion of the docket—26 percent of the identifiable civil cases between 1902 and 1932 across my sampled counties in Illinois, Mississippi, New Jersey, Virginia, North Carolina, and Washington, DC, up from 12 percent during Reconstruction. Black people averaged 31 percent of the population in those counties; they filed 40 percent of the divorces.[2]

These Black divorce-seekers came from all walks of life, making divorce one of the most democratic branches of law. Urban, middle-class people like the Freemans were probably overrepresented in *contested* divorce cases, because they could better afford the fees and had more tangible property to fight over. Some poor and working-class people couldn't afford even a cheap, uncontested divorce. They had to tell themselves that "it ain't worth it," as an Alabama washerwoman did, or just hope that "maybe he will die before long and I won't have to" file papers.[3] Yet the county court ledgers indicate that most of the Black people who came to get divorced were still poor and working-class: washerwomen, tenant farmers, and laborers who owned little or no property.

Although divorce laws basically stayed the same from the 1880s to the 1960s, it became easier to get divorced. Partly this was because judges became more willing to swallow people's tales of cheating and drunkenness and desertion at face value. The central reason, though, was that divorce got to be routine. Routine in a cultural sense, as white newspapers, judges, and legislators slowly recognized women as having a separate legal identity, unwittingly following Black women's decades-long insistence that they wouldn't submit to either a master or a husband. And also routine in a practical sense, a shift that had already been underway in the 1860s, when freedpeople first reached for the right to divorce. In 1800, an unhappy couple needed a special bill from the state legislature. By 1942, when Ethel Reaves, the wife of Annie Holcomb's brother Eugene Reaves, wanted out, all she needed was a decree from Judge Flood of the Cumberland County Circuit Court. Although Judge Flood was supposed to demand "full" and "corroborated" evidence and not hand out judgments by default, in practice, he was just signing off on papers prepared by circuit clerk Lewis Crawley, and Crawley, in turn, was relying on a fill-in-the-blank deposition that Ethel had given her lawyer, William M. Smith. The process became cheaper, too. Ethel Reaves paid $7.20 for the little notice that needed to run in the Farmville *Herald*, as well as $7.50 in court costs plus whatever lawyer Smith charged.[4] The process was so routinized that you might not even need to make a second trip to the lawyer's office. You told your story in his office. Then he would send you the petition—a short version of your story, sandwiched between the requisite pleadings—with a cover letter telling you to "Read this over and if you find the facts . . . correct," then "go before some office, the mayor of your town or a justice of the peace" to get it witnessed, "sign on the line marked in pencil with a cross" and mail it back "in the enclosed stamped envelope." When the hearing came, it was by deposition, meaning it usually took place at a local bank or law office in front of a court-appointed "master" rather than in a courtroom in front of a judge. There would usually be a few basic questions aimed at drawing out the required facts for a divorce into the court record: What is your name? Where do you live? When did he desert you?

Write your answers below each question, and return this paper.

(1) What is your wife's full name? Carrie Biggs

(2) What place does she live on? Alsop X W. P. Stephens

(3) When were you married? 1900

(4) What county were you married in? Sharkey

(5) In what county did the separation between you and her take place? Bolivar

(6) When did you separate? 1903 march 16

(7) Have you lived with or co-habitated with her since the separation? no

(8) What was the cause of the separation? the man that she live with

(9) Did she leave you or did you leave her? she left me

(10) How long have you lived in Bolivar County? 3 years

(11) How long has she lived there? 2 years

(12) Does anybody live in the house cexcept the other man and herself?

yes a Family lives joining her it is on the same Place & Does they are Making a crop to gether

Your Truly

JOHN W. BIGGS. BOX. 83

9/21 1904

John W. Biggs JOHN W. BIGGS. BOX. 83

White lawyer's fill-in form for divorce clients. Papers in file are labeled "John Biggs v. Carrie Biggs."

Have you "lived together since that time?" If you and your lone witness gave the expected answers, and your spouse did not show up to contest the petition, then a divorce decree was almost a sure thing. Although there had been glimmers of it before the Civil War, this routinization of the county courts during Jim Crow opened the floodgates to a steadily rising tide of divorce-seekers, both white and Black, one that still has not ebbed.[5]

Husband, wife, mother: each of these words was a legal status that carried specific rights and duties. When Ethel Reaves filed her divorce petition, she was asking a judge to remap all those rights and duties: the right to give one's paycheck to this person and not that one, to sleep with this person and not be arrested for fornication, to have legitimate children who could inherit whatever was left after the creditors were paid. For women, it also meant the right not to have your property seized to pay a spouse's debts. But many people just wanted out. They just started living apart and didn't bother filing papers until they needed that changed legal status, with its remapped rights and duties. When Ethel Reaves filed for divorce, she and my great-grandfather Eugene had been separated for at least twelve years—since shortly after they left Cumberland County for New Jersey. In fact, they had talked, off and on, about getting back together. The reason Ethel finally filed was probably because she had decided to marry my step-great-grandfather, Alden Wilson.[6] Or, to return to the example that opened this chapter, consider this rare letter Lucy Freeman wrote to Edward four years *after* they stopped living together:

> Washington D.C. Mar. 18, 1885
>
> Mr. Freeman:
>
> I recived your letter today and was glad to hear that you was speaking of a devoast. I never mean to live with you again as long as I live so you have just as well get a devost. and I expect to go to Heaven without living with you and if you dont it's time yous praying And I am perfectly willing for a devost and have been willing for seven years Its true the winter been very hard but still I did not notice it only when I went out doorse you neanter write here again

> for I wont answer them and would not answer this if it was not for a devost. This is all I have to say.
> Lucy Freeman

Or consider Puss Jackson, who "packed up her things," hauled them across the road onto her neighbor's land, cursing, and told her husband "she was going to leave and never come back" and that if he ever came near her again, he "was liable to get killed." Or Mittie Conrad, who went over to her in-laws' house "with a man and a push cart" and said: "Here is your son's trunk, if he is not man enough to leave me, I will show him I am woman enough to leave him, if he wants anything else—tell him to send for it, but if he puts his foot again in that house—I will blow his brains out." The dockets say that when Black couples got divorced, more than half the time it was the husband who sued, whereas with whites, it was usually the wife.[7] But testimony from the case files suggests a subtler story behind the dockets. It may be more accurate to say that men like Edward Freeman went to court armed with depositions about things their wives had done outside of court, in the shadow of the law, emotional acts whose legal significance was widely, if imperfectly understood. Edward Freeman, Robert Jackson, and Dorsey Conrad were the plaintiffs who "won" the cases but it was Lucy, Puss, and Mittie who actually ended things.

Litigants and their lawyers then gathered up the proof: letters, marriage certificates, and especially witness depositions. "Why are you and he not living together?" asked Ethel Reaves's lawyer, at her hearing. Because he "struck me more than once and left me more than eleven years ago," she answered. "Did he leave you because of any fault on your part"? "No, not that I know of. We just couldn't get along." To back up her story, Ethel had asked a beautician she knew, named Jessie Hopkins, to come down from New Jersey. Hopkins explained that the Reaveses had split up eleven or twelve years earlier because "he fought her," and they definitely weren't going to get back together.[8] Witnesses in other cases told of stumbling on adulterous spouses in bed, of "kept . . . wom[e]n," and of sexually transmitted diseases and "loud . . . talk" in half-open doorways. They snorted about husbands who sat "loaf[ing] about" drunk "on the porch all day," or "holding up the side of a bar room."[9] They saw when spouses finally called it quits and hauled "all the things . . . out of the house." They noticed which of the things were "hers." The "common rumor" grew especially loud if a man ran off with a white woman. Such developments were "publicly known," especially "among the Church people," who "often talked about" them and disciplined their members for moral misconduct. Such testimony meant nothing by itself. You had to tell the judge what it meant, to translate a unique story—the story of a marriage—into categories that a court could recognize.[10] Above all else, the courts wanted proof that the couple had not lived together for at least two years—proof that came from the same community knowledge that had anchored Jackson Holcomb's ownership of his boat.

Until the states finally adopted no-fault divorce laws in the 1970s, divorce was officially an adversarial proceeding. My great-grandparents couldn't just tell the judge they didn't want to be married anymore. It had to be somebody's fault. Ethel had to sue Eugene and accuse him of specific things that Virginia law said were grounds for divorce: adultery, impotence at the time of the marriage, imprisonment or conviction of an "infamous" crime, desertion for two years, or that the wife had been a prostitute when they got married. By itself, cruelty only justified a legal separation, and even then, it had to involve "bodily harm" or the kind of "unrelenting" verbal abuse that put "life or health" in danger. And there had to be "full and satisfactory proof," not just "conclusions from unrevealed fact."[11] In order to secure a full divorce, Ethel had to take her six years of life with Eugene and fit it into a morality play, staged for Judge Flood. She had to turn herself and Eugene into stereotypes. But those stereotypes were different for Black women than they were for Black men, or for white men or women.

Jim Crow was the heyday of mass-marketed racist stereotyping—the bits that Disney is busy scrubbing from its back catalog now—and much of that stereotyping specifically slandered Black people's sexual and family values. Black men were supposedly happy-go-lucky "Sambos" who left behind a trail of abandoned "pickaninnies." Black women were portrayed as either Mammies or Jezebels. In 1939, Hattie McDaniel became the very first Black Oscar-winner by playing a character who was literally named "Mammy," in *Gone with the Wind*, a movie that glorified slavery and the Confederacy. African Americans' marital troubles were plastered across newspapers, lampooned in blackface minstrel shows, and turned into racist vignettes to spice up law journals. For years, the Ku Klux Klan, aided by some southern criminal courts, had portrayed Black domestic abuse as a "law and order" issue, one of the many reasons why "the Negroes" had to be prosecuted, imprisoned, and stripped of the right to vote. (Many of today's felon disfranchisement laws were enacted in the 1890s and explicitly targeted bigamy, "wife-beating," and other supposedly "Negro" crimes.)[12] Aghast at such politically charged stereotyping, Black reformers fiercely emphasized that Black families were "respectable," well-behaved, and tidy. The stereotypes had an all-too-credulous audience in the whites who staffed the local court system. Divorce meant revealing, in public, the worst secrets of one's intimate life, at a time when white politicians, doctors, and journalists routinely slandered Black people as lewd, degenerate, and riddled with venereal diseases. All of this raised the stakes for any Black person thinking about a divorce. It is easy to see why modern scholars have agreed with past Black leaders that it was dangerous for Black people to bring their "family quarrel[s]" into the courts. Certainly many Black people stayed in unhappy marriages, or just quit without bothering with a divorce, or quietly lived apart for the sake of the children, just as millions of whites did.[13]

But some Black people *did* take their spouses to court. An undivorced person who wanted to remarry had to move out of town or out of state and hope no one would find out. Churches routinely expelled people for having sex outside of marriage. Inheritance law made out-of-wedlock children legally vulnerable, even if Black cultural norms did not. And as Lucy and Edward Freeman's story suggests, just because Black women were less likely than white women to be the plaintiffs does not mean they were less active in ending their marriages—or that they were afraid to call on government power in other ways. As the historian Cheryl Hicks has shown, Black parents were willing to call the police if that seemed like the only means to push their wayward daughters back onto the straight and narrow.[14] Working-class Black people did not always agree with the Black elite that being respectable meant keeping family affairs private. Judging from how frequently divorce witnesses mentioned earlier proceedings in police courts and before local magistrates, it seems clear that some Black women were also calling the cops to protect them from domestic abuse, abuse that their relatives and neighbors either could not or would not stop.[15]

Indeed, one of the staple cases that first-year law students read today in contract law unwittingly reveals how Black women struggled to cope with domestic violence in an era of racist underpolicing—unwittingly, because the casebooks don't disclose that the people involved were Black. Late on the night of January 7, 1945, Arnisea Taylor went to the Hamlet, North Carolina, police to report that her husband was beating her. The police simply dropped her off at the house of her neighbor, Lena Harrington. The next day, Taylor's husband barged in and assaulted Arnisea again. Arnisea picked up an axe Harrington kept for cutting stove wood, knocked her husband down with the flat of it, hit him again on the neck, and then swung at his head blade-first, saying "Let me kill him! . . . If I don't kill him, he will kill me!" Harrington grabbed for the axe handle trying to stop Arnisea, caught the blade instead, and it severed her fingers against the door. In the aftermath, she struck a deal with Lee Walter Taylor, who promised to compensate her for her maimed hand. When he stopped paying, she sued. By the time her case went to the county superior court, Harrington had paid $59 for doctor's bills (not including medicine) even as her income—previously $26.75 a week, all from washing clothes—dried up.[16] *Harrington v. Taylor* is a classic case that law professors use to teach a key doctrine in contract law, but the reason Lena Harrington made that contract and sued to enforce it had everything to do with an unenforced criminal law.

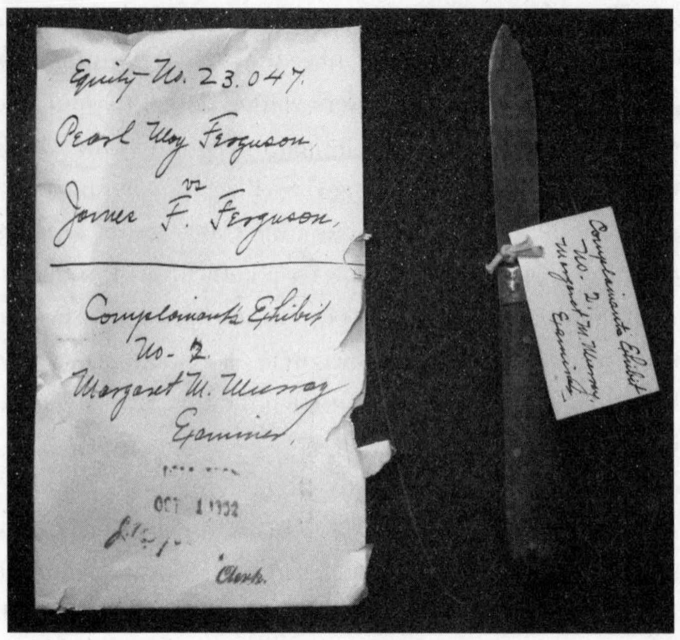

Evidence in Pearl v. James Ferguson, *case 23047, Supreme Court of the District of Columbia, Equity. The Fergusons were white. Litigants and lawyers translated such physical evidence into legally compelling stories.*

In an era when the police and the judges generally did not care about Black people's violence unless it affected somebody white, the only way to make Lee Walter Taylor pay for his violence was through the civil right of contract.[17]

What if Arnisea Taylor had sued him for divorce? Once Black couples entered the divorce process, they and their lawyers and witnesses confronted a grislier version of the problem they faced in any civil suit against whites: the most effective strategy was to lean on a stereotype. In divorce, the "lewd colored female" stereotype did for husbands what the "ignorant negro" did for Black defendants in contract cases: it let them pose as the innocent victims of a broken promise. Under Virginia law, only the wife could be "a prostitute" or have an out-of-wedlock baby. So, men did not get accused of having a bad "reputation for chastity" or of "rov[ing] about" as "a 'Levee Camp strumpet.' " Of course, white women got called "lewd," too. And a Black Illinoisan did accuse her husband of forcing her to let him commit oral "sodomy" on her.[18] But accusations about sex hurt Black women worse than they did Black men, white men, or white women, and worse than the "lazy negro husband" stereotype hurt Black men, confirming an assumption that "colored females" were promiscuous. Yet far from hiding such scandalous details from white eyes, many Black litigants and their witnesses played them up tactically. When the chancery examiner in Edward Freeman's divorce case asked a witness to back up Edward's claim that Lucy threw him out, the witness started talking about adultery instead:

Q [What is] the general opinion as to her not letting [Edward] come there[?]
A I know one thing she had a child that was not his.
Q I have not asked you about that. I am asking you if the people there in that neighborhood . . . generally know that she will not live with him.

Such testimony suggests that some Black men may have been willing to manipulate stereotypes about women's sexuality—especially of Black women—in order to win their cases.[19]

It is easy to think of Jim Crow as a kind of frozen society, in which Black southerners were chained to the land. In fact, they moved all the time, and divorce was both cause and consequence of their moving. Jealousies and suspicions surely festered in the cramped apartments that so many Black migrants wound up in, with their rotating casts of relatives and roomers sleeping in converted bedrooms. Some people, especially women, claimed that their husbands' cruelty or lack of support "forced" them to migrate "in search of work." Others expected their spouses to follow them once they found work, and were disappointed.[20] Or they stayed behind, expecting their migrating spouses to earn some money and come back, only to find that their spouses had created new lives for themselves. "I have written perhaps twenty-five letters for Ned trying to find out where she was, but have never been able to locate her," said a witness about Maggie Alexander. "One of her brothers told me he knew where she was and that she was still alive, but he could not tell me . . . because she did not want Ned to come after her and bother her, and that she was never coming back here." No group of Americans felt the possibilities and risks of movement more keenly than those whose constant hunt for work, in a society that denied them access to decent jobs, could strain even a loving marriage.[21] In one county courthouse after another, many if not most of the Black divorce litigants I found in the dockets were from someplace else—Kentuckians living in Illinois, city dwellers fresh from the countryside, tenant farmers from the next county.

The Great Migration transformed how lawyers handled divorce and how ordinary people experienced it. Each state has its own divorce laws, so as the rising divorce rate merged with the Great Migration, divorce and separation lawsuits increasingly raised questions about "conflict-of-laws," the rules for determining which state's laws should apply when people made a contract (in this case, a marriage contract) in one state and broke it in another. One line of cases was about "migratory divorce," a middle-class option that involved going to a different state where the laws were more forgiving, roosting for the legally prescribed six weeks, and then winging homeward with a new spouse. In 1945, in *Williams v. North Carolina,* a case about a white couple's quickie Nevada divorce, the Supreme Court approved this tactic, holding that a valid divorce in one state was valid nationwide. Few Black people could afford a quick trip to Nevada but millions of them were moving across state lines permanently, fleeing the South. The Black lawyers' *National Bar Journal* carefully followed developments in the law of migratory divorce, Black newspapers avidly reported on Black celebrities who traveled out of the country for "Mexican divorces," and canny divorce lawyers used the publicity to sell, to a rising Black middle class, this latest fad in American divorce-seekers' long love affair with federalism. Long before the "no-fault revolution" of the 1970s, when states like New York finally loosened their conservative divorce laws, the constant press of divorce petitions from migrants—including Black migrants—helped blur the differences between strict and easy divorce states. Those migrants became a voting bloc to be reckoned with on issues relating to divorce. In 1966, New York assemblyman Percy Sutton, soon to become the city's highest-ranking Black elected official, who had handled plenty of divorces in his law practice, pushed the legislature to liberalize New York State's laws and bring them in line with his constituents' assumptions about what it took to end a marriage. African Americans helped change the law and culture of divorce, as more and more Americans of all races came to think of divorce as a right and not as an exceptional privilege bestowed by the state.[22]

Maybe that is why Ethel Reaves sued in Virginia even though she and Eugene had been living in New Jersey for years, and even though, in either state, all she had to prove was that Eugene hadn't been living in the house for two years. But if the right to divorce and the right to move were fundamental civil rights, long-distance divorce in the era of the Great Migration sometimes threw into doubt other civil rights, such as property. Those who didn't get a legal divorce from a spouse down South might face nasty surprises up North. One real estate broker had to postpone a sale because just before the closing he found out that his client, the seller, still had a "legal wife . . . in the South." Because they held property interests in more than one state, couples often had to find two or even three lawyers in each state in question to get the job done. They might write to a lawyer in the South to divide up the property they had bought up north, or hire a northern lawyer to go after the property back home.[23] In fact, for decades Black women had been insisting in local courts that they had rights over marital property, challenging the patriarchal claim that, as one indignant Mississippian put it in 1909, "When a man has a wife he can do her as he wants to" and that "a woman is subject to her husband . . . right or wrong, good or bad." Courts had often sided with women who made such claims, following established principles that certain kinds of things—such as bedding and tableware—were presumed to belong to the wife.[24]

In the era of the Great Migration, women found they could go further. Land had traditionally been presumed to belong to husbands, but now some Black women found that judges would help them reclaim what was theirs. If, after eighteen years of marriage, Gladys Spinner's husband was going to "keep a woman" and be "hugging and kissing . . . on the back porch," then she was going to make him sell that porch. "I own one half of the place in which he is living," she insisted, because "I paid for it with my own money." When Emma Collins decided to leave Mississippi and move to Detroit, she convinced a judge that the farm she and her husband had been working for the past five years really belonged to her because, first, the two of them had never gotten legally married and, second, because all the purchase money came from her earnings before their "pretended marriage." Other women described the work they did during their marriages as part of "a joint enterprise" managed by their husbands.[25] In short, Black women pried open the grip of patriarchal privilege in the 1930s and 1940s by exercising their civil rights—of property, contract, and standing—through divorce proceedings.

As divorce became more routine, better record keeping was making it more difficult for people to vanish. An unhappy husband in 1860 would have just moved away. It was a big country. Who would ever know? But now, as the county clerks' ledgers gave way to the modern bureaucracy of state Departments of Vital Statistics and corporate personnel offices, better record keeping helped nationalize the system of "notice" that anchored marriage and divorce, as well as records that anchored property and contract. It made legal acts visible to a community that sprawled coast to coast. This nationalized system of notice prodded people to seek divorces after years, even decades, of informal separation. It carried summonses and decrees like jolts of electricity along long-forgotten wires—from Chicago to Clarksdale or from Cumberland

County to South Orange—to distant spouses whose reactions nobody could predict.[26]

Once people decided to divorce, they gathered up their memories and whatever scraps of paper they had and brought them to a lawyer. One lawyer tracked down the address of a woman whose husband said he hadn't "known of her whereabouts for 25 yrs." Another guessed his client's marriage date and then wrote to county clerks and state bureaucrats for the rest of the necessary facts. In a 1950 case, William Eskridge Duke, grandson of the Charlottesville lawyer and ex-Confederate "Colonel" introduced in Chapter 3, invited Geraldine Hill and her mother to "come by and talk" at his office about her husband, a Navy cook. "What is your name please, come over here close, pull up a chair and talk," he began, genially, almost conspiratorial. "Well now did you . . . ever hear them have any quarls, not that they do any harm cause most married couples do have a few quarls"? Whites and Blacks were not social equals, Duke seemed to be saying, but we all know that when a marriage falters, each spouse will "try to frame a case," no matter their race.

Perhaps most important, lawyers mediated. As the states' laws slowly loosened their demand for proof of adultery or physical violence, lawyers drafted the most "moderate" complaint bills they thought would persuade a judge, and cooperated with the other spouse's lawyer to work out the details. They talked clients and their spouses off the ropes, coaxed them to lower their gloves. Why fight? they asked. Why delay the inevitable when you could just sign these papers and be done with it, without spending a dime on "alimony or support or even" the cost of the divorce itself? Ruth Cook's problem was that her husband wouldn't mouth the necessary lies: he refused to sign the papers because he wouldn't admit to deserting her, and if she was going to be the plaintiff, she couldn't be the one at fault. "Why should a person have to stay tied to some one they don't love and don't want," she wondered, "it all seems so unfair."[27]

The biggest cost-saver might have been there all along: lawyers still did not segregate their clientele by race, not even in Mississippi. The lawyers totted up white and Black clients' payments on the same ledger books, talked with them in the same offices, and typed them letters on the same letterhead. Southern states' laws required that divorce petitions identify the parties by race, but if six or seven of an attorney's clients happened to change their minds before their divorces were finalized, then he just wrote up a draft order of dismissal that covered them all, and the only hint about which ones were Black was that some of their names didn't begin with "Mrs."[28]

All this helped keep divorce reasonably accessible to working people: not exactly cheap, but within reach. As Black people shifted from farming to paycheck jobs, more of them had cash to pay for divorces. By 1966, when Black men earned about $3,100 a year and Black women $1,300, Black lawyers charged between $120 and $450 for an uncontested divorce. The states helped, too, by setting relatively low costs, creating whole new courts to handle the crush—"Domestic Relations" in Chicago, a "Matrimonial" docket in New Jersey—and by ignoring the trial judges' growing habit of granting nearly every divorce that came before them. In the county courthouses, I opened file after thin file from that era and found just a petition, a summons, and no testimony.[29]

Even in its modern, routinized form, however, the divorce process put special obstacles in front of poor and working-class Black women. Nobody really "won" a divorce case; what people cared about was their rights and duties *after* the marriage, and those were usually determined in pretrial negotiations. (That is why divorce decrees could be so rote: the judge was basically signing off on a deal worked out beforehand.) In this all-important pretrial bargaining stage, conducted where the shadow of the law fell strongest, Black women held a weak hand. They held a weak hand, first, because they earned so much less than men in a job market that was both racist and sexist. Geraldine Hill's husband might have been bluffing when he threatened to divorce her without alimony. But she couldn't call his bluff. "You know dam well you and your people don't have any money to hire a lawyer to fight your case in court," he taunted, "so you had better stop being so lazy and go to work" because "I am not going to support you much longer." Money wasn't the only deterrent. Black women in unhappy marriages also had to reckon with the fact that going to law still meant bringing their grievances to a legal system that was almost all white and male. A woman could ask to have her ex-husband jailed for nonsupport, but what did she gain? As one Philadelphia man pointed out, "You loose a few dollars and I loose my . . . income. . . . Think it over. I will probably get out any way."[30] Nobody wanted an actual trial, but in the high-stakes poker game of pretrial negotiations, husbands held more of the high cards.

That was not all that weakened Black women's position in the divorce process. Divorce petitioners worried not just about outcomes (alimony, child custody) but also about what the process might do to their privacy and reputations—anything that jeopardized the new, better life they hoped to lead afterward. At hearings, some Black women found themselves testifying about being deserted, yelled at, even raped by their husbands, about their husbands' "depraved sexual desires," "horrible experience[s]" that must have been difficult to recount even in the quiet of a lawyer's office, even if—as was so rarely true—their lawyer was also a Black woman. Forty years earlier it had been racist white newspapers that profited from Black people's marital troubles. Now the Black press waded in, gleefully covering Black divorce, from celebrities like Joe Louis to middle-class chauffeurs and stenographers to the "hairdresser" who "threw pots and pans at" her husband.[31] Black women had not necessarily been embarrassed about ending a marriage, but, faced with the harsh glare of a sensationalist Black press, many women did what Lucy Freeman did back in 1886: they chose separation rather than divorce, and if their husbands filed suit, they sat quietly by.

And yet, other things may have encouraged Black women to assert their right to divorce: changes in African Americans' conception of private life, judges' willingness to enforce wives' claims to marital property, and the fact that more Black women were getting paycheck jobs. Josephine Butler, who owned a beauty parlor in Jacksonville, Illinois, and a one-acre lot on the outskirts of town, persuaded the county judge to award her as alimony the adjoining one-acre lot and house, which was actually on the books in her husband's name, on the ground that she had paid for most of it. My great-grandmother Ethel Reaves worked as a live-in maid for a white family in Connecticut, and had fifteen acres of land in Virginia to fall back on. Culturally, marriage didn't mean what it used to, either. In 1908, when she was born, marriage was "a normative legal description" that defined the identities "wife" and "husband" through a set of "inescapable reciprocal duties" they owed both to each other and to the public. By 1942, when she asked Judge Flood for a divorce, more and more people, including African Americans, saw it "as a private choice," as "an expectation," and as a "right."[32]

The Freemans and the Reaveses were just some of the thousands of Black people who helped shape the law and legal culture of marriage in America from the 1880s to the 1940s, a legal culture that increasingly held that there was, in fact, a right to *end* a marriage, a right that was just as important as the right to *make* one. This fledgling right of divorce wasn't equally distributed, because husbands still held so many advantages under the invisible baseline legal rules. And what often came out in the divorce process—stories of cheating, thrown furniture, "vile" and "indecent language," abandonment—undermined the "respectability" that was so central to many Black people's claims not only to status within their communities but also to citizenship in the nation. In the 1950s, as divorce continued to undermine the old ideal that marriage was morally and legally permanent, Black people were appealing to the ideals of the Declaration of Independence to stake out a moral claim on the nation's conscience.[33]

On September 3, 1958, Martin Luther King Jr. got arrested for loitering outside the Recorder's Court of the city of Montgomery, Alabama. The photograph of his booking, instantly flashed around the world, became one of the iconic images of the civil rights movement, a tableau of Black dignity being "trampled over by the iron feet of oppression," as

King had put it on the eve of the famous bus boycott. With its uniformed policemen jamming King against the long wooden counter of the police station, a desk clerk reaching to start the paperwork, and Coretta Scott King quietly looking on, hands clasped, the picture dramatized the moral injustice of Jim Crow.

But what was King doing there in the first place? The newspapers did not say.[34] In fact, he had come to the courthouse to support his top lieutenant, the Rev. Ralph Abernathy, whose marriage was teetering on the brink of a collapse that might damage the entire civil rights movement. Late afternoon that past Friday, Edward Davis, a local schoolteacher, had gone to Abernathy's church, assaulted him in his basement office, and chased him down the street waving a hatchet. Davis was convinced that Abernathy was having an affair with his wife, Vivian. On Wednesday morning, King tried to look in on Davis's arraignment, and got arrested by a short-tempered police sergeant. King's arrest knocked Davis's assault out of the headlines before it could take hold. By the time Vivian Davis was forced, in November, to testify in open court about her

Martin Luther King Jr. arrested for "loitering," Montgomery, Alabama, 1958.

troubled marriage to Davis and extramarital sex with Abernathy, the national papers were distracted by the news that King had been stabbed by a deranged person in New York. An all-white jury acquitted Edward Davis after a one-day trial. Abernathy sat in the basement of King's church, "shocked" that Vivian had testified. Then he gave a prepared statement that the charges against Davis were really a scheme cooked up by the segregationists "to stop me from pressing for the rights of my people." Montgomery's Black ministers piously commended the Abernathys for their "Christian . . . fortitude" during "this unnecessary ordeal."[35] The Davises quietly filed for divorce a few months later. Vivian Davis left town. Edward won a libel suit against the Black-owned *Jet* magazine, one of the few publications that had mentioned why he attacked Abernathy. He used the money to quit teaching junior-high gym and launched a prosperous real estate business. The whole thing was "soon . . . forgotten."[36] In 1885, Lucy Freeman had thought that if anyone ought to be worried about their troubled marriage keeping them out of Heaven, it was her husband, Edward. Perhaps Juanita Abernathy felt the same way in 1958. She said nothing in public about the allegations aired at the Davis trial. But these women, two generations apart, each of them expected to remain steadfast in the role of the preacher's wife, faced very different prospects in exercising their right to leave a marriage.

From the 1890s to the 1950s, for at least three generations after the collapse of Reconstruction's experiment in multiracial democracy, African Americans pressed even further into the institutions and practices of American law. They went to county courthouses, talked with lawyers and quasi-lawyers, filled their newspapers with legal news and commentary. They acquired millions of acres of land and negotiated as best they could over a dizzying variety of contracts, from farm leases to sharecropping contracts to insurance policies to old-age care agreements. As they entered the world of law, they debated about what law could and could not do for them. They grappled with a tension between the rights of an individual and the privileges of status in a collective—whether it was a family, a church, a business, or an activist group. Then, in the 1950s, a new kind of collective purpose and identity emerged, one that was bigger than any church, or lodge, or family—bigger even than "the race" as a whole. It had no headquarters or agreed-on leader. It went by all sorts of names. But the one that stuck was the simplest of all: "The Movement."[37]

The emergence of the mass movement for Black freedom not only helped push marriage and divorce out of the category of civil rights, but many other parts of Black life, too, just as "the King case" quickly shunted "the Davis case" from the newspapers.[38] The Davises' story centered on privileges and rights, but they were ones that did not fit the morally charged, Black-and-white categories of a struggle for "freedom" and racial justice. The era of "civil rights" as rights of everyday use was coming to an end. A new era of civil rights had begun, one that we are still living in today.

PART IV

THE MOVEMENT ERA

11

"Just like any other case with damages"

A few days after Christmas in 1973, Thurgood Marshall, America's first Black Supreme Court justice, sat down with the white journalist Richard Kluger for an interview about Marshall's most famous case. Marshall had argued *Brown v. Board of Education of Topeka* twenty years earlier as head of the NAACP's legal team. Since the day it was handed down, white critics from all over the political spectrum had accused the Court of behaving like nine politicians in robes, imposing their personal values, untethered from statutes and legal

Thurgood Marshall, September 17, 1957. Photograph by Thomas J. O'Halloran.

rules. Many critics singled out one of *Brown*'s footnotes, which cited psychology research purporting to show that segregated schools damaged Black children's self-image, fastening onto them a badge of inferiority that could not be removed simply by making the schools equal. Kluger asked the question that was on everyone's mind: how did the NAACP lawyers decide to rely on these "doll tests"? Marshall did not hesitate. "I said that we had to try this case just like any other case with damages," he said emphatically, just as "if your car ran over me, you'd have to pay up." Kluger let the matter drop. When his book came out a couple of years later, it was titled *Simple Justice,* and it was about the "brave" "black folk" and their NAACP lawyers who waged "Black America's Struggle for Equality."[1] The struggle was simple and it was sacred. So why was its hero talking like a crass ambulance-chasing personal-injury lawyer? Because he wasn't talking just to Kluger; he was talking to Black people in Topeka and all across America, who knew perfectly well what a personal-injury lawsuit was.

In 1866, "civil rights" had meant rights of contract and property, and the right to go to court. By 1954, civil rights meant ending racial discrimination on the job, at school, in voting, and an end to lynching. And by the mid-1960s, activists were saying that the real "struggle was not for civil rights, but for liberation," or "human rights," or "grassroots participatory democracy."[2] Each of these ideas of civil rights carried inside it a story about Black people's relationship to law.

One was about "simple justice": how a powerful protest movement joined forces with civil rights lawyers to write anti-discrimination into federal law. National civil rights groups like the NAACP and the Southern Christian Leadership Conference (SCLC), led by charismatic men such as Martin Luther King Jr. and Thurgood Marshall, mapped out a strategy to tear down the Jim Crow system, and their crowning achievements were the great constitutional cases, like *Brown v. Board of Education of Topeka* (1954), and the landmark federal laws, like the Civil Rights Acts of 1964, the Voting Rights Act of 1965, and the Fair Housing Act of 1968.

The other story about Blacks and the law grew from the 1960s movement, and has been developed by more recent historians. It is a story of struggle for a "larger freedom . . . of the human spirit," a struggle that was more authentically rooted in the lives of "everyday people" than civil rights was. This freedom struggle grew from the grassroots of local communities—it was not handed down by elite leaders like King and Marshall. And the grassroots wanted much more than some federal laws protecting their right to vote, to patronize restaurants, and to attend integrated schools. They wanted to remake American democracy from the ground up.

There was no room for Marshall's personal-injury plaintiff in either of those stories. Both portrayed Black people as untutored in law and alienated from the legal system. But in fact the rights of everyday use were everywhere in the freedom struggle. They permeated the activists' rhetoric. They underwrote the financing that movement activists needed and the legal tools that enabled them to organize. They were the battlefield where much of the fast-growing federal law of antidiscrimination was fought. And just as Thurgood Marshall implied in 1973, civil rights lawyers and activists counted on the fact that ordinary Black people knew something about law.

Since the 1830s, as we have seen, Black people and their allies had thought about Black rights in a variety of different ways. From the welter of status-based privileges and common-law rights that had structured people's lives in the early United States, antislavery leaders had singled out a handful as the fundamental rights of free men, the rights that marked the line between freedom and slavery. In the late 1860s, the Republican-led Congress had written that principle—equality in fundamental rights—into the first Civil Rights Act and the Equal Protection Clause of the Fourteenth Amendment. During those same years, Black leaders had argued that the kind of freedom they had—a freedom marred by exclusion and discrimination in all matters except those fundamental rights—left them "slaves of the community," what a later generation would call "second-class citizens." In the 1870s, 1880s, and 1890s, their pressure had prodded northern states to ban racial discrimination in public accommodations. Black elites in the early 1900s recommitted themselves to "uplifting the race," an almost anti-legal idea that exemplary individuals would convince white people that Black people were worthy of citizenship and at the same time would foster Black enclaves where Black people could flourish. In the 1930s, the idea of "civil rights" became ever more ecumenical. White law professors and judges used the term, sometimes interchangeably with the term "civil liberties," to describe all sorts of personal prerogatives: the right to free expression and to worship freely, the right to earn a living, rights of property, the right to organize a labor union, even the right *not* to join a union. Then, in the late 1940s, activist leaders, law professors, and journalists started talking about "civil rights" in one very specific sense: the struggle to tear down Jim Crow.[3] These leaders reasoned that state officials were denying rights to racial minorities because of their race, that racial minorities could not vote those officials out because the normal democratic process was broken in those states, and that therefore their only redress was in the federal courts, especially the U.S. Supreme Court. This idea of civil rights came to be known as "legal liberalism."

Legal liberalism fused together two of the main strands of thinking about Black rights: the idea of fundamental rights and the idea of civil slavery, now dubbed "second-class citizenship." The legal liberal idea of civil rights was made possible because the Supreme Court was becoming more open to claims by various disfranchised minorities and because President Franklin Delano Roosevelt's New Deal, which vastly expanded the powers of the federal government, fostered a belief that true freedom could come *through* government, not in spite of government. The New Deal also opened the door for lawyers and activists "to describe and attack racial discrimination" not just in the "civil" domain of property and contract but also in the vast domain of "social rights," which whites had always held off-limits: hotels, trains, restaurants, and schools.[4]

In 1947, President Harry S. Truman's new Committee on Civil Rights published an official report that warned of the corrosive impact of treating African Americans as second-class citizens. Then, in a special "civil rights" address, Truman asked Congress to strengthen the old Enforcement Act of 1870, legislate against lynching, protect voting rights, ban discrimination in interstate transportation, create a national commission to end job discrimination, and institutionalize all these reforms in a new Civil Rights Division within the Department of Justice, with its own assistant attorney general.[5] Over the next twenty years, federal law was transformed so dramatically that some observers started referring to a "Civil Rights Revolution," or "Second Reconstruction," a chance to make good on the broken promises of the 1860s. *Brown v. Board of Education,* the Civil Rights Act of 1964, the Voting Rights Act of 1965, and the Fair Housing Act of 1968 didn't just write new rules for people to follow. They also supplied a vocabulary to describe long-cherished aspirations as "rights," protected by the awesome power of the federal government against the whims of local and state officials.

This Second Reconstruction revitalized the public meaning of the term "civil rights." Civil rights became identified with Black people and with federal law, specifically the Equal Protection Clause of the Fourteenth Amendment, and it widened the scope of things that were so fundamental that they must not be infringed "on account of race, color, religion, nationality, etc."[6] The Second Reconstruction revived the Black abolitionists' idea of civil slavery, the idea that freedom required equality not just in basic civil rights but in "all those rights and privileges common to American citizens." "Second-class citizenship contradicts democracy," said Nobel laureate Ralph Bunche to the NAACP's 1951 annual meeting. The struggle for "first-class citizenship," contended Martin Luther King Jr., meant resisting "all forms of racial injustice." Even President Dwight Eisenhower, who was no liberal, assured the United Negro College Fund "that there is no place in the United States for 'second-class' citizenship."[7]

Black lawyers like Thurgood Marshall played a key role in this rethinking of rights and citizenship, but scholars have argued fiercely about what, exactly, that role was. Some have asserted that Black lawyers deradicalized the great social movements of the twentieth century, turning them away from economic populism and democratic rebirth and toward a narrower campaign for formal legal equality. Others have doubted whether it was even possible for Black lawyers or anyone else to truly speak for the interests of "the black community."[8] Yet for most Black lawyers, most of the time, law was a way to make a living, and it was hard to make a living fighting for the cause of Black freedom. So, as Black lawyers remade their professional identities during the 1940s, 1950s, and 1960s, marking out civil rights law as a distinct, morally charged, almost sacred field of practice, they held onto and sometimes still drew from the idea that civil rights were also rights of everyday use.

About thirty years before Marshall spoke with Kluger, a white senator and part-time lawyer in Ruleville, Mississippi, James O. Eastland, won a $7,000 settlement for three Black workers who had been killed or injured by the Delta Electric Company. Eastland went on to write the playbook for today's Republican Party, blockading civil rights legislation and cynically attacking "big government" while milking huge federal subsidies for himself and his friends. In October of that same year, 1947, a Black Baltimore lawyer, William Gosnell, brokered a deal to split the $2,000 payout from a deceased utility worker's life insurance policy between the man's legal wife and his common-law wife.[9] There are no famous names or great constitutional cases in either of these lawyers' papers. Still sitting in the order in which they came out of the file cabinets decades ago, these old file folders offer a glimpse of the day-by-day work of general-practice lawyers. What stood out right away, once I started looking up their clients' names in the Census, is that both Eastland and Gosnell routinely took Black clients. They collected debts *for* Black people as well as from them. They policed debt collectors to make sure their clients got credit for their payments. They brokered real estate sales to Black buyers. They helped secure insurance payouts and pursued veteran benefits for Black families. They filed personal-injury lawsuits for Black clients against construction companies, sawmills, utility companies, trucking companies, and transit companies.[10]

The stunning achievements of the NAACP's litigation strategy has made it easy to forget that most Black lawyers still spent most of their time doing what Gosnell and Eastland did. As Black lawyers became the symbols of the new conception of civil rights, they stayed grounded in the old rights of everyday use. It didn't bother Eastland that the term "civil rights" became supercharged with almost sacred power, because setting apart civil rights as special and sacred meant that white lawyers could keep making money from Black clients without joining the freedom struggle. But Gosnell could not so easily untangle a Black person's rights from "Black rights" because, increasingly, people expected Black lawyers to be part of the freedom struggle. And the higher that "civil rights" floated into the realm of the sacred, the more awkwardly it drifted away from the mundane legal concerns Black people actually brought in.

Eastland, Gosnell, and Marshall came of age at a time when the public meaning of the term "civil rights" was changing. As we have seen, for decades most whites had assumed that there was no "civil right" to dine in a railroad car because dining was a "social" activity, not a civil one, but few had denied that Blacks had the right to sue and be sued, the "right . . . to buy, own, rent and sell property," the right to make and enforce contracts, and some guarantees of protection from corrupt and biased enforcement of criminal laws. Most people still understood that those rights were secured by the states and vindicated by a county clerk, not by Congress or the Justice Department. In the 1930s and 1940s, that wobbly white consensus began to topple. Activists and cause lawyers began using the Fourteenth Amendment's Equal Protection Clause to pry open the American workplace, the schoolhouse, and other domains that whites had long kept hidden behind the old scarecrow of "social equality." A handful of Black lawyers, most famously Marshall and his mentor Charles Hamilton Houston, began working to dismantle Jim Crow, taking cases attacking discrimination in both public institutions like schools and private ones like grocery stores, cases that would confront the system's economic oppression, not just its assault on human dignity. They drew heavily from the school of legal realism, "an approach to legal reasoning and education" that "sought to understand legal rules in terms of their [real-world] social consequences" and "context." As Houston's own mentor, the white Harvard Law School dean Roscoe Pound, once put it, a realistic lawyer or judge had to look at both "the law in the books" and "the law in action." The Court had handed down dozens of book-centered decisions during the previous fifty years. Its most unrealistic decision, the one that most obstinately refused to acknowledge the law in action, was *Plessy v. Ferguson,* where Justice Henry Billings Brown had written that the alleged harms of segregation were all in Black people's heads.[11]

Meanwhile, spurred by letters from Black workers that starkly presented "the economic consequences of racial discrimination," federal government lawyers briefly embraced a vision of civil rights that put work at its center. Still other Black lawyers tried to plant seeds of political change from "within the confines of Jim Crow." These developments helped lead the American Bar Association to announce, in 1940, that "civil rights" was emerging as "a distinct field of law."[12] But if that was true, what made it so distinct?

Ever since they were almost entirely hounded out of the profession in the 1890s, Black lawyers scattered around America's cities had been eking out a living from general practice. Their experiences representing Black farm owners, laborers, cooks, small businesses, and churches profoundly shaped what would become "civil rights lawyering." As the legal historian Kenneth Mack has shown, they had fashioned a vision of race uplift, one that combined legal claims against the white majority with an almost anti-legal inward-looking emphasis on what the race could do for itself. As more and more of those clients moved from the cash-scarce rural economy of promissory notes and deeds of trust to the paycheck jobs of towns and cities, Black lawyers finally found a real market for their services. Their numbers climbed until, by 1966, there were something like 2,200 Black lawyers in the United States, nearly all of them in cities. They still did not make very much money. The typical Black lawyer in the 1950s was a solo practitioner in a "shabby looking" office in the Black section of town. Some of them were so-called Sundowners, people who "practiced law at odd hours" after their day jobs. White corporations still wouldn't hire Black lawyers—that only began to change in the 1980s—and there was no way to build a serious corporate practice from clients who were barbershop owners or small-time criminal defendants.[13]

These realities imposed structural constraints on the nation's leading civil rights organization. Kluger was understandably dazzled by Thurgood Marshall and his all-stars at NAACP headquarters in New York, but it was a self-selected diaspora of solo lawyers in their shabby looking offices who did the all-important local work that led to cases like *Brown*. They were the ones who listened to people's complaints and made the initial decisions about which ones qualified as "civil rights"—cases that would set precedents for "the rights of colored people as a whole"—and which ones stood a chance of winning. Once headquarters decided to take a case, these local branch lawyers carefully pushed it along for months, in whatever time they could spare from their bread-and-butter practice. They fended off their opponent's pretrial motions to dismiss and tried to keep the client from fleeing or talking to the press or doing anything else that might upset the delicate, all-important facts of the case before Marshall or his chief deputy Robert Carter could swoop in for the trial.[14]

Gosnell and his sometimes partner, Dallas Nicholas, may not have made much money, but lawyers like them were setting their sights higher. A few got appointed to judgeships, executive branch staff positions, and other posts in the growing federal government, or blue-ribbon commissions like the 1947 Committee on Civil Rights. For most Black lawyers, however, higher ambitions did not mean lawyering for a cause. It meant professional respect and the fees that came with it.

What they yearned for was to stride out from the professional ghetto of crime and divorce to the green meadows of corporate practice, with its higher fees, steadier clients, air-conditioning, copy machines, dictaphones, and decent office libraries for researching complex legal issues. For some, it was high-profile criminal cases that opened the door—the "impossible" cases that no one else would touch. For others, it was deep-pocketed Black corporations—Atlanta's A. T. Walden was counsel for the National Baptist Convention and the Atlanta State Savings Bank, and Sadie Alexander, a leading lawyer in Philadelphia, transformed her firm when she landed the A.M.E. church as a client.[15] Still others set their sights on attracting white corporate clients, determined to build their reputations as "hard-core litigators," not token hires. However they got their foot in the door, their steady-paying institutional clients—the churches and insurance companies and businesses—brought respect from their professional peers and a chance, as Mack puts it, to "connect with something larger."[16]

Connecting to "something larger" posed practical and conceptual problems when that "something" was a cause rather than a professional network or a large corporation. Conceptually, the problem was how to define what the Black lawyer's duties should be. It was a familiar challenge. The Colored Conventions of the 1840s and 1850s and the NAACP Legal Department in the 1910s and 1920s had confronted something similar. Did it mean only cases that would "benefit Negroes in general"? Cases involving constitutional rights? If the cause was "civil rights," then what, exactly, were those?[17] Some thought that "civil rights" were "more important" than "mere property rights," while others said civil rights were those "basic" property rights common to all Americans. Even at Howard Law—the nation's top Black law school and home to the very first course on Civil Rights—students in the 1940s still spent most of their time taking the same courses their predecessors had in the 1920s: Business Units, Civil Procedure, Contracts, Criminal Law, and Property. Why wouldn't they? That was the business of American courts.[18]

The practical problem was that lawyering for a cause simply didn't (and doesn't) pay much. That is why, before the rise of the Black civil rights lawyer, cause lawyers tended to be men from well-to-do families or men who had steady corporate clients—men like Louis Brandeis. Before he joined the Supreme Court in 1916, Brandeis was already famous as "the people's lawyer," the attorney who refused a fee for any legal work that, in his judgment, raised "public" issues. When young lawyers asked him for career advice, he told them to earn enough money to stay above politics or personal interest, enough to "buy" the "freedom to do as seems to you . . . right." Brandeis could give that kind of advice because he came from a rich family and he had a lot of wealthy clients. Black lawyers who sought to fight for the cause of Black freedom had to break the Brandeis mold. Thurgood Marshall's mother was an underpaid schoolteacher and his father a railroad porter; his clients were working-class people and small businesses. For lawyers, time is money, and Marshall needed money more than Brandeis did. Many other Black lawyers faced similar quandaries. In 1928, Marshall's future mentor, Howard Law School vice dean Charles Hamilton Houston, groused that older Black lawyers were too busy handling divorces and church business to "work[] for racial advancement." But five years later, when Marshall graduated from Howard Law in 1933, Houston advised him not to "drop everything for N.A.A.C.P. work." "Keep a finger on your office practice whatever you do. You can get all the publicity from the N.A.A.C.P. work but you have to keep your eye out for cashing in."[19]

In reality, most Black lawyers' careers in the 1940s and 1950s looked a lot like the careers of their predecessors and of their white counterparts; the difference was that white lawyers had access to bigger and wealthier networks. James Baber, a white graduate of University of Virginia Law School (class of 1961), had a leg up when he moved back home to Cumberland County and hung out his shingle. "A lot of people knew me," he told me in 2016, as we sat in the Cumberland courthouse waiting for one of his clients; people knew "my father, my family, my wife's family," and they sent him clients. Many Black law school graduates did the same thing: they went back home and rustled up clients through friends, family, church, and fraternity. Or they headed out "where the money was," negotiating oil leases for Native Americans in Oklahoma or handling cases related to the new industrial Ship Channel at the Port of Houston. That is what James Nabrit did in the early 1930s, before he started Howard's pioneering civil rights seminar. Like earlier generations, they attached themselves to more established lawyers. They offered free income-tax advice and notarizations. They turned an office remodeling into a grand opening, hoping to parlay the publicity into new clients. The handful of Black women lawyers who managed to resist being relegated to "legal drudgery" in a male lawyer's firm were seen as having a natural affinity for community service and social reform work, yet took a backseat to men during courtroom arguments in civil rights cases.[20] Even those who became famous later on for their anti-discrimination litigation, like Thurgood Marshall and A. Leon Higginbotham, spent their early careers in traditional "bread-and-butter" "neighborhood practice," garnishing workers' paychecks or "dealing with small property matters or little 'two-for-nothing' misdemeanor cases" and selling insurance and real estate on the side, taking "everything that walked through the door."[21]

Marshall never forgot that before he was "Mr. Civil Rights," he had been "the little man's lawyer" in Baltimore, a job so financially meager that, during lean spells, he would bring in sandwiches to keep up his office staff's spirits while they waited for a paying client to walk in. This is why Marshall "stormed around" the NAACP's Legal Defense Fund's New York office after he heard about the 1960 student sit-ins, booming that "he was not going to represent a bunch of crazy colored students who violated the sacred property rights of white folks by going in their stores or lunch counters and refusing to leave when ordered to do so." He was probably half-joking. But by "trespassing on private property,"[22] the sit-inners forced lawyers like Marshall to confront the awkward tension that arose as "civil rights" came to be identified with the Black freedom struggle.

The LDF's big plan was to wage a carefully planned, step-by-step assault on *Plessy*. The LDF won case after case starting in the 1930s, and each victory grabbed bigger headlines: *Murray v. Pearson* (in which the Maryland court of appeals held that the state's law school could not bar nonwhite students without providing them a separate law school), *Gaines v. Canada* (a 1938 decision that a state could not ship nonwhite law students out of state), *Smith v. Allwright* (the 1944 case that ended the voter-suppressing "white primary"), *Brown v. Board of Education of Topeka* (holding unconstitutional racial segregation in public elementary and high schools), *Browder v. Gayle* (the 1956 Montgomery Bus Boycott case, holding racial segregation unconstitutional on city buses), *Griggs v. Duke Power Company* (a 1971 case outlawing most employment practices that have a "disparate impact" on minority workers), and more. The vast majority of Black lawyers were not on the LDF team, though some of them had helped find the plaintiffs and get the cases ready to litigate. For them, these victories vindicated Houston's graduation advice to Marshall back in 1935: they could parlay anti-discrimination cases into "publicity" for "cashing in." Anti-discrimination cases "crowded" the courts "with Negro spectators," who witnessed firsthand the court's respect for a Black lawyer. Black lawyers' "demonstration of competence" made them "a symbol of the Negro's struggle for dignity and respectability." By unlocking the gates of prejudice for their civil rights clients, they would bring new and better-paying clients through the door.[23]

In spotting the professional benefits of public-interest lawyering, Black lawyers were not so different from white lawyers, who did free work for clubs and charities as stealth advertising. For many Black lawyers, what made the 1960s feel like a turning point was the professional freedom that came with better incomes—freedom to choose the cases they wanted, and to fight them how they wanted. "The big insurance companies" and other powerful opponents "couldn't buffalo" Black lawyers anymore, one of them said. "Johnnie Cochran didn't need the money, so he could go ahead" with the cases he felt were worthwhile, whether or not they counted as civil rights.[24] They out-Brandeised Brandeis.

Black lawyers had built their idea of civil rights before *Brown* and the great Civil Rights Acts of the 1960s opened up a toolbox of public-law remedies to use. So they did not draw a bright line between the new "civil rights" of the freedom struggle and the routine private civil rights of everyday use that took up most of their time. The seamlessness of the small-firm Black lawyer's civil rights vision appears even in their file cabinets. Sadie Alexander scribbled notes about a domestic assault case on the back of a typed "Statement on Krushchev Visit," and wrote a draft affidavit for a will on the back of a schedule for "UN Week." Her law partner (and husband) Raymond Alexander filed his copy of the briefs in *Brown v. Board of Education* between divorce papers he was handling for women named Loretta Brown and Pearl Logan Brown. The office was busy. You grabbed a piece of paper and wrote on the back. You filed things in alphabetical order. Oliver Brown's lawsuit against the Topeka school board went under the "B"s.[25]

This is why Marshall thought *Brown* was "just like any other case with damages": Black lawyers' approach to the great constitutional cases of the 1940s and 1950s was subtly shaped by "neighborhood practice" and by their legal-realist emphasis on looking beyond "the law on the books." Marshall wasn't the only one who intended the school desegregation cases to do more than just strike down the *Plessy* doctrine, who wanted the cases "to lead and teach within the communities where [the] cases were being argued." What lesson did they think they were teaching those communities? It was that the *public* laws mandating racial segregation could be described and attacked in the language of *private* law, the language of property, contract, and now tort that wove through people's daily lives. In fact, Black lawyers had been trying for decades to win tort damages for the "shock" of "humiliation," for "injury to the personality," when white railroad conductors mistreated passengers on trains. It was Howard Law graduate Pauli Murray's intuition that public and private harms were related—an intuition later supported by Marshall and Carter—that led the NAACP team to incorporate the social psychology ideas that came to be known as "the doll tests" in its *Brown* briefs.[26] A segregated school was like a car accident: they both injured Black children.

As civil rights became more tightly linked to race discrimination and more intensely charged with universal moral values such as "injustice," "freedom," and "dignity," Marshall's logic—that civil rights were mundane, that a civil rights case was, in some sense, just like any other case—was set aside. Segregation was nothing like a car accident; it was an evil, a wrong in the eyes of God. For example, take Elisha Scott, whose law firm filed the original 1951 lawsuit that became the *Brown* case. Scott's "bread and butter" was oil and gas cases. His clients were people like Lillie Guss Taylor, a Black Louisianan, and Malinda Schuyler, a Black Kansan, trying to negotiate the best leases for their suddenly valuable lands. A gifted litigator—"he could make a jury cry like a Baptist minister," his secretary recalled—Scott was the obvious choice when activists began trying to desegregate the Kansas schools. In both his "private cases" and his NAACP work, Elisha Scott worked to "protect blacks." And yet, a case like *Brown* made some of the habits and practices of "private cases" look downright crass. To a white Kansan who helped to organize the *Brown* litigation, Scott sounded like "a typical southern-midwestern negro lawyer": "unorganized," "not very bright but flamboyant." Worse, he was always asking for money, recalled the white ally, "which surprised me since I just assumed a Negro attorney would work for a civil rights cause for nothing." Indeed, many Black people assumed that, too.[27] The NAACP built its litigation campaign on the skills of local Black lawyers like Elisha Scott, but that campaign forced the association to invent a new model for financing and litigating lawsuits, one that would soon have no room for a lawyer who looked and sounded like Scott.

The problem was that most Black lawyers sounded a bit like Scott, at least sometimes, because they couldn't afford to give away their services for free. And *Brown* was not really "just like any other case with damages" because there was no money in it—not for Linda Brown, the eight-year-old girl whose long walk to school through the dangerous Rock Island Railroad switchyards was the signature story of the school segregation cases, not for her lawyers, not for anyone. No wonder Marshall's mentor warned him not to "drop everything for N.A.A.C.P. work." No wonder Black lawyers in the NAACP branches across the country kept bickering with the national office over fees. No wonder Martin Luther King Jr.'s right-hand man, the Reverend Fred Shuttlesworth, accused the local attorneys handling Birmingham's desegregation lawsuits of trying to milk "big money" out of the "sacred . . . struggle" for "first-class citizenship" and "human rights."[28] The moralizing rhetoric of "sacred struggle," the emphasis on the Fourteenth Amendment to the Constitution, and the presumption that Black lawyers handled "civil rights case[s] for nothing": all these shifts helped lift up "civil rights" as a distinct category of professional practice without any obvious source of cash flow.

For Black lawyers, the presumption that civil rights was a "sacred struggle" for Black freedom generated more than awkwardness about fees and crass behavior. It raised questions about what it even meant to be a Black lawyer. Lawyers had typically played a conservative role in society—"the American aristocracy," Alexis de Tocqueville once called them. It was lawyers who had helped make segregation work—not so much through landmark cases like *Plessy* but through the routine legal work that defined the system and kept it running, from helping a county issue bonds to refinance its "colored" school district, to helping a worried father get his son safely transferred to the "negro unit" of the state mental hospital.[29] This structural role made it almost inevitable that Black lawyers would get squeezed between the imperatives of the emerging idea of civil-rights-as-sacred-struggle and their professional duties as lawyers.

For example, much of the income at Hill, Tucker & Marsh, Richmond, Virginia's premier Black law firm, came from Samuel Tucker's skill in handling partition suits—lawsuits over family land, which Movement activists increasingly blamed for the demise of Black landowning. Other

Black lawyers helped Black people break into all-white neighborhoods or white businessmen hang on in Black ones. Everybody said they hated blockbusters, the notorious real estate brokers who stampeded whites into selling their homes cheap by telling them "Negroes" were moving into the neighborhood, and then turned around and resold those homes to "Negroes" at exorbitant prices. Yet some blockbusting broker-lawyers *personally* opposed racially restrictive covenants for the same reasons the critics did, and some NAACP lawyers wanted to cooperate with them.[30] Then, too, fights over liquor licenses had none of the moral righteousness of a bus boycott or a school suit. Taverns were "public accommodations" just like buses and hotels, but it was harder to portray a tavern-owner's right to sell booze as simple justice than an eight-year-old girl's right to attend a decent school. Hundreds of exasperated "colored residents" showed up at licensing board meetings, crying out that the last thing their neighborhood needed was another liquor store. Would a Black-owned bar be a "breakthrough for blacks"? Would a white-owned bar "keep down crime"?[31] The more morally charged the term "civil rights" became, the more it seemed to pull loose from the varied practice that had kept Black lawyers afloat for so long.

If the demands of orchestrating a sacred struggle through far-flung, cash-strapped branch lawyers helped define our modern concept of "civil rights," the passage of the great civil rights statutes of the late 1960s helped crystallize it. As it had done in its 1866 Civil Rights Act, Congress wrote the Civil Rights Act (1964), the Voting Rights Act (1965), and the Fair Housing Act (1968) so that they did not replace wholesale the fifty states' vast corpus of statutes and common-law rules of property, contract, and tort. Instead, Congress installed "discrimination" as a latchkey to the federal courts. If a person suffered "discrimination or segregation on the ground of race, color, religion, or national origin" in a place of public accommodation, on the job, in a federally funded program, or in the selling or renting of housing, then he or she could either file a complaint at a federal agency or a lawsuit in a federal court. Though the actual texts of these laws were necessarily dry and riddled with carve-outs, their sponsors imbued them with the symbolic power of a righteous cause. "The issue of equal rights for American Negroes" laid bare "the secret heart of America itself," said President Lyndon Johnson, urging Congress to pass the Voting Rights Bill, while the evening news blared images of the Alabama State Police bludgeoning peaceful marchers at the Edmund Pettus Bridge. "The time of justice has come," he said, looking into the television cameras. "And we *shall* overcome." The idea that discrimination was morally wrong shone brightly through the floor debates on the new bills, as liberal congressmen stood up and echoed Martin Luther King Jr.'s wrenching description of his five- and six-year-old children seeing their father "humiliated" by the Jim Crow system.[32]

Yet Black lawyers never lost sight of the older meanings of civil rights, which fused together ideas of race uplift and rights of everyday use with anti-discrimination and anti-humiliation. Oliver Hill, the NAACP specialist at Hill, Tucker & Marsh, spotted opportunity for Black lawyers in the growing field of torts, the same field Thurgood Marshall would later gesture to in his interview with Richard Kluger. Hill "was too busy fighting segregation to take it up" himself, he recalled years later. So he brought George Allen, a white lawyer he had met back in 1930 in the course of an eviction suit, to give lectures to the members of Virginia's Black bar association on a new "theory" Allen was developing for winning negligence cases.[33] The quiet harmony between anti-discrimination work and other kinds of lawyering can be seen, too, in a story I heard from Henry Marsh, the third partner at the same Richmond firm, about a time he did handle a church suit. Marsh's client, a member of one of Richmond's Black Baptist churches, had been summarily disciplined by the church trustees—that is, without the due process spelled out in Baptist by-laws—and he hired Marsh to make them give him a church trial. Marsh was delighted when the judge ruled that his client was entitled to one. He knew he would win. Why was he so sure? I asked him. Marsh explained that during the 1970s he had spearheaded a series of employment-discrimination suits in Richmond and won back-pay settlements, including for many members of this church. "We sued *everybody*" from Philip Morris to DuPont, he chuckled. All those employment-discrimination suits had engendered a fleeting sense among Black Richmonders that "we were all together" in a righteous struggle; his name was everywhere. And as if that wasn't enough of a leg up, Marsh laughed, the church trustees "were dumb enough to get a white lawyer against me in my heyday!"[34] When the church finally held its court-ordered trial, Marsh's client won in a landslide.

Black lawyers helped change popular ideas about law and rights in the 1940s, 1950s, and 1960s. African Americans increasingly viewed civil rights as a cause: a distinct, almost sacred field of practice. But as much as they might have shared those views, Black lawyers' professional training and daily practice never let them forget that civil rights were also the rights of everyday use.

12

Civil Rights, Inc.

On June 1, 1956, ten people filed papers to incorporate a group called The Montgomery Improvement Association. The MIA had been founded six months earlier, at a mass meeting of the city's Black churches and civic groups at Holt Street Baptist Church, on the night Rosa Parks was arrested for violating the city's bus segregation law. There, Martin Luther King Jr., then still relatively unknown, had been the surprising pick to lead what was expected to be a four-day boycott. Now, in front of a notary public, King and nine other members registered the MIA with the county probate judge's office, the place where Alabama law sent citizens who wanted to set up a corporation. In the blank where the form asked the "nature" of the MIA's "business," the members wrote: "to secure and maintain Civil Rights." Mrs. Erna Dungee, of 668 West Jeff Davis Avenue, would be the registered agent. They left membership in the MIA wide open: anyone could join who had "an urge for the enjoyment of freedom and full citizenship."[1]

But the ten incorporators centralized the new corporation's management powers. Under its by-laws, filed along with the form, a board of directors would have power to choose its officers and to propose changes to its articles of incorporation—the companion document that said what the MIA was *for.* The by-laws granted its president (King) and a few officers the power to "supervise and control" its day-to-day "business and affairs": to sign contracts and deeds, to speak and act for the

ARTICLES OF INCORPORATION OF
THE MONTGOMERY IMPROVEMENT ASSOCIATION BOOK 33 55

We, the undersigned, incorporators, hereby associate ourselves together to form and establish a corporation not for profit under the "Alabama Non-Profit Corporation Act", adopted, 1955.

FIRST

The name of the corporation is the Montgomery Improvement Association.

SECOND

The period of existence of this corporation is unlimited.

THIRD

The purposes for which the corporation is formed are:

a. To use effective legal means to secure and maintain Civil Rights in any situation where an individual or a group have been deprived of their Civil Rights.

b. To increase respect for the dignity of the individual in the use of public facilities.

c. To generally improve the living conditions in the community and particularly in the area of housing, health, education, sanitation and recreation.

d. To resolve community problems in a climate of mutual goodwill and understanding; forever remembering that God is first and all problems shall be solved in the Spirit of Christ, without fear, and without violence.

e. To stimulate specific responsibility in the individual so that he will participate fully and effectively in community action.

f. To encourage individuals to become first class citizens by securing the ballot and using it wisely, and

g. To do any and all other acts which will generally improve the City and County of Montgomery so that all of its citizens will receive all the rights and privileges secured to them by the Constitution of the State of Alabama and of the United States and to inform the citizens of their obligations, responsibilities and duties which accompany these rights and privileges.

FOURTH

Membership in the corporation shall be composed of individuals who believe in the purposes for which the corporation is formed and who desire to associate themselves with others so that the purposes of the corporation will become a reality. Membership in the corporation shall not be divided into classes.

Articles of Incorporation of the Montgomery Improvement Association, Book 33, page 55, Montgomery County Probate Records Office, Montgomery, Alabama.

corporation. Ordinary MIA members would have only a few limited rights: to elect the board of directors, and to vote on things it proposed. The boycott lasted nearly seven more months, an astonishing 382 days in all. And during those long, harsh months, King and the other officers turned to their corporate powers again and again: to organize a giant car-pool system, to take in thousands of dollars in donations, to pay the lawyers handling their lawsuit against the city, and, above all, to negotiate with white officials on behalf of its entire membership, representing to the world what the MIA—and by extension all of Montgomery's Black people—wanted.[2]

By contrast, the Student Nonviolent Coordinating Committee (SNCC) refused to act anything like a corporation. Founded by southern Black college students during the lunch-counter sit-in movement of 1960, SNCC workers were deeply influenced by the vision of "group-centered leadership" offered by their mentor, the veteran grassroots organizer Ella Baker, so they "self-consciously avoided" replicating the top-down structure of Black-run organizations like the SCLC and the NAACP. SNCC wasn't just unincorporated; it was *anti*-corporate. Its decentralized, non-hierarchical setup was supposed to keep it responsive to the needs of local people. Indeed, SNCC made leaders out of Black southerners who usually got sidelined. But that anti-corporate structure meant that its leaders could not act or speak for the group or discipline bad field workers. A corporation could be a democracy. Baptist churches certainly were: most important decisions got made by majority vote. But not only was SNCC not a corporation; it wasn't a democracy, either. It made decisions by consensus rather than by vote, and that, said James Forman, one of its key figures, enabled small factions to "bog down" meetings in endless discussion, a tyranny of the minority. Ironically, SNCC only survived its early months by borrowing office space and precious mailing facilities from a corporate partner (SCLC, cofounded by Baker and incorporated in 1958). Even more ironically, the SNCC staffers who actually came from the South—the very kinds of "indigenous" people that SNCC was so fervently trying to mobilize—actually "*wanted* more structure and more organization," precisely because they thought "more structure" would give them a voice in the organization and was likelier to get stuff done.[3]

SNCC stuck with its group-centered leadership model, and just seven years after its founding, it collapsed. As John Lewis, another of SNCC's key figures, lamented years later, the activists refused to confront their governance problems. They insisted that "SNCC is not an organization. It's not a union. It's not a club. It's a *movement.*" SNCC never quite made the leap from a campus protest group to an organization capable of promoting "a broad-based mass struggle" in part because it refused to use the powers of a corporation. The MIA was not a democracy either. But one reason the Montgomery bus boycott worked is that the MIA was a corporation.[4]

Today, progressives use the word "corporate" as an epithet, shorthand for a world distorted by the relentless pursuit of profit. But the Black freedom struggle of the 1950s, 1960s, and 1970s relied again and again on the legal power of corporations. As Philadelphia's Black Methodists had done in 1796, and South Carolina's Black militiamen had done in 1876, Black people once again seized the advantages of incorporation for their own goals, only to confront tensions over corporate authority, rights, and privileges. From churches and mosques to activist groups, Black-owned corporations, as well as unincorporated associations, powered a "freedom struggle" against a white supremacist society that denied their rights as citizens. But that empowerment came with risks. Soon white supremacists tried to turn their corporate status against them. Behind the corporate veil, African Americans fought on a second front: against leaders who sometimes acted like dictators and who said that members did not have rights within the corporation, only privileges. In some cases, members redirected the rhetoric of racial justice inward, demanding rights and justice *within* the corporation. This veiled struggle was not new; it dated from the first Black corporations, established back in the 1790s, and it happened in white ones too. The difference was that now Black corporations were being asked to drive a movement, one whose success seemed to require unwavering solidarity.

Black people had been forming corporations for nearly two centuries: religious corporations (churches and mosques), nonprofit membership corporations (like the NAACP), fraternities and sororities (like Alpha Kappa Alpha), and business corporations. Some were big, like the Baptist Publishing House, with $25 million annual revenue (in 2021 dollars) and a block-long building in downtown Nashville. Most were small—say, a supper-club-turned-restaurant—and some were so small that they could hold back-to-back board meetings for "four or five businesses" by "just changing seats at the table."[5] There were stock corporations with shareholders, mutual companies like North Carolina Mutual Insurance, member-owned cooperatives, and more. The Movement of the 1950s and 1960s drew strength from all these types of corporations.

Black southerners were familiar enough with the advantages of the corporation that local activists in South Carolina tried to establish one right at the dawn of the Movement: during the run-up to *Briggs v. Elliott,* the case that eventually became part of the five-case omnibus suit known as *Brown*. When Harry Briggs, a gas-station worker in the town of Summerton, agreed in 1949 to be the lead plaintiff, he and his wife Liza were fired from their jobs and his credit was cut off at all the local banks. To protect their budding movement from this kind of economic retaliation, Briggs's neighbors created a Clarendon County Improvement Association to supply farm fertilizer, cash loans, and other services, much the same way Charlie Black had rescued Nate Shaw from the "friendship business amongst the white folks." Getting a corporate charter was usually a routine thing by the 1940s. The White Citizens Council that hounded out Harry Briggs had no trouble getting its corporate charter. Neither did the Ku Klux Klan. But the Clarendon County Improvement Association was turned down three times because local whites lobbied the South Carolina secretary of state, much as white ex-Confederate terrorists had disputed the charters of Black militias in 1876. So they had to make do as an unincorporated co-op, each member liable for its debts, each member empowered to stymie its mission at any time.[6]

Black activists understood the power of incorporation, if only because so many of them had grown up in incorporated churches, using hymnals from the Baptist Publishing House, Inc. (a Black-owned Tennessee corporation) and reading about the inventor Elijah McCoy ("the real McCoy") and Atlanta Life Insurance during Negro History Week.[7] They carried that understanding into the 1960s, as they increasingly urged not just ending racial discrimination in schools and public accommodations but also "economic justice." As Ella Baker put it, real change required "something bigger than a hamburger." And in the South, that meant dealing with the men on courthouse square, the insiders who set the local tax assessments and school budgets, decided who received credit, whose land got flooded, and who got to soak up federal subsidies from Washington. In the early 1960s, charitable organizations, such as the Ford Foundation, and the Office of Economic Opportunity (OEO, part of the federal government's War on Poverty) started sending money to help poor people build decent schools and infrastructure for healthcare and food. Like the activists, the OEO had a mandate to make plans and decisions together with the people it was helping, so it listened to Black people's "goat sense," meeting them on the muddy ground between laypeople's and lawyers' expert ideas of what "the law" was. What emerged from those conversations, again and again, was that they needed a corporation.[8]

Black Mississippians incorporated the North Bolivar County Farm Cooperative in 1968. The Poor People's Technical Assistance Corporation, a nonprofit New York corporation, was set up by a SNCC activist to channel donations and purchase orders to and from a dizzying network of women-run sewing co-ops across Mississippi.[9] The Southwest Alabama Farmers Co-operative Association was incorporated in 1967 by local activists and SCLC activists. The Child Development

Group of Mississippi (CDGM) acted as subcontractor for dozens of Head Start programs around that state, and soon turned churches into classrooms and staffed them using federal money. The all-Black settlement of Tougaloo, which learned from the CDGM "how to form a water association and apply for a loan to dig their own well," almost managed to get incorporated as a town (a municipal corporation). The Freedom City Development Fund, Inc., a Mississippi nonprofit, was incorporated in 1970 by Owen Brooks, Ida Mae Lawrence, and Maxine Maxwell and "domiciled" at Brooks's apartment in Greenville. The Freedom Farms Corporation, incorporated in 1970 and domiciled at the activist Fannie Lou Hamer's house in Ruleville, Mississippi, had some 1,500 member families working almost 700 acres; it combined voter education outreach and preschools with economic efforts such as a sewing business (which made quilts and African-style clothes for sale to college kids in Madison, Wisconsin), a catfish enterprise, and a "pig bank." In Oakland, the Black Panther Party (incorporated in 1972) created a whole string of subcorporations to protect themselves from government interference and to run their many initiatives, from the Sickle Cell Anemia Research Foundation (1972) to the "liberation schools" of the Educational Opportunities Corporation (1973). The first thing new community groups should do, the Panthers advised in 1974, was to work "on becoming a nonprofit corporation," which could solicit donations (and justify tax write-offs for the donors). In New York, the Bedford-Stuyvesant Renewal and Rehabilitation Corporation provided a powerful vehicle for everything from renovating houses to securing mortgages to teaching Black history and putting on culture festivals. Some of the new organizations built directly on foundations laid by earlier Black corporations. The Tufts-Delta Health Center—one of the most ambitious OEO initiatives of the 1960s—was set up in the Black-run town of Mound Bayou, Mississippi, in partnership with a local Black hospital that the Knights and Daughters of Tabor, a Black-run fraternal corporation, had been running since 1942.[10] In short, Black-run activist groups held different opinions about what "freedom" entailed and how to achieve it, but they all took advantage of incorporation.

To be sure, a corporate charter was just a tool, and in the mid-twentieth century, Black people wielded their corporate charters in an arena that was tilted against them—indeed, where powerful players sometimes were literally out to get them. Right from the start, white officials almost crushed the civil rights movement by turning activist groups' corporate powers into their Achilles heel. Montgomery's white leaders probably could have beaten the bus boycott in 1955 if they had immediately secured an injunction against the MIA instead of prosecuting Rosa Parks. But the segregationists learned fast. In 1956, white congressmen prodded the IRS to investigate the link between the NAACP (a tax-paying lobbying corporation) and the NAACP Legal Defense Fund (LDF, the tax-exempt "Inc. Fund" spin-off that handled the court cases). That same year, Alabama and six other states outlawed the LDF's usual methods for finding test plaintiffs. The new laws said that if the NAACP was found guilty of either "barratry" (stirring up lawsuits) or "running and capping" (soliciting legal business), then any Alabama lawyer who had ever handled NAACP business would be disbarred.[11]

Then Alabama got downright clever. On the grounds that the NAACP, a New York corporation, was running an unregistered "business" in Alabama, the state's attorney general swore out an injunction barring the NAACP from operating in Alabama until it handed over its membership lists. The NAACP refused, knowing that every person on those lists would suffer the same fate as Harry and Eliza Briggs, and wound up sidelined during the height of the Movement in Alabama. In the middle of that membership lists conflict, Montgomery's police commissioner engineered a $500,000 libel judgment against the *New York Times* and four Black ministers who, as members of a Committee to Defend Martin Luther King and the Struggle for Freedom in the South, had signed an ad accusing the police of unleashing a "wave of terror" against nonviolent protesters. Then, since the unincorporated Committee had no assets to satisfy that judgment, the county court seized and auctioned off the ministers' cars and land.[12]

Organizing boycotts exposed the NAACP to huge civil damages judgments well into the 1970s. Corrupt sheriffs had long used such financial persecution to silence their critics. Now the tactic was part of a campaign to force Black activists to choose between their property rights and the survival of their activist associations. It would be years before the Supreme Court shielded civil rights groups from this kind of state harassment, holding that it violated the groups' rights to freedom of speech and of association—that is, their First Amendment rights as corporate "persons." Yet even without that protection, Black-owned corporations kept helping the movement, from the NAACP down to the little New Orleans restaurant that "would feed the marchers" and "give them some money . . . whenever we can."[13]

Faced with relentless attacks by white outsiders, activist organizations also navigated tensions from inside, tensions over authority, property, and Black people's privileges as association members. Activist groups talked a lot about what they were doing on behalf of "colored people," but what did they owe their "colored" members? The NAACP launched a major membership drive in the 1940s, only to discover that many of the newcomers assumed that membership entitled them to a free lawyer even if their problems weren't about racial discrimination. Indeed, some of the new members grumbled that the NAACP ought to be attending to its members' personal legal needs, not bringing expensive cases on behalf of people like Oliver Brown, who wasn't even a dues-paying member. As for the farm co-ops set up in the 1960s, some members felt that these had turned out to be "just another plantation," "with black agents instead of white" ones.[14]

The question of what racial justice groups owed their members was even starker for employees—the people who worked full-time for them. For years, the board of the Armstrong Association, Philadelphia's largest racial justice group in the 1930s and 1940s, ignored complaints—backed by affidavits and warnings from "the mothers of four Camp Fire groups, a Girl Scout Troop, and several Neighborhood Clubs"—that its executive secretary was sexually harassing and assaulting women staffers. In the 1950s, Ruby Shuttlesworth was convinced that her family's sacrifices, through her husband Fred's relentless toil for the Alabama Christian Movement for Civil Rights (ACMHR), entitled them to a share of its proceeds. At SNCC, whose fiercely anti-corporate leaders were all men, women staffers kept getting assigned to "female" chores and having to endure offhand, sexist remarks. And in 1967, the women leaders who had convinced Senator Ted Kennedy to create New York's Bedford-Stuyvesant Renewal and Rehabilitation Corporation found themselves pushed aside by an all-male band of Black Power activists.[15]

Precisely because they were corporations, the members and employees of groups like the ACMHR, SNCC, the Armstrong Association, and the NAACP believed their status came with certain rights: a right to a lawyer, a decent workplace, a salary, a piece of the pie or "fair treatment" in disputes. Armstrong board member Sadie Alexander argued in 1939 that the "ladies had a right to be heard" on the problem of sexual harassment because "after all . . . they *were* the Armstrong Association." But over and over, the leaders of Black-run associations, like their white counterparts, brushed aside those questions about members' rights.[16] Nowhere did that friction burn hotter than in Black religious corporations—churches and mosques—where justice for the race had always threaded through matters of faith.

"Do you recall the March on Wash. 8/63"? wrote a Washington, DC, resident named Vernita Wimbush to the bishop who had just removed her church's pastor. "I think you urged all C. M. E. Churches to try if possible to participate in that March, so that we could fight for our rights." She and her fellow church members, Wimbush warned, had "decided to take your advice" and "plan a march to *your* house, 7/28/66," to "fight for there rights" to keep their pastor. The marchers of 1963 went to the seat of American government to transform American democracy. The marchers of 1966 aimed at another government, one that was even less democratic: the Christian Methodist Episcopal Church, a Tennessee corporation.[17] If the March on Washington could rally a quarter-million people for "jobs and freedom," then surely a march on the bishop's house could do something for the rights of church members.

Black people had argued for generations about religious leaders' authority and members' privileges. These arguments had unfolded in similar ways across different religions. Members of mosques and churches worshiped each in their own manner, but they all worshiped as members of associations, similarly empowered and regulated by the state. That left spiritual matters up to the believers while putting worldly matters of church property and other civil rights firmly in the hands of laypeople. This doctrine of judicial deference applied to all religious institutions but it fostered a distinctive discourse among Black people, who were blocked by Jim Crow from most of the civic institutions where whites found a sense of purpose and belonging. In the 1950s and 1960s, buoyed by donations from congregations whose members were getting paid cash wages rather than a share of a crop, some churches and mosques grew larger and wealthier than ever.[18] Meanwhile, a self-consciously organized mass movement increasingly looked to Black religious associations for foot soldiers and money. Now, mosque and church members found themselves fighting on two fronts: against a white supremacist society that denied their rights as citizens and against a male supremacist religion that denied their rights as members.

There had always been tension between Black religious leaders' sexism and their traditional insistence that theology needed to be grounded in the realities of life. After all, two obvious realities of Black religious life were that women made up more than half the members and that women contributed an outsize share of the money. And it was precisely because they had civil rights of property and contract that women could fill up collection plates. Take, for example, the Nation of Islam, a religious group that sought to redeem African Americans from a depraved white world and shelter them within a Black-owned parallel economy. In the 1940s and 1950s the Nation recruited new members ravenously for its ever-expanding galaxy of mosques. On the street, in bars, pool halls, and back alleys, the Nation's ministers hustled to out-compete the Baptists, Methodists, and storefront Holiness churches that had dominated the religious landscape of northern cities until then. It found its most famous member in a Boston prison: Malcolm X. The Nation grew fast but it had trouble recruiting women because it treated Muslim women as second-class citizens. Ministers like Malcolm X habitually talked about women as "valuable property" that needed protecting. Not only did the Nation deny women privileges within the faith, but it tried to constrain their rights outside it, even barring women from exercising their constitutional right to use birth control.[19] In some respects, Christian churches weren't much better. According to Ella Baker, the average Black Baptist minister

Mortgage burning ceremony at a Minnesota church.

thought of women as pretty ornaments and faithful workers who carried out the minister's agenda. Everyone knew that a man always preached at the mortgage-burning, an event where the church celebrated paying off the loan that had financed their building, but often it was women who had cosigned on the promissory note that backed that mortgage and had raised the money to pay it off. Did women's contributions give them rights in their churches? Bishop Richard R. Wright thought so, reasoning that "'taxation without representation is tyranny' both in Church and State." By the 1940s some churchmen were starting to think that biblical commands such as "Let your women keep silence in the churches" were just excessive "legalism," unworkable "in a modern church." Women's rights in church ought to reflect what they did for the church.[20]

But what rights? Rights to religious property, pulpits, salaries, and emoluments, which were the only rights a court would protect, were all

Cartoon accompanying an article entitled "High-Flying 'Sky Pilot' Grounded as Deacons Take Him From Pulpit," Pittsburgh Courier, December 19, 1959. "Bedlam broke loose" after this Cleveland pastor, recently charged with adultery, mounted the pulpit to "humble" himself before the congregation. Note the irreverent use of the hallowed Black spiritual, soon to become an anthem of civil rights marchers.

attached to religious offices still dominated by men: trustees, ministers, bishops, elders. At the same time, the departure-from-faith doctrine—which awarded rights to those who, as the Supreme Court had ruled way back in Rev. Bouldin's case, stayed true to "the organization" and its "doctrines"—inevitably helped those same male officials during conflicts because they were the ones who got to tell judges what the true faith was. Yet men's power was not airtight, because, in the mid-twentieth century, Baptist and Holiness churches habitually put women in supposedly minor church offices. At First Baptist South Orange, where Thomas and Annie Holcomb were worshiping, the Keeper of Membership Records—the one who "knew everything"—was a woman named Lula Slackman. The *Bouldin* doctrine also told courts to enforce majority rule in congregational churches like the Baptists, and that gave women such as Slackman an indirect influence over church constitutionalism and the privileges it protected. By the 1950s, nearly eighty years after Rev. Bouldin had "made a rush for the Books and Papers of the church," with their precious lists of voting-eligible members, women often served as church clerks or secretaries, whose control of church records made them powerful players in intrachurch battles. (It is worth remembering that Rosa Parks, as the secretary of Montgomery's NAACP branch, kept the meeting minutes and membership list.) In 1968, when another pulpit dictator expelled trustee William Baugh from First Baptist South Orange, Baugh demanded the membership rolls as part of his lawsuit—rolls that happened to be kept by his cousin, Lula Slackman. He and his lawyer knew the same thing Henry Marsh counted on for his Richmond client: the *Bouldin* doctrine, which required judges to defer to the wishes of the majority of the members, meant that the Essex County court could reinstate him if valid members had been kept from voting. "Packing" the deacon board was an old game in Baptist churches, and activists had traded accusations of packing the Colored Conventions back in the 1830s, but as women became church secretaries, the deference doctrine may have let some women stack the *membership,* who were the church.[21]

In the 1940s and 1950s, just as the Supreme Court, Congress, and

"Church Ann[iversary] 1947." Undated photograph, inside First Baptist Church, South Orange, New Jersey. Deacon Robert Baskerville (my grandfather) is on the left. Ethel Reaves and Thomas and Annie Holcomb "fellowshipped" here after they moved to New Jersey but kept their membership at Midway Baptist (Virginia). Church anniversary celebrations like this one helped raise money, bonded members together, and ensured that legally important facts—some of which became crucial during lawsuits—became matters of public "notice." They were also just plain fun.

presidents Truman and Eisenhower were beginning to confront the problem of whether Black people had rights as American citizens, state judges and religious leaders once again confronted the problem of whether Black people had rights in their own religious bodies. The issue loomed large, not only because Black religious associations had grown in membership and property holding, but because changes in legal doctrine had cracked open a door to revisit the question at last. Some judges wanted to rethink the deference doctrine, which, they worried, was licensing "lawlessness," encouraging church tribunals to ignore the "substantive and procedural due process" that a court of law required. A federal district judge in Pennsylvania criticized the "almost absolute control" that AME bishops exerted over the "so-called trials" of an accused minister. Behind the veil of the First Amendment, the judge warned, churches were using " 'steamroller' tactics." An increasing number of religious leaders agreed. Churches were supposed to be ruled by their constitutions and disciplines, but what were Christians to do, asked an exasperated lawyer-member, if their pastor acted as if *he* were "the law, not the discipline"? Even *Watson v. Jones,* the 1871 touchstone case for deference, had drawn a line, saying that religious freedom must "not violate the laws of morality and property" nor "infringe personal rights." Now, warned Benjamin Mays in 1957, some leaders were using even more "crooked" methods to suppress their religious rivals than white Mississippi Democrats used to suppress Black voters. It was high time to stamp out church "dictatorship."[22]

For a moment in the 1950s and 1960s, amid mounting disgust with church centralization and "dictatorship," it seemed as if the law might finally turn the privileges of church membership into civil rights, justiciable in court. In 1953, after Rev. Joseph H. Jackson expelled more than four hundred people who had voted him out of the pulpit of Chicago's Olivet Baptist, his critics sued to vindicate "their rights as church members." Their years of faithfully giving "their time, their money, and their services" had made them like "stockholders" in a "religious corporation," the parishioners argued. And they had an even more significant investment in "the hand of fellowship," the communion with God that every member entered into when they joined a church, a communion that carried with it all the rights, privileges, and duties of membership, a communion whose loss, they believed, would "damn them to hell's fires." At First Baptist South Orange, William Baugh's young lawyer Benjamin Michel took that argument a step further, convinced that Baugh sincerely believed that his membership was "a precious thing" and that his expulsion was a "cause [that] needed to be addressed for other people as well." Alluding to "a great expansion of our concept of what is civil rights," Michel argued to the New Jersey supreme court in 1969 that Baugh's membership was "a 'property,' " just like land or money but "far more precious and valuable to him," and that, because of his investment in that property, he had "a 'civil right' to remain a member" until he either quit or was expelled under normal church rules.[23]

These ideas didn't come out of nowhere. Michel was obviously alluding to the Movement when he said that "our concept of what is civil rights" had expanded. But his main argument was about developments in private law. That is where the possibility of recognizing membership as a civil right lay. For decades, state courts had said that although membership in churches and other voluntary associations was not itself a civil right, it was "a valuable privilege," one that "indirectly" involved the civil right of property.[24] Then, in 1930, two of the country's most famous and influential law professors—Zechariah Chafee and Roscoe Pound, both of Harvard—had invited courts to reinterpret this judicial protection of membership as affirming something more than a privilege: as being itself a kind of "property rights." Moreover, the professors contended, this notion that members of associations had property rights in the association wasn't really much of a stretch. In the modern American economy, they pointed out, all kinds of valuable but intangible interests were coming to be seen as property: from corporation stock to patents and news, from "privacy" to "business goodwill," and, of course, a property in one's capacity to work. In other words, lawyer Michel reasoned in 1969, the modern impulse to think of everything as a kind of "property" implied that people might also have justiciable "rights" in church.[25] Everyone knew that members had privileges within their churches, but were those also civil rights? Extending law's protection to church membership, either as a share of property or an intangible spiritual interest, could have upended long-standing assumptions about the rights of laity in churches—a laity that was still composed mostly of women. Baugh won: "The opportunity to worship in familiar surroundings is a valuable right which deserves the protection of the law," the New Jersey supreme court held, more valuable even than "property or contract rights."[26]

But few other courts were willing to go that far. However much they worried about church "lawlessness," and however they felt about the civil rights movement, most midcentury judges rejected Baugh's argument that church membership itself was a legally protected "interest" or "civil right." If you were expelled, you lost whatever "interest" you had in your church. At the same time, courts hollowed out the meaning of religious due process, making it easier to expel members in the first place. Critics warned that if courts would not guarantee due process in church proceedings, if church constitutionalism was accountable only to church leaders, then members' privileges were worthless. Just when movement activists and lawyers were sharpening the term "civil rights" into a sword "specifically for the legal battle against Jim Crow"—just when a new body of secular law was arising to define and protect Black people's "civil rights" as racial subjects in the housing market and workplace, in schools and public accommodations—most judges returned to the idea that *within* churches, there were only privileges, to be defined outside the realm of the civil, according to church law.[27] And that idea tended to hurt members. Church members' inability to turn their privileges into rights that a court could protect cleared the way for ministers to centralize church and mosque authority in their hands, further disempowering a membership composed mostly of women.

Judges may have decided that members did not have rights in religious associations, but judges could not put the question to rest in the 1960s any more than they could in the 1870s. The question played out all over American religious life, and nowhere as prominently as in a pair of spectacular showdowns between America's most famous Black churchmen, Joseph H. Jackson and Martin Luther King Jr., over the presidency of the National Baptist Convention (NBC), the world's largest Black-owned institution. Today, only scholars of Black religion pay much attention to these confrontations, but in their own time they were front-page news in Black newspapers and a matter of serious concern among civil rights activists. Politically, the battle between Jackson and King was over whether the NBC, which is the corporation that oversees the entire Black Baptist denomination, should throw its weight behind the Black freedom struggle. Legally, it was a larger version of the same battle that had always driven church lawsuits: the right of members to control the NBC's assets, to examine its books, and to vote in its elections. The conflict over the NBC presidency drew from both men's own legal experiences and from the distinctive discourse developed since the Civil War about rights within Black churches.

Charges of "czarism" and "iron rule" had dogged the NBC for a long time before King tried to topple Jackson from its presidency. The Baptists finally wrote a four-year term limit into their Convention's constitution in 1953, just before Jackson was first elected. Four years later, presiding over the 1957 meeting, Jackson abruptly announced that the term-limit amendment was void because of a technicality, and that he was therefore eligible for reelection after all. "All hell broke loose," one of the reformers remembered. A whole day before the election was scheduled to take place, Jackson's allies "swept into the auditorium," thumping a "bass drum" and waving "Jackson for President" banners." As "ministers broke down and wept," shouting " 'No, no, no,' " the Jacksonites seized the microphone, and moved to "suspend the rules and re-elect our president by acclamation" immediately. Ten ministers sued Jackson in federal court, hoping that a secular judge might correct what they saw as a breakdown in the Baptists' normal democratic process, much the same way Henry Marsh had gotten a court-ordered church trial for his client in Richmond. Their lawsuit went nowhere and Jackson had them expelled "for taking court action." The 1958 election repeated the charade. Jackson was "hoisted aloft" by "wildly cheering delegates," who immediately voted him "a money tree complete with $3,000 worth of crisp new bills on it and a new Chrysler." A generation before, Booker T. Washington's personal lawyer had warned NBC leaders that incorporating their organization could eventually turn Baptists into "a denominational oligarchy."[28] Now that prophecy seemed to be coming true.

At the NBC's 1960 convention in Philadelphia, Martin Luther King led a reform faction that upstaged Jackson's supporters with a convention "sit-in" and savvy media interviews. They won a court order to force an accounting of the NBC's assets as well as a real election, rather than

Joseph H. Jackson, President of the National Baptist Convention, at the podium during the Convention election of 1960.

the "old convention trick" of having a single candidate affirmed by a roar of "acclamation." And the reform candidate, Gardner Taylor, won in a landslide. But Jackson's legal team got that court-ordered election overturned. For days, flanked by several of America's leading Black lawyers, some of them fresh from victory in *Brown v. Board of Education,* the two sides pelted each other with court filings, each claiming to represent the real majority and accusing the other of being a disruptive "small faction." The conflict kept boiling. At the next year's convention, in Kansas City, King's reformers tried again to remove Jackson. This time the floor fight ended in tragedy when an elderly delegate fell off the high stage and broke his neck. In the stunned aftermath, Jackson was again reelected, and he vindictively blamed King for the accident and stripped his NBC title (vice president of the Sunday School Board) from him. Once all the lawsuits were dismissed, leaving Jackson in full control, he moved to keep members from taking governance questions to court ever again: he had the NBC's constitution amended to make "the Convention itself" an unappealable "supreme court."[29]

Jackson has gone down in history as a Baptist dictator, the law-and-order conservative who kept the world's biggest Black religious organization on the sidelines of the Black freedom struggle. But Jackson was not a straightforward reactionary. He had a deep faith in law's power to advance Black interests, a faith rooted in his youth in the Jim Crow South, when Black people had exercised common-law civil rights routinely. His criticism of the civil rights movement was quite specific: lunch-counter sit-ins and tenement take-overs undermined "property rights" without regard for the owners' right to "due process." The U.S. Supreme Court worried about the same thing. So did NAACP Legal Defense Fund executive director Thurgood Marshall, who, as recounted in Chapter 11, half-jokingly called the lunch-counter sit-inners "a bunch of crazy colored students who violated the sacred property rights of white folks." To Jackson, civil disobedience was "a form of lawlessness . . . not far removed from open crime," indistinguishable from the practices that sustained segregation. And there was no better proof of the lawlessness of civil disobedience, Jackson warned, than the chaotic NBC meetings of 1960 and 1961.[30]

Why did Jackson have such faith in civil rights of everyday use? Because in his experience and that of his predecessors in the Baptist leadership, they *worked.* Jackson had been attuned to the power of property, contract, and the law of religious associations since he first stepped into a pulpit in 1925. As other Black religious leaders had done since the early 1800s, Jackson wrote thick books stuffed with long stories about church lawsuits, verbatim copies of decades-old court orders, and letters from lawyers. Just as denomination leaders urged ministers to "know the law thoroughly," Jackson's first move on being elected NBC president in 1953 had been to embark on "a thorough study of . . . the constitution and by laws," its "charter of incorporation," and its "legal relationship" to its "auxiliary corporations . . . state conventions, individual churches, and [their] members." Jackson's grasp of both religious and secular legal rules gave him a keen intuition about what judges would do in church disputes, and this enabled him to strike the pose that *Bouldin* told judges to look for: the pose of the orthodox adherent, the church constitutionalist, the one who stayed true "to our governing document." Like the trustees who sued Albert Bouldin in 1867, Jackson blithely ignored the contradiction of using a lawsuit to condemn others for "going to law." By making the NBC leadership an unappealable "supreme court," he turned the deference doctrine into a justification of Baptist dictatorship, horrifying those who thought that preachers must answer not only to God but also to their congregations.[31]

Jackson's faith in the civil rights of everyday use was constantly reinforced by ideas and practices that were almost generic in twentieth-century Black religious life. It may have begun even before he became a minister. Born around 1900 in tiny Rudyard, Mississippi, Jackson had seen plenty of poverty and white supremacist violence growing up. He also saw his father "inherit[] forty acres of land from an aunt," which gave the Jacksons a degree of independence. This experience probably instilled in him a lifelong faith in what he later called the power of "production" and, perhaps, a sense that some kinds of law could work *for* Black people, without fuss or protest marches. Jackson was not alone in that faith. Black civil plaintiffs crowded Mississippi's trial courts when he was young, including the one in Jackson's home county, Coahoma, where nearly one-third of the civil cases I sampled for 1902, 1912, and 1922 had Black plaintiffs. Those twin faiths in Black-owned property and the efficacy of private law would have been reinforced as Jackson moved into the Black religious world of the early 1900s, where leaders extolled building associations ("the poor man's antidote") and "accumulating property." Such things were supposed to shift the terms of the "color line" debate. "If we would help control the country, we must help own it," Savannah's Rev. E. K. Love had preached in 1891. "Buy land . . . Be a free holder, and no powers on earth can keep you down."[32] The language of contract and property resounded in Black churches throughout Jackson's lifetime, in mortgage-burning ceremonies, gospel songs, and sermons that described Christian salvation as forming "an uncancellable contract" "on record in heaven." When Martin Luther King criticized a sheriff's abuse of the injunction, when he stood at the Lincoln Memorial in 1963 and described the Declaration of Independence and Constitution as "a promissory note to which every American was to fall heir," when he entitled his last published essay "A Testament of Hope," he was taking an inward-looking tradition forged in Jim Crow–era Black churches, a tradition rooted in ideas of property, contract, and associational privileges, and redirecting it toward race relations. These were more than metaphors. They were civil rights, powerful but ill-fitted categories into which religious people knew they had to squeeze their most precious interests if they wanted help from a court.[33]

In short, when Jackson refused to enlist Black Baptists in the freedom struggle, when he elevated "a gospel of soy beans" over the gospel of nonviolent resistance and desegregation, he was revealing a deep faith in the ordinary workings of private law, a faith that still resonated among many middle-class African Americans, from Baptist ministers to Black nationalists. For him and many others, the best strategy for African Americans to win respect and "economic independence" was to exercise common-law civil rights, the kind of rights they so proudly hailed at mortgage burnings and annual conventions. But within churches, the country's biggest "all-Negro" institutions, he seemed to insist, civil rights did not apply—only the associational privileges of status did, which no secular court could protect.[34]

There is no denying that Jackson was an autocrat, frequently vengeful and petty.[35] There is also no doubt that he had a vision of civil rights. And, in fact, if we move from the heady scene of national conventions back to the level of a single church, that vision doesn't look so different from the vision of his famous opponent, Martin Luther King. King was first called to the pulpit at Dexter Avenue Baptist Church, in Montgomery, Alabama, and he began his pastorate with a showdown over authority. Dexter was famous at the time as a "deacons' church," where ministers were unusually vulnerable. King had been warned about this by his own father and by Dexter's most recently booted pastor, Vernon Johns. So, on his first Sabbath as pastor, September 5, 1954, King announced a breathtaking plan to reorganize every part of the church, place it firmly under his authority, and strip "voting privileges" from members who did not contribute to the church's finance. "Leadership," he declared that morning, "descends from the pulpit to the pew," and so long as the minister did not take "unnecessary dictatorial authority," he had to "be respected and accepted as the central figure around which the policies and programs of the church revolve." It was a "coup," the kind of thing that had sparked lawsuits, but in this case it worked beautifully. Dexter's membership swung in behind him.[36]

King's persona is so closely associated with the transformation of public law in the landmark civil rights statutes of the 1960s that it has obscured how deeply private law informed his ideas about rights. Like any other church, Dexter's property—from robes to pews to the building itself—was held by its trustees, who also signed employment contracts with its pastors and mortgages with its lenders. It had had its share of lawsuits over the years. In 1932, for example, Dexter could not pay its pastor's salary and had avoided a messy lawsuit only by selling the church's car. Just nine years before King arrived, the deacons had gone to court to shoo out another pastor—the one before Vernon Johns—for abusing his wife, and had had to sidestep that pastor's by-now-familiar defense—that courts could only judge "temporalities"—by calling in an expert witness on Baptist rules. So, when King took the pulpit at Dexter, he was stepping into a very old, ongoing debate over members' rights in that particular religious association. A year later, early the morning after Rosa Parks's arrest, when E. D. Nixon phoned asking permission to hold a meeting of about fifty of Montgomery's Black leaders in Dexter's basement to discuss a massive and dangerous bus boycott, King's muscular view of ministerial leadership gave him the confidence to simply say yes.[37]

As King became the public face of the civil rights movement, he articulated a powerful vision of law, one that not only built on the writings of

Martin Luther King Jr. behind the pulpit at his church in Montgomery, Alabama. Notice the preponderance of women in the pews.

Henry David Thoreau and Mohandas Gandhi but also justified his view of the minister's authority in a religious corporation. A church was governed by rules, he preached in 1966, just as school districts were. Just as the brand-new Civil Rights Act cut off federal funds to any school district that discriminated by race, "the funds of grace" would be "cut off from the divine treasury" if church members failed to "follow the guidelines." And "the guidelines made it very clear that God anointed" the pastor to run his church. King answered critics who felt "they talk too much about civil rights in that church" with an even more forceful declaration of the pastor's calling than he had dared when he first came to the Dexter pulpit in 1954. He told the congregation of Atlanta's Ebenezer Baptist Church, where he had been hired to be co-pastor with his father, that he would not "pay any attention" to such criticism from members because the members did not anoint the minister to preach. "You called me to Ebenezer, and you may turn me out of here, but you can't turn me out of the ministry," King declared, "because I got my guidelines and my anointment from God Almighty. And *anything* I want to say, I'm going to say it from this pulpit. It may hurt somebody, I don't know about that; somebody may not agree with it. But when *God* speaks, who can but prophesy? The word of God is upon me like *fire* shut up in my bones, and when *God's* word gets upon me, I've got to say it, I've got to tell it all over *every*where. And God has called me to deliver those that are in captivity." There was no chance that Ebenezer was going to fire Martin Luther King Jr. in 1966. Yet for generations, churches had been turning out ministers who hurt or steamrollered members in the name of God Almighty. If King had not been so famous, Ebenezer might have tried to turn him out, too. Many Baptists, including Joseph Jackson, believed that God had *not* called their ministers "to deliver those that are in captivity"—not in the way King claimed. Ironically, to make sure his church was on the front line of the fight for democracy and equality in America, King fashioned his own ministry in undemocratic ways, daring his critics to divide "the word of God" from the man who spoke it and exploiting the principle, developed partly through Black church cases, that civil rights did not apply to churches' internal affairs. Today, if anyone remembers Jackson, it is as the Baptist dictator who kept the Black church out of the freedom struggle. But because King became the most famous leader of the freedom struggle, almost nobody remembers the anti-democratic tradition lurking in his dealings with his congregations.[38]

In the Nation of Islam, the long argument over members' rights and ministers' authority curdled into violence. The Nation's leader, Elijah Muhammad, had amassed power in ways Joseph Jackson could only dream of. This was manifest in his treatment of Malcolm X, his onetime disciple whom he came to see, by the early 1960s, as a threat to his leadership. Muhammad used his arbitrary and "untouchable" authority to silence Malcolm. The Nation's own rules said that an accused minister had a "right to a judicial hearing before members of his own mosque," but when Malcolm insisted on having his day in Muslim court, Elijah Muhammad refused, tacitly inviting Muslims to inflict the thuggish punishments meted out to any member who violated his personal version of the Nation's "law." Not only that, but the Nation asserted its civil right of property, suing to evict Malcolm and his family from their parsonage home in Queens, New York. Malcolm bitterly criticized the Nation for "bringing me . . . to the white man's court" rather than "a Muslim court."[39]

But Malcolm was no fool: he went to the white man's court, too, to protect his civil rights as a citizen of New York. There he argued that, as "one of 'the original incorporators' " of Mosque Number 7 and a minister suspended but not expelled, he still had the right to live in the parsonage. Like C. P. Jones, the minister whose faith healings at Mt. Helm Baptist in the 1890s touched off the explosion of Holiness Pentecostalism across the Deep South, Malcolm's actions in 1963 and 1964 sparked a struggle within the Nation over orthodoxy, and over the power to say *what* was orthodox, a struggle that lurched from religious tribunals to secular courts and back again. Like Jones, like generations of Black Christians, both Elijah Muhammad and Malcolm X freely resorted to both religious and secular authorities as they argued over who was entitled to call himself a Muslim. Stripped of his mosque and rethinking his own worldview, Malcolm left the Nation of Islam and filed incorporation papers for a new group, Muslim Mosque, Inc. (MMI), preparing, as so many others had done since the 1790s, to seed a new faith: this time oriented around orthodox Sunni Islam. But before that faith could take root, Elijah Muhammad had Malcolm murdered.[40]

From Muslims to Baptists to Methodists, the ultimate challenge religious leaders faced in the 1960s was that once they started fusing the language of "civil rights" to the cause of Black freedom, they could not fully control what members did with it.[41] Working-class Chicagoans described contract buying as a biblical confrontation; through their grassroots Contract Buyers League, they urged one another to "take up your bed and walk," like Lazarus, downtown to fight their crooked landlords. "C.B.L. is built on solid rock," members said, alluding to a well-known hymn, and their meetings were "just like church." At one

Mississippi church, a member whose name was on the deed "threatened to take the church away" unless the congregation let voting-rights organizers come in. At another, a member bluntly asserted the rights of a corporate shareholder, ordering the deacons to open the doors for civil rights activities by reminding them that "she had put more money in the church than anyone else." There is nothing surprising about Black people mixing rights talk with religious rhetoric to challenge racial injustice. But once King had supplied a morally charged rhetoric of "civil rights" as *racial* justice, parishioners seized it for their ongoing debate about *church* justice, as when Vernita Wimbush threatened to reenact the March on Washington in front of her bishop's house to keep the pastor they wanted. When Black church members "got together to see what [they] could do as Christians," they sometimes redirected the outward-looking rhetoric of Black freedom toward the internal problems of their churches.[42]

And yet, by the time Wimbush wrote to her bishop, the public meaning of "civil rights" had become firmly associated with federal law and the anti-discrimination principle, its scope and logic articulated in *Brown v. Board of Education* (1954) and the Civil Rights Act of 1964. The powerhouse lawyers of the NBC suits are hailed today as civil rights trailblazers for their work in the areas of desegregation, job discrimination, criminal justice, and voting, even though they spent some, if not most, of their careers litigating the kinds of rights Wimbush was demanding. A horrific 1963 Ku Klux Klan bombing turned Birmingham's Sixteenth Street Baptist into a monument to the sacred cause of Black freedom, but almost nobody remembers Lizzie Jenkins's challenge, forty-two years earlier, against "church injustice" in that same church. The things we remember about that era—and the things we forget—reflect our modern concept of civil rights, a concept built on an implicit divide between public and private law, between the rights of racial subjects and those of religious subjects. That divide arose from many sources, not just the shifts within Black churches and mosques. But it perpetuated the gendered problems of authority and rights that had plagued Black religious associations for generations. It belied the creative ways that Black people had built a mass movement on the foundation of property, contract, and the law of associations. It defied the wishes of myriad worshipers such as Wimbush and Jenkins and Baugh, who kept asking courts to vindicate their rights in their churches. It keeps us from seeing the full range of what civil rights did in the past—and what they might do now.[43]

13

The New Property

From the 1940s to the 1970s, just as the disparate strands of Black protest that had long tugged against the Jim Crow system coalesced into the Movement, there was another, quieter shift in Black life: a revolution in property. It was driven by many factors. The streams of migration out of the South, which had added several hundred thousand Black people to places like Harlem and Los Angeles during the 1920s and 1930s, now widened to a flood, more than a million almost every decade from 1940 to 1980.[1] Equally crucial were far-reaching changes in the law and culture of property in America. Just as the end of slavery had made it possible for Jackson Holcomb to own land and not just coins and a rowboat, the Civil Rights era once again changed the *kinds* of property Black people owned: from farms to apartments, and from tangible goods like farms and mules to intangibles such as government entitlements, employee benefits, and even intellectual property. Many of these things weren't quite "property," in the traditional sense. Some of them weren't even things. At the same time, the Great Migration changed *how* Black people owned property, putting hundreds of miles between family land back in places like Cumberland and the people who had a stake in it, like Thomas and Annie Holcomb. In some cases, family land that had lasted generations suddenly went out of the family and got carved up for golf courses or housing developments. In cities, Black homebuyers found themselves drowning in exploitative installment-purchase contracts.

As activists and legal professionals in the mid-twentieth century tried to make sense of all this, two stories emerged. One was about deep structural flaws in the law, what we might today call "systemic racism." The other was cultural, a story about people rich in folk wisdom but so alienated from the legal system that they were ignorant of their rights. To be sure, some activists and lawyers—such as Thurgood Marshall—still appealed to Black people's "goat sense." But more and more during the 1960s and 1970s they attributed Black people's lack of economic opportunity to a combination of structural oppression and Black legal ignorance and alienation. This required downplaying evidence that Black people did have working knowledge of property law.[2] It required downplaying the differences between white lawyers who steamrollered Blacks out of land and those who helped them keep it. It focused on an ideal of "the Black family" rather than the complex reality of privileges and duties within actual Black families. And it involved ignoring the fact

Thomas Holcomb, Annie Reaves Holcomb, and Yolanda Reaves, undated photo probably taken in South Orange.

that sometimes, when Black people said they had been cheated out of their land, the people they accused were their own relatives.

These twin revolutions—the civil rights revolution and the revolution in property—completed the long journey of "civil rights" toward its familiar, modern meaning. Black people's cases had played a significant role in the development of contract law and property law during the nineteenth century, and law school casebooks in the Jim Crow era had included cases involving Black people and other racial minorities, often with overtly racist language. By the 1970s, though, casebooks had scrubbed those overt racial references from the old cases, or simply cut out the cases altogether. Law professors, judges, and lawyers continued to cite and discuss them and other cases involving Black people—but without mentioning that Black people were involved. Similar to the way some "colored" people were allowed to "pass" as white, "'colored' cases" were "passed" silently into the heart of private law and naturalized as white. Contract and property law came to seem "white," except in a few niches of legal doctrine that were portrayed as being "about race."[3] And civil rights became "Black."

Sitting in my great-great-uncle Tom's house in 1976, my uncle Craig asked why they left Virginia. It turned out Uncle Tom hadn't wanted to leave. He had promised to take care of his father. "But times got so tough," he recalled, "couldn't get no money." In 1927, he sold his things, gave his car to his brother Robert, and came up north to work on a farm in Monmouth County, New Jersey. Then Annie and her parents (Willie and Mary Frances Reaves) went north, and the four of them settled in South Orange, just outside Newark. Later, Annie's younger brother Johnny and his wife Lena moved in with them, along with her brother Eugene and his two children, Osborne and Yolanda, after Eugene and Ethel Reaves separated. They all lived in a little apartment at 51 Church Street, a couple of blocks from Annie's other brother, Irving, and near the town's main Black church, First Baptist. Yolanda slept in the dining room most nights. Ozzie doubled up with Eugene. On Thursdays, when the town's maids usually had the night off, the children would be bundled off to some other relative's house, then Johnny or Eugie or Irving would go pick up Cousin Lottie, and the grownups would settle down with a bottle of gin and blow off steam.[4] South Orange wasn't segregated—at least, not officially. There weren't any "white" or "colored" signs on the water fountains. Many of the neighbors were Italian immigrants. Ozzie and Yolanda went to school and made friends with white children in the 1930s and, twenty years later, so did Yolanda's children, Craig and Penelope. Somehow, though, they never got invited over to any of the white children's homes. Somehow, most of the women in the family worked for white people as maids, the men as butlers, car washers, and chauffeurs. And somehow, most of South Orange's small Black population lived within a few short blocks of one another.

As described in Part III, whites reacted to the Great Migration by writing explicitly racist rules into property law, trying to "save the neighborhood" by keeping out Black migrants like the Holcombs. But the story of zoning and restrictive covenants goes far beyond racial segregation. Black property owners used those legal devices to pursue their own interests as they saw them. While open-housing activists sought to end housing discrimination, other Black people tried to channel it. They formed all-Black homeowners' associations to keep out "riff-raff bars" and nightclubs, boarding houses, multifamily homes and the "rowdy" welfare recipients who lived in them, and even "ghetto churches." Black homeowners did not dispute that cities should zone off certain areas as "blighted"—the infamous euphemism for what James Baldwin called "Negro removal." They just wanted city planners to stop funneling all of the low-income housing and prostitution into *their* neighborhoods.[5] "When you're black, anybody else who is black can move in beside you," one Baltimorean lamented, because real estate speculators "don't care whether people are able to take care of the house or not," whether they are "high class people" or "poor class" or even "the kind of people who" would throw bottles into the street. The lament was about "neighborhood

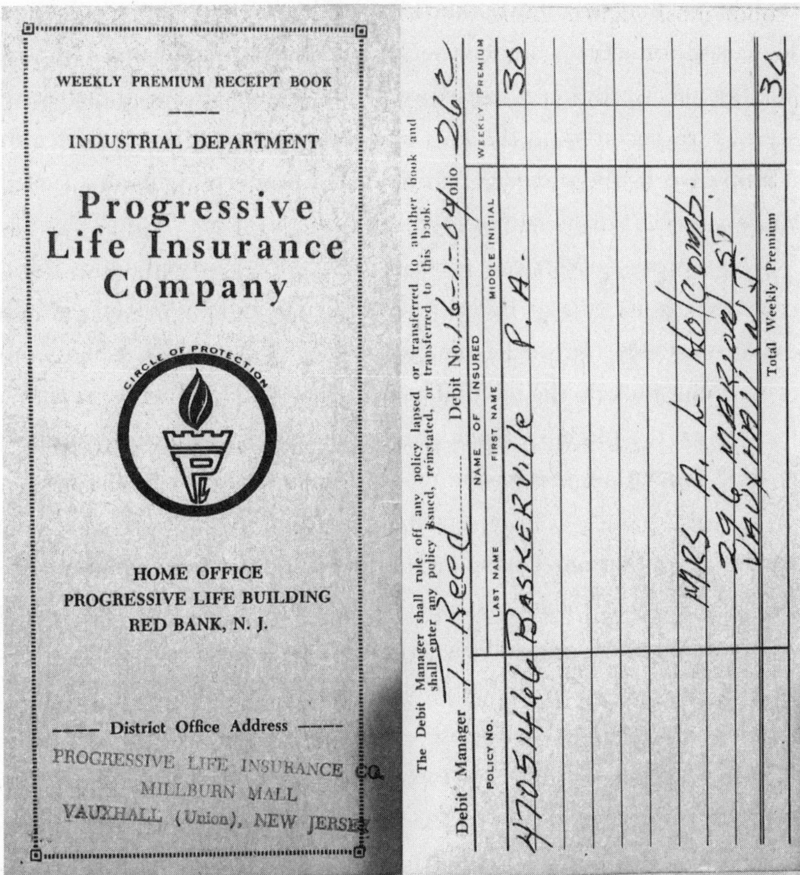

WEEKLY PREMIUM RECEIPT BOOK

INDUSTRIAL DEPARTMENT

Progressive
Life Insurance
Company

CIRCLE OF PROTECTION

HOME OFFICE
PROGRESSIVE LIFE BUILDING
RED BANK, N. J.

District Office Address

PROGRESSIVE LIFE INSURANCE CO.
MILLBURN MALL
VAUXHALL (Union), NEW JERSEY

The Debit Manager shall rule off any policy lapsed or transferred to another book and shall enter any policy issued, reinstated, or transferred to this book.

Debit Manager I. Reed Debit No. 16-1-04 Folio 262

POLICY NO.	NAME OF INSURED LAST NAME	FIRST NAME	MIDDLE INITIAL	WEEKLY PREMIUM
4705146	Baskerville	P. A.		30
	MRS A. L Holcomb 296 Marion St. Vauxhall N.J.		Total Weekly Premium	30

Annie Holcomb's insurance book. Entries are for March and April 1966, when her grandniece, Penelope Baskerville, was a sophomore in college.

character," a pleasant-sounding term that masks an aggressive idea of property rights, in that it asserts that a homeowner has a right to control things far beyond the walls of her own home, beyond what the law on the books actually says. Today, "neighborhood character" is almost a shorthand for white racism, a justification for everything from the Detroit mob that drove out Ossian Sweet's family in 1925 to the college-town liberals who have repeatedly blocked affordable housing in the 2010s in order to preserve backyard vegetable gardens and supposedly "historic" bungalows. But "neighborhood character" has no necessary connection to racism. Some Black homeowners have historically appealed to it, too, and not necessarily because they wanted to preserve Black culture or be seen as "respectable" in the eyes of a racist society.[6] They appealed to it motivated by the same aggressive idea of property rights that fueled white defenders of "neighborhood character."

This history—of African Americans in the 1950s and 1960s using covenants, zoning, and homeowner associations to ward off "ghetto blight"—quickly vanished from public memory. In 1968, when Congress finally took up the bill that became the Fair Housing Act, senators focused on the plight of Black professionals who were trapped in "the ghetto." Once Congress passed that bill, cause lawyers refashioned the grievances of Black homebuyers and apartment dwellers into claims of racial discrimination.[7] Politicians, lawyers, and movement activists overlooked how middle-class Black people had sometimes redirected their associational privileges and civil right of property against poor Black people, and they enshrined in public memory the struggle between the forces of "white flight" and those who fought for "full equality in housing." In doing so, they narrowed both the concept of civil rights and the complex reality of mid-century Black life to a story of simple justice.

The growing tendency to conflate civil rights with nondiscrimination also obscured how African Americans were adapting to shifts in the very nature of property itself. These shifts were just as profound as redlining and covenants, and were provoking complicated debates among Black people about the meaning of family and of community. Claiming resources like Social Security and fringe benefits pulled African Americans toward new areas of law and new legal institutions. They had to get acquainted with new legal language ("dependents" and "entitlements") and with lawyers and bureaucrats and company "personnel departments," some of whom encouraged them to think of these resources as "rights."[8] For many, it meant reaching across state lines to gather written documentation of their status and family relations, or to legalize relations that had never been documented at all. In 1964, Annie Reaves

Holcomb, now living in Vauxhall, New Jersey, gathered these official documents to get her Social Security card: a form from the Cumberland County, Virginia, circuit clerk certifying her marriage to Thomas Holcomb in 1915; a transcript page from the Census Bureau; and a Delayed Certificate of Birth from the Virginia Bureau of Vital Statistics. This was probably the most intense bout of bureaucratic dealings she had had in her life. When her card finally came, she kept it, just as the instructions said to do, along with all the documents that had gone into getting it, until the day she died. Her monthly benefit was $64.80 (about $749 in 2021 dollars). That was smaller than what most white men got, and she only got to enjoy it a few years before she died, but applying for Social Security drew her just as surely into the new legal rules and culture. So did insurance. Like generations before her, my great-great aunt tried to hedge the costs of mortality. Every week, an industrial life insurance collector came to her door, and she paid a nickel on a policy insuring her grandniece, Penelope Baskerville. She kept her premium book carefully, since a lapsed policy would mean forfeiting the payout. It wasn't a longing for soul food or the simple life that made the bluesman Sonny Boy Williamson sing: "I don't live up North; my home is back down in Tennessee." It was something much more mundane: he was begging a door-to-door "insurance man" not to cancel his burial policy.[9]

A new cadre of professionals arose to administer these benefits and their daunting technicalities. Like the quasi-lawyers of the 1880s and 1900s, the HR reps and welfare bureaucrats of the 1950s, 1960s, and 1970s met Black people on the muddy ground between popular understanding and official written rules. Big companies and universities established personnel departments to oversee the growing array of employee benefits like pensions, health insurance, and tuition remission. By 1980, workers at large and medium-sized companies received almost one-third of their pay in the form of such benefits.[10] Although it was stigmatized as the "boring" domain of "the personnel gal," an office far down the corporate ladder, sharp-eyed observers realized that Personnel—eventually renamed "Human Resources"—was becoming crucial, if only because employee benefits ate up so much of "the almighty bottom line." And in a field that was feminizing fast, a disproportionate number of Human Resources workers were Black women: 12 percent of the clerks and frontline personnel specialists by 1980, and 9 percent of the personnel managers.[11] One of them was my mother—Annie Holcomb's grandniece—Penelope Baskerville, who worked as a personnel representative at Princeton University and then Rider College. Although white male CEOs and white female HR vice presidents still made the big decisions (setting benefits, choosing the company health plan), frontline benefits workers like Baskerville kept track of the deadlines and patiently explained the glossy brochures that went out every year to shipyard and cafeteria workers and college professors, just as the insurance man had done for her great-aunt Annie twenty years earlier. As she put it in the Rider newsletter: "We make sure the benefits work the way they're supposed to."[12] Like the quasi-lawyers described in Chapter 7—the knowledgeable nonprofessionals who encouraged Mary Woodson in 1892 to "seek[] into the law" when her white relatives tried to snatch her inheritance, and like Sam Jennings, who urged Felix Brown to get back his fraudulently taken land, saying "he knew what law was and that he could tell me how to work it"—people like my mother helped turn benefits into something like property.[13]

But benefits were not property. Neither was a welfare check or a McDonald's franchise or an airline subsidy or a real estate broker's license or most of the other kinds of valuables that Americans increasingly relied on. They could not be sold, passed down to loved ones, or borrowed against except in limited circumstances. They could be hedged with conditions, withheld, or revoked entirely.[14] My mother's tuition-grant benefit helped put me through college but she knew it lasted only as long as she kept her job at Rider. Moreover, these new licenses, privileges, and entitlements were not all created equal. Some enjoyed protection because they were held by powerful corporations, such as Delta Airlines and CBS, or powerful white individuals, like James Eastland, the Mississippi lawyer-senator (see Chapter 11), who, in just the year 1967, was paid $170,000 worth of federal subsidies *not* to farm his land. Other kinds of privileges and benefits were treated as sacrosanct because they were associated with white people: Social Security, GI Bill benefits, the homeowner's tax deduction. And still others—especially welfare benefits and public housing—were denigrated as "handouts," liable to be cut without warning, because they were associated with racial minorities.

As Johnnie Tillmon, head of the National Welfare Rights Organization pointed out, calling these resources "handouts" hurt the people who relied on them the most. Worse, contended Yale Law School professor Charles Reich, the vast expansion of these valuables—whether they were denigrated as "handouts" or applauded as "entitlements"—was corrupting officials, stunting research, stifling the free market, and eroding the Bill of Rights. Reich called for the law to recognize these valuables as a new kind of property: "the New Property." He argued that welfare and other government benefits ought to be given all of the safeguards of traditional property: protection against being arbitrarily deprived of it without due process, the right to spend it freely, and the right to keep it if one changed jobs or moved to a new state.[15] Inspired by Reich's theory, and building on earlier efforts by bureaucrats in the 1930s, activists and cause lawyers in the 1960s won a string of what they called "welfare rights" cases.

Turning benefits and privileges into rights came at a cost, especially in the context of welfare. As the historian Karen Tani puts it, welfare put recipients under the pitiless gaze of state and county officials—required them to be "*seen,* in one's most private spaces"—often by the very same insiders who ran courthouse square. For example, the rules specified that women could lose their welfare benefits if they had a man in the house, or if they earned too much, so county welfare workers routinely poked into closets and medicine cabinets and then wrote up reports for the administrative-law judges who supposedly safeguarded "due process" in welfare cases. Of course, nobody snooped around Senator Eastland's bedroom, because crop subsidies were not seen as "welfare." For Black people, whose resources tended to be disproportionately composed of the most tenuous forms of the New Property, the eclipse of the "old" property was a mixed blessing. Future Supreme Court Justice Clarence Thomas felt that welfare "takes away your manhood." Johnnie Tillmon contended that it actually entrenched a new kind of patriarchy—"you trade in *a* man for *the* man." Despite their radically different politics, both Black feminists like Tillmon and would-be Black patriarchs like Thomas decried what government largess did to Black people's status and authority within the family.[16]

The New Property included much more than welfare. In 1885, as we saw, the Atlanta city council had tried to break up a laundry-workers' strike by imposing a licensing requirement, and the Washerwomen's Association had creatively reinterpreted the new requirement as "a protection, so we can control the washing for the city"—a franchise. Eighty years later, a new generation of African Americans sought to turn a new kind of franchise—the business franchise—into an engine of Black freedom. Pioneered in the 1950s by chain companies like McDonald's and Motel 6, the business franchise was a private legal structure that enabled a company to outsource risk while centralizing control. Rather than own its restaurants, McDonald's left restaurant ownership to thousands of individual "franchisees." Each "franchisee" signed a contract that granted him the right to operate a store under the McDonald's trademark, on the condition that he follow a thick binder full of rules covering everything from the size of the big yellow-and-red sign out front to the temperature of the French fries. After McDonald's belatedly started granting franchises to Black businesspeople in the late 1960s, some of the most successful and visible Black entrepreneurs in the nation emerged from the fast-food business, among them Charles Griffis, who ran a fleet of Los Angeles–area McDonald's outlets under his C. M. Griffis, Inc., umbrella.[17] In 1970, the Black entrepreneur seemed like a natural sequel to the freedom struggle: an engine of Black empowerment, roaring with the promise of jobs and much-needed revenue for Black neighborhoods.

Franchising gave McDonald's enormous control over franchise-owners and over the people who worked in its restaurants, while at the same time letting the company dodge the normal legal consequences of that control. When a store failed, the franchisee took the hit, not the McDonald's Corporation itself. Cooks and greeters could not form a union to bargain with McDonald's because, even though their paper hats and nametags said "McDonald's," they actually worked for the franchisee. And McDonald's invariably plunked Black franchisees, as Griffis put it, "right in the middle of the ghetto," where the risks and costs were highest. McDonald's could treat Black franchisees this way—even incorporated ones like Griffis—because a franchise was a contract, not a property. The only truly valuable asset was the brand—the big golden arches—and that belonged to the McDonald's Corporation. As bright as franchising had seemed in 1970, over the next thirty years Black-owned fast-food franchises looked more and more like a drain funneling wealth out of Black neighborhoods. The franchisees themselves charged that McDonald's kept them "imprisoned in the ghetto," and, as the historian Marcia Chatelain has shown, they enlisted Movement tactics and rhetoric to try to break out. Al Sharpton and Jesse Jackson led a protest march. Griffis sued McDonald's for racial discrimination. By the 2010s, it was clear that nothing was coming to "inner city" neighborhoods but minimum-wage jobs, nutritional crisis, and gauzy Black History Month ads in *Ebony* magazine. The business franchise was a powerful example of the swelling importance of the New Property in American life, but most of its benefits flowed upward, away from Black franchisees and their workers.[18]

Meanwhile, a handful of Black artists, ministers, and associations increasingly asserted rights to a kind of valuable that was rapidly consolidating into something called "intellectual property." Fighting over "IP" sounded even less like a civil rights struggle than fighting for the right to open a McDonald's store. The language of racial justice rang especially hollow here precisely because, much as in Black church disputes, the rise of Black-owned management companies ensured that some of the nastiest intellectual-property disputes would erupt *between* African Americans. Berry Gordy—who once accused white executives of offering him "a slave contract"—repeatedly swindled his business partners and singers at Motown Records.[19] Chuck Berry was sued by his own pianist. Intellectual-property disputes shook Black-owned corporations far beyond Motown. Church schisms spawned lawsuits not only over membership but also over naming rights: just like "Coca-Cola" in the soft-drink market or "Cadillac" in the car market, a name such as "House of Prayer for All People" was a valuable trademark in a competitive religious marketplace. Martin Luther King Jr. sued to stop people from selling bootleg recordings of his speeches, and, after he was assassinated, one of the first things his grieving SCLC colleagues did was form "a legal committee" to control the use of his name and image. (That effort continues today. In 2014, the makers of the movie *Selma* had to invent speeches for him because they could not obtain a license from the King estate to use his words.)[20] Entering the modernizing American workplace and its national commerce did not make Black people rich, but it pressed them up against the limits of what rights of everyday use could do.

Nearly everyone was affected by the shift toward the New Property in one way or another. African Americans experienced it differently, however, because of the race discrimination baked into the institutions that created it. The 1935 Social Security Act rescued millions of elderly Americans and their families from poverty, but at the request of key senators and congressmen from the South, it excluded domestic workers and farm workers. Nationwide, that left out 40 percent of whites and 65 percent of Black people—up to 80 percent in some parts of the South. Because Social Security intentionally left African Americans out in the cold, Black property owners may have had to rely longer than whites did on the risky strategy of securing old-age care by promising future gifts—the promise that "someday all this will be yours."[21] The racist exclusions built into Social Security may also have ratcheted up pressure on Black northerners to cash out their interests in family land down South. After

World War II, the GI Bill paid for millions of new homes, provided start-up money for millions of farms and new businesses, sent a huge wave of students to college, and paid for the training of hundreds of thousands of doctors, scientists, and engineers, but the Mississippi congressman who wrote the law made sure that very little of that bonanza went to Black veterans. The immense federal farm subsidies of the era, too, went through local white power brokers, who funneled most of it toward their cronies on courthouse square, who, in turn, spent it on cutting-edge farm equipment—giant harvesters, advanced fertilizers—and got rid of the sharecroppers and tenants who had worked the land for generations.[22]

In short, much of the New Property amounted to "affirmative action for white people": invisible and ostensibly color-blind, but biased in practice. Its biases worked imperfectly: more like a sieve than a scalpel. Sometimes whites got snagged: white farmworkers lost when Congress left farmworkers out of Social Security. And sometimes Black people slipped through: Oliver Brown, the plaintiff in *Brown v. Board of Education,* bought his home with GI Bill benefits. But when the civil rights movement erupted in southern counties and towns, white officials weren't satisfied with the sieve; they wanted to target specific people. They did it by turning the New Property into an anti-Black scalpel. Tax exemptions, business licenses, crop allotments, and welfare checks all became weapons for enforcing segregation. In Greenwood, Mississippi, the county welfare department kicked the activist Laura McGhee "and her children off the Welfare roll," complained fellow activist Amzie Moore, and "they are still trying to get her land." Now the courthouse ring was coming for Moore, too. The Federal Housing Administration (FHA) was threatening to sue over his gas station loan, the post office had slashed his job hours, and the County Health Officer refused to issue him a permit for his new café. "They are trying . . . to put me out of business," Moore wrote, because they "are *mad* about the movement." Meanwhile, county officials weaponized the property tax rolls against protesters; anyone who was spotted marching or boycotting

Roland Freeman, "Family Garden. South Bronx, New York, September 1978."

received a huge tax bill in next month's mail. Even churches opening their doors to activists had to worry about losing their valuable tax exemptions.[23]

To cope, local activists in the Deep South focused on three things. First, as we have seen, they looked once again to the power of association, joining forces with national corporations like the NAACP and creating new ones, like the Montgomery Improvement Association. Second, they emphasized the New Property in their voter registration campaigns. Presidents come and go, they said; the biggest reason to register and vote was to get rid of the white county tax assessor and his cronies, along with the all-white county crop-allotment committee—a federal program that handed out subsidies while limiting how many acres of cotton each farmer was allowed to plant.[24] Third, they turned to the "old" civil rights of property and contract, improvising their own mechanisms for lending and repayment.

So, for example, some northern donors preferred to act as a friendly

Roland Freeman, "Arabing, East 21st Street and Greenmount Avenue, South Baltimore, Maryland, July 1972." Note the mix of produce: some commonly used in older southern foodways and other, newer produce, such as bananas from Ecuador. Freeman's text indicates that by the 1970s, the "Arabers bought their vegetables . . . at the [city-run] produce center."

but temporary substitute for local lenders, much as Charlie Black had temporarily broken up the "friendship business amongst the white folks" for Nate Shaw in 1919, as we saw in Chapter 8. One new organization was Operation Freedom, which sent money to activists who faced economic retaliation. Operation Freedom did not donate money outright to endangered activists. It loaned the money, taking a promissory note and mortgage at "the prevailing interest rate," and it did a title search at the county courthouse first, because the land they were rescuing was also their collateral if the activists defaulted.[25] For bailing activists out of jail an official at the Congress of Federated Organizations (a coalition of the main civil rights groups working in Mississippi) had another idea. Instead of draining the NAACP's funds or making working-class locals put up their land, why not sign a contract with some big out-of-state company like Aetna to handle bail bonds for all the civil rights organizations at once? Of all the activists who worked in the South during the 1960s, it was probably the younger, northern activists who were the most surprised by how much "the movement for freedom" relied on the ordinary tools of property and contract and the law of associations, and by how familiar "local people" were with those tools.[26] Like their newly freed forebears in 1865, Black southerners needed money and political power, not tutoring in law.

These struggles over credit and over new forms of intangible property—licensing, welfare, benefits—occurred against the backdrop of a profound shift in Black people's rights in *tangible* property: from landownership to apartment-leasing. Most of the people who came north during the Great Migration did not buy houses. Instead, they rented. Renting an apartment was a lot like renting a farm, in that you paid a landlord out of what you earned at work. The difference was that your landlord was not also your boss. For those who came out of sharecropping, the difference was even bigger: instead of getting paid *by* the landlord, now they paid rent *to* him. In legal terms, the Great Migration shifted Black people's property rights into a different branch of landlord-tenant law, one that separated the rights and duties of work from those of residence.

Yet, even as they moved into northern apartments, Black migrants carried with them important aspects of the property regime they had helped create in the southern countryside. One consequence was that, just as the Great Migration was mixing together different regional Black cultures, it was also pushing Black people to think nationally about property. Take gardening. We often think of Black migrants as city-dwellers but in 1940, the Holcombs and half a million other Black people lived in the suburbs. These Black suburbanites planted collard greens and butter beans in Richmond, California, and they kept pigs and chickens in the Cleveland suburbs. The last and largest wave of Black migrants who went North and West in the 1950s and 1960s extended the tradition into the city itself. They planted family gardens nestled between South Bronx housing projects, and farmed corn and vegetables on vacant lots

Cover, Edna Lewis's The Taste of Country Cooking, *with Penelope Baskerville's Post-its.*

in Detroit. Much as enslaved market women had done a century before, "Arabers" pulled carts along the rowhoused streets of Baltimore and Washington, DC, selling peaches, corn, bananas, green beans, and collard greens but now their customers came from all over the South. A few

Black migrants turned their knowledge of southern gardening, farming, and hunting traditions—all practices deeply tangled with property concepts and laws of trespass, fencing, and capture—into bestselling cookbooks. Verta Mae Grosvenor's *Vibration Cooking* (1970) and Edna Lewis's *The Taste of Country Cooking* (1976) opened white New Yorkers' eyes to the diversity and possibility of African American foodways by sketching razor-sharp portraits of the specific communities they came from: the all-Black settlement of Freetown, Virginia; and Daufuskie Island, in the Geechee region of South Carolina. These authors also provided a wry, proud, often humorous language for Black city-dwellers and suburbanites to bond over what they were doing in their gardens and kitchens and front stoops. Boiled greens "need not be greasy," Lewis wrote. "Throw out all" your pots "except . . . the cast-iron ones like your mother used to use," Grosvenor joked. "Can't no Teflon fry no fried chicken."[27]

Whether they saw themselves as temporary sojourners in the North or never intended to go back, a significant number of Black migrants remained invested in the South—they literally owned land there. By the 1950s, it is likely that millions of the Black people living in rental apartments in cities like Newark and Chicago held rights to land they did not live on—family land, or heir property. Family land required them to make important decisions jointly with far-flung relatives they did not necessarily know or like very much.[28] Family land posed a challenge in the age of the Great Migration, and Black people's response to that challenge helped position civil rights more firmly as matters of racial discrimination.

Black people's efforts to weave together their civil rights with their status-based privileges and duties tightened the threads between city and country. Many migrants sent money to fulfill obligations back home: obligations to support aging parents, to keep departed relatives' graves clean, to pay taxes on family land, to pay the pastor's salary, or to sponsor a communion table at the old church. In the 1910s,

Thomas Holcomb had taken seasonal jobs in New Jersey to help his parents keep their land in Virginia; when he and Annie Reaves Holcomb finally moved north, they not only kept sending money home to Thomas's brother Robert but remained "nonresident members" back at Midway Baptist Church in Cumberland, Virginia, where they planned to be buried. That is, they never officially joined First Baptist South Orange in New Jersey. Instead, for forty years, they attended as "fellowshipping" nonmembers. Plenty of migrants shared the Holcombs' sense of duty to southern relatives and institutions. A Chicago migrant wrote to his pastor back in Alabama using highly possessive language: he promised to "send my church some money" and to "influence our members here to do the same," and in the next breath he wanted news about "our church" back home, warning that his "wife [was] always talking about her seat in the church want[ing] to know who [was o]ccupying it." In the mid-1900s, my great-uncle Henry Smith told me, people living in New Jersey and Connecticut and New York sent their children back to Cumberland County each summer to help their grandparents on the farm. In August, parents came down to fetch the children back to school. This kicked off "Homecoming Week," the biggest fundraiser of the year, a parade of church festivals that yoked the joy of family reunion to the never-ending job of raising money. The "family members who are away" working up north "brought money home and put it on the table" for everyone to see.[29]

When members of the Holcomb family died in New York or New Jersey, their bodies went back to Farmville for burial, the expenses paid from their shares of family property they still owned in Cumberland. Those donations and visits were heartfelt, and they were also part of a complex negotiation over migrants' duties and privileges within the families and churches they had left behind but still considered "theirs."[30]

For some, landownership became the heart of a "back to the land" nationalist politics in the 1970s, part of a pastoral critique of urban decay that invoked Black farm owners as carriers of what Edna Lewis called a "spirit of pride in community and . . . cooperation." Lewis did not identify as a Black nationalist, yet in her writing she unmistakably linked the wholesomeness of her Freetown upbringing to the fact that it was a *Black* settlement, owned and governed by the descendants of slaves. The Nation of Islam and the National Baptist Convention bought farmland and set up model enterprises, on the theory that farming was the answer to factory shutdowns and deadly junk food diets. In 1957, Myers Anderson started farming some long-ignored family land out in Liberty County, less to make money than to keep his teenage grandsons Myers and Clarence Thomas busy with wholesome farm chores and off the streets of Savannah during the summers. "Once, years later," Clarence recalled, "I got up the nerve to tell him that slavery was over. 'Not in *my* house,'" Anderson retorted. But unlike with Nate Shaw in 1904 or John Henry Martin in 1928, young Clarence's farm work was supposed to build up his character, not keep the family afloat. Black southerners, wrote the literary critic Addison Gayle, still held the anticapitalist "values and ethics" of their African ancestors, who had valued "people, not things." For the novelist Alice Walker, "the bond of black kinship" had been "so sturdy, so resilient" in the South, so full of an ethic of "mutual caring," but it had "finally been broken in the cities of the North."[31]

Others rang the alarm about a crisis among the Black farmers who had stayed in the South. In 1910, Black people had owned more than fifteen million acres in the region. By 1969, it was less than six million, and plummeting. How had this happened? Black "ignorance" and "white chicanery," said *Ebony* magazine. As major companies relocated to the South and the "Sun Belt" boom was making Black-owned land suddenly valuable, *Ebony* contended, "southern white lawyers, land speculators and county officials" were using "legal trickery" to drive "unsophisticated rural blacks" from "the sacredness of rural landownership."[32] Scholar-activists, many of them veterans of the civil rights campaigns of the early 1960s, organized to save the vanishing Black farmer. And the Black farmer's Achilles heel, the scholar-activists argued, was "heir property"—family land, the tenancy in common.

The activists collected data suggesting that Black landowners lapsed into tenancy in common because they harbored dangerously incorrect assumptions about how property law worked, and they stayed ignorant because they did not trust the legal system enough to learn otherwise. In particular, the activists found, Black farmers wrongly assumed that no heir's interest could be sold without the consent of all the other heirs and were shocked when some fourth cousin in Cleveland got a court order to auction the land and divide the proceeds. Those distant relatives, the activists argued, were selling off their interests in family land because they lived far away and had "no idea how" valuable it was becoming, or what it meant to their relatives who still lived on it. Perhaps because no activist organization could afford to bail out all the farmers who needed money, activists focused on the part of the crisis they thought they could address: Black fear and ignorance. They would ease Black landowners' anxiety about facing "the local Courthouse Establishment" and they would teach Black landowners "their rights." They fanned out with pamphlets titled *Got Land Problems?* and pored over the back pages of small-town newspapers to warn people whose land was about to be auctioned. Today, scholars and journalists continue to frame partition sales in the South alongside predatory lenders in the North as one grand panorama of racist "dispossession." As Ta-Nehisi Coates memorably put it in 2014, Black landowners were "plundered" in Mississippi and plundered again in Southside Chicago.[33] That story is true as far as it goes. Yet it has flattened complex, often very personal family dynamics, and washed away the long history of Black people's engagement with law.

For years, my great-great-uncle and aunt had been telling everyone they were going to retire back to Cumberland County and move next door to Thomas's brother-in-law, George Smith. During the thirty-odd years they had been living in South Orange, New Jersey, Thomas and Annie Reaves Holcomb had kept up their ties back home. They visited often, and they sent money to his brother Robert to help pay taxes on all two hundred acres, which all the Holcomb descendants owned as tenants in

Outside Midway Baptist Church after Thomas Holcomb's funeral service, September 1976. Still from home movie by Robert L. Baskerville. Holcomb's nephew, Osborne Reaves is on the left with arms folded. I am the child at the far right. Funerals were important occasions for migrants to reaffirm and renegotiate their emotional, familial, and legal ties to the South.

common because Jackson and Louisa Holcomb had not left wills. Somewhere along the way, Thomas and Annie Holcomb started preparing for their move back by buying out some of Thomas's brothers' and sisters' shares of the family land, using the conventional method: "friendly" lawsuits at the Cumberland courthouse (that is, where there is no genuine controversy and people are just asking a judge to approve what they have agreed outside of court). Then, in 1961, in the middle of one of those "friendly" suits, Thomas's niece, Arnetha Brown, demanded credit for years of tax payments, claiming that her father was the one who had paid them. It started to look as though Thomas's brother Robert had been taking the tax payments Thomas had sent each year from New Jersey and putting them on the county assessor's ledgers in his own name. The parcel brought $5,300 at a courthouse auction that September.

Taking its best guess at the truth, the circuit court deducted $400 from Thomas's share.[34]

My uncle Henry—Thomas's nephew—told me the story a few years ago. He made it clear how hurtful this all was. "Aunt Annie didn't want to move here after that because she was upset with" Thomas's nieces, my uncle Henry said; "Why would she move some[place] where everybody arguing with her?" She felt "she just couldn't come down here and be" in the "same church Sunday sittin' next to them, the way they had acted." Besides, all of her own brothers—John, Irving, and my great-grandpa Eugene—"were still up there in South Orange!" For his part, Thomas, elderly and usually mild-mannered, was so upset that "they had him cursing. Had Uncle Tom cursing!" "Oh, they had *big* words." So, after decades dreaming of spending their old age back home in Cumberland, Thomas and Annie decided, in 1961, to "just stay right in Jersey with her family."[35]

What had been a family dispute soon became an incident of racial injustice. From New Jersey, Thomas hired a white Cumberland lawyer named William C. Carter, who had done routine legal work for him before. He asked Carter to sell the land he had assembled along Guinea Road from his siblings, again following the form of a friendly partition lawsuit nominally "against" them. Carter ran the usual ad in the Farmville *Herald* and soon the court auctioned the land to Lucille and Clarence Ferguson, white landowners with thousands of acres. But Thomas had told Carter, before the sale, to pull the land off the market, either because Arnetha had phoned asking him to, or because the Fergusons' offer was too low. Ignoring a client's wishes was a serious violation of legal ethics. Could Thomas prove that had happened? Henry Smith, my uncle, didn't think so when he told me the story in 2015. The white Cumberland lawyers "all are friends!" They took his money and "just . . . put it in their pocket and that was the end. It never went nowhere," Smith told me angrily. "They *stole* the land."[36]

My uncle Henry was right: the Holcombs never got that land back from those white people. But it wasn't for lack of trying. In 1967, one of Thomas's sisters-in-law, Mary Holcomb, asked the local judge to rescind the 1962 sale to the Fergusons, alleging that lawyer Carter had never actually looked for all the relatives who owned interests in the land, many of whom lived right there in Cumberland. In 1972, Thomas joined her suit, adding an allegation that Carter had ignored his specific instruction to have the court vacate its sale decree before the auction.[37] In short, Mary and Thomas Holcomb were saying that Carter had colluded with the Fergusons to commit fraud. And to prove it, they went outside Cumberland's courthouse ring and got a new lawyer all the way from Richmond: Samuel W. Tucker, the partition specialist at Virginia's premier Black law firm, Hill, Tucker and Marsh.

At the trial, Carter (now represented by his own high-powered Richmond lawyer) described Thomas Holcomb as an elderly client who "just up and [filed] a partition suit without saying anything to anybody," a confused old man who could not "give . . . a straight answer" even now. Thomas's niece Arnetha complained that "it wasn't fair" for him to sell his interest in the land "when he knew we all owned part of it." But Thomas Holcomb had every right to demand a partition and he seems to have assumed that it was Carter's job, not his, to notify the relatives. Perhaps, at a time when he was angry with some of those relatives, it had felt better to turn the whole thing over to a lawyer. Most importantly, he insisted that he *had* told Carter to stop.[38]

And so, my great-uncle's newly hired Black lawyer told a story very different from Carter's, a story about a negligent white lawyer. Confronting Carter with damning written evidence and methodically knocking down each of Carter's excuses for not stopping the auction process, S. W. Tucker demonstrated that Carter had knowingly pushed the sale through. He showed that Carter knew most of the Holcombs personally, so he had no reason to have addressed the crucial sale notice to "parties unknown." "I certainly wasn't being dishonest," Carter squirmed. "It was an oversight." Judge Meredith Dortch was openly skeptical. "Your client said, stop," he chastised Carter. So "why . . . didn't [you] stop"? As a white lawyer had done for the Pinn family back in 1882, Tucker was putting a white lawyer on trial for breaching his duty to a Black client. And Carter's breach of duty went to the heart of the rules that had enabled Black property since the days of slavery: he had failed to provide notice. Virginia law required Carter to do "the best that can be done" to notify all the heirs, and he hadn't.[39]

But even though Judge Dortch hinted that he would overturn the sale, the Holcombs still lost, for reasons that the file does not make clear. They appealed to the Virginia supreme court, which refused to hear the appeal because the trial transcript, which was based on a tape-recording, was flawed.[40] Still, three broad observations seem warranted. The first is that the standard rules of property law were completely inadequate for the era of Civil Rights and Great Migration. In 1850, cropping a pig's ear or counting off chickens in front of one's cabin was all that an enslaved person could do to put people on notice of her claim to property. In 1900, when Black people could own land and not just pigs and chickens, it had made sense for the law to presume that posting a notice on the courthouse door and in the local newspaper for three weeks would give everyone who had an interest in the land—the aunts, the cousins, the local bank, the hardware store—a reasonable chance to see or hear about the sale and to raise an objection. In fact, for generations, judges had discouraged partition sales for whites as well as Blacks, not just because of the challenges of deciding what was adequate notice but also because, as Black nationalists would later contend, the judges had felt that the real value of family property—whether land or slaves—couldn't be measured in dollars and cents. But in 1962, when nearly eleven million southern-born people lived outside the South, a three-week box ad in the local paper was, as lawyer Tucker put it, "a poor substitute for notice." Judges made a serious mistake when, in the mid-1900s, swayed by the neoclassical economic view that land is just a commodity, they began routinely ordering partition sales—a mistake that affected people of all races.[41]

Second, if the Great Migration exposed flaws in the way pro-business judges handled tenancies in common, the Holcombs' lawsuit suggests that it also produced, as we have seen numerous times in this book, tensions within Black landowning families: between the idea of land as a privilege of membership in a family association and the idea of land as a civil right. Tenancy in common was a frail "knot rope" for keeping land in the family; it worked only as long as relatives felt, as the activist Shirley Sherrod put it in a 1994 interview, that "we have this sort of pact that if anyone wants to sell their portion," the others will make sure "it stays in the hands of family." (Or else "they just whupped his ass," as one Mississippian half-jokingly told me in 2010.) The knot rope had been fraying since the 1860s but the combination of mass migration and rising land prices strained it to the point that white people could sometimes break

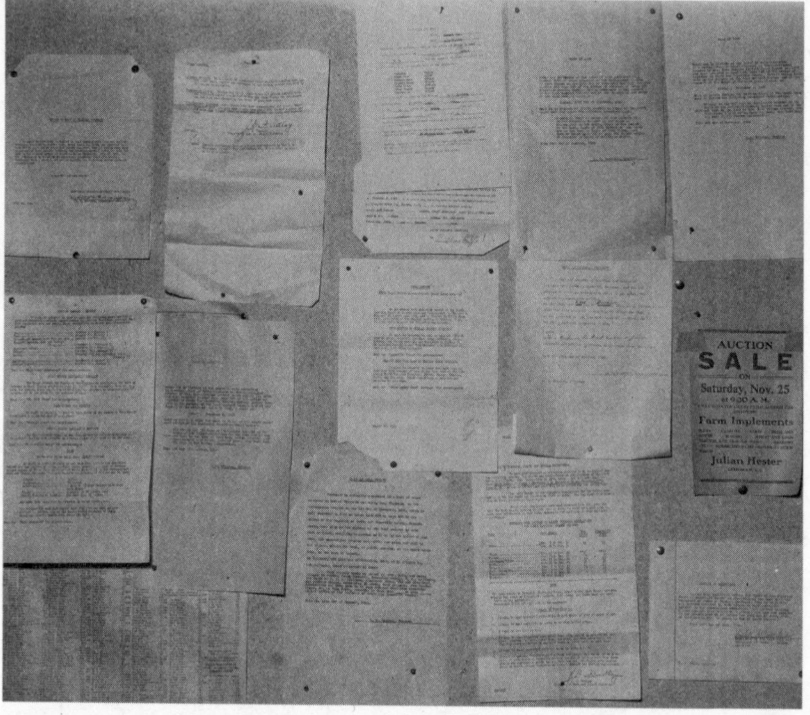

Marion Post Wolcott, "Bulletin board showing variety of notices: sales, wills, forclosures, game laws, hunting season, and etc. in hallway of Granville County Courthouse. Oxford, North Carolina," Nov. 1939.

it. "Why Uncle Tom and Aunt Annie didn't move" back to Cumberland "had nothing to do with this sale" to the Fergusons, Henry Smith told me in 2016. "The land "was stolen from him" after he put it on the market, but "he put it on the market because he had had an argument with his nieces."[42]

The third observation about *Holcomb v. Ferguson* is that none of the participants used the term "civil rights." Samuel W. Tucker was the bread-and-butter partner at Hill, Tucker & Marsh, the one who normally *didn't* handle "civil rights" matters. Yet only a few years before their trial at Cumberland County courthouse, the same two lawyers, Tucker and Carter, had squared off in federal court over a major voting rights case, a case one Black newspaper dubbed the "Civil Rights Vote Act" of 1965.[43] By the 1970s, few people thought of landownership as a civil rights issue anymore unless it was clearly connected to racial injustice.

In the fall of 1972, my mother, Penelope Baskerville, became one of a handful of Black students at the University of Pennsylvania Law School. She dropped out after three semesters. Once, I asked her why. She said she just didn't want to be a lawyer. I didn't push the question. She died in 2014. A year later, I started a job that is partly in a law school. Many of the students expressed deep frustration that the core curriculum—especially the courses on contract law, property law, and civil procedure—did not meaningfully engage with race. By then, my research assistants and I had uncovered hundreds of Black litigants in the county courthouse dockets and when we began examining the casebooks that my students were assigned for their core courses—thick, hardcover anthologies of carefully selected appeals court cases and related materials—we found Black litigants there, too. But they were invisible. To paraphrase the late Toni Morrison, I realized that Black people's absence from the canon of contract law was an illusion, that legal professionals had had to perform "intellectual feats" to erase Black people from a world of contracts literally "seething with their presence." And as I set out to discover what those intellectual feats had done to the law of contract, as I wrestled with the implications of all this, I wished I could ask my mother: what was it really like for you?[44]

When my mother started at Penn, elite law schools, under intense pressure from students, were introducing new courses on "Blacks and the Law," "Civil Rights," "poverty and minority law," "Legal Problems of the Poor," and "consumer credit." First-year courses were also starting to cover various kinds of inequality, incorporating insights from the growing fields of "law and economics" and what is known as the "law and society movement." But the law school curriculum, and the academic movements that were reshaping it, still stumbled when it came to race. The curriculum tended to equate "civil rights" with "minorities," implying that contract and property law were not "civil rights."[45] Well-meaning colleagues underlined that conceptual divide when they urged newly hired minority law professors "not [to] get too caught up in civil rights or other 'ethnic' subjects." So did white students who refused to talk about race in the "core" courses where, they supposed, race was extraneous. Many students and faculty found the situation frustrating, but it seemed as though all that law schools could do was offer more specialty courses and hands-on clinics and pro bono opportunities where students could use their training to help minorities directly, and issue vague pleas for faculty to "face head-on the pain . . . and lingering injustices" of the law.[46] By treating "civil rights" as a special, minority-focused body of law, the law schools obscured what cases brought by Black people had contributed to "core" areas like contract law during the field's formative years, as well as the complex ways that contract jurists had used those cases to fashion their theories of voluntariness, capacity, reasonableness, assent, and more.

This was understandable, because the leading casebooks of the 1960s and 1970s made it seem as though contract law had nothing to do with either minorities or civil rights. I discovered this almost by accident. A few years ago, I got curious about *Harrington v. Taylor*, the 1945 case we saw in Chapter 10. *Harrington* is one of a trio of cases that are often used to teach the doctrine of "past consideration." Taylor orally promised to compensate Harrington, whose hand had been maimed when she stopped Taylor's wife from killing him with an axe. Taylor broke his promise and Harrington sued. Neither the casebooks nor the North Carolina supreme court report say anything about who Lena Harrington and Lee Walter Taylor were. It wasn't until I ordered a copy of the original case file from Raleigh that I realized that all of the people who were there when Lena Harrington sacrificed her hand to keep her daughter from killing her abusive son-in-law were Black.

And so, I started ordering more case files—several hundred by the end—from state and federal archivists across the country, and as each file arrived, I looked up the names of the litigants in the Census. Unlike with the county court dockets, I did not try to build a statistical sample because a casebook is a teaching tool, not a snapshot of real life. I did enough research to be confident that cases involving African Americans are flecked across the pages of some of the leading law journals, treatises, dictionaries, and annotated codes from the late 1800s and early 1900s, the formative era of modern contract law, and that they continue to appear in current ones. White judges and lawyers have frequently relied on "'colored' cases" to develop common-law rules and to think through major doctrinal and theoretical problems in contract. But they did not mention that Black people were involved. In fact, many of the most influential cases involving Black people are the ones that do *not* talk about race. Similar to the way some "colored" people were allowed to "pass" as white, "'colored' cases" have been "passed" silently into the heart of contract law when legal professionals elided the fact that a litigant was Black, and when they turned slavery into an abstraction, detached from race. The result was to make "civil rights" and "contract" seem like completely separate categories of law, darkening one, whitening the other, and impoverishing both.[47]

In their editing and case selection, the law professors inadvertently muffled the role that Black litigants, racial ideas, and the legacy of emancipation had played in the development of contract law. That encouraged white students to think of race as something tangential to "real" contract law. Whether made out of embarrassment or a desire to "modernize" law teaching, law professors' casebooks and classroom choices treated Black students as guests to a white limestone cathedral built by white men. In the fall of 1972, when my mother opened her Contracts casebook, she would have seen just one case that involved Black people: *Williams v. Walker-Thomas Furniture Co.* That was a case where a Washington, DC, store sold—on the installment plan—furniture, curtains, and children's toys to Ora Lee Williams, a single mother of "limited education" and on welfare, and waited until she had nearly cleared her debt, and then clawed back all the goods when she started missing payments. Law professors used *Williams* to teach the doctrine of unconscionability, but nobody thought unconscionability was central to contract law. Penn's new course on Consumer Credit—which used Homer Kripke's recently published casebook—taught my mother how to decipher the installment-purchase contracts and nickel-a-week insurance policies that she had seen her great-aunt Annie and uncle Thomas Holcomb wrestle with, but it veiled what people like the Holcombs had done to help make the law of consumer credit.[48] This veil was woven from lawyers' and judges' tactical decisions in pursuit of the broadest winning rule, combined with the assumption—ironically strengthened by the 1960s civil rights movement—that Black people encountered law meaningfully only in criminal justice, voting, the workplace, schools, and public accommodations—that is, in cases "about" race.

In 1866, contract and property had been considered the very heart of "civil rights." In 1970, James Alan McPherson, a Black Harvard Law student just two years ahead of my mother at Penn, wrote in *The Atlantic* that for Black students, learning about civil procedure and contracts and esoteric "thirteenth-century property law" meant betraying their "true interests" in "civil rights and civil liberties," posing "a problem of fidelities" that would haunt their careers.[49] Like my mother, McPherson decided not to be a lawyer.

Far from the classrooms, activists unknowingly helped widen this growing conceptual divide between "civil rights" and private law. They mirrored scholars' habit of treating Black people as outsiders to the world of law, except that, unlike the law professors, the activists were keenly interested in Black people's encounters with law. The activists recast Black people's experiences with property and contract—sometimes even their own—in nostalgic, almost anti-legalist terms. The white-dominated legal system, they contended, was eroding Black cultural values of "independence," "dignity," and "community."[50]

To be sure, the activists' views on the matter were complex. A number of the most dedicated and influential Black activists of the 1950s, 1960s, and 1970s—Medgar Evers, Ralph Abernathy, Rosa Parks, Malcolm X, Ella Baker, Martin Luther King Jr., and Shirley Sherrod—came from landowning southern families, and in some settings they described property and contract just as their parents' generation did: as rights of everyday use, or privileges of status within an association. "My father always said that land would be the means by which we would rise in the world," recalled Abernathy in his 1989 autobiography. W. L. Abernathy's reputation as the owner of five hundred acres of prime farmland, as a man with good credit who paid his bills, Ralph believed, gave him "standing . . . in the community," and a "fragile . . . kind of equality based on mutual respect and a certain standoffishness." Sherrod remembered that her extended family owned hundreds of acres in Baker County, Georgia, with hired laborers and tenants doing much of the work. Baker described her grandfather's purchase of his former master's plantation as the seedling of her family's local prominence in ministry and politics, and said it taught her her first lessons in the power of "community."[51]

Moreover, activists like Baker and Sherrod and Abernathy drew on the rights of everyday use as they worked within the larger freedom struggle. But in doing so, they began to talk differently about those rights and about Black legal life. In Summerton, South Carolina, as activists gathered signatures for the fateful school petition that would launch the *Briggs* case, they approached landowners first—people like Harry and Eliza Briggs. As school petitions gave way to a mass movement,

Black landowners let out-of-town activists turn their spare bedrooms into offices and their farms into meeting grounds, signed bonds against their farms to bail civil rights workers out of jail, fed the marchers from their restaurants, and often worked hard on voter registration drives. The famous 1965 voting rights march from Selma to Montgomery, Alabama, might never have happened if Black landowners along Highway 80 had not given marchers permission to camp on their land.[52] Activists knew that the landowners were sticking their necks out. They winced as the Briggses lost their jobs, their cotton crop, and their mortgage loan. They fumed as Joseph DeLaine, a key local organizer behind the *Briggs* suit, tried in vain to protect his own property from a spurious slander judgment. Largely helpless to protect local activist landowners against such full-blast economic retaliation, and profoundly aware that they were witnessing history, the out-of-town activists tried to make sense of what they were seeing.[53]

They found their explanation in culture. The activists figured that some Black people were already primed to get involved in the movement because they had grown up in landowning families, "relatively protected from white racism and unafraid of it." In Madison County, Mississippi, Congress of Racial Equality (CORE) activists were awestruck by C. O. Chinn, a restauranteur and landowner locally known as "the type of person that didn't take shit from anyone." In Holmes County there was Hartman Turnbow, who in spring 1963 fired back at white terrorists and then warned "the sheriff and everybody else that anybody he caught on his land after dark was going to get lit up like a Christmas tree." Another Holmes County landowner, Laura McGhee, delivered a similar warning when the Greenwood sheriff tried to stop a SNCC rally at her farm. "She gave him to understand that *he* was on *her* property, that *he* was trespassing, and that if he couldn't offer her protection from the nightriders who kept shooting up her home, she didn't need his advice now. He left, which actually seems to have surprised her."[54]

Hugely impressed by such bravery, SNCC activists came to believe that landowning instilled in Black farmers a certain "independence" that sharecroppers lacked. Sharecroppers suffered from what the activists called "the 'plantation mentality,' an ingrained sense of helplessness and dependence on whites."[55] In the mid-twentieth century, such "cultural" theories were everywhere, from Marcus Garvey's idea that racial oppression produced "mental slavery," to the Moynihan Report's assertion that the crumbling of "the Negro family in the urban ghettos" was seeding a "culture of poverty," and to the Supreme Court's urgent warnings about the harm school segregation inflicted on the "hearts and minds" of "Negro children."[56] Movement activists, especially those who had not grown up in the rural South, passed their cultural theory of Black landowning, along with their open admiration for plainspoken "local people," to scholars. The cultural theory explained and justified what they were doing in the South.

What the cultural explanation left out was law. The cultural explanation tended to treat legal relations, such as share tenancy or landownership, as talismans that somehow produced lifelong patterns of behavior. It overlooked copious evidence that the "Negroes of the Black Belt" viewed a tenancy contract as a contract. The "local people" the civil rights workers were trying to teach were already quite familiar with legal rules and concepts, a familiarity born as much from legal relations *among* African Americans as from legal relations between Black people and white people. Many of the youthful northern activists lionized Hartman Turnbow for his plainspoken defiance of white authority, but Turnbow himself emphasized an example of a Black landowner manipulating property law to defy *Black* authority: leaders of a certain church who wouldn't let him preach the gospel of voter registration. Even Ella Baker—who, unlike some of the main SNCC field workers, did come from the rural South—encouraged this anti-legalist, cultural explanation. When Baker told oral historians that her philosophy of community organizing grew out of the "cooperative," sharing spirit of her southern upbringing—out of a "deep sense of community" that had supposedly gotten lost when Black people migrated to the cities—historians relied on those interviews to assert that her grandparents "never regarded the land . . . as private property." In doing so, they were downplaying the tenancies in common, contracts, mortgages, donative gifts, and associational charters that by Baker's own account her parents and neighbors had actually relied on. When Shirley Sherrod told her story for an oral history project in 1994, she insisted that the laborers who worked her parents' farm "were like family," ignoring the enormous difference in power between them.[57] Both Baker and Sherrod, in fact, glossed over the inherent contradictions of a "cooperative" "community" where one family owned and controlled most of the land.

The McGhees, a landowning family from just outside Greenwood, Mississippi, venerated for their bravery during the 1960s campaigns, offer another example of how culture displaced law in the stories being told of Black life in the South. When asked in 1980 by the sociologist Charles Payne how they persevered through so much violence and violent threats, Silas McGhee explained by way of a story from the 1950s, before the Movement came to Mississippi. At that time, they were having trouble with some white neighbors who coveted their land. Their animals kept going missing, their fences were cut. One morning, Silas's mother, Laura McGhee, spotted one of the neighbors on a bulldozer, carving a drainage ditch on her side of the property line. She "went down there, climbed up on that bulldozer and pulled that man off . . . and shook him so," Silas recounted. Payne continued: "When the sheriff arrived, she told him they had ten minutes to get that bulldozer off her land before she burned it." It was a stunning act of bravery. Black women had been lynched for less. "The McGhees represent a tradition of defiance," Payne concluded, one that "stripped" white violence of its mystique and helped persuade "Black Greenwood that the old order might be passing." For Payne, the episode illustrated that "the crucial break with the past" was not the passage of the federal civil rights laws, and not the arrival of "the somewhat mysterious SNCC workers." It was when "people like the McGhees" began to insist that those federal laws be enforced. Payne was right. But by reading local activists' stories through the prism of community organizing, Payne and other scholars overlooked something important. Why didn't these white men kill Laura McGhee? Because they were on her land. The clue was right there in the moral of the story: " 'My mother would always tell me,' " Silas recalled, "I don't care what you do as long as you be within the law. You stay within the law and you can do anything you want to."[58]

Landowners acted differently than sharecroppers because landowners owned the land they lived on. The distinction was simple but profound: all three of the people in the story—white sheriff, white neighbor, Black landowner—believed that McGhee had a right under Mississippi law to burn that bulldozer. It was almost beside the point whether that right existed on the books, though she probably would have had a strong case if the white neighbor had sued her.[59] What mattered was that her assertion made sense to her and to the sheriff as they stood arguing there in the shadow of the law, each relying on the broadly shared assumptions about what lay "within the law"—not federal anti-discrimination law, but Mississippi property law.

It was the same "goat sense" that guided Ben Houston in his 1903 dispute with Oliver M. Ellis, that Nate Shaw relied on when he refused to sign "the paper" in his jail cell in 1932, and that made sharecroppers so nervous in front of the young SNCC activists talking earnestly on their front porches about voting. The sharecroppers knew that the activists were "trespassers" when they tried to organize them on a landlord's land, just as McGhee's covetous white neighbor was a "trespasser" when he went on her land. It was almost beside the point what the law on the books said. (In fact, that question was up in the air at the time, doctrinally, partly because of challenges from activists trying to give legal advice to migrant farmworkers.) From their long experience living in the shadow of the law, sharecroppers knew, better than the activists, that they could not do whatever they pleased on their front porches because they did not own the porch. Their pile of chips—the legal endowment that Mississippi law granted them—was smaller than their landlord's, smaller even than Ben Houston's had been in 1903, because Houston had a lease. It would have been easier to add sharecroppers to

Herbert Randall, "Local teenager Doug Smith (left) and SNCC field secretary Sandy Leigh explaining to elderly African American Hattiesburg resident Sylvester Magee the procedures required to register to vote at the Forrest County Courthouse."

the voter rolls if the SNCC field workers had seriously challenged this principle of property law—say, by carving out a right to register voters in their rented homes, as New Jersey legal aid lawyers managed to do for migrant farmworkers in 1971, a right the Supreme Court practically erased in 2021. But claiming a right to go onto someone else's land to organize voters would also have thrown into question the "sense of the community" about "the law" that enabled Black landowners to help movement activists in the South.[60] If a white landlord had no right to keep unwanted strangers off his property, perhaps Laura McGhee had no right to keep the white neighbor off hers.

Black southerners' decisions during the 1960s campaigns were shaped by their working knowledge of state-based private law. Yet movement activists interpreted those behaviors as part of a southern way of life that, they believed, had kept generations of Black southerners alienated from the law and afraid to approach the courthouse. In their memoirs and oral interviews, activists created a documentary record of what "local people" said and did in the 1960s, sometimes underlining the grassrootedness of the freedom struggle with earthy, profane language, just as many activists had taken to wearing denim work clothes on protest marches. The McGhees, marveled SNCC's Bob Zellner, "simply just didn't take no shit." Of another local man, Matt Suarez, another SNCC worker, from New Orleans, recalled that "you didn't fuck with C. O. Chinn because he would kick your natural ass."[61] To be sure, some SNCC activists derided "local-people-itis—the romanticization of poor Mississippians" as "an excuse" for SNCC's own inaction and disorganization. And some activists did recognize that local people understood basic legal terms and principles.[62] Yet again and again, the movement lifted civil rights up from the house porch and the county courthouse into the universal values of freedom, justice, and dignity and then returned them, transfigured, as moral arguments.

Something, of course, got lost in that transfiguration: the long, rich history of Black people's legal experiences and ideas about rights. By the 1960s, movement activists were urging a "grassroots approach" to help "the millions of exploited, disfranchised and degraded Negroes of the Black Belt" to understand "the meaning of first class citizenship"—help them "gain enough confidence in themselves to seek and assert their rights." In 1965, SNCC unwittingly harked back to a long and tangled history to describe three delegates for the Mississippi Freedom Democratic Party who had unsuccessfully challenged the white Mississippi Democrats' right to represent the state at the Democratic National Convention. Much as white Union officers in 1865 had thought that they needed to teach newly freed slaves about property rights, much as NAACP lawyers in 1931 had thought that the "black masses were still ignorant of their rights," much as white southern lawyers had presented their clients as "ignorant negroes," and much as white liberals at that very moment were describing Ora Lee Williams as uneducated and helpless, SNCC asserted that "Mrs. Hamer, Mrs. Devine and Mrs. Gray do not know much about legal things." That alleged homespun innocence about "legal things" helped validate SNCC's agenda; it affirmed the activists' belief that they were faithfully representing the wishes of the South's poor Black "folk." The three women "do not know much about legal things," SNCC said. "But they know what we want," and that, as Ella Baker put it, was "much bigger than a hamburger." African Americans wanted the right to vote, to use public facilities, to have jobs and decent schools—as well as "a larger freedom," a "freedom of the human spirit." But, of course, Black people had known about "legal things" for a long time and they were still highly active in local courts during the 1950s and 1960s.[63] Thus activists bequeathed to historians three deeply flawed assumptions: first, that common-law rights under state law, and the local courts that judged those rights, had been a closed book to Black people before the modern freedom struggle; second, that those rights were not civil rights; and, third, that they were essentially irrelevant compared with protection from discrimination or subordination as defined by Congress and the Supreme Court, much less compared to the broader human freedoms that activists now sought.

As historians in the 1980s turned away from top-down approaches to the history of civil rights, they relied heavily on accounts about (and sometimes by) movement activists that positioned "local people" at the center of "the freedom struggle" while explaining those "local people's" actions in cultural, almost anti-legalist terms. The first generation of civil rights historians had told a story of "simple justice" won at the Supreme Court; those who rewrote that story from the bottom up wound up limiting what counted as "civil rights," or even veered away from law altogether. As civil rights historians shifted from celebrating *Brown* to lamenting its "lost promise," from the Montgomery-to-Memphis frame (popularly consecrated by the campaign for a King national holiday) to a nationwide "long movement," from national leaders to the grassroots—and especially as historians sought a "freedom struggle" that was bigger and more authentically rooted in the lives of "rural black folk" than "civil rights"—that trio of assumptions has remained their North Star. But in portraying Black history as an ongoing quest for something "more robust . . . than . . . civil rights"—whether "dignity," economic justice, or "full citizenship"[64]—historians missed the vast fields of common-law civil rights and associational privileges that Black people had been plowing for more than a hundred years. The "freedom struggle" version of Black history shrank what counted as civil rights and distorted what Black people actually thought about law and did with law. And because so much of what Black people thought and did with law had to do with other Black people, it also narrowed what counts as Black history.

Others were wondering about what counts as "law." Just a few years after my mother left Penn Law, a loose group of law professors from around the country began holding small meetings to talk about the place of race in the law. Mixing history, personal narrative, and rigorous doctrinal analysis, and building on some of the insights of the old legal realists, their conversations and law journal articles coalesced by the 1990s into an academic subfield called Critical Race Theory (CRT). Today, as right-wing politicians caricature CRT to get elected, American law schools are slowly awakening to its message that race still matters in America, and that law schools must confront and critique the many ways law continues to play a crucial role in perpetuating racial inequality.

The history of Black legal life before the Movement suggests that law schools are still teaching two important legends, even if only implicitly. The first is that civil rights, African Americans, and race are marginal to "real law"—the "core curriculum" centered on contract and property law. The second is that the history of civil rights, African Americans, and race is a story of legal liberalism and its failures—how Black communities banded together with lawyers and activist organizations, won a landmark victory over state-mandated white supremacy in *Brown v. Board of Education*, and have fought ever since to realize its promise. In fact, uncovering the hidden history of Black civil rights suggests that these two legends reinforce one another. The legal liberal interpretation and its critical heirs triumphed by throwing away alternative traditions of civil rights, including ones rooted in contract law. Modern contract law, in turn, was created in part by exiling "race" to the seldom-used niche of unconscionability and to other branches of law, especially criminal law and constitutional law, and by taking the massive legal-theoretical struggle over the meaning and limits of market freedom in a post-slavery society and turning it into abstract hypotheticals about "the negro" and "the slave." Many of the cases reprinted or cited today in first-year contracts casebooks were chosen during the decades between the end of slavery and the end of Jim Crow. Those cases were chosen not because they were representative or frequently cited, but because some Ivy League law professors thought that they illustrated certain legal principles.[65] "Contract law" exists today as a conceptually unified field partly because white judges, lawyers, and law professors buried their complicated choices about race.

Now, there is nothing necessarily wrong with legends, especially if they serve a useful purpose. Legal professionals have always ransacked history to lend gravitas to their preferred version of what "the law" is. But when the needs of the legal profession change, it may be worth asking whether the particular legends being taught are still useful or not. For fifty years now, law schools have struggled to attract and keep talented minority students and faculty, and to convince them that "the law" being taught is relevant to them and worth devoting their careers to. Yet the leading casebooks make it seem as though contract law has almost nothing to do with race or racial minorities or the struggle to define freedom in a world without slavery. And this doctrinal "passing" has come at great cost to law schools and the American people whom they serve. By making *Williams v. Walker-Thomas Furniture* the only " 'colored' case" first-year law students read, contracts teachers have inadvertently reinforced racial stereotypes and relegated racial minorities to the marginal, seldom-used doctrine of unconscionability. The point is general. There is no principled reason why only some parts of the law school curriculum—chiefly courses in constitutional and criminal law—should be responsible for teaching about the role of race and racial minorities in law, or why students interested in corporate law or contracts should be taught that those areas of law have nothing worthwhile to say about race. The right to contract is a civil right. Understanding how long and how deeply Black people have engaged with the law of contract can help ease the damaging perception that racial minorities contribute only to cases that are "about" race. This is one reason why law students are once again demanding that the law school curriculum be desegregated.[66]

But this might be easier than it appears. To paraphrase Toni Morrison once more, "It only seems that the canon of American" contract law "is 'naturally' or 'inevitably' 'white.' In fact, it is *studiously* so."[67] And the canon becomes more fascinating and more powerful when we begin to notice the unspoken presence of race and how studiously legal professionals have dealt with it. "'Colored' cases" offer a useful window on judges' decision making, lawyers' tactics, and case reporting, precisely *because* they obscure race. They belong at the core of how we think about the law. Indeed, more than we know, they are already there.

Conclusion

Near the beginning of Ava DuVernay's Oscar-nominated 2014 film *Selma,* Annie Lee Cooper (played by Oprah Winfrey) crosses the echoing marble floor of her county courthouse and tries to register to vote. Nervously, she slides her papers through the registrar's window. The white registrar sneers at first. Then Cooper aces the questions and he gets annoyed. Finally, he stumps her with an impossible, nonsensical question and she turns away, fighting back tears of humiliation. By the middle of the movie, she is punching the county sheriff in the mouth during a protest at the courthouse steps.

"Dahmer, demonstrations, Jan 1966." Photograph taken on the morning of slain civil rights leader Vernon Dahmer's funeral in Hattiesburg, Mississippi.

I gasped, and maybe you did, too. Hers is an inspiring journey: from humiliation to dignity, from second-class citizenship to full citizenship, an epochal change powered by ordinary people. And it really is based on a true story.

Just as Rosa Parks in 1955 turned a bus into a "moving theater" of injustice,[1] voting rights activists in the 1960s turned county courthouses into a made-for-television drama, in which ordinary Black people suddenly seemed to shake off centuries of fear, confronting racist white sheriffs and county clerks to demand their rights. The notorious police attack at the Edmund Pettus Bridge, where SNCC chairman and future congressman John Lewis had his skull cracked open, happened at the start of a march headed to the Montgomery County courthouse. Over and over, in one county seat after another, Black marchers kneeled to pray on the courthouse steps as white cops glowered down on them from in front of the tall, heavy double doors.[2] Photographers captured the moment when the first Black registrants stood in the inner sanctum.

In fact, though, many of the marchers probably had already been there before, for one reason or another: to pay property tax, to have a deed recorded, to get divorced. They had seen the metal wall cabinets full of trial papers. Some of them had consulted the ledgers of property deeds that sat behind the counter. Though Black people had sometimes been mistreated at the courthouse, or outright defrauded, like my great-great-uncle Thomas Holcomb, few southern whites had denied that African Americans held the common-law civil rights embodied in those ledgers.

For more than a hundred years after slavery's end, white people maintained a legal system that refused to recognize Black people's dignity as full citizens. Whites used the criminal justice system to discipline Black workers, barred them from voting or holding office, and constantly reinforced their inferior status through violence and a thousand humiliating acts of discrimination and exclusion. But whites could not impose their racial preferences on every part of the law. During those same years, as we have seen, African Americans exercised a whole range of civil rights. They bought and sold property, talked with notaries and lawyers, and

"Integration voter, Jan and Feb 1964," print no. 13. Photograph taken Jan. 22, 1964, in Hattiesburg. Forrest County circuit clerk Theron C. Lynd is shown at left. Note the ledger books stored horizontally behind Lynd. The deed books, by then too numerous to fit behind the desk, would have been stored in a side room and brought out for consultation. Seemingly polite here, Lynd was truculent when the television cameras left, as described by historian John Dittmer.

"Integration voter, Jan and Feb 1964," print no. 20. Note the metal file cabinets behind the unnamed voter. Those would have contained loose papers of circuit court cases, trifolded and either tied with string or slotted into cardstock envelopes designed specially for courthouse use.

made oral and written contracts scrawled on the backs of receipts and scraps of paper. They had a working knowledge of law. They refined it through daily experience and discussed it at church, in school, and in Black-owned newspapers. Their "goat sense" didn't always match the law on the books but neither did white people's. The system needed Black people to be legally competent. They built activist organizations, banks, fraternities, and churches under the sheltering umbrella of corporation law. When they sued, they did it in county court, not the U.S. Supreme Court. They sued on the law of contract and property and wills and torts, not the Constitution's Equal Protection Clause. This private-law tradition of civil rights helped pave the way for the more familiar modern vision of civil rights that finally began to tear down discrimination in voting, schools, the workplace, and public accommodations.

From the 1920s to the 1960s, five seemingly unrelated developments shook the views that Americans—including African Americans—held about Blacks and the law. One was the rise of new forms of property and the strain that mass migration put on older forms of property, such as family land. Another was the continued spread of the corporation as a tool for pursuing collective goals. The third was a growing conviction among African Americans that the internal rules of Black-run corporations were failing to protect the rights of their members, a conviction that led to particularly painful conflicts within Black religious corporations—churches and mosques. Fourth, prominent white judges and law professors elaborated a legal theory about associational privileges and common-law rights, a theory that, for a fleeting moment, seemed poised to grant rights to members of religious corporations, including Black religious people. Finally, more and more racial justice advocates began to coalesce around an agenda of fighting racial discrimination and subordination through law, and they increasingly identified that agenda as "civil rights."[3] As brave people like Annie Lee Cooper put the whole edifice of racial oppression on trial, the rights of everyday use faded from the public memory of Black life.

Today, right-wing politicians and judges insist that racism is history, and that the only way to sweep away its remnants is to be color-blind.[4] For such people, there might be no better proof of this proposition than the long history of Black people's engagement with property and contract, rights that even Jim Crow laws did not deny. To be clear: the fact that Black people participated in contract and property law does not mean that Black people had power equal to white people, nor does it mean that law was color-blind—much less that it should be color-blind now. It does mean that it was harder to segregate some areas of law than others—that it was easier to padlock the railcar and voter rolls than the deed books or even the courts.

This book is not a lament for the path not taken; it is not about the lost promise of private-law civil rights. What I have tried to do in these pages is to replant a familiar story in the soil where it first grew. The past is anything but "dead and buried," as Barack Obama put it. As James Baldwin wrote, it "is literally *present* in all that we do." But how? Mass incarceration is the "New Jim Crow," some scholars contend. Murderous policemen are the direct descendants of the slave patrollers and lynchers. Republicans' attacks on democracy are "downstream" from the feverish proslavery politicians of the 1850s. And, many scholars and activists lament, the Supreme Court's eagerness to help demolish the achievements of the Civil Rights era shows that legal liberalism—the basic faith that courts could be an engine of progressive social change—was always based on a fundamental misunderstanding of the role the Court has played for most of American history.[5] It is right and good to make these connections.

But if we want to learn from our shared history, then we must open up our vision of Black legal lives beyond the Constitution and the criminal justice system. If we want to understand why Sunday morning is still the most segregated day of the week, why African Americans continue to invest so much in their churches, and why women, LGBTQ, nonbinary, and trans members so often find themselves subordinated there, we must recall the massive church walkouts of the 1800s and the corporation laws that made them possible. To grasp more fully why so many people are willing to countenance voter restrictions for public elections, we must remember the centuries of sharp struggles over voting in private elections within churches and other associations. To imagine how Americans may cope with the looming destruction of Medicare and Medicaid, we might consider how people like Eliza Brown bargained for care. To understand why the Supreme Court's Republican justices believe that the Constitution requires government to be colorblind, we must remember how the party of Lincoln replaced the complicated world of privileges and "community opinion" with the seductively simple principle of equal civil rights, how Republican judges struggled to take account of racial inequality without violating the principle of nondiscrimination, and how judges, lawyers, litigants, and law professors have been treating race opportunistically ever since. If we want to understand why only 17 percent of Black Democrats consider themselves liberal, why Justice Clarence Thomas angrily described eminent domain as a constitutional fig leaf for "Negro removal," or why some Black professionals have embraced gun ownership, we have to look at what Black people actually thought and did with law.[6] Most of all, if we want to understand why so many Black people put their faith in law at all when the Movement came, we have to know what law meant to their ancestors before the Movement. In short, if we want to understand Black people's demands for the rights that America denied them, we must pay more attention to how they talked about and used the rights that were *not* denied them—the associational privileges and common-law civil rights they had been exercising for generations in county clerks' offices and church basements—rights of everyday use.

Yet there is more at stake in these questions than how we tell the story of Black *legal* lives. The challenge is to talk about Black people's lives in full. We must grasp Black people's political and economic and religious and family commitments as more than episodes in race relations, echoes of America's original sin, signposts on the road to a more perfect Union, or facets of a struggle for Black freedom. We must put Black people at the center of their own history. When we take that broader view, we can better see the rich diversity of Black life: the ways they loved each other, exploited each other, fought each other, got annoyed with each other, helped each other, joked with each other; how they dealt with getting old, how they imagined God, how they imagined "the law," and how they imagined what either God or law could do for them—or to them. The basic premise of this book is that Black people's lives are worth studying in themselves.

Today, county courthouses are still seats of power. Circuit clerks still have enormous discretion over the civil rights of everyday use. But now, some of the clerks are Black, and nearly all of them courteously entertain inquiries about Black history. Because of the freedom struggle waged in the 1960s, an African American researcher like me can consult, without special pleading, the ledgers and loose papers that, for more than a century, embodied civil rights. Yet, because of that same freedom struggle, people today do not think of those documents as the stuff of "civil rights," much less as the stuff of "freedom." And that is one reason why I was able to use these documents to write this book: very few people care about old court records. Rather than being suppressed, like records of the Attica prison uprising, or locked away by the descendants of famous leaders, or reverently preserved, like oral histories of activists, the documents that hold these precious glimpses of the past have simply been neglected.[7] Many of the documents are rotting away because counties do not have money to keep them dry, or are being destroyed because most states do not consider county court records to be historically valuable unless they are connected to someone famous or to the freedom struggle. But for now, they are still there, for anyone willing to look. And they have stories to tell.

ACKNOWLEDGMENTS

This book took many years to research and write. I am indebted to Adrienne Frie and Nicole Viglini, who did the lion's share of data entry, lookups, and database troubleshooting that underpin the trial court numbers. Additional research assistance was provided by Derek Burk, Maya Campbell, Christopher Eckels, Brianne Felsher, Sophie Fitzmaurice, Grace Goudiss, Kavitha Iyengar, Robert Kutchin, Diana Lee, Eliza Meredith, Jesse Nasta, Sally Nuamah, Daimeon Shanks, Rashmee Singh, Craig Spencer, Alycia Tulloch, Samantha Turner, and Cristina Violante.

I owe a great debt to the librarians at Northwestern and Berkeley, including Douglas Avila, Ramona Collins, Jennifer Dorner, Edna Lewis, Harriet Lightman, James McMasters, Dean Rowan, and I-Wei Wang, who repeatedly fielded my queries about obscure materials and somehow managed to track them down. I received invaluable guidance from archivists, librarians, and records managers at the New Jersey State Archives—especially the incomparable Bette Epstein—the New Jersey Superior Court Public Information Center, the New Jersey State Law Library; Robert Ellis, the late Brenda French, and Jermaine (Jody) Scott (the National Archives); Donna Wells (Moorland-Spingarn at Howard University); Vincent Brooks, Amy Judd, and Minor Weisiger (Library of Virginia); Earl Ijames, Doug Brown, Erin Fulp, and Lauren McCoy, (State Archives of North Carolina); Jessica Hopkins (NARA Kansas City); Stacey Skeeters and staff of Illinois Supreme Court Archives; Julia

Marks Young, Betty Uzman, and staff of the Mississippi Department of Archives and History; Gary Saretsky, Mary Ann Kiernan, and George Joynson (Monmouth County Archives); Leigh McWhite (University of Mississippi Archives); Mimi Miller (Historic Natchez Foundation); Cecilia Brown (University of Virginia Law Library Special Collections); and many other specialists around the country.

Much of the evidence in this book does not come from archives or libraries but from county circuit clerks and their staffs, who permitted me to conduct historical research in their hectically-busy offices. Some of them unlocked seldom-used basements and back rooms and, in one case, a converted pie factory warehouse where old dockets were being kept. I thank Bill Carlin, Kate McCann, Octavia Gurley, and others at Jersey Street Superior Court Records Management Center; Valerie Wallace (Camden County); Sheri Parish, Nancy Kessler, Sueann Billelo, George Punnoose, Larry Couram, and Paulyn Holandez (Essex Vicinage); Torey King and Lauren Wiley (Mercer County); Diane Gerofsky and Ludovico Iezzo (Mercer Surrogate's Office); Josie Catalano and Shawn McIlvaine (Salem County); Debra Shipp (Albemarle County); Deidre Martin, Ciera Morris, and Madison Lewis (Cumberland County); Kathleen Torrence and Debbie Szymanski (Isle of Wight County); Michelle Gordon (Mecklenburg County); Traci Johnson (Northampton County); Machelle Eppes (Prince Edward County); Bevill Dean (Richmond City); Chaz Evans-Haywood (Rockingham County); Rick Francis (Southampton County); Paul Jones (Alexander County); Philip Costello and Thomas Sobun (Cook County); staff of the Illinois Regional Archives Depository at Carbondale; Janet Carril and Lamark Kirkwood (Madison County); Marcus Grace (Massac County); Theresa Lonergan (Morgan County); Cindy Kennedy (Pulaski County); staff (St. Clair County); Eddie Walker and Thomas O'Beirne (Adams County); Carolyn Parham and Ed Peacock (Coahoma County); Zack Wallace (Hinds County); Sherry Wall (Lafayette County); and Lucy Carpenter (Marshall County).

A book like this one also requires time to think and to write, and money to travel to where the evidence is. I have been fortunate to have received such support along the way. Bob Nelson, then Director of the American Bar Foundation (ABF), was steadfast early on, and encouraged me to think big while tutoring me in the lingo and imperatives of law-and-society scholarship. I am grateful for the generous financial support the project received from the ABF, the Northwestern University Dean's Office (through term appointments as Charles Deering McCormick Professor of Teaching Excellence and Wayne V. Jones Research Professor in History), and more recently at UC Berkeley from an appointment to the Alexander F. and May T. Morrison Professorship of American History and American Citizenship. Year-long fellowships from the American Council of Learned Societies (ACLS), the Stanford Humanities Center, and the Newberry Library's National Endowment for the Humanities afforded me precious blocks of time to think and to write. When I began this project, I thought it would be about Washington DC and Virginia. Thanks to the expert guidance of Katherine Hannaford and Lucinda Underwood at the ABF, a grant from the National Science Foundation (award #0921883) enabled me to think much bigger. Since my move to Berkeley, I very much appreciate the support this project has received from the History Department and Division of Social Science, and from the Berkeley Law School, whose dean, Erwin Chemerinsky, has consistently championed the value of law-school-based interdisciplinary scholarship and teaching. A five-year Fellowship from the John D. and Catherine T. MacArthur Foundation was transformative and I am deeply grateful for the trust they placed in me.

I have benefited from conversations and criticism by Gregory Ablavsky, Abbye Atkinson, Bernadette Atuahene, the late Penelope Baskerville, Shana Bernstein, Wallace Best, Eric Biber, Traci Burch, Carolyn Chen, Jane Dailey, Stephen Daniels, Adrienne Davis, Shari Diamond, Myisha Eatmon, the late Lauren Edelman, Laura Edwards, Elizabeth Emens, Brodie Fischer, Adrienne Frie, Barbara Fried, Stavros Gadinis, Mark Gergen, Risa Goluboff, Sarah Barringer Gordon, David Grewal, Joanna Grisinger, James Grossman, John Hagan, Terence Halliday, Hendrik

Hartog, Alexandra Havrylyshyn, Carol Heimer, John Heinz, Bonnie Honig, Martha Jones, Stephanie Jones-Rogers, Stephen Kantrowitz, David Konig, Robert Kutchin, the late David Lieberman, Kenneth Mack, Waldo Martin, Kate Masur, Leslie McCall, Kevin McCarthy, Ajay Mehrotra, Elizabeth Mertz, Jesse Nasta, Laura Beth Nielsen, Osagie Obasogie, Peter Paris, Frank Partnoy, Stephen Penningroth, Claire Priest, Emily Prifogle, Jothie Rajah, Osborne Reaves, Richard Roberts, Russell Robinson, Carol Rose, David Schoenbrun, Christopher Schmidt, Susan Shapiro, Richard Shragger, Justin Simard, Henry and Margaret Smith, Amy Dru Stanley, Karen Tani, Robert Tobias, Arielle Tolman, Chris Tomlins, Ann Twitty, Nicole Viglini, Kimberly Welch, Barbara Welke, John Witt, Vicky Saker Woeste, and Magdalene Zier. Early conversations with Michael P. Johnson and Calvin Morrill helped me formulate my approach to sampling, and toward the end Leslie McCall gave me an emergency tutorial in interpreting sampled evidence, as well as astute comments along the way. Melvin Ely searched his files to point me to the images of Appomattox boatmen. Kenneth Snowden referred me to resources on real estate finance. Frank Partnoy pointed me in the right direction on corporation law with his usual grace and good humor.

Carolyn Chen, Brian Delay, Laura Edwards, Dirk Hartog, Waldo Martin, Kate Masur, Ailey Penningroth, and Christopher Tomlins read the whole manuscript and gave me astute and invaluable criticism. I received helpful comments on portions of this book from Abbye Atkinson, Mark Gergen, Stephanie Jones-Rogers, Ken Mack, Leslie McCall, Stephen Penningroth, Russell Robinson, Christopher Schmidt, seven anonymous reviewers for the *Journal of American History,* the editors of the *University of Pennsylvania Law Review*, and from presentations at legal history workshops at Stanford Law, the University of Pennsylvania Law School, Yale Law School, Columbia Law School, the University of Virginia Law School, the American Bar Foundation, the University of Wisconsin-Madison, the University of Minnesota Law School, and Harvard Law School; at annual meetings of the American Society for Legal History, the American Historical Association, and the Law and

Society Association; at the University of Chicago History Department, the Northwestern Black Law Students Association, Northwestern History Department, the Berkeley Center for the Study of Law and Society, the American Studies Program of Princeton University, the Princeton History Department, the History Colloquium at Southwestern University; and from audiences at the University of Miami Center for the Humanities, Vanderbilt Law School, Boston College, and the National Museum of African American History.

My literary agent, the incomparable Tanya McKinnon, grasped what I was driving at from our very first conversation and always kept the big picture in view. I could not have asked for a better editor than Dan Gerstle. At every stage, Dan's thoughtful questions and suggestions drew out the essence of the project. Zeba Arora kept the train on schedule while Dan was on leave. Nancy Green's superb copyediting improved the book immensely. I thank Dassi Zeidel, Lauren Abbate, and the entire team at Norton/Liveright for helping get the right words on the page. Fanta Diallo, Peter Miller, Elizabeth Shreve, and Lauren Hodapp made sure the word got out.

Bernadette Atuahene, Wallace Best, Paul Bertoni, Chuck Bush, Reginald Butler, Gerry Cadava, Laura Edwards, Adrian Gaskins, Leslie Harris, Dirk Hartog, Kate Masur, Leslie McCall, Russell Robinson, Christopher Schmidt, David Schoenbrun, and Wilhelmina and Travis Webber were steadfast friends when I needed them most. My aunt and uncle Bob and Susan Tobias, my South Orange aunts Agnes Buchanan-Warner, Dorothy Sparrow, Mamie Austin, Nancy Smith, and Helen Harris, my Reaves cousins Karen and Ed, Greg and Beth, Mike, Steven, Michele, Martine, Jeff, Renée, Reggie, Jackie, Mark, Jackie, Stephany, Alisha, Danielle, Jordan, Josh, Mia, my sister Ailey and brother-in-law Bob Williams, my father Stephen and stepmother, Judy Roberts, my uncle Ozzie, uncle Henry and aunt Margaret, and my mother, listened patiently to me going on and on about tenancies in common, and only teased me a little. In the middle of one memorably difficult Mississippi research trip, Greg, Mike, Steve, and uncle

Ozzie rescued me for a much-needed Mardi Gras at Aunt Jeannette's house in New Orleans.

For all the time I spent looking at documents, my inspiration often came from interviews. I am grateful to the lawyers who shared their memories with me, including the Hon. Henry Marsh, Professor (emeritus) Curtis Reitz, the late James "Penny" Baber, and the late Benjamin Michel. Members of my own family let me interview them and cheered me on, including my grandmother, Mary Baskerville; my mother, Penelope Baskerville; my father, Stephen Penningroth, who also gave me a quick tutorial in catalysis; my great-uncle, the late Osborne Reaves; my aunt Agnes Buchanan; my aunt, Adunni Slackman Anderson; my aunt Margaret Smith and my great-uncle, the late Henry Smith. My mother never let me officially interview her but much of the inspiration and substance of this book came from years of talking with her. She explained "packing the deacon board" to me. She went with me to some of the archives. She was there whenever I had an academic talk anywhere in the tri-state/DC area. She was there when my Uncle Ozzie first reconnected me with Uncle Henry, whose memories proved crucial to the writing. She kept her brother's recorded interview of my Uncle Tom for many years, and gave it to me at just the right time. And she cheered me on every step of the way. I miss her more than words can express.

Two years ago, I donated one of my kidneys to someone I love dearly. Along the way, I learned that donors can help ease the enormous shortage of donors that plagues this country by talking about their experiences, by letting people know that it is possible. So here goes: donating is not only possible, it is surprisingly simple. I did some health screenings. I flew out for a full workup. Then again for the surgery. I took a couple of weeks off work afterward. And I was back jogging a couple of weeks after that. The whole thing was beautiful and joyous. To Laurie Shore, Sherry Matthias, Santa Rosario, Aidee Alaniz Molina, Dr. Heidi Pearson, Dr. Chole Wang, and the entire transplant team at Tampa General Hospital, to Uncle Herman Anderson, to the anonymous family with whom we paired, to my family, and especially to Ailey: thank you. You gave me a gift for which I will always be grateful.

This project is older than my children. August and Julien have done their level best to distract me with backyard basketball and badminton and Jeffrey-ball and tag and tickle fights, and I am grateful for every minute of it. Carolyn Chen has put up with this thing even longer. She read drafts and talked shop with me after the boys were in bed, talked trash during family hoops games, researched and published her own second book, covered for me while I went off on weeks-long trips to the courthouses, held the phone up to the boys' ears so I could say goodnight, and gently but pointedly described all the fun vacations we would take After The Book Is Finally Done. Like the song goes, what is there to say?

ABBREVIATIONS

AFIC	Records of the American Freedmen's Inquiry Commission, File O-328 (1863), Entry 12, Letters Received, 1805–89, Correspondence, 1800–1947, General Records of the Adjutant General's Office, Record Group 94, National Archives, Washington, DC
Afro	*Baltimore Afro-American*
AHM	Atlanta History Museum
ALDAH	Alabama Department of Archives and History
AHR	*American Historical Review*
Am. Jur.	*American Jurisprudence*
b	box
BAP	C. Peter Ripley et al., eds. *The Black Abolitionist Papers.* 5 vols. Chapel Hill: University of North Carolina, 1985.
Bouvier 1843	John Bouvier, *Law Dictionary, Adapted to the Constitution and Laws of the United States of America, and of the Several States of the American Union* (T. and J. W. Johnson, 1843).
Bouvier 1868	John Bouvier, *A Law Dictionary, Adapted to the Constitution and Laws of the United States of America and of the Several States of the American Union* (G. W. Childs, 1868).
Bouvier 1871	John Bouvier, *A Law Dictionary, Adapted to the Constitution and Laws of the United States of America, and of the Several States of the American Union: With References to the Civil and Other Systems of Foreign Law* (J. B. Lippincott, 1874).

Bouvier 1883	John Bouvier, *A Law Dictionary, Adapted to the Constitution and Laws of the United States of America* . . . 2 vols. (J. B. Lippincott, 1883).
Bouvier 1897	*Bouvier's Law Dictionary* by John Bouvier, a New Edition Thoroughly Revised and Brought up to Date by Francis Rawle, new, rev. ed. (Boston Book Company, 1897).
Bouvier 1914	*Bouvier's Law Dictionary and Concise Encyclopedia.* 8th ed. (Vernon Law Book Company, 1914).
BRFAL	Records of the Bureau of Refugees, Freedmen, and Abandoned Lands, Record Group 105, National Archives, Washington, DC
BTV	Behind the Veil Project, Duke University Archives
CBMB	Cumberland Baptist Church Minute Book, 1836–1856, Library of Virginia
CBRB	Cumberland Baptist Church Record Book, 1856–1896, microfilm reel 88, Local Government Records Collection, Library of Virginia
CCA	Clerk of the Circuit Court Archives, Richard J. Daley Center, Chicago, IL
CD	*Chicago Defender*
CG	*Congressional Globe*
CHM	Chicago History Museum, Archives and Manuscripts
CirCtCh	Circuit Court, Chancery
CirCtLaw	Circuit Court, Law
CLR	*Columbia Law Review*
CoCtCh	County Court, Chancery
CoCtLaw	County Court, Law
CR	*Christian Recorder*
DB	Deed Book
DLJ	*Duke Law Journal*
DNWG	The Legal Papers of Dallas Nicholas and William Gosnell, Thurgood Marshall Law Library, The University of Maryland School of Law, Baltimore, MD
DUKES	The Papers of Duke and Duke, MSS 79-6, Archives & Special Collections, University of Virginia School of Law

EASTLAND	James O. Eastland Collection, MUM00117, Department of Archives and Special Collections, University of Mississippi
EDC	Entry 69, Equity Case Files, Supreme Court of Washington, DC, Record Group 21, National Archives, Washington, DC
f	folder
FDHE	René Hayden, Anthony E. Kaye, Kate Masur, Steven F. Miller, Susan E. O'Donovan, Leslie S. Rowland, and Stephen A. West, eds. *Freedom: A Documentary History of Emancipation, 1861–1867*, ser. 3, vol. 2: *Land and Labor, 1866–1867* (University of North Carolina, 2013)
FPMS	E. Franklin Frazier Papers, Moorland-Spingarn Collection, Howard University, Washington, DC
FJ	*Freedom's Journal*
FSDC	Freedom Summer Digital Collection
FSSP	Records of the Freedmen and Southern Society Project, College Park, Md. (with document identification number)
FWP	Federal Writers' Project, Works Progress Administration
GSA	Archives of the State of Georgia, Morrow, GA
GWIN	Gwin and Mounger Records, Z 2299.000 S, Mississippi Department of Archives and History
HLR	*Harvard Law Review*
ILSA	Illinois State Archives, Springfield, IL
JAH	*Journal of American History*
JNH	*Journal of Negro History*
JSH	*Journal of Southern History*
KLUGER	Kluger Collection, Yale University Archives
KPP	Martin Luther King, Jr. Papers Project, Stanford University
LHR	*Law and History Review*
LSI	*Law & Social Inquiry*
LSR	*Law & Society Review*
LV	Library of Virginia, Richmond, VA
LVRC	Library of Virginia State Records Center, Richmond, VA
MDAH	Mississippi Department of Archives and History, Jackson, MS

NAACP Papers	Papers of the NAACP, Library of Congress, ProQuest History Vault
NARA	National Archives and Records Administration, Washington DC
NCSA	State Archives of North Carolina
NJLL	New Jersey State Law Library, Trenton, NJ
NJSA	New Jersey State Archives, Trenton, NJ
NYAN	*New York Amsterdam News*
NYT	*New York Times*
OWEN	Thomas Scott Owen Papers, MDAH
PC	*Pittsburgh Courier*
PERCY	Percy Family Papers, Z 0209.003, MDAH
PLR	*University of Pennsylvania Law Review*
RG 393, Part I	Records of Geographical Divisions and Departments and Military (Reconstruction) Districts, Part I, Records of United States Army Continental Commands, 1821–1920, Record Group 393, National Archives, Washington, DC
RG 393, Part IV	Provost Marshal Field Organizations of the Civil War, Part IV, Records of Military Installations, Records of United States Army Continental Commands, 1821–1920, Record Group 393, National Archives, Washington, DC
RP	*Richmond Planet*
RPA	Raymond Pace Alexander Papers, UPT 50 A374R, University Archives & Records Center, University of Pennsylvania
SCC	Case Files, Southern Claims Commission, Records of the Third Auditor, Allowed Case Files, Records of the U.S. General Accounting Office, Record Group 217, National Archives, Washington, DC
Schomburg	Schomburg Center for Research in Black Culture, New York Public Library
SHC	Southern Historical Collection, Wilson Library, University of North Carolina at Chapel Hill
SLR	*Stanford Law Review*
SOHP	Southern Oral History Program Collection, Southern

	Historical Collection, Wilson Library, University of North Carolina at Chapel Hill
STMA	Sadie Tanner Mossell Alexander Papers, UPT 50 A374S, University Archives & Records Center, University of Pennsylvania
TSLA	Tennessee State Library and Archives
UVALaw	Special Collections, University of Virginia Law Library
VFC	Voices of Freedom Collection, Virginia Commonwealth University Libraries Digital Collections
VHS	Virginia Historical Society
WAITS	Hilton Waits Collection, MUM01706, Department of Archives and Special Collections, University of Mississippi
WMQ	*William & Mary Quarterly*
YLJ	*Yale Law Journal*

Citations to proceedings of the Colored National Conventions are to the Colored Conventions Project website: https://omeka.coloredconventions.org

NOTE: All money figures converted using the "production worker compensation" measure at www.measuringworth.com.

NOTES

INTRODUCTION

1 Interview of Thomas Holcomb by Craig Baskerville (1976). This puzzlement was also partly because at first my uncle Tom said it was Union general Ulysses S. Grant's men.

2 U.S. Census Bureau, Twelfth Census of the United States: 1900: Virginia, Cumberland County, Randolph District, Sheet 11; deed from Rebecca F. Blanton to Jackson Holcombe, Apr, 9, 1883, DB 33, 59; Jackson Holcombe to Louisa Holcombe, Jan. 24, 1899, DB 38, 344, Office of Circuit Clerk, Cumberland Co., VA; Holcomb interview (1976); deed from Jackson and Louisa Holcomb to "Phillip Blanton Colored," Apr. 26, 1915, DB 52, 147; deed from Robert L. Holcomb, Grand Noble et al. to Florence E. Lantigua, July 12, 1951, DB 90, 188; E[dward] T. Hiscox, *The Star Book for Ministers* (1878), 226, 239; *Community Leaders of Virginia, 1976–1977,* ed. Harry Hone (American Biographical Center, 1977), 61; "Robert Holcomb, Church Leader, Is Eulogized," *New Journal and Guide,* Oct. 25, 1958, C5.

3 Interview of Osborne Reaves, Mar. 25, 2016; interview of Henry Smith, Mar. 25, 2016; deed from Thomas Holcomb and Annie Holcomb to Stonewall J. Holcomb et al., trustees of Midway Baptist Church, Nov. 1, 1965, DB 111, 3.

4 James Baldwin, "The White Man's Guilt," *Ebony,* August 1965, 47-48. On historians' positionality, see Kendra T. Field, "The Privilege of Family History," AHR 127, no. 2 (2022), 600–33; Martha Biondi, *The Black Revolution on Campus* (University of California Press, 2012), 1–4, 179–80; August Meier and Elliott Rudwick, *Black History and the Historical Profession, 1915–1980* (University of Illinois Press, 1986), 176–77, 189–93; Clayborne Carson, *In Struggle: SNCC and the Black Awakening of the 1960s* (Harvard University Press, 1981), 4; Vincent Harding, *There Is a River: The Struggle for Black Freedom in America* (Harcourt Brace & Co., 1981), 3.

5 On the vibrant interconnections between scholarship and social movements, see Robin D. G. Kelley, *Freedom Dreams: The Black Radical Imagination* (Beacon Press, 2022), esp. xviii. A classic example of "grassroots" historiography is John Dittmer,

Local People: The Struggle for Civil Rights in Mississippi (University of Illinois Press, 1994).

6 For examples, see Jacquelyn Dowd Hall, "The Long Civil Rights Movement and the Political Uses of the Past," JAH 91 (March 2005), 1233–63; Glenda Gilmore, *Defying Dixie: The Radical Roots of Civil Rights, 1919–1950* (W. W. Norton, 2008), 4–11; Thomas J. Sugrue, *Sweet Land of Liberty: The Forgotten Struggle for Civil Rights in the North* (Random House, 2008), xvi–xvii; Mia Bay, *Traveling Black: A Story of Race and Resistance* (Harvard University Press, 2021), 3, 17. For criticism of the "long movement" paradigm, see Thomas C. Holt, *The Movement: The African American Struggle for Civil Rights* (Oxford University Press, 2021); Christopher W. Schmidt, *Civil Rights in America: A History* (Cambridge University Press, 2021), 3–10; Sundiata Keita Cha-Jua and Clarence Lang, "The 'Long Movement' as Vampire: Temporal and Spatial Fallacies in Recent Black Freedom Studies," *Journal of African American History* 92 (Spring 2007), 273–80.

7 Carson, *In Struggle,* 1; Ta-Nehisi Coates, "The Case for Reparations," *The Atlantic,* June 2014, 54–71 ("plunder"); Keeanga-Yamahtta Taylor, *Race for Profit: How Banks and the Real Estate Industry Undermined Black Homeownership* (University of North Carolina Press, 2019); Beryl Satter, *Family Properties: Race, Real Estate, and the Exploitation of Black Urban America* (Picador, 2009). Black history has veered between narrative frames of resistance and (more recently) despair, precisely because scholars have tended to conceive of Black politics and Black self-definition almost entirely along the axis of race. Vincent Brown, "Social Death and Political Life in the Study of Slavery," AHR 114, no. 5 (2009), 1235, 1244.

8 Richard Kluger, *Simple Justice: The History of Brown v. Board of Education and Black America's Struggle for Equality* (1975; Vintage, 2004), 136; Sugrue, *Sweet Land of Liberty,* 54–55. On dispossession as the foundation of Black collective identity, see Saidiya Hartman, *Lose Your Mother: A Journey Along the Atlantic Slave Route* (Farrar, Straus & Giroux, 2007), 233–34. On law as social control, see Charles S. Johnson, *Shadow of the Plantation* (University of Chicago Press, 1934), 191–92; Neil R. McMillen, *Dark Journey: Black Mississippians in the Age of Jim Crow* (University of Illinois Press, 1989), 197–223, 385n11; David M. Oshinsky, *"Worse Than Slavery": Parchman Farm and the Ordeal of Jim Crow Justice* (Free Press, 1996), esp. 131–32, 238–48. The "afreaid" quotation is from Risa L. Goluboff, *The Lost Promise of Civil Rights* (Harvard University Press, 2007), 80 (spelling in original).

9 Speech of Sen. Jacob Howard, CG, 39th Cong., 1st Sess. (Jan. 30, 1866), 504.

10 "Smart Answer," FJ, May 25, 1827; "Business Law," CR, Aug. 9, 1877; Catalogue of the Tuskegee Normal and Industrial Institute, 1895–96 (Normal School Press, 1896), 42, 45; "Mortgage Burning and Laying of Cornerstone at the Hamlett Temple Christian Methodist Episcopal Church," Nov. 23, 1975, f 17, b 11, Bunton Papers, Schomburg; John Hope Franklin, *From Slavery to Freedom: A History of American Negroes,* 2nd ed. (Knopf, 1964).

11 "Bottom-up" legal historians have long debated a theoretical distinction between

"lay" and "legal" consciousness. Another influential strand focuses on lawyers as intermediaries. Christopher Tomlins, "What Is Left of the Law and Society Paradigm after Critique? Revisiting Gordon's 'Critical Legal Histories,'" LSI 37 (Winter 2012), 155–66; Goluboff, *Lost Promise;* Tomiko Brown-Nagin, *Courage to Dissent: Atlanta and the Long History of the Civil Rights Movement* (Oxford University Press, 2011), 8, 11, 269, 434. I build on those insights. Also, lest anyone think that digitization is the solution, I should add that when properly kept, paper is much more durable than any computer or cloud storage yet invented.

12 I created a purposive interval sample of county, circuit, and justice-of-peace court dockets and "order books" in Illinois, Virginia, Mississippi, New Jersey, North Carolina, and the District of Columbia. I visited circuit clerks' offices in twenty-two counties; other dockets are held in state or regional repositories. New Jersey's Chancery Court was statewide until 1947; thereafter, equity cases went to a division of the state Superior Court. I took photographs on-site. Research assistants and I transcribed docket entries from those docket photographs. We usually sampled twenty-five cases per decade per county, from both "Law" and "Chancery" dockets, for years ending in 2, from 1872 through 1962, evenly across a calendar year whenever possible. For each sampled case, we coded the names of parties, cause of action, and other relevant information into a FileMaker database. We then searched party names in the manuscript Census on Ancestry.com, coded each party as either "no match," "low-confidence match," or "high-confidence match," and filled in the party's race, sex, and other information. To date, we have coded 14,016 civil cases, plus a smaller sample of 2,393 criminal cases. Of these, we have low- or high-confidence matches for at least one party in 10,394 civil cases, of whom 1,542 involved Black individuals or entities, and for 7,351 civil plaintiffs, of whom 998 were Black individuals or entities. In both the percentages of cases involving Black plaintiffs and the mix of case types, the findings here differ sharply from those derived from keyword searches of state supreme court reports.

13 For criticism of the resistance model in legal history, see Laura F. Edwards, *Only the Clothes on Her Back: Clothing and the Hidden History of Power in the Nineteenth-Century United States* (Oxford University Press, 2022). On the inadequacy and instability of rights, see Barbara Ransby, *Ella Baker and the Black Freedom Movement: A Radical Democratic Vision* (University of North Carolina Press, 2003), 254, 319; Mark Tushnet, "An Essay on Rights," *Texas Law Review* 62, no. 8 (1984), 1363–403; Saidiya V. Hartman, *Scenes of Subjection: Terror, Slavery, and Self-Making in Nineteenth-Century America* (Oxford University Press, 1997), 118–51. See also Patricia J. Williams, *The Alchemy of Race and Rights: Diary of a Law Professor* (Harvard University Press, 1991), 153.

14 A. E. Keir Nash, "Fairness and Formalism in the Trials of Blacks in the State Supreme Courts of the Old South," *Virginia Law Review* 56, no. 1 (1970), 64–100. Compare Melvin Patrick Ely, *Israel on the Appomattox: A Southern Experiment in Black Freedom from the 1790s through the Civil War* (Random House, 2004), 116.

15 Khalil Gibran Muhammad, *The Condemnation of Blackness: Race, Crime, and the Making of Modern Urban America* (Harvard University Press, 2010), 226–68.

16 William J. Novak, "The American Law of Association: The Legal-Political Construction of Civil Society," *Studies in American Political Development* 15 (Fall 2001), 167, 172–74; Kate Masur, *An Example for All the Land: Emancipation and the Struggle over Equality in Washington, D.C.* (University of North Carolina Press, 2010), 5.

17 Eric Foner, *Free Soil, Free Labor, Free Men: The Ideology of the Republican Party before the Civil War* (1970; Oxford University Press, 1995), 290–91; Hendrik Hartog, "The Constitution of Aspiration and 'The Rights That Belong to Us All,'" JAH 74 (Dec. 1987), 1033; Alice Walker, "Everyday Use," in *In Love and Trouble: Stories of Black Women* (1967; Harcourt, 1973), 47–59. In seeking to bring private law into the genealogy of Black rights discourse, I am building on Williams, *Alchemy of Race and Rights*, 164–65.

A NOTE ON TERMINOLOGY

1 Tiya Miles, *All That She Carried: The Journey of Ashley's Sack, a Black Family Keepsake* (Random House, 2021), 287–89; Dylan C. Penningroth, "The Claims of Slaves and Ex-Slaves to Family and Property: A Transatlantic Comparison," AHR 112 (2007), 1048–53, 1060, 1068–69.

2 Walter Johnson, "On Agency," *Journal of Social History* 37 (2003), 113–21.

CHAPTER 1: THE PRIVILEGES OF SLAVERY

1 Caitlin Rosenthal, *Accounting for Slavery: Masters and Management* (Harvard University Press, 2018); Jean M. Humez, *Harriet Tubman: The Life and the Life Stories* (University of Wisconsin Press, 2003), 175–77; Stephanie E. Jones-Rogers, *They Were Her Property: White Women as Slave Owners in the American South* (Yale University Press, 2019); Sven Beckert, *Empire of Cotton: A Global History* (Knopf, 2015).

2 Bouvier 1843, 369; Henry James Holthouse, *A New Law Dictionary* [. . .] (Lea and Blanchard, 1847), 339.

3 Edlie Wong, *Neither Fugitive nor Free: Atlantic Slavery, Freedom Suits, and the Legal Culture of Travel* (New York University Press, 2009), 8; Laura F. Edwards, *The People and Their Peace: Legal Culture and the Transformation of Inequality in the Post-Revolutionary South* (University of North Carolina Press, 2009), 28–29, 58. Testimony of Joseph Bacon, 1873, Claim No. 21447, SCC.

4 Arthur Linton Corbin, *Corbin on Contracts: A Comprehensive Treatise on the Working Rules of Contract Law,* §231 (1963) ("community opinion"). See also Dylan C. Penningroth, "Race in Contract Law," PLR 170, no. 5 (2022).

5 Frederick Law Olmsted, *A Journey in the Seaboard Slave States, with Remarks on Their Economy* (Dix & Edwards, 1856), 436; Philip D. Morgan, *Slave Counterpoint: Black Culture in the Eighteenth-Century Chesapeake and Lowcountry* (University of North

Carolina Press, 1998), 184–87; Frederick Law Olmsted, *A Journey in the Back Country* (Mason Brothers, 1860), 483; Justene Hill Edwards, *Unfree Markets: The Slaves' Economy and the Rise of Capitalism in South Carolina* (Columbia University Press, 2021), 16–23.

6 Orville Vernon Burton, *In My Father's House Are Many Mansions: Family and Community in Edgefield, South Carolina* (University of North Carolina Press, 1985); 161 (South Carolina patches); Frederick Law Olmsted, *The Papers of Frederick Law Olmsted,* ed. Charles E. Beveridge and Charles Capen McLaughlin, vol. 2, *Slavery and the South, 1852–1857* (Johns Hopkins University Press, 1981), 183–85, 217–18 (Mississippi patches); *Advice Among Masters: The Ideal in Slave Management in the Old South,* ed. James O. Breeden (Greenwood Press, 1980), 2, 71–72 (Alabama patches); Sojourner Truth, *Narrative of Sojourner Truth* (Vintage, 1993), 3; Rosenthal, *Accounting for Slavery,* 96–97, 115–16; Betty Wood, *Women's Work, Men's Work: The Informal Slave Economies of Lowcountry Georgia* (University of Georgia Press, 1995), 12–15; Jessica Marie Johnson, *Wicked Flesh: Black Women, Intimacy, and Freedom in the Atlantic World* (University of Pennsylvania Press, 2020), 183; Morgan, *Slave Counterpoint,* 137–38.

7 Charles Ball, *Slavery in the United States: A Narrative of the Life and Adventures of Charles Ball, a Black Man* (John S. Taylor, 1837), 191; Melvin Patrick Ely, *Israel on the Appomattox: A Southern Experiment in Black Freedom from the 1790s through the Civil War* (Random House, 2004), 150–74; Dylan C. Penningroth, *The Claims of Kinfolk: African American Property and Community in the Nineteenth-Century South* (University of North Carolina Press, 2003), 61–66; *Broadhead v. Jones,* 39 Ala. 96, 97 (1863); Laura F. Edwards, *Only the Clothes on Her Back: Clothing and the Hidden History of Power in the Nineteenth-Century United States* (Oxford University Press, 2022), 31–32, 173–89; Jean Fagan Yellin, *Harriet Jacobs: A Life* (Basic Civitas, 2004), 12.

8 On the geographic incidence of the overwork systems, see Steven Hahn, *A Nation Under Our Feet: Black Political Struggles in the Rural South from Slavery to the Great Migration* (Harvard University Press, 2003), 22–23; Charles Dew, *Bond of Iron: Master and Slave at Buffalo Forge* (W. W. Norton, 1994). On caulking and wages, Frederick Douglass, *My Bondage and My Freedom* (1855), 318–20; Seth Rockman, *Scraping By: Wage Labor, Slavery, and Survival in Early Baltimore* (Johns Hopkins University Press, 2009), 8–9, 57–59; William Wetmore Story, *A Treatise on the Law of Contracts Not Under Seal,* 2nd ed. (1847), 1 ("undertakes").

9 On slaveowners' financial calculations about slaves' aging and disabilities, see Sharla M. Fett, *Working Cures: Healing, Health, and Power on Southern Slave Plantations* (University of North Carolina Press, 2002), 18–20; Rosenthal, *Accounting for Slavery,* 36, 126, 141–45. On state efforts to counter such cost shifting, see Hendrik Hartog, *The Trouble with Minna: A Case of Slavery and Emancipation in the Antebellum North* (University of North Carolina Press, 2018), 61–67; Shane White, *Somewhat More Independent: The End of Slavery in New York City, 1770–1810* (University of Georgia Press, 1991), 111–13; Sarah Levine-Gronningsater, "Delivering

Freedom: Gradual Emancipation, Black Legal Culture, and the Origins of Sectional Crisis in New York, 1759–1870," PhD diss., University of Chicago, 2014, 108–10; Truth, *Narrative,* 26–27.

10 Todd L. Savitt, "Slave Life Insurance in Virginia and North Carolina," JSH 43, no. 4 (1977), 583–85; Frederick Douglass, *Narrative of the Life of Frederick Douglass, an American Slave, Written by Himself* (1845; W. W. Norton, 1997), 37–38; Moses Grandy, *Narrative of the Life of Moses Grandy* (Oliver Johnson, 1844), 51; Alix Lerner, "Aging in Bondage: Slavery, Debility, and the Problem of Dependency in the Antebellum South," PhD diss., Princeton University, 2017, 14, 91–101, 131, 149–58.

11 Walter Johnson, *Soul by Soul: Life inside the Antebellum Slave Market* (Harvard University Press, 1999), 217–19 ("chattel principle"); Hartog, *Trouble with Minna,* 9–11 ("infected").

12 Edwards, *Only the Clothes on Her Back,* 141–47, 202–6; Andrea G. McDowell, "From Commons to Claims: Property Rights in the California Gold Rush," *Yale Journal of Law & the Humanities* 14, no. 1 (2002), 11–17.

13 Jesse Dukeminier et al., *Property,* 8th ed. (Wolters Kluver, 2014), 147–50, 842; Restatement (Second) of Contracts, §222, illustrations 1 (shingles), 5 (fourteen days).

14 Maureen E. Brady, "The Forgotten History of Metes and Bounds," YLJ 128, no. 4 (2019), 902–7; Claire Priest, *Credit Nation: Property Laws and Legal Institutions in Early America* (Princeton University Press, 2021), 46 (quoting Blackstone).

15 Priest, *Credit Nation,* 46–49.

16 R. Q. Mallard, *Plantation Life before Emancipation* (1892), 18; Penningroth, *Claims of Kinfolk,* 91–99.

17 Testimony of Henrietta McLaughlin, claim of Lucy Lee, Hinds County, Mississippi, SCC; testimony of Samson Bacon, claim of Prince Stevens, Liberty County, Georgia, SCC.

18 Testimony of George Richardson, claim of Emily Frazier, Limestone County, Alabama, SCC.

19 Testimony of Samson Bacon and Brister Fleming, claim of Prince Stevens, Liberty County, Georgia, SCC.

20 Carol M. Rose, "Possession as the Origin of Property," *University of Chicago Law Review* 52, no. 1 (1985), 77–78, 82–84. For a complementary, but different interpretation, see Edwards, *People and Their Peace,* 4–10, 134–35, 238–56. Bouvier 1897, 703, s.v. "possession" (citing *Bryan v. Spivey,* 109 N.C. 57 [1891], a case involving a large settlement of ex-slaves).

21 Albert Pike, "Letters from Arkansas," 213, repr. in *Travels in the Old South: Selected from the Periodicals of the Times,* ed. Eugene L. Schwaab (University Press of Kentucky, 1973) ("some mark"); testimony of John Keyser, Spencer Cummins, James Clarke, all in *Matthews v. Clarke,* Dec. 21, 1867, Provost Court at Berkeley, 1867–1868, RG 393, Part IV. See also Frederick Law Olmsted, *The Cotton Kingdom:*

A Traveller's Observations on Cotton and Slavery in the American Slave States, 1853–1861 (1861; DaCapo Press, 1996), 185; *Richardson v. Broughton,* 3 Strob. 1 (1848); William Howard Russell, *My Diary North and South,* vol. 1 (Bradbury and Evans, 1863), 196; testimony of Meyer Levy in claim of Jackson French, 24–25, Claiborne County, MS, SCC.

22 *State v. John Davis* 24 N.C. 153 (1841); A. R. Newsome, "The A. S. Merrimon Journal, 1853–1854," *North Carolina Historical Review* 8, no. 3 (1931), 313; *The Revised Statutes of the State of North Carolina,* vol. 1 (Turner and Hughes, 1837), ch. 17, §1; "Record Book of Marks & Brands No. A," 037.908.1, Stock Marks, 1732–1809, 1835, Misc. Records, Edgecombe Co., NCSA; Brady, "Forgotten History of Metes and Bounds," 872–953.

23 Revised Statutes of the State of North Carolina, ch. 111, §24; *McNamara v. Kerns,* 24 N.C. 66 (1841); *White v. Cline,* 52 N.C. 174, 176 (1859); *Hobson v. Perry,* 1 Hill (SC) 277 (1833).

24 Testimony of John Hill, James Murray, and George G. Murray in *Matthews v. Clarke,* Dec. 21, 1867; testimony of George S. Simmons, claim of Horace Herndon, Lauderdale Co., Alabama, SCC.

25 Revised Statutes of North Carolina, 1837, ch. 111, §§23, 28, 82–85 ("certain articles"); Rev. Stat. ch. 34, § 75 ("lawful"); Dukeminier et al., *Property,* 99 (the rights to possess, use, exclude, and dispose (or "alienate") by sale or gift); Yellin, *Harriet Jacobs,* 12.

26 *Stanley v. Nelson,* 28 Ala. 514 (1856) (enslaved subcontractor); *Barker v. Swain,* 57 N.C. 220 (1858) (hiring white man); Ulrich B. Phillips, *Life and Labor in the Old South* (Little, Brown, 1929), 248 (accounts, probate); Yellin, *Harriet Jacobs,* 21–22 (Molly's auction). On the role of public signaling in contract law, see Lon L. Fuller, Melvin Aron Eisenberg, and Mark P. Gergen, *Basic Contract Law* (West Academic, 2018), 10th ed., 16.

27 *Batten v. Faulk,* 49 N.C. 233 (1856) (enslaved borrower); *Webb v. Kelly,* 37 Ala. 333, 336 (1861); *Broadhead v. Jones,* 39 Ala. 96 (1863); *Jenkins v. Brown,* 25 Tenn. 299 (1845) (enslaved lender); *Love v. Brindle,* 7 Jones (NC) 560 (1860); *Gregg v. Thompson,* 9 S.C.L. 331 (1818) ("note"); Harriet Jacobs, *Incidents in the Life of a Slave Girl* (1861), 10; Phillips, *Life and Labor,* 283 ($1,000). On enslaved lenders, see also *Webb v. Kelly,* 37 Ala. 333 (1861); Juliet E. K. Walker, *The History of Black Business in America: Capitalism, Race, Entrepreneurship,* 2nd ed., vol. 1, *to 1865* (University of North Carolina Press, 2009), 83–86. On "banking hubs" controlled by enslaved and free Black women, see Nicole Viglini, "'She Is a Very Smart Woman and a Great Trader': Enslaved and Free Women's Economic Strategies and Gendered Geographies of Credit in the Nineteenth-Century South," PhD diss., University of California-Berkeley, 2023, ch. 3. On cash-poor accounting, see Ely, *Israel on the Appomattox,* 107ff.

28 *Black's Law Dictionary,* 11th ed. (Thomson Reuters, 2019), s.v. "consideration"; Jacobs, *Incidents,* 13, 20; Walter Johnson, "Inconsistency, Contradiction, and

Complete Confusion: The Everyday Life of the Law of Slavery," LSI 22, no. 2 (1997), 418; *Lenoir v. Sylvester,* 1 Bail. 632 (1830).

29 Frederick Douglass, *Narrative of the Life of Frederick Douglass, an American Slave. Written by Himself* (1845), 98–103; Douglass, *Life and Times of Frederick Douglass, Written by Himself, His Early Life as a Slave, His Escape from Bondage, and His Complete History to the Present Time* (Park Publishing Co., 1882), 210; Truth, *Narrative,* 26–27; *Broadhead v. Jones,* 39 Ala. 96, 97 (1863), at 97; *Stanley v. Nelson,* 28 Ala. 514, 515–16 (1856); Walker, *History of Black Business in America,* 79; Wood, *Women's Work, Men's Work,* 61–70.

30 Douglass, *My Bondage and My Freedom,* 328–30; Ball, *Slavery in the United States,* 298–301; Henry Bibb, *Narrative of the Life and Adventures of Henry Bibb, an American Slave, Written by Himself* (1849), 37; *Gist v. Toohey,* 31 S.C.L. 424 (1846).

31 David Thomas Konig, "The St. Louis Slave Freedom Suit Trial Court Records: An on-Line Database of Legal Challenge to Slavery," *Trends in Law Library Management and Technology* 18 (2008), 26; George M. Stroud, *A Sketch of the Laws Relating to Slavery in the Several States of the United States of America* (1856), 121–32; Bouvier 1868, s.v. "slave," 527; Edwards, *People and Their Peace,* 153 (the "peace"); *Bryant v. Sheely,* 35 Ky. 530, 531–32 (1837) (presumption of agency relationship).

32 Kimberly M. Welch, *Black Litigants in the Antebellum American South* (University of North Carolina Press, 2018), 155–56 (indictment for theft from slave); *Waddill v. Martin,* 38 N.C. 562 (1845); *McNamara v. Kerns,* 24 N.C. 66 (1841) ("as if they were"). My interpretation of these cases is inspired in part by Edwards, *People and Their Peace,* 149. *Jenkins v. Brown,* 25 Tenn. 299 (1845) (Black barbers' loan). See also *Sterett's Ex'r v. Kaster,* 37 Ala. 366 (1861). Henry E. Baker, "The Negro in the Field of Invention," JNH 2, no. 1 (1917), 24 (patenting).

33 *Rice v. Cade,* 10 La. 288, 294–95 (1836) (steamboats); *Jones v. Allen,* 38 Tenn. 626, 636–37 (1858) ("absurd"). On regulations and their transient effect, see Thomas D. Morris, *Southern Slavery and the Law, 1619–1860* (University of North Carolina Press, 1996), 349; Wood, *Women's Work, Men's Work,* 87; Michael P. Johnson and James Roark, *Black Masters: A Free Family of Color in the Old South* (W. W. Norton, 1984), 174–76; Penningroth, *Claims of Kinfolk,* 67–70; Luther Porter Jackson, *Free Negro Labor and Property Holding in Virginia, 1830–1860* (Appleton-Century, 1942), 181; Christopher Waldrep, *Roots of Disorder: Race and Criminal Justice in the American South, 1817–80* (University of Illinois Press, 1998), 24–25.

34 Olmsted, *Papers,* 185 (emphasis in original) (fowling piece); Waldrep, *Roots of Disorder,* 33 (groceries and taxis); Johnson, *Soul by Soul,* 64–65, 167–68 (slave pens).

35 Ira Berlin, *Many Thousands Gone: The First Two Centuries of Slavery in North America* (Harvard University Press, 1998), 313 (percentage of whites who owned slaves); *Rice v. Cade* 10 La. 288 (1836) ("trifling"); Breeden, *Advice Among Masters,* 270–71, 273–75, 320–22, 331.

36 On divisions of opinion among whites, see "Greely Take Notice," *Jackson Daily News,* Mar. 16, 1860; Wood, *Women's Work,* 52–80; Waldrep, *Roots of Disorder,* 32–35;

Johnson and Roark, *Black Masters,* 173–84; Morris, *Southern Slavery and the Law,* 351–52, Edwards, *Unfree Markets,* 163–71. On regulation as implying legality, see Morris, *Southern Slavery and the Law,* 349–52; John Belton O'Neall, *The Negro Law of South Carolina* (Columbia, 1848), 21, 43; Thomas R. R. Cobb, *An Inquiry Into the Law of Negro Slavery in the United States of America* (1858), 235, 237; Martha S. Jones, *Birthright Citizens: A History of Race and Rights in Antebellum America* (Cambridge University Press, 2018), 96; *Waddill v. Martin,* at 565 ("a sort of ownership").

37 *Waddill v. Martin* at 563–64; *State v. Negro Will,* 18 N.C. 121 (1834); *Hobson v. Perry,* 19 S.C.L. 277 (1833); *Rice v. Cade,* 10 La. 288 (1836); *Lea v. Brown,* 58 N.C. 379 (1860); *Oswald v. McGehee,* 28 Miss. 340 (1854). See also *Jenkins v. Brown,* 25 Tenn. 299 (1845); Olmsted, *Slavery and the South,* 183.

38 *Shanklin v. Johnson,* 9 Ala. 271, 275 (1846) (free person's dealing with slave creates trust or "moral duty" that could "impose[] a legal obligation" to slave).

39 Record in *Wilson v. James,* at 4–5, 13; *Wilson v. James,* 79 N.C. 349, 352 (1878). Italics modified.

40 O'Neall, *Negro Law of South Carolina,* 43; Cobb, *Inquiry Into the Law of Negro Slavery,* vol. 1, 237, 241; Edwards, *Only the Clothes on Her Back,* 52–53.

41 *McNamara v. Kerns,* 24 N.C. 66 (1841) ("ownership"); *Lea v. Brown,* 58 N.C. 379, 382 (1860) ($1,500).

42 *Rice v. Cade,* 10 La. 288, 294–95 (1836).

43 On justice-of-the-peace court locations, see Edwards, *People and Their Peace,* 69, 75–79, 87; Rhys Isaac, *The Transformation of Virginia: 1740–1790* (University of North Carolina Press, 1982), 88–94; Ariela Gross, *Double Character: Slavery and Mastery in the Antebellum Southern Courtroom* (Princeton University Press, 2000), 24–26. On plantation courts, see Jacob Stroyer, *My Life in the South* (1879; Newcomb & Gauss, 1898), 59–62; "Family History Written by Mrs. Washington," ca. 1931, f 10, b 131–82, FPMS; Thomas D. Turpin, "May and New River Mission, S.C. Con[nection], to the Blacks," Oct. 6, 1833, *Christian Advocate and Journal,* Oct. 25, 1833, 34, 90. See also Ulrich Bonnell Phillips, *American Negro Slavery: A Survey of the Supply, Employment and Control of Negro Labor as Determined by the Plantation Régime* (D. Appleton & Co., 1918), 296; Charles C. Jones, *The Religious Instruction of the Negroes. In the United States* (Thomas Purse, 1842), 131; Albert Raboteau, *Slave Religion: The 'Invisible Institution' in the Antebellum South* (Oxford University Press, 1978), 180–81; Sylvia R. Frey and Betty Wood, *Come Shouting to Zion: African American Protestantism in the American South and British Caribbean to 1830* (University of North Carolina Press, 1998), 186.

44 J. Vance Lewis, *Out of the Ditch: A True Story of an Ex-Slave* (Rein & Sons, 1910), 16–21.

45 Uniform Commercial Code, Art. 1, §303(c); Restatement (Second) of Contracts, §§219, 222.

46 On slaves' alleged knowledge of warranty and redhibition, see Johnson, *Soul by Soul,* 183–87; Gross, *Double Character,* 43–45. On slaves' knowledge of other areas

of private law, see "Didn't Know Nothing, Never Thought of Nothing But Slavery," in *American Slave,* vol. 18, Tennessee Narratives (Fisk), 73; narrative of Ellen Claibourn, Augusta, Georgia, Georgia Narratives, in *American Slave,* vol. 12:1, 185; Douglass, *Narrative,* 35–38; "Every Thursday Was 'Whipping Day' for Slaves," in *Unwritten History of Slavery: Autobiographical Accounts of Negro Ex-Slaves* (Fisk University, 1968), 113; testimony of Hanson Brooks, Sept. 2, 1867, *Hume and Crosby v. Beale;* Solomon Northup, *Twelve Years a Slave. Narrative of Solomon Northup, a Citizen of New-York, Kidnapped in Washington City in 1841, and Rescued in 1853, from a Cotton Plantation near the Red River, in Louisiana* (Derby and Miller, 1853), 106–17. See also the brutal hanging scene in the movie *Twelve Years a Slave* (2013, dir. Steve McQueen). Testimony of Townley Johnson, Aug. 30, 1867, *Hume & Crosby v. Beale,* case 919, EDC. See also Jones-Rogers, *They Were Her Property,* 37–39, 46–48, 64–65.

47 Narrative of Katie Rowe, Oklahoma Narratives, *American Slave,* v. 7:1, 277–78. Rowe's narrative is subtly analyzed in Jones-Rogers, *They Were Her Property,* 47.

48 Edwards, *People and Their Peace*; *Jones v. Allen,* 38 Tenn. 626, 628 (1858); *Waddill v. Martin,* at 563–65; Penningroth, "Race in Contract Law," 1246; Rose, "Possession as the Origin of Property," 82–88.

CHAPTER 2: THE RIGHTS OF FREEDOM

1 "The Great National Convention," *North Star,* Aug. 11, 1848; Emily Morry, "Retrofitting Rochester: Talman Building," *Democrat & Chronicle,* Feb. 13, 2015.

2 Eric Foner, *Free Soil, Free Labor, Free Men: The Ideology of the Republican Party before the Civil War,* 2nd ed. (1970; Oxford University Press, 1995), 290; Kate Masur, *Until Justice Be Done: America's First Civil Rights Movement, from the Revolution to Reconstruction* (W. W. Norton, 2021); Report of the Colored National Convention, 1848, 18; H. F. D. to editor, *Provincial Freeman,* Mar. 8, 1856; "For Governor, James S. Wadsworth," Nov. 1862, *Douglass' Monthly*; Proceedings of the Colored National Convention, Held in Rochester [. . .] (1853).

3 William J. Novak, "The American Law of Association: The Legal-Political Construction of Civil Society," *Studies in American Political Development* 15 (Fall 2001), 167, 172–78; Joseph K. Angell and Samuel Ames, *A Treatise on the Law of Private Corporations Aggregate* (Hilliard, Gray, Little & Wilkins, 1832), 1; Kate Masur, *An Example for All the Land: Emancipation and the Struggle over Equality in Washington, D.C.* (University of North Carolina Press, 2010), 5; Stephen Kantrowitz, *More Than Freedom: Fighting for Black Citizenship in a White Republic, 1829–1889* (Penguin, 2012), 44. A white Delaware congressman once described the United States itself as a gigantic "association . . . of white people." Masur, *Until Justice Be Done,* 49.

4 Minutes of the State Convention of the Colored Citizens of Pennsylvania (1849), 23.

5 Martha S. Jones, *Birthright Citizens: A History of Race and Rights in Antebellum America* (Cambridge University Press, 2018), 90–137; Kimberly M. Welch, *Black Litigants in the Antebellum American South* (University of North Carolina Press, 2018),

115–33. Melvin Patrick Ely, *Israel on the Appomattox: A Southern Experiment in Black Freedom from the 1790s through the Civil War* (Random House, 2004), 13, 87, 89, 103–8; Michael P. Johnson, and James Roark, *Black Masters: A Free Family of Color in the Old South* (W. W. Norton, 1984), 23, 76–79; *Stanley v. Nelson,* 28 Ala. 514 (1856); John Hope Franklin, *The Free Negro in North Carolina, 1790–1860* (University of North Carolina Press, 1943), 83–85.

6 Abbye Atkinson, "Rethinking Credit as Social Provision," SLR 71 (2019), 1093–162; Ira Berlin, *Slaves Without Masters: The Free Negro in the Antebellum South* (Pantheon, 1974), 224–26.

7 Luther Porter Jackson, *Free Negro Labor and Property Holding in Virginia, 1830–1860* (Appleton-Century, 1942), 31–32, 200–229; Berlin, *Slaves Without Masters,* 97; Franklin, *Free Negro in North Carolina,* 150–51; Johnson and Roark, *Black Masters,* 23–25, 50–51, 65–106; Welch, *Black Litigants,* 13–15, 149–52; Loren Schweninger, *Black Property Owners in the South, 1790–1915* (University of Illinois Press, 1990), 96; Luther Porter Jackson, "The Virginia Free Negro Farmer and Property Owner, 1830–1860," JNH 24, no. 4 (1939), 414–16, 438.

8 Jackson, "Virginia Free Negro Farmer and Property Owner," 398–400. The difference is that Chisman would have fewer procedural protections if he defaulted. Jesse Dukeminier et al., *Property,* 8th ed. (Wolters Kluver, 2014), 649. On prenups, see Suzanne Lebsock, *The Free Women of Petersburg: Status and Culture in a Southern Town, 1784–1860* (W. W. Norton, 1984), 101–109; Reginald Dennin Butler, "Evolution of a Rural Free Black Community: Goochland County, Virginia, 1728–1832," PhD diss., Johns Hopkins, 1989, 108–13.

9 *Christenbury v. King,* 85 N.C. 229 (1881); deposition of W. M. Edwards, ca. 1906, f 30, b 5, GWIN.

10 Administrator's report, *Stewart v. Stewart et al.,* case 1829-038, CirCtCh, Mecklenburg Co., VA.

11 Martha L. Benner and Cullom Davis et al., eds., *The Law Practice of Abraham Lincoln: Complete Documentary Edition,* 2d ed. (Illinois Historic Preservation Agency, 2009). See also Richard E. Hart, *Lincoln's Springfield: The Early African American Population of Springfield, Illinois (1818–1861)* (Spring Creek Series, 2008), 105, 142, 156; Jones, *Birthright Citizens,* 41. On white lawyers' motives, see Justin Simard, "Slavery's Legalism: Lawyers and the Commercial Routine of Slavery," LHR 37, no. 2 (2019), 587; Welch, *Black Litigants,* 86–90.

12 On personalism, see Butler, "Evolution of a Rural Free Black Community," 36–37, 353; Ely, *Israel on the Appomattox,* 247, 436; Johnson and Roark, *Black Masters,* esp. 25, 35–36, 96–97, 239. On repeat players, see Stewart Macaulay, "The Use and Non-Use of Contracts in the Manufacturing Industry," *The Practical Lawyer* 9 (Nov. 1963), 17. Administrator's report, *Stewart v. Stewart et al* ("exonerated"). Here I am adapting a key tenet of Critical Race Theory. See Derrick A. Bell Jr., "*Brown v. Board of Education* and the Interest-Convergence Dilemma," HLR 93 (1980), 518.

13 Kunal M. Parker, *Making Foreigners: Immigration and Citizenship Law in America, 1600–2000* (Cambridge University Press, 2015), 108–13; Barbara Young Welke, *Law and the Borders of Belonging in the Long Nineteenth Century United States* (Cambridge University Press, 2010); James H. Kettner, *The Development of American Citizenship, 1608–1870* (University of North Carolina, 1978), 252.

14 Kettner, *Development of American Citizenship*, 248–61; *Corfield v. Coryell*, 6 F.Cas. 546, 551–52 (1823).

15 Theophilus Parsons, *The Law of Contracts*, vol. 1 (1857), 327; Christopher L. Tomlins, *Law, Labor, and Ideology in the Early American Republic* (Cambridge University Press, 1993), 223–70. Bouvier 1843, 529, 592.

16 *Girod v. Lewis*, 6 Mart. (o.s.) 559 (1819) ("deprived"); Parsons, *Law of Contracts* (1857), vol. 1, 337–42; *Lenoir v. Sylvester*, 1 Bail. 632, 642 (1830) (So. Car.) (slave cannot enforce promise in court); *Bailey v. Poindexter's Exr.*, 55 Va. 132 (1858), 142 ("whatsoever").

17 Robert J. Steinfeld, *The Invention of Free Labor: The Employment Relation in English and American Law and Culture, 1350–1870* (University of North Carolina Press, 1991), 125 (quoting the Philadelphia Cordwainers' case). Judges did not count wife-beating as coercion because it was a "private" issue. See Reva B. Siegel, "'The Rule of Love': Wife Beating as Prerogative and Privacy," YLJ 105, no. 8 (1996), 2117–2207.

18 Joseph C. G. Kennedy, *Population of the United States in 1860* (Government Printing Office, 1864), 600–604; Masur, *Until Justice Be Done*, 3–30, 50, 59–60; Foner, *Free Soil*, 261; The Second Constitution of New York, 1821, Art. III, §1; Paul Finkelman, "Prelude to the Fourteenth Amendment: Black Legal Rights in the Antebellum North," *Rutgers Law Journal* 17 (1986), 425, 471, 476.

19 Parker, *Making Foreigners*, 94–97; Masur, *Until Justice Be Done*, 84; C. Vann Woodward, *The Strange Career of Jim Crow* (1955; Oxford University Press, 2002), 17.

20 Masur, *Until Justice Be Done*, 44–45, 92.

21 Foner, *Free Soil*, 288–92; Abraham Lincoln, First Lincoln-Douglas Debate, Ottawa, Illinois, Aug. 21, 1858, in *Speeches and Writings*, vol. 1 (1989), 512; "Colored People of Cincinnati," *The Colored American*, Oct. 17, 1840.

22 Masur, *Until Justice Be Done*, 244–45 ("Slave Power"); "The Great National Convention," *North Star*, Aug. 11, 1848 ("entirely free"); "Report of the Proceedings of the Colored National Convention, Held at Cleveland, Ohio," Rochester, 1848 ("slaves of the community"). See also "Sound and Important Advice," *The National Era*, Nov. 16, 1848; St. George Tucker, *A Dissertation on Slavery* (Mathew Carey, 1796), 18–22; "The Work of the Future," *Douglass' Monthly*, Nov. 1862; H.F.D. to editor, *Provincial Freeman*, Mar. 8, 1856; *Argument of Charles Sumner, Esq. Against the Constitutionality of Separate Colored Schools, in the Case of Sarah C. Roberts vs. The City of Boston* (B. F. Roberts, 1849), 6.

23 *Dred Scott v. Sandford*, 60 U.S. 393 (1857); Jamal Greene, "The Anticanon," HLR 125, no. 2 (2011), 384, 406–12.

24 Kettner, *Development of American Citizenship,* 320–21; *Scott v. Sandford,* 60 U.S. 393, 533, 537 (Maclean, J., dissenting), 572–76 (Curtis, J., dissenting) (1857).

25 Masur, *Example for All the Land,* 5–7; Sydney R. Wrightington, *The Law of Unincorporated Associations and Similar Relations* (Little, Brown, 1916), 3, 336 ("acting together"); Juliet E. K. Walker, *The History of Black Business in America: Capitalism, Race, Entrepreneurship, vol. 1, to 1865* (University of North Carolina Press, 2009), 86–88; Kantrowitz, *More than Freedom.*

26 Herbert A. Smith, *The Law of Associations: Corporate and Unincorporate* (Clarendon Press, 1914), 18–19; Wrightington, *Law of Unincorporated Associations,* 208; Robert Charles Clark, *Corporate Law* (Little, Brown, 1986), 2; Angell, *Law of Corporations,* 58.

27 Walker, *History of Black Business,* 108–63.

28 John N. Still to Henry Bibb, Feb. 3, 1852, BAP: 4, 108–12. See also Patrick Rael, *Black Identity and Black Protest in the Antebellum North* (University of North Carolina Press, 2002), 193; *Proceedings of the Colored National Convention* (1853), 28.

29 Angell, *Law of Corporations,* 35; Theda Skocpol, Ariane Liazos, and Marshall Ganz, *What a Mighty Power We Can Be: African American Fraternal Groups and the Struggle for Racial Equality* (Princeton University Press, 2006), 35; Walker, H*istory of Black Business in America,* 90–100, 120–21, 149; Daniel Perlman, "Organizations of the Free Negro in New York City, 1800–1860," JNH 56, no. 3 (1971), 182; Leslie M. Harris, *In the Shadow of Slavery: African Americans in New York City, 1626–1863* (University of Chicago Press, 2003), 86; W. P. Burrell and D. E. Johnson Sr., *Twenty-Five Years History of the Grand Fountain of the United Order of True Reformers, 1881–1905* (1909), 395–97.

30 Perlman, "Organizations of the Free Negro in New York City," 183; "Notice," FJ, Mar. 21, 1829. On Black institutional life in New York and its larger context, see Harris, *In the Shadow of Slavery,* 86–90. "Notice," *Colored American,* Feb. 23, 1839. For Ann Hacket's loan, see Dorothy Sterling, *We Are Your Sisters: Black Women in the Nineteenth Century* (1984; W. W. Norton, 1997), 107.

31 Here I am borrowing from the literary theorist Henry Louis Gates Jr. See *The Signifying Monkey: A Theory of African-American Literary Criticism* (Oxford University Press, 1988), 137–38, 156–58, 171.

32 Rael, *Black Identity,* 3; Jones, *Birthright Citizens,* 63–64, 71–88; Kantrowitz, *More than Freedom;* 6 Fletcher-Cyc. §2414; *New-York Society for Mutual Relief v. Varick,* 13 Johns. 38, 39, Supreme Court of New York (1816). Varick was the first bishop of the African Methodist Episcopal Zion Church. Harris, *Shadow of Slavery,* 84. *Varick* appeared in several nineteenth-century treatises and is still occasionally cited today.

33 Hendrik Hartog, *Public Property and Private Power: The Corporation of the City of New York in American Law, 1730–1870* (University of North Carolina Press, 1983), 66; "Important," *Colored American,* April 12, 1838; Wrightington, *Law of Unincorporated Associations,* 208–10; Novak, "American Law of Association," 172–74.

34 *Negro Year Book,* ed. Monroe N. Work (Negro Year Book Pub. Co., 1919), 159; Walker, *History of Black Business in America,* 108–62.

35 Sylvia R. Frey and Betty Wood, *Come Shouting to Zion: African American Protestantism in the American South and British Caribbean to 1830* (University of North Carolina Press, 1998), 166–69; Rev. W. Morgan, in "Speech by J. W. C. Pennington," BAP 1, 111.

36 CBRB, frames 46, 55, 62–63, 50–55, 66.

37 CBMB, frames 55, 71–73; Frey and Wood, *Come Shouting to Zion,* 197–201; *Newman v. Proctor,* 73, Ky. 318, 319–20 (1874); "Burke Mission, Ga. Con.," *Christian Advocate and Journal,* Aug. 22, 1834, 206; W. P. Harrison, *The Gospel Among the Slaves* (1893), 132–33. I thank Michael P. Johnson for the references to Harrison and *Christian Advocate.*

38 Frey and Wood, *Come Shouting to Zion,* 199, 187; CBRB, frame 55; William Crowell, *The Church Member's Hand-Book: A Guide to the Doctrines and Practice of Baptist Churches* (Gould, Kendall and Lincoln, 1850), 42–44.

39 On separate churches, see Albert Raboteau, *Slave Religion: The 'Invisible Institution' in the Antebellum South* (Oxford University Press, 1978), 181; Sarah Barringer Gordon, "The African Supplement: Religion, Race, and Corporate Law in Early National America," WMQ 3d ser., 72, no. 3 (2015), 395. On parallel legal system, see Orville Vernon Burton, *In My Father's House Are Many Mansions: Family and Community in Edgefield, South Carolina* (University of North Carolina Press, 1985), 58–59. On prosecuting injuries to slaves, see Thomas D. Morris, *Southern Slavery and the Law, 1619–1860* (University of North Carolina Press, 1996), 171–81; Edwards, *People and Their Peace,* 101–11. On sex ratios in nineteenth-century churches, see Raboteau, *Slave Religion,* 180–87; Edwards, *People and Their Peace,* 194–95; Frey and Wood, *Come Shouting to Zion,* 163–66.

40 Richard Allen, *The Life, Experience, and Gospel Labours of the Rt. Rev. Richard Allen* (Martin & Boden, 1833), 12; Frey and Wood, *Come Shouting to Zion,* 177; "More Facts and Memories of Jenkins Church," 13, in Gail McClure, *Jenkins Church: Historical Notes and Memories* (2008), CBMB; Sylvia Frey, *Water from the Rock: Black Resistance in a Revolutionary Age* (Princeton University Press, 1991), 305.

41 Gordon, "African Supplement," 396, 403–4; Allen, *Life, Experience,* 13; Frey and Wood, *Come Shouting to Zion,* 174–80; A. M. Chreitzberg, *Early Methodism in the Carolinas* (1897), 156–57; F[rancis] A[sbury] Mood, *Methodism in Charleston* [. . .] (1856), 130–33. These sources do not indicate what date the Charleston walkout happened. Novak, "The American Law of Association," 183–86.

42 "Report of the Proceedings of the Colored National Convention, Held at Cleveland, Ohio" (1848), 10, 13; testimony of Hon. James Speed, Rev. Mr. Bradwell, and Rev. Mr. Ebbett, File 7, AFIC; Luther P. Jackson, "Religious Development of the Negro in Virginia from 1760 to 1860," JNH 16, no. 2 (1931), 229–34; Schweninger, *Black Property Owners in the South,* 138–39; Raboteau, *Slave Religion,* 179.

43 Minutes of the Fifth Annual Convention . . . (1835), 11; "Railroad Corporations," *Colored American,* May 1, 1841; Minutes and address of the State Convention of

the Colored Citizens of Ohio . . . (1849), 13; "Toadyism Rebuked," *Frederick Douglass' Paper,* Aug. 27, 1852; *Autographs for Freedom. By Mrs. Harriet Beecher Stowe, and Thirty-Five Other Eminent Writers* (1853), 110.

44 Jones, *All Bound Up Together,* 155–56 (restrictions on women); Minutes of the Fifth Annual Convention . . . (1835), 18; Minutes of the State Convention of Colored Citizens of Pennsylvania (1848), 23 (voting restrictions); Proceedings of the Colored National Convention (1853), 4 ("our people"); Minutes of the National Convention of Colored Citizens (1843), 7–8; Rael, *Black Identity and Black Protest,* 31–32 (convention-packing); Minutes of the State Convention of the Colored Citizens of Pennsylvania (1849), 23 ("all the Rights").

45 Levi Jenkins Coppin, *Unwritten History* (A. M. E. Book Concern, 1919), 44–46; Wallace D. Best, *Passionately Human, No Less Divine: Religion and Culture in Black Chicago, 1915–1952* (Princeton University Press, 2005), 52.

46 Gordon, "African Supplement," 415–19; Kantrowitz, *More than Freedom,* 21.

47 Daniel Alexander Payne, *History of the African Methodist Episcopal Church* (Publishing House of the A. M. E. Sunday School Union, 1891), 230–32; "Fight in Church," *Sunday Dispatch,* Mar. 4, 1849; James T. Campbell, in *Songs of Zion: The African Methodist Episcopal Church in the United States and South Africa* (Oxford University Press, 1995), 43, also attributes the attack to a dispute over reforms to worship practices.

48 Jones, *All Bound Up Together,* 2–4, 67.

49 Kennedy, *Population of the United States in 1860,* vii; "Interview with a Colored Delegation respecting Suffrage," in *A Hand Book of Politics for 1868,* ed. Edward McPherson (Philp & Solomons, 1868), 52.

50 Civil Rights Act of 1866 §1 (codified as amended at 42 U.S.C. §§1981–82); Masur, *Until Justice Be Done,* 327.

51 Speeches of Senators Jacob Howard, Charles Sumner, and Lyman Trumbull, CG, 39th Cong., 1st Sess., 503–4, 91, 43.

52 Dylan C. Penningroth, *The Claims of Kinfolk: African American Property and Community in the Nineteenth-Century South* (University of North Carolina Press, 2003), 139–41.

CHAPTER 3: DOES COLOR STILL MATTER?

1 "Address at Gettysburg, Pennsylvania," in *Abraham Lincoln: Speeches and Writings, 1859–1865,* ed. Don E. Fehrenbacher (Library of America, 1989), 536; P. Houston Murray [writing from Natchez], "Negro Suffering and Suffrage in the South," CR, July 1, 1865 (quoting a "hard-working colored man"); Samuel Thomas to O. O. Howard, Sept. 6, 1865, quoted in Eric Foner, *Reconstruction: America's Unfinished Revolution, 1863–1877* (1988; Perennial Classics, 2002), 149–150 ("any rights at all"); W. E. B. Du Bois, *Black Reconstruction: An Essay toward a History of the Part Which Black Folk Played in the Attempt to Reconstruct Democracy in America, 1860–1880* (Russell & Russell, 1935), 30.

2 Thomas D. Morris, *Southern Slavery and the Law, 1619–1860* (University of North

Carolina Press, 1996), 424; Walter Johnson, "Inconsistency, Contradiction, and Complete Confusion: The Everyday Life of the Law of Slavery," LSI 22, no. 2 (1997), 430; Justin Simard, "Citing Slavery," SLR 72, no. 1 (2020), 81–82, 85, 94–97; *Slaughter-House Cases,* 83 U.S. 36, 77 (1873); Giuliana Perrone, "'Back into the Days of Slavery': Freedom, Citizenship, and the Black Family in the Reconstruction-Era Courtroom," LHR 37, no. 1 (2019), 125–61.

3 The case counts are 54/436 for 1872, and 66/440 for 1882. *Slaughter-House Cases,* at 77.

4 Suzanne Lebsock, *The Free Women of Petersburg: Status and Culture in a Southern Town, 1784–1860* (W. W. Norton, 1984), 252–56; Luther Porter Jackson, *Free Negro Labor and Property Holding in Virginia, 1830–1860* (Appleton-Century, 1942), xiii–xiv.

5 Dylan C. Penningroth, "Race in Contract Law," PLR 170, no. 5 (2022), 1199–301.

6 *Slaughter-House Cases,* at 68, 71, 47–48 (emphasis added); Brief of Plaintiff at 3–8, 17–31, *Slaughter-House Cases,* 83 U.S. 36 (1872) (Nos. 475–480).

7 Transcript of Record at 11, 15–16, *S. Express Co. v. Byers,* 240 U.S. 612 (1916) (No. 201); *Byers v. S. Express Co.,* 81 S.E. 741, 742 (N.C. 1914); Barbara Young Welke, *Recasting American Liberty: Gender, Race, Law, and the Railroad Revolution, 1865–1920* (Cambridge University Press, 2001), 358–59; Myisha Shuntez Eatmon, "Public Wrongs, Private Rights: African Americans, Private Law, and White Violence during Jim Crow," PhD diss., Northwestern University, Sept. 2020.

8 Record in *Byers* at 21–22.

9 Walter F. Murphy, "In His Own Image: Mr. Chief Justice Taft and Supreme Court Appointments," *Supreme Court Review* (1961), 159, 166; *Aldridge v. United States,* 283 U.S. 308, 316–18 (1931) (McReynolds, J., dissenting); *Nixon v. Condon,* 286 U.S. 73, 105 (1932) (McReynolds, J., dissenting); *Byers,* at 615; *Slaughter-House Cases,* at 69.

10 Laura F. Edwards, *A Legal History of the Civil War and Reconstruction: A Nation of Rights* (Cambridge University Press, 2015), 106.

11 Rev. Code Miss. (1880), ch. 42, §1147; *Code of Virginia* (1873), ch. 104, §15, 845; Miss. Code (1906), §1671; Miss. Code (1930), ch. 24, §1426; Miss. Code (1930), ch. 20, §1103; Peggy Pascoe, *What Comes Naturally: Miscegenation Law and the Making of Race in America* (Oxford University Press, 2009), 9–10.

12 Thanks to Laura Edwards for pointing this out.

13 [Voter] Reg[istration] Book, 1902–3, Brown's Church Precinct, Randolph Magisterial District, Office of Circuit Clerk, Cumberland Co., VA; General Index to Deeds, 1749–1918, Grantee A–K, and Deed Books cited above, Office of Circuit Clerk, Cumberland Co., VA.

14 Testimony of Felix Brown, 1, *Brown v. McWilliams,* case 1451, CirCtCh, Coahoma Co., Clarksdale, MS ("were you ever"); testimony of Albert Southall, *Southall v. Jones et al* (1918), ended case 2841, CirCtCh, Albemarle Co., VA; testimony of Gus Turner, Record in *Bailey v. Johnson* (1916), VASC ("Uncle"); wrapper, n.d., in

Southall v. Jones; testimony of James Pinn, *James Pinn v. Frank H. Fall,* 1882–006, CirCtCh, Fauquier Co., LV ("Of course").

15 *Dred Scott v. Sandford,* 60 U.S. 393, 412 (1857).

16 Powhaten Lockett (1876), quoted in Foner, *Reconstruction,* 355; Michael Willrich, *City of Courts: Socializing Justice in Progressive Era Chicago* (Cambridge University Press, 2003), 3–4, 13; "Moses Jeffries," Arkansas Narratives, vol. 2, pt. 4, 41–42, FWP; Irvin C. Mollison, "Negro Lawyers in Mississippi," JNH 15, no. 1 (1930), 61–62. For relatively open courthouse access, see "Georgia District Meeting," CR, July 18, 1878; "A Sunday in Chicago," CR, Aug. 22, 1868; "Neighborhood News and Gossip," *Huntsville Gazette,* July 1, 1882. For examples of violent struggles over courthouse control, see Foner, *Reconstruction,* 342–43, 425–37, 550–53, 561; Steven Hahn, *A Nation under Our Feet: Black Political Struggles in the Rural South from Slavery to the Great Migration* (Harvard University Press, 2003), esp. 266.

17 On convict leasing, see Rev. Code Miss. (1880), ch. 79. On "color," see Bouvier 1868, 292–93; Noah Webster, *An American Dictionary of the English Language* (Converse, 1828), s.v. "color," "colored"; Bouvier 1883, 335; Bouvier 1897, 353. On judicial notice, see *Brown v. Piper,* 91 U.S. 37, 42 (1875); Bouvier 1897, 41–42; *Jacobson v. Massachusetts,* 197 U.S. 11, 23–24 (1905); *Plessy v. Ferguson,* 163 U.S. 537, 554 (1896), Harlan, J., dissenting.

18 *Plessy,* at 559 (1896); Linda Przybyszewski, *The Republic According to John Marshall Harlan* (University of North Carolina Press, 1999), 85.

19 For example, see Morton J. Horwitz, *The Transformation of American Law, 1870–1960: The Crisis of Legal Orthodoxy* (Oxford University Press, 1992), 267–68.

20 Cheryl I. Harris, "Whiteness as Property," HLR 106, no. 8 (1993), 1707–91; Rebecca J. Scott, "Public Rights, Social Equality, and the Conceptual Roots of the *Plessy* Challenge," *Michigan Law Review* 106, no. 5 (2008), 777–804.

21 Brandi Clay Brimmer, *Claiming Union Widowhood: Race, Respectability, and Poverty in the Post-Emancipation South* (Duke University Press, 2020).

22 "Death on the Rail, *Savannah Tribune,* Sept. 9, 1876; "Special Damages," *North American,* May 3, 1878; "South Carolina Correspondence," CR, July 21, 1866; "Laws of New York Relating to Religious Corporations," CR, Sept. 21, 1876; "Law Debating Society," *Washington Bee,* Feb. 10, 1883; "Bishop Cain's Civil Rights Suit," *Sentinel* [Trenton, NJ], Jan. 21, 1882; "Expensive Prejudice," *Sentinel* [Trenton, NJ], Mar. 11, 1882.

23 "Business Law," CR, Aug. 9, 1877; Oliver Wendell Holmes, "The Path of the Law," HLR 10, no. 8 (1897), 497.

24 "The Sandy Hill *Herald* Says," *The Elevator,* Dec. 26, 1874; "The Sad Results," *Huntsville Gazette,* Jan. 3, 1885; "Smart Answer," FJ, May 25, 1827; [Untitled], FJ, May 25, 1827; "Varieties," FJ, Nov. 23, 1827.

25 "Negro Suffrage," CR, Feb. 25, 1865. See also John B. Russwurm and Samuel Cornish's well-known mission statement, "To Our Patrons," FJ, Mar. 16, 1827.

26 "Virginia and Maryland," CR, Sept. 30, 1880; "Arkansas to Georgia," CR, Sept.

3, 1885; "John Blye: Or The Trials and Triumphs of a White-Washer's Son," CR, Aug. 15, 1878.

27 Holmes, "Path of the Law," 497.

28 Edward A. Pollard, *The Lost Cause: A New Southern History of the War of the Confederates* (E. B. Treat & Co., 1866), 49; collection description, The Papers of Duke and Duke, Special Collections, UVALaw, https://archives.law.virginia.edu/resources/papers-duke-and-duke.

29 Richard Thomas Walker Duke, Jr., *Recollections,* unpublished manuscript, vol. 3, 122–23, Special Collections Library, University of Virginia.

30 Joshua D. Rothman, *Notorious in the Neighborhood: Sex and Families across the Color Line in Virginia, 1787–1861* (University of North Carolina Press, 2003), 86; Duke & Jones Fee Book, 1870–1874, DUKES; Ledger c. 1880–87, 206, 240, 242, 295, DUKES; *Scott v. Raub,* 88 Va. 721 (1891).

31 William H. Beveridge, *Extracts from the Law for the Benefit of the Householder and the Laboring Man* (n.d.), VHS; Lauranett L. Lee, "Giles B. Jackson (1853–1924)," in *Encyclopedia Virginia,* https://encyclopediavirginia.org/entries/jackson-giles-b-1853-1924; Dunbar Rowland, *Courts, Judges, and Lawyers of Mississippi, 1798–1935* (Hederman Bros., 1935), 220–22.

32 *Mississippi* [. . .] ed. Dunbar Rowland (Southern Historical Publishing, 1907), vol. 3, 824.

33 Peter Karsten, "Enabling the Poor to Have Their Day in Court: The Sanctioning of Contingency Fee Contracts, a History to 1940," *DePaul Law Review* 47 (1997–1998), 249–50.

34 3 *Bench and Bar* 374 (1873–74); "A Negro's Knowledge of an Oath," 5 *Chicago Legal News* 547 (1872–73); "Sayings and Doings," 2 *Bench and Bar* 191 (1872–73); George Warville (1920), quoted in Karsten, "Enabling the Poor," 255–56 ("sordid hucksters"); [untitled], *Chicago Inter-Ocean,* Jan. 18, 1876; *The New High Priests: Lawyers in Post-Civil War America,* ed. Gerard W. Gawalt (Greenwood Press, 1984).

35 "The Alabama State Bar Association," 2 *Southern Law Journal,* no. 10 (1879), 537; "Special Damages," *The North American,* May 3, 1878; "The Lawyer's Boy," *Huntsville Gazette,* June 18, 1881.

36 Kitty Calavita, *Invitation to Law & Society: An Introduction to the Study of Real Law* (University of Chicago Press, 2010), 34. I do not know Sandy's exact kin connection to all the Pinns but "cousin" seems both handy and likely, based on the evidence. Petition of James Pinn et al., Dec. 15, 1881, in *James Pinn et al v. Frank Fall and Grenville Gaines,* 1882-006, CirCtCh, Fauquier Co., LV; City Directory, 405, 1879, Washington, DC, U.S. City Directories, 1822–1995, Ancestry.com.

37 Testimony of Thomas Miller, in *Pinn v. Fall.*

38 F. H. Fall to the President of the United States, Aug. 6, 1880, in *Pinn v. Fall.* On taxpayer rhetoric as a superficially race-neutral restriction on Black rights, see

Kate Masur, *An Example for All the Land: Emancipation and the Struggle over Equality in Washington, D.C.* (University of North Carolina Press, 2010), 10, 194–207, 220–24. Testimony of Frank Fall, Mar. 30, 1882, in *Pinn v. Fall.*

39 Testimony of Alice Pinn, Feb. 20, 1882, cross-examination of Charles Smith, and testimony of Charles Smith, in *Pinn v. Fall.*

40 Testimony of James Pinn, Grenville Gaines, Edward Pinckney, and Alice Pinn, in *Pinn v. Fall.*

41 Testimony of Alice Pinn, Betsy Pinn, and George Corkhill, in *Pinn v. Fall.*

42 Sally Engle Merry, "Everyday Understandings of the Law in Working-Class America," *American Ethnologist* 13, no. 2 (1986), 258. Hayes may have commuted Sandy's sentence because Sandy was dying of tuberculosis. "The Gallows in Washington," *Montgomery County Sentinel,* Nov. 26, 1880. Judge Keith cancelled the deeds on the Pinn's house. He did not explain. Decree, Sept. 16, 1882, *Pinn v. Fall.*

CHAPTER 4: FROM THE RUINS OF SLAVERY

1 Nathan Womack & wife to Cha[rles] Palmore & others, Aug. 22, 1875, DB 31, 44–45; R. F. Blanton to Jackson Holcomb, Apr. 9, 1883, DB 33, 59, Office of Circuit Clerk, Cumberland Co., VA.

2 Jane Dailey, *Before Jim Crow: The Politics of Race in Postemancipation Virginia* (University of North Carolina Press, 2000), 119–24.

3 Mark Schultz, *The Rural Face of White Supremacy: Beyond Jim Crow* (University of Illinois Press, 2005), 45. Older work, much of it by African American scholars, paid closer attention to Black landowning. For example, see Monroe N. Work, *Negro Year Book* [. . .] (Negro Year Book Company, 1916), 1–8, 29, 57, 300–334.

4 Adrienne D. Davis, "The Private Law of Race and Sex: An Antebellum Perspective," SLR 51 (1999), 221–88; Julie Saville, *The Work of Reconstruction: From Slave to Wage Laborer in South Carolina, 1860–1870* (Cambridge University Press, 1994), 84–85.

5 Manning Marable, "The Politics of Black Land Tenure, 1877–1915," *Agricultural History* 53, no. 1 (1979), 146; Loren Schweninger, *Black Property Owners in the South, 1790–1915* (University of Illinois Press, 1990), 160.

6 Thomas W. Merrill and Henry E. Smith, "Optimal Standardization in the Law of Property: The *Numerus Clausus* Principle," YLJ 110 (2000), 3–4, 69; Jesse Dukeminier et al., *Property* (Wolters Kluver, 2014), 221–22.

7 Wesley Newcomb Hohfeld, "Some Fundamental Legal Conceptions as Applied in Judicial Reasoning," YLJ 23, no. 1 (1913), 20–24, 30–33; Carol M. Rose, "Property as the Keystone Right?," *Notre Dame Law Review* 71 (1996), 363. Recurrent problems in the recordation system underscore this basic insight. See Myres S. McDougal and John W. Brabner-Smith, "Land Title Transfer: A Regression," YLJ 48, no. 7 (1939), 1126–29; Dukeminier, *Property,* 669, 709–14, 754. On southern

whites' property views, see Steven Hahn, *The Roots of Southern Populism: Yeoman Farmers and the Transformation of the Georgia Upcountry, 1850–1890* (Oxford University Press, 1983); Edward L. Ayers, *The Promise of the New South: Life after Reconstruction* (1992; Oxford University Press, 2007), 127.

8 Lon L. Fuller, Melvin A. Eisenberg, and Mark P. Gergen, *Basic Contract Law* (West Academic, 2018), 10th ed., 16–17.

9 On the bright line, see Eric Foner, *Free Soil, Free Labor, Free Men: The Ideology of the Republican Party before the Civil War* (1970; Oxford University Press, 1995), 290–91; William E. Nelson, "The Impact of the Antislavery Movement Upon Styles of Judicial Reasoning in Nineteenth Century America," HLR 87 (1974), 525–26, 534–44, 550–52. On the chattel principle, see Walter Johnson, *Soul by Soul: Life inside the Antebellum Slave Market* (Harvard University Press, 1999), 218–19; Foner, *Free Soil*, 73–85, 114; E. L. Godkin (1867) and Christopher G. Tiedeman (1900), both quoted in Stanley, *From Bondage to Contract: Wage Labor, Marriage, and the Market in the Age of Slave Emancipation* (Cambridge University Press, 1998), 2, 74. For examples of the persistence of nineteenth-century antislavery thinking, see "Texas Essential Knowledge and Skills for Social Studies," §113.C., Texas Education Agency, Aug. 2022 update; Nikole Hannah-Jones, "The Idea of America," *New York Times Magazine*, Aug. 18, 2019, 16–19.

10 Foner, *Reconstruction*, 460–64, 477–78; George Fitzhugh (1857) and William West (1847), both quoted in Stanley, *From Bondage to Contract*, 20. See also Christopher L. Tomlins, *Law, Labor, and Ideology in the Early American Republic* (Cambridge University Press, 1993), 223–26 (1993).

11 Foner, *Free Soil*, 73.

12 Stanley, *From Bondage to Contract*, 20.

13 Willie Lee Rose, *Rehearsal for Reconstruction: The Port Royal Experiment* (Bobbs-Merrill, 1964); Foner, *Reconstruction*, 50–60.

14 Foner, *Reconstruction*, 1.

15 Stanley, *From Bondage to Contract*, 20.

16 "Free Labor Experiments in Louisiana," NYT, Jan. 16, 1863; "What Shall Be Done With the Emancipated Slaves," NYT, June 12, 1865; "Memorandum of an agreement," June 7, 1865, Mss 1B2924a 1669–1684, VHS; Thomas C. Holt, "An Empire over the Mind: Emancipation, Race, and Ideology in the British West Indies and the American South," in J. Morgan Kousser and James M. McPherson, *Region, Race, and Reconstruction: Essays in Honor of C. Vann Woodward* (1982), 300–302; Brig. Gen. Davis Tillson to W. F. Eaton, Apr. 17, 1866, FDHE, 294; Howard (1907), quoted in Stanley, *From Bondage to Contract*, 123–24.

17 Nelson, "Impact of the Antislavery Movement," 551–52, 565–66; William E. Forbath, "The Ambiguities of Free Labor: Labor and the Law in the Gilded Age," *Wisconsin Law Review* 1985, no. 4 (1985), 783; Morton J. Horwitz, *The Transformation of American Law, 1870–1960: The Crisis of Legal Orthodoxy* (Oxford University

Press, 1992), 10–19; Thomas C. Grey, "Langdell's Orthodoxy," *University of Pittsburgh Law Review* 45 (1983–1984), 1–53; Barbara H. Fried, *The Progressive Assault on Laissez Faire: Robert Hale and the First Law and Economics Movement* (Harvard University Press, 1998), 48–56.

18 Forbath, "Ambiguities of Free Labor," 783–86, 797, 811; *Slaughter-House Cases,* at 90, 110; Nelson, "Impact of the Antislavery Movement," 556–57.

19 Stanley, *From Bondage to Contract,* 108–24; Saville, *Work of Reconstruction,* 18–19, 60–71, 79–87, 188–95; Foner, *Reconstruction,* 102–10, 137–75, 586.

20 Foner, *Reconstruction,* 166; Stanley, *From Bondage to Contract,* 127; Civil Rights Act of 1866 §1 (codified as amended at 42 U.S.C. §§1981–82); U.S. Const. amend. XIV; Foner, *Reconstruction,* 199; Reports of Assistant Commissioners of Freedmen, and Synopsis of Laws on Persons of Color in Late Slave States, S. Exec. Doc. No. 6, 39th Cong., 2d Sess. (1866), at 170–230; CG, 39th Cong., 1st Sess. (1866), at 686 (statement of Sen. Charles Sumner); Kate Masur, *Until Justice Be Done: America's First Civil Rights Movement, from the Revolution to Reconstruction* (W. W. Norton, 2021), 44–45; CG, 39th Cong., 1st Sess. (1866), at 474–75 (statement of Sen. Lyman Trumbull).

21 Stanley, *From Bondage to Contract,* 125–27; Foner, *Reconstruction,* 134; Liz Donovan and Muriel Alarcon, "Long Hours, Low Pay, Loneliness and a Booming Industry," NYT, Sept. 26, 2021, section BU, 1; Fried, *Progressive Assault on Laissez-Faire,* 48–49, 211–212; see also Dylan C. Penningroth, "Race in Contract Law," PLR 170, no. 5 (2022), 1248–52.

22 Abbye Atkinson, "Rethinking Credit as Social Provision," SLR 71 (2019), 1106–1107; FDHE, 94, 360; NYT (1865), quoted in Amalia D. Kessler, *Inventing American Exceptionalism: The Origins of American Adversarial Legal Culture, 1800–1877* (Yale University Press, 2017), 266.

23 Kessler, *Inventing American Exceptionalism,* 19, 112–32, 301–02; "'Judges Are Not Politicians in Robes,' Gorsuch Tells Senate," *National Law Journal,* Mar. 20, 2017; FDHE, 99; Joseph William Singer, "Legal Realism Now," *California Law Review* 76 (1988), 477; Penningroth, "Race in Contract Law," 1216–25.

24 Harold D. Woodman, *New South—New Law: The Legal Foundations of Credit and Labor Relations in the Postbellum Agricultural South* (Louisiana State University Press, 1995), 44; FDHE, 368, 438.

25 FDHE, 438–39, 544–45, 379–80, 374, 580–81, 414, 608.

26 FDHE, 687–89, 643–48; Title 24, §1977–1978, *Revised Statutes of the United States* [. . .] (Government Printing Office, 1878).

27 *Joel P. Holland v. Robert Holland,* case 1882-011, CirCtCh, Isle of Wight Co., LV. He seems to have held onto the land. A Robert Holland appears in the 1900 Census as a "farmer" who owned mortgage-free land.

28 Contract dated May 1, 1866, in *Robertson v. Wright and Thompson,* case 1871-001, CirCtCh, Amelia Co., LV.

29 Petition, Feb. 5, 1867, and Robertson to Godsey, Jan. 11, 1867, both in *Robertson v. Wright.* The handwriting suggests that Robertson's notice was written by Justice of the Peace J. M. Gills, later a minor player in the local Readjuster Party. Dailey, *Before Jim Crow,* 100–101.

30 Testimony of John A. Jeter, F. P. Anderson, Petition, Feb. 5, 1867, and Decree, Oct. 7, 1867, in *Robertson v. Wright.* William Waller Hening, *The Virginia Justice, Comprising the Office and Authority of a Justice of the Peace, in the Commonwealth of Virginia . . . ,* 4th ed. (Shepherd & Pollard, 1825).

31 Robertson also recovered some of his property in the local Freedmen's Bureau court.

32 Hening, *The Virginia Justice,* 569. Today, such statutes are fairly empty promises; they may have been then, too. Kevin R. Johnson, "Integrating Racial Justice into the Civil Procedure Survey Course," *Journal of Legal Education* 54, no. 2 (2004), 250.

33 Testimony of F. P. Anderson ("a man of color"), in *Robertson v. Wright.*

34 Testimony of George D. Anderson; Answer of James E. Wright, both in *Robertson v. Wright.* Or perhaps they intended to sell it back to Robertson at cost, stepping into Thompson's shoes as his creditor.

35 *Cherokee Nation v. Georgia,* 30 U.S. 1, 13 (1831) (Marshall, C. J.); *Hunt v. Wing,* 57 Tenn. 139, 146 (1872); Susanna L. Blumenthal, "The Default Legal Person," *UCLA Law Review* 54, no. 5 (2007), 1217–19.

36 *Embry v. Morrison,* 63 Tenn. 186 (1874); *Bowen v. State,* 68 Tenn. 45 (1876); *Hart v. Diggs et al.,* 1879 WL 10427 (Ky.); *Marwilsky v. State,* 9 Tex. App. 377 (1880). Other scholars date this strategy to around 1900. See Melissa Milewski, *Litigating across the Color Line: Civil Cases between Black and White Southerners from the End of Slavery to Civil Rights* (Oxford University Press, 2018), 123; Royal Dumas, "The Muddled Mettle of Jurisprudence: Race and Procedure in Alabama's Appellate Courts, 1901–1930," *Alabama Law Review* 58 (2006), 440–41. Kimberly M. Welch [*Black Litigants in the Antebellum American South* (University of North Carolina Press, 2018), 72] finds it being used much earlier, in the early 1800s Natchez region. The trope plays a similar role in criminal law today. See Gabriel J. Chin, "Race and the Disappointing Right to Counsel," YLJ 122 (2012–2013), 2241.

37 Record in *Talley v. Robinson's Assignee, &c,* 9-10, case 1068, Court of Appeals of Virginia (Richmond), RG 100, Supreme Court Records and Briefs, acc. 35441, box 17, LVRC; *Talley v. Robinson's Assignee,* case 1873-050, LV.

38 Eric Foner, *The Fiery Trial: Abraham Lincoln and American Slavery* (W. W. Norton, 2010), 5; Dukeminier, *Property,* 752–53.

39 "Memorandum of an Agreement," Sept. 2, 1864, *Talley;* FDHE, 926–27.

40 The modern rule relies partly on *Talley.* See *Williston on Contracts,* 4th ed., May 2022 update, ch. 71:22. For a fuller discussion, see Penningroth, "Race in Contract Law," 23–28.

CHAPTER 5: DO FOR LOVE

1 Testimony of Ann Middleton, Henrietta Jefferson, and James H. Saville, in *Stewart v. Jefferson,* case 9368, EDC.

2 Testimony of Henrietta Jefferson and Ann Middleton, in *Stewart v. Jefferson.*

3 Testimony of James H. Saville, Mary Jackson, and Francis Hall, in *Stewart v. Jefferson.*

4 Testimony of Henrietta Jefferson and James H. Saville, in *Stewart v. Jefferson.* I am inferring from the testimony that it was a pocket deed.

5 Testimony of James H. Saville, in *Stewart v. Jefferson.*

6 Testimony of Ann Middleton, in *Stewart v. Jefferson.*

7 Testimony of George R. Dent; amended bill of complaint, Nov. 5, 1885, both in *Stewart v. Jefferson.*

8 Order dismissing bill, Feb. 9, 1887, in *Stewart v. Jefferson.*

9 *John Stewart v. Euphemia Stewart* (1885), case 9538, EDC.

10 For an example of a free Black family bargaining over old-age care, see Lindsay Gellman, "A Hamptons Property Fight over a Black Whaler's Homestead," NYT, Nov. 1, 2022. For a brilliant rethinking of the history of Black marriage, see Tera W. Hunter, *Bound in Wedlock: Slave and Free Black Marriage in the Nineteenth Century* (Harvard University Press, 2017).

11 FDHE, 879, 898–99, 902–903, 414.

12 This discussion builds on Hendrik Hartog's groundbreaking argument about inheritance among white middle-class Americans. Hartog, *Someday All This Will Be Yours: A History of Inheritance and Old Age* (Harvard University Press, 2012), 26.

13 Hunter, *Bound in Wedlock,* 199–200; Chery Williams to Hardy Williams, Tennessee, Freedmen's Bureau Field Office Records, 1865–1872, Assistant Commissioner, Roll 33 (T142), Letters received, registered series W-Z, 1866, T142, NARA, images, *FamilySearch.*

14 On the race and class dimensions of marital rights in the mid-1800s, see Reva B. Siegel, "'The Rule of Love': Wife Beating as Prerogative and Privacy," YLJ 105, no. 8 (1996), 2122–25; Laura F. Edwards, *Gendered Strife and Confusion: The Political Culture of Reconstruction* (University of Illinois Press, 1997), 177–83; Noralee Frankel, *Freedom's Women: Black Women and Families in Civil War Era Mississippi* (Indiana University Press, 1999).

15 Divorces were 34 of the 217 cases in 1872 and 1882 where I can identify at least one of the litigants as Black. Harriet Jacobs, *Incidents in the Life of a Slave Girl* (Published for the Author, 1861), 17, 44–48, 58–66; Frederick Douglass, *Narrative of the Life of Frederick Douglass, an American Slave. Written by Himself* (Anti-slavery Office, 1845), 12–14; Laura F. Edwards, "'The Marriage Covenant Is at the Foundation of All Our Rights': The Politics of Slave Marriages in North Carolina after Emancipation," LHR 14, no. 1 (1996), 101.

16 Hunter, *Bound in Wedlock,* 6–7, 30–31, 54, 200; Gerald David Jaynes, *Branches*

without Roots: Genesis of the Black Working Class in the American South, 1862–1882 (Oxford University Press, 1986), 158–73, 180; Susan Eva O'Donovan, *Becoming Free in the Cotton South* (Harvard University Press, 2007), 193.

17 "Memorandum of an agreement," June 7, 1865, Mss 1B2924a 1669–1684, VHS; Suzanne Lebsock, *The Free Women of Petersburg: Status and Culture in a Southern Town, 1784–1860* (W. W. Norton, 1984), 23; Frankel, *Freedom's Women,* 128–29; FDHE, 196–97, 558, 609–10, 370.

18 Laura F. Edwards, *The People and Their Peace: Legal Culture and the Transformation of Inequality in the Post-Revolutionary South* (University of North Carolina Press, 2009), 169–201; FDHE, 575–76, 626–27, 635–36; Noralee Frankel, *Freedom's Women,* 136–38, 154–58; Amy Dru Stanley, *From Bondage to Contract: Wage Labor, Marriage, and the Market in the Age of Slave Emancipation* (Cambridge University Press, 1998), 46–55; W. P. Burrell and D. E. Johnson Sr., *Twenty-Five Years History of the Grand Fountain of the United Order of True Reformers, 1881–1905* (1909), 412.

19 Adrienne D. Davis, "The Private Law of Race and Sex: An Antebellum Perspective," SLR 51, no. 2 (1999), 272–73; Gilbert Thomas Stephenson, "Racial Distinctions in Southern Law," *American Political Science Review* 1, no. 1 (1906), 47.

20 Hunter, *Bound in Wedlock,* 282–92; *Francis v. Francis,* 72 Va. 283 (1879).

21 Hendrik Hartog, *Man and Wife in America: A History* (Harvard University Press, 2000), 380n 45, 281–82; Carroll D. Wright, *A Report on Marriage and Divorce in the United States, 1867 to 1886* (Government Printing Office, 1889), 79–80; *Buford v. Buford* (1871), case 1337, CirCtCh, Lafayette Co., MS; Decree, Mar. 14, 1882, in *Wooldridge v. Wooldridge,* case 1882–001, CirCtCh, Amelia Co., LV; Petition of Edward Johnson, in *Johnson v. Johnson,* case 1875–002, CirCtCh, Amelia Co., LV.

22 *In re Campbell's Estate,* 12 Cal. App. 707, 108 P 669 (1910); *Speese's Heirs v. Shores,* 81 Neb. 593 (1908); "Validity of a Slave Marriage," 1 *Chicago Legal News* 119 (1868–69); *Irving v. Ford,* 179 Mass. 216 (1901); *McDowell v. Sapp,* 39 Ohio St. 558 (1883); *Morris v. Williams,* 39 Ohio St. 554 (1883); *Adams v. Sneed,* 41 Fla. 151 (1899); *Christopher v. Mungan,* 61 Fla. 513 (1911); Estate of John H. White, Orphans Court, Camden, NJSA; Record in *Francis v. Tazewell* (1917), LVRC. Slavery continued to crop up in inheritance cases well into the late twentieth century. See *Anderson v. Anderson,* 52 Tenn. App. 241 (1962); *Evans v. Young,* 299 S.W. 2d 218 (Tenn. 1957); *Pouncy v. Garner,* 626 S.W. 2d 337 (Texas 1981).

23 Estate of Maria Parker, case 388, CirCtCh, Adams Co., MS; Maria Parker, Mississippi, Wills and Probate Records, 1780–1982, Ancestry.com.

24 Davis, "Private Law of Race and Sex," 221–88.

25 For an excellent summary of many of the key legal issues, see Hunter, *Bound in Wedlock,* 283–92.

26 *Girod v. Lewis,* 6 Mart. La. (1819), 559 ("civil rights"), 560 ("dormant"); William Blackstone, *Commentaries on the Laws of England* (J. B. Lippincott, 1870), 355–56 ("wing").

27 *Howard v. Howard,* 6 Jones N.C. (1858), 235 (all are void).

28 Joel Prentiss Bishop, *Commentaries on the Law of Marriage and Divorce* [. . .] (Little, Brown, 1864), 134–42.

29 Petition of Leah Francis in *Francis v. Tazewell* (1917), LVRC ("never married"); Answer and Cross-bill of Ellen Mayes, Oct. 11, 1900, in *Thompson v. Mayes* (1900), case 3057, CirCtCh, Lafayette Co., Oxford, MS; *Buffington v. Tyner,* 95 Okla. 120 (1923) ("of a slave marriage"); Defendants' Answer, Nov. 11, 1879, in *Johnson v. Saunders,* case 7000, EDC ("lawful wedlock"); *Jones v. Jones,* 36 Md. 447 (1872); *Scott v. Raub,* 88 Va. 721 (1891) ("heritable blood"); testimony of Belle Gregory, in *Goode v. Gregory,* case 1912-51CC, CirCtCh, Mecklenburg Co., LV ("illegal heirs").

30 Michael Grossberg, *Governing the Hearth: Law and the Family in Nineteenth-Century America* (University of North Carolina Press, 1985), 134–35; 2 Kent, Com. 211, and quotations in *Jones v. Jones,* 243 U.S. 615 (1914) at 937.

31 Grossberg, *Governing the Hearth,* 64–83; Ariela R. Dubler, "Wifely Behavior: A Legal History of Acting Married," CLR 100 (2000), 969; *Colston v. Quander,* 1 Virginia Law Journal 689 (1877) at 692; *Middleton v. Middleton,* 77 N.E. 1123 (1906); *Prescott v. Ayers,* 114 N.E. 557 (1916); "Current Decisions," 28 YLJ 516 (1919); *McDowell v. Sapp,* 39 Ohio St. 558 (1883); *Butler v. Butler,* 44 N.E. 203 (1896); Brandi Clay Brimmer, *Claiming Union Widowhood: Race, Respectability, and Poverty in the Post-Emancipation South* (Duke University Press, 2020), 128–29, 138–40, 151–62, 192–97.

32 Thomas S. Stephens, quoted in *In re Campbell's Estate,* 12 Cal. App. 707 (1910); affidavit of Tabitha S. Andrews, Oct. 23, 1912, Record in *Francis et al v. Tazewell et al* (1917), LVRC.

33 Testimony of Ann Middleton, Feb. 24, 1886, in *Stewart v. Jefferson,* case 9368, EDC; testimony of Judson Brooks in *Judson Brooks v. Maria Jackson,* case 6876, EDC.

34 Handwritten list, in *Dallard v. Monroe's Admr.,* case 1912-099, CirCtCh, Rockingham Co., LV; Commissioner's report, in *Gladys Spinner v. Sherman Spinner* (1932), ended case 3411, CirCtCh, Albemarle Co., Charlottesville, VA; testimony of John A. Nottingham, ca. June 9, 1884, in *Fitchett v. Smith's Admr,* CirCtCh, Northampton Co., VA; testimony of Jinnett Lea and Mary Bradsher in *Thompson v. Mayes* (1900), case 3057, CirCtCh, Lafayette Co., MS.; Gwin & Mounger to James A. Townes, Jan. 15, 1910, GWIN; Commissioner's Report, *Jesse Simmons v. Robert Farrar's Admr.,* case 1902-31CC, CirCtCh, Mecklenburg Co., LV ("never been heard"); testimony of Samuel Miller, Feb. 1, 1901, *Estate of John H. White* ("cried").

35 Testimony of John Quinn, *Ryan v. Wallace* (1902), case 23109, EDC; deposition of W. M. Edwards, ca. 1906, f 30, b 5, GWIN (italics added); testimony of William Main, June 20, 1884, *Marks v. Main,* case 8276, EDC. For similar cases, see *Sneed's Admr. v. Harriett Sneed,* case 1892–42CC, CirCtCh, Mecklenburg Co., LV; and *Buckley v. Scott* (1892), case 14103, EDC.

36 Deborah Gray White, *Ar'n't I a Woman? Female Slaves in the Plantation South* (1985; W. W. Norton, 1999), 28–32, 46–49; Edwards, *Gendered Strife,* 186; Gwin &

Mounger to James A. Townes, Jan. 15, 1910, GWIN; Davis, "Private Law of Race and Sex," 270.

37 Edward L. Pierce (1862), and H. Styles [Stiles] (1865), both quoted in Dylan C. Penningroth, *The Claims of Kinfolk: African American Property and Community in the Nineteenth-Century South* (University of North Carolina Press, 2003), 158; Julie Saville, *The Work of Reconstruction: From Slave to Wage Laborer in South Carolina, 1860–1870* (Cambridge University Press, 1994), 18; Eric Foner, *Reconstruction: America's Unfinished Revolution, 1863–1877* (1988; Perennial Classics, 2002), 163 (quoting *Savannah Weekly Republican*); E. Franklin Frazier, *The Negro Family in the United States* (University of Chicago Press, 1939), 562–67; Will of Louisa Warren, Nov. 20, 1866, in *Polk v. Costley,* case 1911, EDC.

38 Sydney Nathans, *A Mind to Stay: White Plantation, Black Homeland* (Harvard University Press, 2017), 218–19; R. S. Bennett to A. Pleasanton, May 16, 1871, FSSP, Z-31; Thomas W. Mitchell, "From Reconstruction to Deconstruction: Undermining Black Landownership, Political Independence, and Community through Partition Sales of Tenancies in Common," *Northwestern University Law Review* 95 (2001), 505–80; Saville, *Work of Reconstruction,* 18; Elizabeth Ware Pearson, *Letters from Port Royal, 1862–1868* (W. B. Clarke Co., 1906), 234; Samuel Boles to Bvt. Maj. Gen. Birge, June 16, 1865, FSSP, A-5863; J. M. Simms to "General," enclosure in Tillson to "General," FSSP A-5161.

39 Testimony of Robert H. Ward, Robert Bowie, Horace Scott, and Brief of Defendant, in *Thomas Henson [Henton] v. Hill,* case 6806, EDC.

40 Hartog, *Someday All This Will Be Yours,* 345–62; testimony of Charity Butler, Ann E. Middleton, Henrietta Jefferson, and James Bowser, in *Stewart v. Jefferson.* Emphasis in original. See also "An Old Woman with Memories Extending Back to Slavery Days," b 131-93, FPMS.

41 Testimony of Charity Butler and Ann E. Middleton, in *Stewart v Jefferson*; testimony of Jacob Bell, Mar. 28, 1885, in *Booth v. Fraser,* case 9185, EDC; testimony of Sancho Richardson in *Richardson v. Richardson,* Apr. 24, 1868, Provost Court Beaufort, South Carolina, Box 2, Provost Courts North and South Carolina, 1866–1868, Entry 4257, RG 393, Part I; Muster Roll, 21 U.S.C.T., U.S. Colored Troops Military Service Records, 1863-1865 [database on-line], Ancestry.com. See also *Goode v. Gregory,* 1912-51CC, Mecklenburg Co., LV.

42 Here I draw from Dubler, "Wifely Behavior" and Wyatt MacGaffey, "Changing Representations in Central African History," *Journal of African History* 46, no. 2 (2005), 189–207.

43 Steven Hahn, *A Nation under Our Feet: Black Political Struggles in the Rural South from Slavery to the Great Migration* (Harvard University Press, 2003), 5–9, 35–36, 135–46, 166–69, 333–34, 459–61; Brimmer, *Claiming Union Widowhood,* 8, 101; Saville, *Work of Reconstruction,* 16–18; Thomas C. Holt, "'An Empire over the Mind': Emancipation, Race, and Ideology in the British West Indies and the American South," in *Region, Race, and Reconstruction: Essays in Honor of C. Vann Woodward,* ed. J.

Morgan Kousser and James M. McPherson (Oxford University Press, 1982), 299–301. Compare Gregory S. Alexander, *Commodity and Propriety: Competing Visions of Property in American Legal Thought, 1776–1970* (University of Chicago Press, 1997), 1; Jesse Dukeminier et al., *Property* (Wolters Kluver, 2014), 364; C. Scott Graber, "A Blight Hits Black Farmers," *Civil Rights Digest* 10, no. 3 (1978), 21–22. On pop nostalgia for the country, see James N. Gregory, *The Southern Diaspora: How the Great Migrations of Black and White Southerners Transformed America* (University of North Carolina Press, 2005), 72–74.

CHAPTER 6: WHO IS THE CHURCH?

1 Record in *Alexander v. Bouldin,* case 1054, EDC; *Bouldin v. Alexander,* 82 U.S. 131, 135 (1872). Emphasis added.

2 *Watson v. Jones,* 80 U.S. 679, 714 (1871) (the white Presbyterian case); *Godfrey v. Walker,* 42 Ga. 562, 569 (1871) (rights to church property are civil rights).

3 Steven Hahn, *A Nation under Our Feet: Black Political Struggles in the Rural South from Slavery to the Great Migration* (Harvard University Press, 2003), 461–62; Elsa Barkley Brown, "Uncle Ned's Children: Negotiating Community and Freedom in Postemancipation Richmond, Virginia," PhD diss., Kent State, 1994, 398–406.

4 Justin Behrend, *Reconstructing Democracy: Grassroots Black Politics in the Deep South after the Civil War* (University of Georgia Press, 2015), 49–53, 67–68, 144; Nell Irvin Painter, *Exodusters: Black Migration to Kansas after Reconstruction* (Knopf, 1977), 115–16; Juliet E. K. Walker, *The History of Black Business in America: Capitalism, Race, Entrepreneurship* (Simon & Schuster, 1998), 152–53, 171–81; Rebecca J. Scott, "Public Rights, Social Equality, and the Conceptual Roots of the Plessy Challenge," Michigan Law Review 106, no. 5 (2008), 797–800; Eric Foner, *Reconstruction: America's Unfinished Revolution, 1863–1877* (1988; Perennial Classics, 2002), 111–12; Henry W. Bellows, *Historical Sketch of the Union League Club of New York* (1879), 166–67.

5 Behrend, *Reconstructing Democracy,* 49; *Biennial Report of the Secretary of State of Texas* (1882), Appendix, Miscellaneous Charters . . . , 11–17; "Laws of the State of Louisiana," *Weekly Louisianan,* July 9, 1871; "Notice," FJ, Mar. 21, 1829; W. P. Burrell and D. E. Johnson Sr., *Twenty-Five Years History of the Grand Fountain of the United Order of True Reformers, 1881-1905* (1909), 5.

6 Sydney R. Wrightington, *The Law of Unincorporated Associations and Similar Relations* (Little, Brown, 1916), §§55–58; "Odd Fellows Department," *Cleveland Gazette,* Mar. 8, 1884.

7 "Notice!" *The Elevator,* Mar. 26, 1869.

8 Hendrik Hartog, *Public Property and Private Power: The Corporation of the City of New York in American Law, 1730–1870* (1983; Harvard University Press, 1989); William J. Novak, *The People's Welfare: Law and Regulation in Nineteenth-Century America* (University of North Carolina Press, 1996), 240; Bouvier 1871, 483, s.v.

"disfranchisement"; Burrell and Johnson, *Twenty-Five Years History,* 18; "Newark Notes," New York Globe, Mar. 29, 1884. See also "Virginia Building and Saving Company," *People's Advocate,* June 17, 1876; FDHE, 966–67, 524–25.

9 Michele Mitchell, *Righteous Propagation: African Americans and the Politics of Racial Destiny after Reconstruction* (University of North Carolina Press, 2004), quotation on 67; Walker, *History of Black Business in America,* 183–87, 204–13.

10 Burrell and Johnson, *Twenty-five Years History,* 15–27, 90, 35–42, 77–78.

11 Burrell and Johnson, *Twenty-five Years History,* 56, 63–69, 81–86.

12 E. A. Williams et al., *History and Manual of the Colored Knights of Pythias* (np, 1917), 118, 186–89, 276; *Grand Lodge v. Barnard,* 9 Ga. App. 71 (1911); *Little v. Grand Lodge K. P. of South Carolina,* 81 S.E. 152 (1914); Theda Skocpol et al., *What a Mighty Power We Can Be: African American Fraternal Groups and the Struggle for Racial Equality* (Princeton University Press, 2006), 80–81.

13 Skocpol et al., *What a Mighty Power,* 139–65.

14 Williams et al., *History and Manual,* 327, 401–402; Skocpol et al., *What a Mighty Power,* 152, 148–49. The *Atlanta Independent* even compared *Creswill* to the *Dred Scott* decision (1857). J. Blaine Poindexter, "Pythians Invade Chicago City," CD, Aug. 20, 1927.

15 "A Drawn Battle," RP, Sept. 21, 1912; "Ohio Pythians Balk New Tax Levy," PC, Oct. 26, 1929; "The Supreme Chancellor's Proclamation," RP, July 14, 1917; "Pythian Election Left Bitter Taste," *Afro,* Aug. 2, 1930; "Pythian Steam Roller Was Well Oiled," *Afro,* Sept. 3, 1927; *Knights of Pythias v. Grand Lodge Knights of Pythias,* 49 App.D.C. 19, 258 F. 275 (1919); Williams, *History and Manual,* 839.

16 Charles Edward Dickerson II, "The Benevolent and Protective Order of Elks and the Improved Benevolent and Protective Order of Elks of the World: A Comparative Study of Euro-American and Afro-American Secret Orders," PhD diss., University of Rochester, 1982, 287–89; Charles H. Wesley, *History of the Improved Benevolent and Protective Order of Elks of the World, 1898–1954* (1955), 426; Skocpol et al., *What a Mighty Power,* 184, 176, 174 (quoting Robert H. Johnson (1956)).

17 Williams, *History and Manual,* 255–56, 287, 310, 356–58, 403, 513–61, 288, 184, 313, 439–40, 401; Burrell and Johnson, *Twenty-five Years History,* 345, 434.

18 Hahn, *Nation Under Our Feet,* 224–25; Stephen Kantrowitz, "One Man's Mob Is Another Man's Militia: Violence, Manhood, and Authority in Reconstruction South Carolina," in *Jumpin' Jim Crow: Southern Politics from Civil War to Civil Rights,* ed. Jane Dailey et al. (Princeton University Press, 2000), 67–87; U.S. Senate Misc. Doc. No. 48, 44th Cong., 2nd Sess., vol. 1 (1877), 156–59, 199–205, 537–38, 557–58, 616, 623, 836, 1024; *An Address to the people of the United States, Adopted at a Conference of Colored Citizens . . .* (Columbia, SC, 1876), 5.

19 Tera W. Hunter, *To 'Joy My Freedom: Southern Black Women's Lives and Labors after the Civil War* (Harvard University Press, 1997), 76–88, 93; Gerald David Jaynes, *Branches without Roots: Genesis of the Black Working Class in the American South, 1862–1882* (Oxford University Press, 1986), 116–20; "To the Citizens of Atlanta," *Daily*

Constitution, July 24, 1881; FDHE, 501–2, 510–15, 545; "The Washing Amazons," *Daily Constitution*, Aug. 3, 1881; Bouvier 1897, 224 (s.v. "license"), 839 (s.v. "franchise"). Bouvier clarified: "A license fee is a tax."

20 *Freedom*, 924–26; Foner, *Reconstruction*, 173; Behrend, *Reconstructing Democracy*, 70–72; Jaynes, *Branches Without Roots*, 116–20, 184–90, 205–206.

21 F. J. A. Bouman, "Indigenous Savings and Credit Societies in the Developing World," in *Rural Financial Markets in Developing Countries: Their Use and Abuse*, ed. J. D. Von Pischke et al. (Johns Hopkins University Press for the Economic Development Institute of the World Bank, 1983), 268; Jaynes, *Branches Without Roots*, 289–95; Behrend, *Reconstructing Democracy*, 101–06; *Freedom*, 880.

22 Record at 12, 28, 200, 9, 6, *Hamilton v. Halpin*, MDAH; *Hamilton v. Halpin*, 8 So. 739, 741–42 (1890). Halpin resold it to Regina Meirs, his sister-in-law and wife of his partner. Both the justice of the peace and circuit clerk were Black.

23 Record at 108, 167–70, 111, 116, 137–38, 157–60, 194, *Hamilton v. Halpin*, MDAH; *Hamilton v. Halpin*, 8 So. 739, 742 (1890).

24 Barbara Dianne Savage, *Your Spirits Walk Beside Us: The Politics of Black Religion* (Harvard University Press, 2008), 56; Benjamin Elijah Mays and Joseph William Nicholson, *The Negro's Church* (Institute of Social and Religious Research, 1933), 100–101; St. Clair Drake and Horace R. Cayton, *Black Metropolis: A Study of Negro Life in a Northern City* (Harcourt, Brace, 1945), 612.

25 Sarah Barringer Gordon, "The First Disestablishment: Limits on Church Power and Property before the Civil War," PLR 162 (Jan. 2014), 311–16, 324–25.

26 Nathan Womack & wife To Cha. Palmore & others, Aug. 23, 1875, DB 31, 44–45, Circuit Clerk of Cumberland County, Cumberland, VA; Sarah Barringer Gordon, "The African Supplement: Religion, Race, and Corporate Law in Early National America," WMQ 72 (July 2015), 385–422.

27 CBMB, 71–73 ("Treasury act" for 1836–1837), LV.

28 William Crowell, *The Church Member's Hand-Book: A Guide to the Doctrines and Practice of Baptist Churches* (1850), 43–44.

29 Paul G. Kauper, "Church Autonomy and the First Amendment: The Presbyterian Church Case," *Supreme Court Review* (1969), 351–52, 362–63; *Shannon v. Frost*, 42 Ky. 253, 259 (1842). Kellen R. Funk, "Church Corporations and the Conflict of Laws in Antebellum America," *Journal of Law and Religion* 32 (2017), 281–82; *Bouldin*, at 139–140. Emphasis added. Minutes, July 12, 1858, CBRB; *Schnorr's Appeal*, 67 Pa. 138, 147 (1870).

30 Lucas P. Volkman, "Church Property Disputes, Religious Freedom, and the Ordeal of African Methodists in Antebellum St. Louis: *Farrar v. Finney* (1855)," *Journal of Law and Religion* 27, no. 1 (2011), 123–33; Charles Elliott, *History of the Great Secession from the Methodist Episcopal Church* [. . .] (Swormstedt & Poe, 1855), 221–23, 243.

31 Foner, *Reconstruction*, 70–71; "Minutes of an Interview . . . ," Jan. 12, 1865, in *The Wartime Genesis of Free Labor: The Lower South*, ed. Ira Berlin et al. (Cambridge

University Press, 1990), 331–38; Record in *Jacob Godfrey v. Robert Walker* (1871) at 2-8, Supreme Court of Georgia, GSA; Proceedings of the Forty-Seventh Session of the Baltimore Annual Conference of the African M. E. Church (Apr. 26, 1864), 20. Thanks to Dennis C. Dickerson for generously sharing this rare document. A. W. Wayman, *My Recollections of African M. E. Ministers, or Forty Years' Experience in the African Methodist Episcopal Church* (A. M. E. Book Rooms, 1881), 104–6.

32 Record in Godfrey, at 10, 12; *Godfrey v. Walker,* 42 Ga. 562, 567, 572 (1871); *Gartin v. Penick,* 5 Bush 110, 150–52 (1868).

33 Ira Berlin, *Generations of Captivity: A History of African-American Slaves* (Harvard University Press, 2003), 208–9; Luther Porter Jackson, *Free Negro Labor and Property Holding in Virginia, 1830–1860* (Appleton-Century, 1942), 77, 159–63; W. Harrison Daniel, "Virginia Baptists and the Negro in the Antebellum Era," JNH 56, 1 (1971), 2; Sylvia R. Frey and Betty Wood, *Come Shouting to Zion: African American Protestantism in the American South and British Caribbean to 1830* (University of North Carolina Press, 1998), 191–203; Foner, *Reconstruction,* 113; *Bouldin v. Alexander,* 82 U.S. 131, 140 (1872).

34 CBRB, frames 72–75, 92–94.

35 Albert Raboteau, *Slave Religion: The 'Invisible Institution' in the Antebellum South* (Oxford University Press, 1978), 212–88; Foner, *Reconstruction,* 88–95, 612; Hahn, *A Nation Under Our Feet,* 230–37.

36 Gordon, "African Supplement," 415–19; Levi Jenkins Coppin, *Unwritten History* (A. M. E. Book Concern, 1919), 123–28.

37 Daniel Alexander Payne, *History of the African Methodist Episcopal Church* (Publishing House of the A. M. E. Sunday School Union, 1891), 320. For the quotations regarding the African Methodist Episcopal Church, see Edward W. Lampton, *Digest of Rulings and Decisions of the Bishops of the African Methodist Episcopal Church from 1847 to 1907* (Record Publishing Co., 1907), 7–8, 11, 15, 27, 159, 224, 314. R. de Baptiste, "A Gospel Church," in *The Negro Baptist Pulpit,* ed. E[dward] M. Brawley (American Baptist Publication Society, 1890), 117. For the "arbitrary" quotation, see E. Franklin Frazier, *The Negro Church in America* (Schocken, 1963), 42–43. Randal Maurice Jelks, *Benjamin Elijah Mays, Schoolmaster of the Movement: A Biography* (University of North Carolina, 2012), 7–16, 49–50.

38 Douglas Laycock, "Towards a General Theory of the Religion Clause: The Case of Church Labor Relations and the Right to Church Autonomy," CLR 81 (Nov. 1981), 1395. State and local judges did not have to follow the deference doctrine, because the Supreme Court decided *Watson* and *Bouldin* under federal common law.

39 *American Law Reports Annotated,* vol. 8 (1920), 112, 115; Calvin White Jr., *The Rise to Respectability: Race, Religion, and the Church of God in Christ* (University of Arkansas Press, 2012), 39–54, 135; John M. Giggie, *After Redemption: Jim Crow and the Transformation of African American Religion in the Delta, 1875–1915* (Oxford University Press, 2008); Record in *Mt. Helm Baptist Church et al. v. C. P. Jones* (1901), 14, 47,

case sc0000010041, ser. 6, Supreme Court Case Files, MDAH; *Mt. Helm v. Jones*, 30 So. 714 (1901). On judges using their own religious common sense, see Linda Przybyszewski, *The Republic According to John Marshall Harlan* (University of North Carolina Press, 1999), 52–60.

40 *Mt. Helm v. Jones*, 30 So. at 716; White, *Rise to Respectability*, 21–54.

CHAPTER 7: "GOAT SENSE"

1 *Civil Rights Cases*, 3 S.Ct. 18 (1883), 29, 31. Eric Foner, *Free Soil, Free Labor, Free Men: The Ideology of the Republican Party before the Civil War* (1970; Oxford University Press, 1995); Jonathan Lurie, "Mr. Justice Bradley: A Reassessment," *Seton Hall Law Review* 16, no. 2 (1986), 349–50, 365. This paragraph relies heavily on Linda Przybyszewski, *The Republic According to John Marshall Harlan* (University of North Carolina Press, 1999), 91–97.

2 *Civil Rights Cases*, at 21–32.

3 Przybyszewski, *Republic According to John Marshall Harlan*, 90–95; Christopher W. Schmidt, *Civil Rights in America: A History* (Cambridge University Press, 2021), 49.

4 "First Annual Meeting of the Corporation," *The Crisis*, Feb. 1912, 158. See also Susan D. Carle, *Defining the Struggle: National Organizing for Racial Justice, 1880–1913* (Oxford University Press, 2013), 277–78. W. E. B. Du Bois, "Postscript," *The Crisis*, vol. 34, no. 7 (Sept. 1927), 239–40. It is probably no accident that Du Bois chose to make his archetypal non–civil rights plaintiff a woman.

5 Kevin Boyle, *Arc of Justice: A Saga of Race, Civil Rights, and Murder in the Jazz Age* (Holt, 2005), 219, 241 (quoting press release). See also W. E. B. Du Bois, "Violations of Property Rights," *The Crisis* 2, no. 1 (May 1911), 28–32; "First Annual Meeting of the Corporation"; Du Bois, "Postscript."

6 "The N.A.A.C.P. Battle Front," *The Crisis*, Feb. 1930, 68.

7 "The Man of Color and His Rights," *Wichita Searchlight*, June 4, 1904; CR, Feb. 24, 1887; *Afro*, July 6, 1929. See also "Interposition Is Nullification," [Norfolk] *New Journal and Guide*, Feb. 4, 1956.

8 "Social Equality," *Weekly Louisianan*, May 27, 1882; "Why Should Gov. Terrell Utter Deliberate Falsehoods," *Savannah Tribune*, Jan. 26, 1907; [untitled], *The Appeal* (St. Paul), June 11, 1910; "Women to Fight Tax on Incomes," *Washington Bee*, Jan. 10, 1914; "Thank God," *The Appeal*, Nov. 24, 1917; Carle, *Defining the Struggle*, 35; J. Clay Smith Jr., *Emancipation: The Making of the Black Lawyer, 1844–1944* (University of Pennsylvania Press, 1993), 45.

9 *Civil Rights Cases*, 3 S.Ct. 18, 26 (1883); Ashley Nkadi, "100 Things Not To Do #WhileBlack," *The Root*, Oct. 26, 2018.

10 For suits against Black insurers, see *Slaughter v. Grand Lodge*, 68 So. 367, 367 (Ala. 1909); *Pollock v. Household of Ruth*, 63 S.E. 940, 940–41 (N.C. 1909); *Wallace v. Circle Lodge No. 2* (1935), case 3169, Docket 15, 1935, City Court Chancery Dockets, Alton, IL, Southern Illinois University at Carbondale, 7–9. For suit against white

insurer, see *Ins. Co. v. Wilkinson,* 80 U.S. 222, 223 (1871). For Black insurer's suit against Black policyholder, see Decree, Sept. 20, 1962, in *North Carolina Mutual v. Johnson,* 468, Chancery Order Book, vol. 16, Southampton County, VA.

11 *Gregory v. Seward,* Dec. 24, 1926, Justice's Judgment and Execution Book—Auto, 2, Gloucester County, VA, LVRC; *Harris v. American Motorist Insurance Co.,* 240 Miss. 870 (1961) (car accidents); *Seaboard Air Line Railway Co. v. Blackwell,* 244 U.S. 640 (1917) (railroad accidents); *Gomillion v. Forsythe,* 218 S.C. 297 (1950) (work accidents); *Robertson v. Wright,* case 1871-001, CirCtCh, Amelia County, VA, LV (farm); *Davis v. Jones,* Feb. 16, 1892, JP docket, Brunswick, VA, LV (rent); *Richmond v. Richmond,* Feb. 25, 1952, case 5546, 225, General Civil Docket 3, Office of Circuit Clerk, Marshall County, MS (personal property).

12 Richard H. Brodhead, ed., *The Journals of Charles W. Chesnutt* (1993), 49 (writ for asssault); *McKinney v. City of Holly Springs,* Feb. 19, 1902, case 4401, CirCtLaw, Marshall County, MS (town officials); *Baskervill v. Ellis,* Jan. 25, 1915, Justice of the Peace Records, 1887–1915, Brunswick County, VA, LV (pregnancy); *Matter of Morning Star Colored Baptist Church,* case 1919-007, CirCtCh, Isle of Wight County, VA (easement); *Estate of Maria Parker,* case 388, CirCtCh, Adams County, MS (will); *Estate of John Dennis,* case 4226 (1912), CirCtCh, Lafayette County, MS. (probate); *Shaw v. Wheat Street Baptist Church,* 234 S.E.2d 711 (1977) (towing); "The Legal Problems of the Rural Poor," DLJ 17, no. 3 (1969), 495, 524–25.

13 Record at 19 *Seaboard Air Line v. Blackwell* (farm in wife's name); Thavolia Glymph, *Out of the House of Bondage: The Transformation of the Plantation Household* (Cambridge University Press, 2008), 157, 174; Tera W. Hunter, *To 'Joy My Freedom: Southern Black Women's Lives and Labors after the Civil War* (Harvard University Press, 1997), 64, 74–78, 111–14, 131–36; Gerald David Jaynes, *Branches without Roots: Genesis of the Black Working Class in the American South, 1862–1882* (Oxford University Press, 1986), 116–20, 288–89 (credit sales); Elsa Barkley Brown, "Womanist Consciousness: Maggie Lena Walker and the Independent Order of Saint Luke," *Signs* 14 (1989), 610, 616–22; Sarah Barringer Gordon, "The African Supplement: Religion, Race, and Corporate Law in Early National America," WMQ, 3d ser., 72, no. 3 (2015), 385; Dylan C. Penningroth, "Everyday Use: A History of Civil Rights in Black Churches," JAH 107, no. 4 (2021), 875, 880; Evelyn Brooks Higginbotham, *Righteous Discontent: The Women's Movement in The Black Baptist Church, 1880–1920* (Harvard University Press, 1993), 57–60; Kenneth W. Mack, *Representing the Race: The Creation of the Civil Rights Lawyer* (Harvard University Press, 2012), 28, 40–41.

14 Theodore Rosengarten, *All God's Dangers: The Life of Nate Shaw* (1974; University of Chicago Press, 2000), 289. Shaw is a pseudonym. The man's real name was Ned Cobb. Hendrik Hartog, *Someday All This Will Be Yours: A History of Inheritance and Old Age* (Harvard University Press, 2012), 14–15; Lawrence M. Friedman, *Contract Law in America* (1965; Quid Pro, 2011), 55.

15 Compare Rosengarten, *All God's Dangers,* 151, 32, 230–31, with 1 Williston, *Law of*

Contracts 605 (1920); 2 Code of Alabama ch. 95, §4486 (1907), and Christopher Gustavus Tiedeman and Edward Joseph White, *The American Law of Real Property*, 3rd ed., Part 1, ch. 2, §§16, 20 (1906). Penningroth, "Everyday Use," 878–80, 893–96; *Catalogue of the Tuskegee Normal and Industrial Institute* (1895–96), 42, 45; "Business Law," CR, Aug. 9, 1877; "Pith and Point," *Huntsville Gazette*, June 10, 1882; "Basic Law for Women," PC, Mar. 13, 1976.

16 *Redmond v. Hartsfield*, case 4102, 1911, CirCtCh, Lafayette Co., MS (exceptional challenge to white supremacy); 177/2103, counting 1902–1932 sample slices, excluding cases where I could not identify both litigants. Patricia J. Williams, *The Alchemy of Race and Rights: Diary of a Law Professor* (Harvard University Press, 1991), 146–65; Kevin K. Gaines, *Uplifting the Race: Black Leadership, Politics, and Culture in the Twentieth Century* (University of North Carolina Press, 1996), 1–5; Kenneth W. Mack, "Rethinking Civil Rights Lawyering and Politics in the Era before Brown," YLJ 115, no. 2 (2005), 272–80; "From the Field," *A.M.E. Church Rev.* (1891), 334; E. K. Love, "Emancipation Oration!" (Georgia Baptist Job Press, 1891), 9, Daniel Murray Pamphlet Collection, [https://perma.cc/8KTE-4VC7].

17 Barbara Young Welke, *Recasting American Liberty: Gender, Race, Law, and the Railroad Revolution, 1865–1920* (Cambridge University Press, 2001); Myisha Shuntez Eatmon, "Public Wrongs, Private Rights: African Americans, Private Law, and White Violence During Jim Crow," PhD diss., Northwestern University, 2020; [untitled], *Nicodemus Cyclone*, Mar. 16, 1888; "Newsy Newark Notes," *New York Freeman*, Aug. 21, 1886; "Ducks and Mule Cause of Feud," RP, May 16, 1908; Speech by J[ames] C. Napier to law graduates of Central Tennessee College, June 1 [no year], f 31, b 1, Fisk University Archives; "Negro Business League," *Nashville Globe*, Jan. 5, 1917; "Algiers Anglings," *Weekly Pelican*, April 23, 1887; [untitled], *Cleveland Gazette*, April 2, 1887; [untitled], *Cleveland Gazette*, Mar. 14, 1885.

18 *Trustees of Dartmouth College v. Woodward*, 17 U.S. 518, 636 (1819) (Marshall, J.).

19 Harold D. Woodman, *New South—New Law: The Legal Foundations of Credit and Labor Relations in the Postbellum Agricultural South* (Louisiana State University Press, 1995), 82; *McElmurray v. Turner*, 86 Ga. 215 (1890).

20 Welke, *Recasting American Liberty*, 299–300, 302, 358–60; Richard Thomas Walker Duke Jr., "The Recollections of Richard Thomas Walker Duke Jr.," Richmond: Library of Virginia, comp. 1899–1926, transcr. 2001 by Gayle M. Schulman for the Albemarle County Historical Society; R. T. W. Duke to C. Venable Minor, May 3, 1937, in f "Fleming v. Garth," C-2062, DUKES.

21 Chauncey Eskridge to Martin Luther King Jr., Nov. 29, 1961, Morehouse College Martin Luther King Jr. Collection ("sky"); King v. Yellow Cab Company, f 6, b 79, Dr. Martin Luther King, Jr., Archive, Howard Gotlieb Archival Research Center, Boston University; *Alice Freeman v. L. D. Hill*, case 2456 (1944), CoCtLaw, Coahoma Co., MS. See also "Court Completes Second Week Here," *Daily Clarion-Ledger*, Mar. 4, 1934.

22 "Restriction of the Jurisdiction of the United States District Courts as to Contracts between the United States and Citizens," *Mississippi Law Journal* 7, no. 2 (1934), 188; Kay Mills, *This Little Light of Mine: The Life of Fannie Lou Hamer* (University Press of Kentucky, 2007), 13, 22.

23 *Charley Bradley v. Federal Compress & Warehouse Co.*, case 5121 (1944), CoCtLaw, Coahoma Co., MS; Motion for costs, Feb. 24, 1919, in *Wicks v. Cox*, case 4817, CirCtLaw, Marshall Co., MS; *Skinner v. Baker & Cagel*, case 1457 (1912), CirCtCh, Coahoma Co., MS; jury instructions in *Wicks v. Cox;* final decree, Nov. 19, 1903, in *Houston v. Ellis*; *Harris v. Holland*, no case number (1920), CirCtLaw, Southampton Co., VA; Record in *Cheney v. Louisville & Nashville R. R. Co.*, 1907, A-29748, GSA; Charles S. Johnson, *Shadow of the Plantation* (University of Chicago Press, 1934), 108; *Fisher v. Roper Lumber Co.*, 183 N.C. 485 (N.C. 1922); Brittany Farr, "Breach by Violence: The Forgotten History of Sharecropper Litigation in the Post-Slavery South," *UCLA Law Review* 69 (2022), 34 (pegging damages); Estate of Edgar Walker, case 4991 (1932), CirCtLaw, Coahoma Co., MS; Sadie Alexander to Bishop Cornelius Range, Oct. 27, 1942, in f "Lilbert Waters," 1942–43, STMA (coaxing settlements).

24 Nan Elizabeth Woodruff, *American Congo: The African American Freedom Struggle in the Delta* (Harvard University Press, 2003), 81–109.

25 William L. F. Felstiner, Richard L. Abel, and Austin Sarat, "The Emergence and Transformation of Disputes: Naming, Blaming, Claiming . . . ," LSR 15, no. 3/4 (1980–1981), 634–35.

26 "Mr. Eagleton" to John W. Cox, June 7, 1918, in *Wicks v. Cox* ("household plunder"); testimony of Alex Herring, in *Herring v. Sutton*, case 11623, MDAH; interview of Henry Smith, Aug. 9, 2015 (friendly tip); cross-examination of W. A. Stinebeck, 57, in *Reno v. Stinebeck* ("lending money"); Record in *Reno v. Stinebeck* ("What would you do?").

27 "Roger T. Stevenson, Justice of the Peace" [1939 interview by Bernice Kelly Harris], in *Such As Us: Southern Voices of the Thirties*, ed. Tom E. Terrill and Jerrold Hirsch (University of North Carolina), 260–69; Michael Willrich, *City of Courts: Socializing Justice in Progressive Era Chicago* (Cambridge University Press, 2003), 4; Aaron C. Porter, "The Career of a Professional Institution: A Study of Norris, Schmidt, Green, Harris, Higginbotham, and Associates," PhD diss., University of Pennsylvania, 1993, 32.

28 Neil R. McMillen, *Dark Journey: Black Mississippians in the Age of Jim Crow* (University of Illinois Press, 1989), 197–206; Howard N. Rabinowitz, *Race Relations in the Urban South, 1865–1890* (Oxford University Press, 1978), 31–36; W. E. B. Du Bois, "Race Relations in the United States, 1917–1947," *Phylon* 9, no. 3 (1948), 237. States then squelched challenges to those color-blind statutes through "subconstitutional rules" about things like standards of proof and access to federal courts. Michael J. Klarman, *From Jim Crow to Civil Rights: The Supreme Court and the Struggle for Racial Equality* (Oxford University Press, 2004), 42–43, 59. On Black

subsidizing, see Andrew W. Kahrl, "The Power to Destroy: Discriminatory Property Assessments and the Struggle for Tax Justice in Mississippi," JSH 82, no. 3 (2016), 584–93.

29 Pressly Spinks Sikes, "Judicial Administration in Mississippi," PhD diss., University of Illinois, 1934, 10–13; Frank H. Andrews (1917), quoted in Woodruff, *American Congo,* 58–59; Nicholas R. Parrillo, *Against the Profit Motive: The Salary Revolution in American Government, 1780–1940* (Yale University Press, 2013), 44–45; *Tulane's admr. v. Vanzandt* (1888), case 12-458, Mercer Co., Chancery Court of New Jersey, NJSA.

30 [W. S. Welch], "The Squire's Court," *Mississippi Law Journal* 8 (Dec.1935), 175–76. See also Willrich, *City of Courts,* 13.

31 Testimony of Warner D. Bundens, Feb. 24, 1927, in *Green v. Green,* case 61-170, Chancery Court of New Jersey, NJSA; "Stevenson, Justice of the Peace," 262, 264, 266, 269. See also Federal Writers' Project Works Progress Administration, *These Are Our Lives* (University of North Carolina Press, 1939), 312–13. For similar behavior by a Black JP, see *Reminiscences of an Active Life: The Autobiography of John Roy Lynch,* ed. John Hope Franklin (University of Chicago Press, 1970), 63–65. Future Supreme Court justice Hugo Black behaved similarly while serving as a trial judge in Birmingham. John P. Frank, *Mr. Justice Black: The Man and His Opinions* (Knopf, 1949), 17–19.

32 On clerks' role, see Alfred E. Cohen, "Notes on Divorce Procedure," *Virginia Law Register* 7, no. 11 (1922), 804; *Annotated Code of* [. . .] *Mississippi* (1892), 215, ch. 20, §§468–70; *Mississippi Code 1942,* §§1248, 1250, 1251. Cost bill, Dec. 2, 1921, in *Wicks v. Cox.* On "security," see *Mississippi Code 1942 Annotated,* §§1566–1568; *Revised Statutes of the State of Illinois. A.D. 1874,* comp. Harvey B. Hurd (Illinois Journal Co., 1874), ch. 33, §1 (still in effect in 1922 Code); *The Virginia Code of 1942* (Michie Co., 1942), vol. 1, pt. 1, 1234, §3519; Code 1887 §3539; *General Statutes of New Jersey* (Frederick D. Linn & Co., 1896), 404.

33 Parrillo, *Against the Profit Motive,* 113–24.

34 Ann. Code of Mississippi (1917), §§194, 207. See also Lauren Sudeall, "The Overreach of Limits on 'Legal Advice,'" YLJ *Forum* 131 (2022), 637–55. *Leatherwood v. Wilkerson* (1922), case 3119, CirCtCh, Coahoma Co., MS; Answer of John Henry Rives, Apr. 14, 1880, in *Dice v. Cole's Exr.,* case 1882-003, CirCtCh, Albemarle Co., LV; testimony of W. L. Lyon, record in *Bond v. Branning Mfg. Co.,* 58, NCSA.

35 V.C. Butt[?], Sheriff, to Oliver Clifton, Clerk, n.d. (1884), Clifton Papers, Z0378.000, MDAH (strained budgets); Thomas Scott Owen to Cooke, Gray & Co., April 25, 1911, f 22, b 7, OWEN; Gwin & Mounger to O. F. Bledsoe, Aug. 18, 1911, f 18, b 5, "Wesley v. Henrietta Sykes," GWIN; W. A. Percy(?) to Will Hardie, Mar. 25, 1910, f 1, b 30, PERCY (signing over crop); Petition, Aug. 29, 1892, in *Cleveland v. Cleveland,* case 2547, CirCtCh, Lafayette Co., MS; handwritten bearer's note, ca. 1903, in *Estate of George Carter,* case C-1912, CirCtCh, Adams Co., MS (handwritten

guarantees); *Jane Tillman et al v. Alice Tillman,* case 23133, EDC; testimony of H. M. Smith, Nov. 20, 1911, Record in *Jackson v. Hewlett,* LVRC (repeat client).

36 Cross-examination of Felix Brown, [P1100717], in *Brown v. McWilliams* (1909), CirCtCh, Coahoma Co., MS. Black newspapers warned about court costs and risks. See "The Lawyers Won," *Savannah Tribune,* Dec. 3, 1910; "A Smooth Scoundrel," *Rocky Mountain News,* Mar. 11, 1890.

37 R. B. Eggleston to Gwin & Mounger, Aug. 12, 1902, in *Hale v. Edwards,* GWIN ("manage"); John Brunini to E. L. Mounger, July 15, 1912, in f 50, b 10, GWIN (divorce suit by wife of white doctor).

38 "*McShane Cotton Co. v. Means Johnston et al* (1911–1912)," b 12, GWIN (enforcing lien against white family); William Alexander Percy(?) to Senator LeRoy Percy, Mar. 25, 1910, and William Alexander Percy(?) to Judge C. C. Moody, May 3, 1910, both in f 1, b 30, PERCY (fee chasing).

39 On courthouses' relative openness, see "The Manager's Weekly Letter," CR, Feb. 10, 1898; "Alabama Conference Statistics," CR, Feb. 3, 1881; "A Most Worthy Pastor," CR, June 22, 1882. On Black activity around courthouse square, see cross-examination of Jessie Reno, in *Reno v. Stinebeck,* 1916, case 4692, 47–48, CirCtCh, Lafayette Co., MS. See also John H. Gwathmey, *Legends of Virginia Lawyers: Anecdotes and Whimsical Yarns of the Old Time Bench and Bar* (Dietz Printing Company, 1934), 45; Pauli Murray, *Proud Shoes: The Story of an American Family* (1956; Beacon, 1999), 229–30; Juliet E. K. Walker, *The History of Black Business in America: Capitalism, Race, Entrepreneurship, 2nd ed.,* vol. 1, *to 1865* (University of North Carolina Press, 2009), 184–87.

40 The typology comes from Marc Galanter, "Why the 'Haves' Come out Ahead: Speculations on the Limits of Legal Change," LSR 9, no. 1 (1974), 95–160.

41 Only 52 of the 148 Cook County plaintiffs between 1902 and 1932 listed a lawyer. William C. Sprague, *The Commercial Lawyer and His Work* (n.p., 1918), 334; Joseph Lacy Seawell, *Law Tales for Laymen* (Alfred Williams & Co., 1925), 97, 109.

42 Clarksdale, MS, City Directory 1916–1917 (Oulla Printing & Bindin[g] Co., 1916), vol. 2, 201; "Time Takes Its Toll on Friars Point Cemetery," *Clarksdale Press Register,* May 16, 2005; James Clark Fifield, *The American Bar* [. . .] (James C. Fifield Co., 1918), 347; George A. Torrey, *A Lawyer's Recollections in and out of Court* (Little, Brown, 1910), 79–141; *Shireman v. Wildberger,* 125 Miss. 499 (1921); Willrich, *City of Courts,* 20–21; Sprague, *Commercial Lawyer,* 4.

43 Here I am referring only to plaintiffs identifiable in the Census and with lawyers listed in the sample's 1892–1922 decades. George Anderson to Gwin & Mounger, Aug. 14, 1909, in "*Baskin v. Southern Railway,*" GWIN (wrongful death suit by family of white doctor); Lawrence J. Nelson, *King Cotton's Advocate: Oscar G. Johnston and the New Deal* (University of Tennessee Press, 1999), 9, 17; "Roosevelt Roasted," *Greenville Times,* Sept. 24, 1903; "Freeland Chew Is Dead," *Memphis Daily Commercial Appeal,* Aug. 1, 1890.

44 LeRoy Percy to J. N. Johnson, May 25, 1906, f 10, b 1; Percy to J. B. Ray, Dec. 28,

1906, f 14, b 1; Percy to Williams, Wells & Croome, May 18, 1905; Judge Robert B. Mayes to Percy, ca. 1905; Percy to Ike Muckle, July 16, 1906, f 11, b 1, all in PERCY.

45 *Sunflower Oil Co. v. Wilson,* 142 U.S. 313 (1892); testimony of Henry Michaux, James Archer, N. B. Clark, and H. M. Smith, in Record in *Jackson v. Hewlett,* LVRC; testimony of Jennie Hanson, Record in *Williams v. White,* ILSA; account of T. H. Somerville, in *Banks v. Cochran* (1922), case 5433, CirCtCh, Lafayette Co., MS.

46 Testimony of Addison Day, Aug. 28, 1886, *Sparks v. Philips,* case 9343, EDC; testimony of Retta Lum and Anna Campbell, both in *Estate of John H. White,* Orphans Court, Camden, NJSA; "Miscellany," 7 Virginia Law Register 282 (Aug. 1901); Geoffrey R. Watson, "In the Tribunal of Conscience: *Mills v. Wyman* Reconsidered," *Tulane Law Review* 71, no. 6 (1997), 1787–89.

47 Brandi Clay Brimmer, *Claiming Union Widowhood: Race, Respectability, and Poverty in the Post-Emancipation South* (Duke University Press, 2020), 5; Will of John Dennis, case 4226 (1912), CirCtCh, Lafayette Co., MS.

48 Wilson Bowles to Thomas Scott Owen, Aug. 31, 1911, Emily Smith to Owen, July 17, 1911, both in f 11, b 8, OWEN; Jeff Arrington to Thomas Scott Owen, April 1, 1912, f 20, b 10, OWEN; Affidavit of James H. Smith, Dec. 22, 1892, affidavit of Frederick Johnson, Dec. 23, 1892, both in *Buckley v. Scott,* case 14103, EDC; testimony of Felix Brown, in *Brown v. McWilliams* (1909), CirCtCh, Coahoma Co., MS.

49 Final Report of the Committee on Code of Professional Ethics, American Bar Association (1908), 579; Kaufman to Rinehart & Dennis, Mar. 29, 1915, f "Tommy Nowlin" (1915), b 65, DUKES.

50 "Thomas Smith Son of Harrison Smith v. Y.&M.V.R.R. Co.," typescript notes, ca. 1911, in GWIN; Record in White v. Tolliver, ADAH; *White v. Tolliver,* 110 Ala. 300 (1896).

51 Letters from Susie Brooks to Raymond Pace Alexander, June 5, Feb. 9, and Apr. 30, 1943, all in f "Susie Brooks," 1942–44, RPA; Master's Report, n.d.; Answer of Mary Bacon, May 17, 1943, both in "Mary Bacon," 1943–45, STMA.

52 E. Franklin Frazier, *The Negro Family in the United States* (University of Chicago Press, 1939), 379. Compare S[idney] F[ant] Davis, *Mississippi Negro Lore* (McCowat-Mercer, 1914), 23–25. The script was the original when a conveyance of property title was signed in "part and counterpart." Henry Campbell Black, ed. *A Law Dictionary . . .* (West, 1910), 875, 1061. "Dilsey Chambliss," b 131-92, FPMS. On formalist ideas of law today, see Patricia Ewick and Susan S. Silbey, *The Common Place of Law: Stories from Everyday Life* (University of Chicago Press, 1998), 28–29, 106; Tess Wilkinson-Ryan, "Intuitive Formalism in Contract," PLR 163 (2015), 2122–26.

53 J. M. Huffstickler to Mr. Umphrys Circuit Clerk, Nov. 7, 1903, Loose Papers, GWIN.

54 John Simms to J. J. Scruggs, Sept. 10, 1918, *Scruggs v. Scruggs,* DUKES. See also unsigned letter to Alfred Manning, Sept. 29, 1911, f 17, b 8, OWEN.

55 Irvin C. Mollison, "Negro Lawyers in Mississippi," JNH 15, no. 1 (1930), 45–51;

Mack, *Representing the Race,* 28; *Bradwell v. Illinois,* 83 U.S. 130 (1872); *Matter of Taylor,* 48 Md. 28 (1877).

56 "Legal Facetiae," 13 Western Jurist, no. 8 (1879), 384; "Notes," 5 *Green Bag* 51 (1893); "Some Southwest Georgia Court Scenes," *American Bar Association Journal,* 9, no. 3 (1923), 164; "Obiter Dicta," 1 Mississippi Law Review 34 (Dec. 1922); "In Wholesale Lots," 2 *West Publishing Company Docket* 1456; "Legal News," 1 Albany L. J. 263 (1870); Gwathmey, *Legends of Virginia Lawyers,* 20, 31, 39, 46, 58, 72–73, 81, 99–100, 111–15, 141–45; John H. Gwathmey, *Legends of Virginia Courthouses* (Dietz Printing Co., 1934), 18–19, 22, 59–61, 69–73, 79–82, 93, 106–7, 120, 131.

57 "The Smallest Law Suit?" *Commercial Law Journal* (1924), 490; Theodore W. Dwight, "Columbia College Law School New York," 1 *Green Bag* 141–60 (1889).

58 Maxwell Bloomfield, "From Deference to Confrontation: The Early Black Lawyers of Galveston, Texas, 1895–1920," in *The New High Priests: Lawyers in Post Civil War America,* ed. Gerard W. Gawalt (Greenwood Press, 1984), 152–53; W. E. Burghardt Du Bois, *The Philadelphia Negro: A Social Study* (University of Pennsylvania, 1899), 114–15; Porter, "Career of a Professional Institution," 63–65; Mack, *Representing the Race,* 28–32, 39–48.

59 J. Clay Smith Jr., *Emancipation: The Making of the Black Lawyer, 1844–1944* (University of Pennsylvania Press, 1993), 57–58; Robert T. Swaine, *The Cravath Firm and Its Predecessors, 1819–1948,* vol. 2 (Ad Press, 1946–48), 1–12, 122–32; Mack, *Representing the Race,* 41, 55–56; J. Vance Lewis, *Out of the Ditch: A True Story of an Ex-Slave* (Rein & Sons, 1910), 84–85; Thomas C. Walker, *The Honey-Pod Tree: The Life Story of Thomas Calhoun Walker* (John Day Co., 1958), 167–68; Bloomfield, "From Deference to Confrontation," 156–60.

60 "Notes," 5 *Green Bag,* 51 (1893); John Hope Franklin, *Mirror to America: The Autobiography of John Hope Franklin* (Farrar Straus and Giroux, 2005), 32; Mollison, "Negro Lawyers in Mississippi," 59.

61 Lewis, *Out of the Ditch,* 38–56; Carter Godwin Woodson, *The Negro Professional Man and the Community, with Special Emphasis on the Physician and the Lawyer* (1934; Negro Universities Press, 1969), 202; Mollison, "Negro Lawyers in Mississippi," 64–67; Mack, *Representing the Race,* 148; "The Brother in Black—Some High-Sounding Names," 7 Virginia Law Register 890 (1901–1902); Ariane Liazos and Marshall Ganz, "Duty to the Race: African American Fraternal Orders and the Legal Defense of the Right to Organize," *Social Science History* 28, no. 3 (2004), 520–26; A. Briscoe Koger, *The Negro Lawyer in Maryland* (Clarke Press, 1948), 6–7, 10–11.

62 Record in *Karr v. Freeman,* 12, ILSA.

63 *Karr v. Freeman,* 46 N.E. 717, 718 (1897); Record in *Karr* at 19–22.

64 *Karr* at 720.

65 Felstiner, "Emergence and Transformation of Disputes," 631–54; testimony of Henry Michaux and of James Archer, Record in *Johnson v. Michaux* (1908), LVRC; Record in *Bullen v. Dawson,* 42, case 25751, ILSC; Record in *Bryan v. Nash* (1909), LVRC; Record in *Ackley v. Croucher,* 70; testimony of Solicitor Benders, Record

in *Fisher v. Roper Lumber Co.*, NCSA; testimony of Mary Woodson, 59, Record in *Hannah v. Woodson,* LVRC; testimony of Felix Brown, in *Brown v. McWilliams.* See also testimony of Sam Farkas, Record in *Farkas v. Powell* (1891), GSA; testimony of James H. Saville in *Stewart v. Jefferson.* Compare Brimmer, *Claiming Union Widowhood,* 101–22; Felice Batlan, *Women and Justice for the Poor: A History of Legal Aid, 1863–1945* (Cambridge University Press, 2015), 4–14; Barlow F. Christensen, "The Unauthorized Practice of Law: Do Good Fences Really Make Good Neighbors—or Even Good Sense?" *American Bar Foundation Research Journal,* vol. 5, no. 2 (1980), 177–80.

66 Mollison, "Negro Lawyers in Mississippi," 52–53, 67–71; Du Bois, *Philadelphia Negro,* 114–15; "Some Kentucky Lawyers of the Past and Present," 9 *Green Bag* (1897), 260–73. See also Lester F. Russell, *Profile of a Black Heritage* (Graphicopy, 1977), 52; Smith, *Emancipation,* 625.

CHAPTER 8: THE SHADOW OF THE LAW

1 Bouvier 1897, 810, s.v. "forcible entry or detainer"; amended bill, Feb. 16, 1903, Record in *Houston v. Ellis,* case 631, CirCtCh, Coahoma Co., MS.

2 Decree, Nov. 19, 1903, Record in *Houston v. Ellis.*

3 Freeman has said he regrets doing the show, probably because it sometimes sank into broad stereotypes of the "soul brother."

4 Alexis de Tocqueville, *Democracy in America,* transl. Henry Reeve (Saunders and Otley, 1835), vol. 1, 205; Michael Grossberg, *A Judgment for Solomon: The d'Hauteville Case and Legal Experience in Antebellum America* (Cambridge University Press, 1996), 2–3; Herbert Jacob, "The Elusive Shadow of the Law," LSR 26, no. 3 (1992), 565–66.

5 Contrast with Robert C. Ellickson, "Of Coase and Cattle: Dispute Resolution among Neighbors in Shasta County," SLR 38, no. 3 (1986), 672, 685. Ellickson theorizes that disputes "are generally resolved . . . *beyond*" the shadow of the law, because "ordinary people" are "committed to an overarching norm of cooperation among neighbors." One obvious problem with Ellickson's theory is that it rests on a study of a racially homogeneous community of white California ranchers.

6 Question by Cutrer on cross-examination of Austin Johnson, Feb. 13, 1903, *Houston v. Ellis; McCorkle v. Yarrell,* 55 Miss. 576, 577 (1878); *Paden v. Gibbs,* 40 So. 871 (1906) (both parties probably white); *Moring v. Ables,* 62 Miss. 263, 270 (1884).

7 Testimony of O. M. Ellis and Ben Houston, both in *Houston v. Ellis.*

8 Ejectment is a suit to determine who has title to a property. Herbert Thorndike Tiffany, *The Law of Real Property and Other Interests in Land* (Keefe-Davidson, 1903), §63 ("expel a tenant"); David McAdam, *The Rights, Duties, Remedies and Incidents Belonging to and Growing out of the Relation of Landlord and Tenant,* 4th ed. (Baker, Voorhis & Co., 1910), 1493–96 ("force"); *Paden,* at 871 (proof of force).

9 On the "force, fraud, or stealth" standard, see Annotated Code of [. . .] Mississippi

(Marshall & Bruce, 1892), §4461; *McCorkle* (at least one of the parties was Black). On verbal objection, see *State v. Earp,* 196 N.C. 164 (1928) (white man convicted of trespassing on Black tenant's leased land); *Rhodes-Carroll Furniture Co. v. Webb,* 230 Ala. 251 (1935). On unlawful entry, see Annotated Code of [. . .] Mississippi (1892), chap. 142. For an example of a Black tenant winning an unlawful entry and detainer suit (with damages for withheld crops), see *State v. Smith,* 100 N.C. 466 (1888).

10 Testimony of Ben Houston and Priscilla Houston, in *Houston v. Ellis.*

11 *Holman v. Gulf Refining Co. of Louisiana,* 76 F2d 94 (1935); *Minor v. Young,* 148 La. 610 (1921); *Taylor v. Allen,* 151 La. 82 (1920); *Soule v. West,* 185 La. 655 (1936). For a similar fact-pattern involving fraud rather than violence, see *Johnson v. Umsted,* 64 F.2d 316 (C.A.8 1933). Lester F. Russell, *Profile of a Black Heritage* (Graphicopy, 1977), 44–53 ("no property rights"); *Primus v. Feazel,* 189 La. 932, 935 (1938) ("affect the title"). The notorious "Reign of Terror" against the Osage of Oklahoma is an exception that proves the rule. Those targeted murders benefited whites largely through strategic marriages, and whites could not legally marry Black landowners. David Grann, *Killers of the Flower Moon: The Osage Murders and the Birth of the FBI* (Doubleday, 2017); Rennard Strickland, "Osage Oil: Mineral Law, Murder, Mayhem, and Manipulation," *Natural Resources & Environment* 10, no. 1 (1995), 42.

12 Maureen E. Brady, "The Forgotten History of Metes and Bounds," YLJ 128, no. 4 (2019), 899–900, 932; Theodore Rosengarten, *All God's Dangers: The Life of Nate Shaw* (1974; University of Chicago Press, 2000), 231–32; T. C. Johnson & w[ife] to Jackson Holcomb, Jan. 27, 1900, DB 39, 378, Office of Circuit Clerk, Cumberland Co., VA; Emmitt Jenkins, quoted in Gail M. McClure, "Jenkins Church: Historical Notes & Memories," dictated ca. 1960, 12, in Cumberland Baptist Church (Cumberland County, VA) Minute Book & booklet, LV. See also Exhibit A, handbill for "Sale of Farm . . . The Ada Brown Place," in *Crosson v. Brown,* case 1840, ended file 9 (1964), Circuit Court of Mecklenburg Co., VA, Boydton; *Howard v. Harrell,* 275 Ala. 454 (1963). *Harrell* is cited in *Spiller v. Mackereth,* 334 So. 2d 859 (1976), which today is a teaching case on the law of co-ownership in Jesse Dukeminier et al., *Property* (Wolters Kluver, 2014), 372.

13 Rosengarten, *All God's Dangers,* 148–49; Pete Daniel, "Up from Slavery and Down to Peonage: The Alonzo Bailey Case," JAH 57, no. 3 (1970), 668; Petition, Nov. 25, 1922, in *Leatherwood v. Frazer and Wilkerson,* case 3119, CirCtCh, Coahoma Co., MS; Anne Fleming, *City of Debtors: A Century of Fringe Finance* (Harvard University Press, 2018), 4–5.

14 Rosengarten, *All God's Dangers,* 267–68.

15 Rosengarten, *All God's Dangers,* 148, 155.

16 Rosengarten, *All God's Dangers,* 155–60.

17 Edward L. Ayers, *The Promise of the New South: Life after Reconstruction* (1992; Oxford University Press, 2007), 13, 64, 87–96, 105–23, 190–98; Adrienne Monteith Petty,

Standing Their Ground: Small Farmers in North Carolina since the Civil War (Oxford University Press, 2013), 88–89; Gavin Wright, *Old South, New South: Revolutions in the Southern Economy since the Civil War* (Basic, 1986), 34–47; Record at 8, *Houston v. Ellis.*

18 Wright, *Old South, New South,* 97; Melvin Patrick Ely, *Israel on the Appomattox: A Southern Experiment in Black Freedom from the 1790s through the Civil War* (Random House, 2004), 87 (referring to antebellum Virginia).

19 John T. Castle, "Arkansas Supreme Court," *The Law* 3 (1907), 687–88 ("confidence"); Zechariah Chafee Jr. and Sidney Post Simpson, *Cases on Equity: Jurisdiction and Specific Performance* (Langdell Hall, 1934), 1304; *Grimsley v. Singletary,* 133 Ga. 56 (1909); *Bates v. Harte,* 124 Ala. 427 (1899), both cited at 12 *Am. Jur.* 630 §137 ("fine print"; "minds"). On precautions for nonliterate people, see Joel Prentiss Bishop, *Commentaries on the Law of Contracts* (T. H. Flood & Co., 1907), 136–38, citing, inter alia, *Jones v. Gurlie,* 61 Miss. 423 (1883) and *Jackson v. Lemle,* 35 La. Ann. 855 (1883). Rosengarten, *All God's Dangers,* 151 ("tellin him"). See also Record at 22, *Nashville, Chattanooga, and St. Louis Railway v. Nance,* case SC 02719, ALDAH (white releasor). For "touching the pen," see *Sparks v. Philips,* case 9343 (1886), EDC; Record at 46, *Reno v. Stinebeck*; *F.S. Royster Guano Co. v. Hall,* 68 F.2d 533, 534 (1934); and Bishop, *Commentaries on the Law of Contracts,* 136–37.

20 Patricia J. Williams, *The Alchemy of Race and Rights: Diary of a Law Professor* (Harvard University Press, 1991), 155–59; Melissa Milewski, *Litigating across the Color Line: Civil Cases between Black and White Southerners from the End of Slavery to Civil Rights* (Oxford University Press, 2018), 10–11, 123–43.

21 Thomas Dixon Jr., *The Leopard's Spots: A Romance of the White Man's Burden* (Doubleday, 1903), 84; Appellee's Brief at 7–8, n.d., Record in *Johnson v. Michaux*; Record in *Reno v. Stinebeck,* 36, 17. See also *Toles v. Stowers,* case 4533 (1915), CirCtCh, Lafayette Co., MS; and Record at 44–45, *Bond v. Branning Mfg. Co.,* 140 N.C. 381 (1906) (No. 22524), NCSA; Record at 32b, *Beaden v. Bransford Realty Co.* 144 Tenn. 395 (1921) (No. 4162), TSLA. On stunts, see Record at 16, *Scott v. Raub,* 88 Va. 721 (1891), LV; Record at 209–10, *Estate of John H. White.*

22 Record at 29–30, *Reno v. Stinebeck.* See also Deposition of Felix Brown at 63, in *Brown v. McWilliams,* case 1451 (1909), CirCtCh, Coahoma Co., MS. Record at 3, 27, *Houston v. Ellis.*

23 Record at 15–16, 27, *Houston v. Ellis*; Royal Dumas, "The Muddled Mettle of Jurisprudence: Race and Procedure in Alabama's Appellate Courts, 1901–1930," *Alabama Law Review,* vol. 58 (2006), 440–41; *Dickerson v. Thomas,* 7 So. 503, 504–5 (1890); Appellant's Brief at 9, *Brown v. McWilliams*; *Norfleet v. Beall,* 34 So. 328 (Miss. 1903).

24 *Alabama Construction Co. v. Continental Car & Equipment Co.,* 62 S.E. 160, 163 (1908); *Hartford Fire Insurance Co. v. Kirkpatrick,* 111 Ala. 456, 459 (1896).

25 Record at 40, *Bond v. Branning Manufacturing Co.,* 140 N.C. 381 (1906), NCSA. For

a fuller discussion, see Dylan C. Penningroth, "Race in Contract Law," PLR 170, no. 5 (2022), 1232–38.

26 Carter Godwin Woodson, *The Mis-Education of the Negro* (1933; Africa World Press, 1990), 84.

CHAPTER 9: "BE MY SOCIAL SECURITY"

1 Holcomb interview by Baskerville (1976). For the jail's location, see Charles Edward Burrell, *A History of Prince Edward County, Virginia* [. . .] (Williams Printing Co., 1922), 40. W. E. B. Du Bois, *The Negroes of Farmville, Virginia: A Social Study* (Government Printing Office, 1898), 4, 18; Lynda J. Morgan, "Samuel P. Bolling (1819–1900)," *Encyclopedia Virginia*, www.encyclopediavirginia.org; Melvin Patrick Ely, *Israel on the Appomattox: A Southern Experiment in Black Freedom from the 1790s through the Civil War* (Random House, 2004), 420–21; *Negro Population, 1790–1915,* Department of Commerce (Bureau of the Census, 1918), 459, 577, 571, 625, 579; W. E. Burghardt Du Bois, *The Negro Farmer,* Bulletin No. 8 (Government Printing Office, 1904), 84; Edward L. Ayers, *The Promise of the New South: Life after Reconstruction* (1992; Oxford University Press, 2007), 69–70; Loren Schweninger, *Black Property Owners in the South, 1790–1915* (University of Illinois Press, 1990), 169, 174, 180; Chicago Commission on Race Relations, *The Negro in Chicago: A Study of Race Relations and a Race Riot* (University of Chicago Press, 1922), 216–30.

2 Stewart E. Tolnay and E. M. Beck, *A Festival of Violence: An Analysis of Southern Lynchings* (University of Illinois Press, 1995), 29–31, 271–72. These numbers cover only ten southern states. Register of Deaths, Lunenburg Co., 1888, Virginia Deaths and Burials, 1853–1912, Ancestry.com; Crystal Feimster, *Southern Horrors: Women and the Politics of Rape and Lynching* (Harvard University Press, 2011), 89–93.

3 Gregory S. Alexander, *Commodity and Propriety: Competing Visions of Property in American Legal Thought, 1776–1970* (Chicago: University of Chicago Press, 1997); Sara Berry, *No Condition Is Permanent: The Social Dynamics of Agrarian Change in Sub-Saharan Africa* (University of Wisconsin Press, 1993).

4 Bonnie Martin, "Slavery's Invisible Engine: Mortgaging Human Property," *Journal of Southern History* 76, no. 4 (2010), 817–66; *Ellis v. Butterfield,* 570 P.2d 1334, 1336 (1977); Eric T. Freyfogle, "Vagueness and the Rule of Law: Reconsidering Installment Land Contract Forfeitures," DLJ no. 4 (1988), 610–15; Allan G. Bogue, *Money at Interest: The Farm Mortgage on the Middle Border* (1955; Russell & Russell, 1968), 214–15. On contract terms, see Record in *Brown v. McWilliams* (1909), MDAH; Record in *Sadler v. Jefferson* (1905), ALDAH. On title transfer, see Record in *Grimsley v. Singletary* (1907), GSA; *Hodge v. Powell,* 96 N.C. 64 (1887). See also *Federal Writers' Project: Slave Narrative Project,* vol. 4, Georgia, pt. 2, 307–9, www.loc.gov/resource/mesn.042/?sp=310. Some sellers transferred title once

half the price was paid, thus converting the instrument into a mortgage. Ernest M. Fisher, *Urban Real Estate Markets: Characteristics and Financing* (National Bureau of Economic Research, 1951), 27.

5 *Wainwright v. Rolling Acres,* 269 So.2d 123, 125 (Ala. 1972); *The Code of the State of Georgia* (Atlanta, 1896), vol. 2, §§4813–22; Asher L. Cornelius, *The Law of Land Contracts* (Callaghan & Co., 1922), 312–15; Brief of Plaintiff in Error, Nov. 4, 1945, *Higdon v. Bransford Realty Co.*, no. 29335 (1914), TSLA, 12.

6 Carol M. Rose, "Crystals and Mud in Property Law," SLR 40 (1988), 583–85; Arthur L. Corbin, "The Right of a Defaulting Vendee to the Restitution of Instalments Paid," YLJ 40, no. 7 (1931), 1022–23; *Lytle v. Scottish American Mortg. Co.*, 50 S.E. 402, 403–6 (1905).

7 Bill of complaint, Record in *Sadler v. Jefferson* (1905), ALDAH ("belonged"); testimony of John Washburn, 14, Record in *Hodge v. Powell,* NCSA (witnessing payments). On "acts and conduct," see Bouvier 1914, 1840, s.v. "landlord and tenant"; *Sohio Corp. v. Gudder,* 375 Ill. 622 (1941). Oliver Wendell Holmes, "The Path of the Law," HLR 10, no. 8 (1897), 466; Morton J. Horwitz, *The Transformation of American Law, 1870–1960: The Crisis of Legal Orthodoxy* (Oxford University Press, 1992), 38.

8 *Soutier v. Kellerman,* 18 Mo. 509 (1853). In fact, courts during the late 1800s and early 1900s increasingly relied on sustained conduct to interpret contracts, rather than manifest expressions at the moment of the contract's inception. Ariela R. Dubler, "Wifely Behavior: A Legal History of Acting Married," CLR 100 (2000), 1007; Horwitz, *Transformation of American Law,* 35–39.

9 Dylan C. Penningroth, "Race in Contract Law," PLR 170, no. 5 (2022), 1245–46.

10 Theodore Rosengarten, *All God's Dangers: The Life of Nate Shaw* (1974; University of Chicago Press, 2000), 233–36, 278–85, 266–68, 295, 305–16; Robin D. G. Kelley, *Hammer and Hoe: Alabama Communists During the Great Depression* (University of North Carolina Press, 1990), 49.

11 Rosengarten, *All God's Dangers,* 327–29.

12 Rosengarten, *All God's Dangers,* 328–30.

13 For example, see *Foster v. Johnson,* 70 Ala. 249 (1881). Perhaps this is why Sheriff Beall had no qualms threatening to auction off Shaw's property: duress was a much harder case to make.

14 Record in *Higdon v. Bransford Realty Co.*

15 Record in *Higdon,* 21; *Patterson v. Davis,* 28 Tenn. App. 571 (1945).

16 *Beaden v. Bransford Realty Co.*, 144 Tenn. 395 (1921).

17 *Patterson v. Davis,* 28 Tenn. App. 571, 574–78 (1945); Arthur L. Corbin, "The Right of a Defaulting Vendee to the Restitution of Instalments Paid," YLJ 40, no. 7 (1931), 1023–24, citing at least one case involving Black plaintiff: *Ward Real Estate v. Childers,* 223 Ky. 302 (1928).

18 James N. Gregory, *The Southern Diaspora: How the Great Migrations of Black and White Southerners Transformed America* (University of North Carolina Press, 2005), xii,

330, 354; Andrew Wiese, *Places of Their Own: African American Suburbanization in the Twentieth Century* (University of Chicago Press, 2004), 1.

19 Richard R. W. Brooks and Carol M. Rose, *Saving the Neighborhood: Racially Restrictive Covenants, Law, and Social Norms* (Harvard University Press, 2013), 8, 34, 42.

20 Jesse Dukeminier et al., *Property* (Wolters Kluver, 2014), 892; Brooks and Rose, *Saving the Neighborhood,* 92.

21 Brooks and Rose, *Saving the Neighborhood,* 60–62, 72–78; Deed from North End Land Company to A. E. Bousfield, Aug. 22, 1916, Contra Costa County, CA.

22 Kevin Boyle, *Arc of Justice: A Saga of Race, Civil Rights, and Murder in the Jazz Age* (Holt, 2005), 159; Brooks and Rose, *Saving the Neighborhood,* 79–80, 83, 91–92.

23 Brooks and Rose, *Saving the Neighborhood,* 130, 187–210; Thomas J. Sugrue, *Sweet Land of Liberty: The Forgotten Struggle for Civil Rights in the North* (Random House, 2008), 202–12; Richard Rothstein, *The Color of Law: A Forgotten History of How Our Government Segregated America* (Liveright, 2017), 84–91.

24 Dylan C. Penningroth, "The Claims of Slaves and Ex-Slaves to Family and Property: A Transatlantic Comparison," AHR 112, no. 4 (2007), 1039–69.

25 Dukeminier, *Property,* 343–44, 361; Claire Priest, *Credit Nation: Property Laws and Legal Institutions in Early America* (Princeton University Press, 2021), 61–67.

26 Margaret Davis Cate and Orrin Sage Wightman, *Early Days of Coastal Georgia* (St. Simons Island, 1955), 170–71; "Nora Parker, [age] 50," b 131-92, FPMS. For a somewhat different interpretation, see Sydney Nathans, *A Mind to Stay: White Plantation, Black Homeland* (Harvard University Press, 2017), 219.

27 Rosengarten, *All God's Dangers,* 236–37. See also "Rev. Handy Williams," vol. 11, pt. 2, North Carolina Narratives, 387, FWP.

28 See also interview, Rhetta and Edward Eppse, July 17, 1934, b 131-92, FPMS; Record at 20, *Proctor v. Lowe,* 1929, Court of Errors & Appeals, New Jersey, NJLL. Rosengarten, *All God's Dangers,* 236–37; *The Impact of Heir Property on Black Rural Land Tenure in the Southeastern Region of the United States* (Emergency Land Fund, 1980), 252.

29 *Negroes in the United States, 1920–32* (Government Printing Office, 1935), 569–70; "Interview with James Sawyer," b 131-92, FPMS; Narrative of William Hamilton, in *American Slave,* Texas Narratives, vol. 4:2, 108; "Interview with James Sawyer"; "Woman Who Ran Away from Home at 14 Years," b 131-81, FPMS; "[interview] of J. B. Jeter, 58 and Wife, 35," b 131-92, FPMS; "Archertown," box 131-92, FPMS; E. Franklin Frazier, *The Negro Family in the United States* (University of Chicago Press, 1939), 256–60.

30 On the image of Black communitarianism, in addition to the citations above, see Barbara Ransby, *Ella Baker and the Black Freedom Movement: A Radical Democratic Vision* (University of North Carolina Press, 2003), 36–38. For a nuanced exploration of one long-lived settlement, see Ely, *Israel on the Appomattox,* esp. 89. "Mooretown," Hertford County Documents, 131-92, FPMS. Elsewhere, Frazier acknowledged that "the oldest head" was often a woman, and incorporated such

women into his famous thesis about the female-headed "Negro family." Frazier, *Negro Family in the United States,* 149–62, 258–59; *The Negro in Virginia* (Hastings House, 1940), 331.

31 Susan J. Pearson, *The Birth Certificate: An American History* (University of North Carolina Press, 2021), 25–33; *Gaskins v. Madre,* 39 App. D.C. 19, 1912 WL 19600; Record in *Ackley v. Croucher,* ILSA; *Ackley v. Croucher,* 68 N.E. 86, 88 (1903).

32 Rosengarten, *All God's Dangers,* 54, 37, 257–58.

33 Sherman A. James, "The Narrative of John Henry Martin," *Southern Cultures* (1993), 96–98.

34 Rosengarten, *All God's Dangers,* 223.

35 W. E. B. Du Bois, "The Negro American Family," *Atlanta University Publications,* no. 13 (1908), 139–40 ("strict discipline"); Howard Snyder, "Traits of My Plantation Negroes," *The Century* 102, no. 3 (1921), 367–68 ("assets"); Gerald David Jaynes, *Branches without Roots: Genesis of the Black Working Class in the American South, 1862–1882* (Oxford University Press, 1986), 185–86 ("cheap labor"); Du Bois, *Negro American Family,* 139–40 ("father is head"). See also Tera W. Hunter, *Bound in Wedlock: Slave and Free Black Marriage in the Nineteenth Century* (Harvard University Press, 2017), 112–14; Reva B. Siegel, "'The Rule of Love': Wife Beating as Prerogative and Privacy," YLJ 105, no. 8 (1996), 2122–25.

36 Eloise Anderson family history, FPMS. See also Rosengarten, *All God's Dangers,* 132; Marilyn Mildred White, "'We Lived on an Island': An Afro-American Family and Community in Rural Virginia, 1865–1940," PhD diss., University of Texas-Austin, 1983, 114; B. A. Botkin, *Lay My Burden Down: A Folk History of Slavery* (University of Chicago Press, 1945), 240.

37 *Illinois Central v. Dunson,* 63 So. 280 (1913); Randal Maurice Jelks, *Benjamin Elijah Mays, Schoolmaster of the Movement: A Biography* (University of North Carolina Press, 2012), 35; Eloise Anderson family history, FPMS; testimony of Ike Dunston, Record in *Ill. Central Ry. v. Dunston* (1913), case 16105, MDAH.

38 Rosengarten, *All God's Dangers,* 37, 54 ("boss"); "Frank Brown," Dec. 9, 1929[?], b 131-81, FPMS. See also "Amanda Harris," Mar. 29, 1930, Clarksville, Tenn., FPMS; Nell Irvin Painter, "Soul Murder and Slavery: Toward a Fully Loaded Cost Accounting," in *U.S. History as Women's History,* ed. Linda Kerber et al. (University of North Carolina Press, 1995), 125–46; *McElmurray v. Turner,* 86 Ga. 215, 12 S.E. 359, 360 (1890); Kevin D. McCarthy, "Fit Custodians: Gender, Race, and the Law in Lower-South Trial Courts, 1830–1925," PhD diss., University of Mississippi, 2005, 184–89.

39 Record at 41, *Bond v. Branning Mfg.*; Jelks, Schoolmaster, 35, 21; Record at 19, *Seaboard Air Line Railway Co. v. Elizabeth Blackwell,* 244 U.S. 310 (1917) (no. 213); Hendrik Hartog, *Someday All This Will Be Yours: A History of Inheritance and Old Age* (Harvard University Press, 2012).

40 Lisa Groger, "Tied to Each Other Through Ties to the Land: Informal Support of Black Elders in a Southern U.S. Community," *Journal of Cross-Cultural Gerontology* 7 (1992), 205–6; Ayers, *Promise,* 197–98.

41 Testimony of Sophia Selden, July 28, 1870, in *Jennings v. Wilkinson* (1873), case 1915, EDC; Cost bill by Nancy D. Savage, Record in *Francis v. Tazewell* (1917), LVRC; Answer of Angus Weaver, Oct. 9, 1900, Record in *Banks v. Weaver and Rising Sun Lodge,* NJSA; "I Has a Garden" [Tom Doyle], in Federal Writers' Project Works Progress Administration, *These Are Our Lives* (University of North Carolina Press, 1939), 47; handwritten receipts dated Oct. 12, 1911 and [illeg.] 11, 1912, in *Bowers v. Carter*; Deposition of Charles T. Reekes, in *Goode v. Gregory,* Mecklenburg County Chancery Causes, 1912-51CC, LV. Neighbors and tenants also sometimes thought they deserved pay for "waiting on" the dying. Testimony of Frank Price, Nov. 20, 1911, Record in *Jackson v. Hewlett,* LVRC.

42 Penningroth, *Claims of Kinfolk,* 85–91; "My WPA Man" [Marguerite Jonas], New Orleans, ca. 1938–39, in *Such as Us: Southern Voices of the Thirties,* ed. Tom E. Terrill and Jerrold Hirsch (University of North Carolina Press, 1987), 226 ("my social security"). See also Hortense Powdermaker, *After Freedom: A Cultural Study in the Deep South* (1939; University of Wisconsin Press, 1993), 199; "Interview—Blanch Robinson (1807 Malloy's Alley)," b 131-82, FPMS. For similar sentiments among whites, see Nancy MacLean, *Behind the Mask of Chivalry: The Making of the Second Ku Klux Klan* (Oxford University Press, 1994), 34.

43 *Ivy v. House of Ruth et al* (1910), case 3986, CirCtCh, Lafayette Co., MS; *Odd Fellows' Ben. Ass'n. v. Ivy,* 105 Miss. 423 (1913); Hartog, *Someday All This Will Be Yours,* 11, 125.

44 *Halbert v. Turner,* 233 Ill. 531 (1908); *Davis v. Patty,* 76 Miss. 753 (1899); testimony of Sam Clements, Record in *Clements v. Clements* (1917), MDAH; testimony of Gertrude Jackson, Nov. 18, 1911, Record in *Jackson v. Hewlett,* LVRC. On white southerners cutting relatives out of their wills for not offering old-age support, see "Family History Secured by Teacher," b 131-92, FPMS. On taking offense at request for writing, see testimony of Florence Bailey Neal, Feb. 13, 1912, in *Neal v. Bailey,* case 30814, EDC.

45 On older people's worries, see petition in *McMillon v. McMillon* (1912), case 4199, CirCtCh, Lafayette Co., MS; "Research Report" on Mrs. Humphrey, Jan. 29, 1931, folder 10, box 131-82, FPMS; Hartog, *Someday All This Will Be Yours,* 166.

46 Depositions of Carrie L. London and John London, Feb. 6, 1886, in *London v. Flood et al.,* case 9378, EDC; *Bowers v. Carter,* CirCtCh, Mecklenburg Co., 1912-63CC, LV; *Huddleston v. Huddleston,* 132 Miss. 55 (1923); *Scott v. Ivy* (1909), case 3861, CirCtCh, Lafayette Co., MS; *Carter v. West et al.,* 14 Ky. L. Reporter 191 (1892–93).

47 Testimony of Florence Bailey Neal, Feb. 13, 1912, in *Neal v. Bailey*; testimony of Jennei Clements, Record in *Clements v. Clements* (1917), 45–46, MDAH.

48 Charles Ball, *Slavery in the United States: A Narrative of the Life and Adventures of Charles Ball, a Black Man* (John S. Taylor, 1837), 192–93; testimony of Priscilla Warren, Apr. 16, 1881, *Douglass v. Brent,* case 7562, EDC; testimony of Mariah Kinling, Sept. 8, 1913, Record in *Bailey v. Johnson,* LVRC; "Research Report" on Mrs.

Humphrey, FPMS; testimony of Margaret Taylor, Mary Jackson, Ann E. Middleton, and Mason Harrison, in *Stewart v. Jefferson;* Nathans, *A Mind to Stay,* 161-62.

49 Bill, Nov. 5, 1941, *Frierson v. Lewis,* case 7561, CirCtCh, Lafayette Co., MS; Answer of Laura Williams, May 13, 1932, *Jackson v. Williams,* case 6215, CirCtCh, Adams Co., MS; Record at 21, 25, 68–69, 79–82, in *Crosson v. Brown,* case 1840, ended file 9 (1964), CirCtCh, Mecklenburg Co., VA.

50 Thomas J. Ward Jr. and H. Jack Geiger, *Out in the Rural: A Mississippi Health Center and Its War on Poverty* (Oxford University Press, 2017), 42–43. White migrants also returned south in the 1960s to care for sick and aging relatives. Rex R. Campbell, Daniel M. Johnson, and Gary Stangler, "Return Migration of Black People to the South," *Rural Sociology* 39, no. 4 (1974), 526.

51 Interview of Henry Smith, Apr. 14, 2007; "Impact of Heir Property," 128–29; C. Scott Graber, "Heirs Property: The Problems and Possible Solutions," *Clearinghouse Review* 12, no. 5 (1978), 281; Powdermaker, *After Freedom,* 132.

CHAPTER 10: THE PREACHER'S WIFE

1 Historic weather data from www.weather.gov/wrh/climate?wfo=lwx, accessed Feb. 1, 2023; depositions of Henry Ware, Alfred Webb, and Robert E. Gilchrist, Jan. 27, 1886, and Decree, June 4, 1886, in *Freeman v. Freeman,* case 9446, EDC.

2 Walter F. Willcox, "The Divorce Problem: A Study in Statistics," *Columbia University Studies in History, Economics and Public Law* 1, no. 1 (1897), 22, 30–32 (Willcox disagreed); Chester G. Vernier, *American Family Laws* (Stanford University Press, 1932), vol. 2, 332–33. Divorces accounted for 830 of the 3,178 cases (26%) in my sample for 1902–1932, excluding cases for which I cannot identify a cause of action. Blacks filed 166/419 (40%) of the divorces in my sample for 1902–1932. Unlike for most other kinds of cases, I am interpolating the race of missing parties where I can identify one party, on the assumption that no interracial divorces were recorded in those years.

3 *Such as Us: Southern Voices of the Thirties,* ed. Tom E. Terrill and Jerrold Hirsch (University of North Carolina Press, 1978), 269; "A Negro Cook's Day," [Dale Co., Ozark, AL], Federal Writers Project Papers, no. 3709 (1936–1940), SHC.

4 Norma Basch, *Framing American Divorce: From the Revolutionary Generation to the Victorians* (University of California Press, 1999), 7; Nelson Manfred Blake, *The Road to Reno: A History of Divorce in the United States* (Macmillan, 1962), 121–30, 226; Tera W. Hunter, *Bound in Wedlock: Slave and Free Black Marriage in the Nineteenth Century* (Harvard University Press, 2017), 304, 6; Glenda Riley, "Legislative Divorce in Virginia, 1803–1850," *Journal of the Early Republic* 11 (Spring 1991), 51–67; Decree, Sept. 29, 1942, in *Ethel v. Eugene Reaves,* CirCtCh, Cumberland Co., VA; Vernier, *American Family Laws,* 140; Petition of John Biggs, ca. 1904, GWIN. On divorce fees in the 1910s and 1920s, see K[arl] N. Llewellyn, "Behind the Law of Divorce: II," CLR 33, no. 2 (1933), 285–86.

5 Gwin to John Biggs, Oct. 7, 1904, in *John v. Carrie Biggs*, GWIN; *Casteel v. Casteel*, case 3191 (1922), CirCtCh, Madison Co., IL; Basch, *Framing American Divorce*, 97; Lawrence M. Friedman and Robert V. Percival, "Who Sues for Divorce? From Fault through Fiction to Freedom," *Journal of Legal Studies* 5, no. 1 (1976), 61–82; Sheela Kennedy and Steven Ruggles "Breaking up Is Hard to Count: The Rise of Divorce in the United States, 1980–2010," *Demography* 51, no. 2 (2014), 587–98.

6 Hendrik Hartog, *Man and Wife in America: A History* (Harvard University Press, 2000), 285; Lawrence M. Friedman, *A History of American Law* (1973; Simon and Schuster, 1985), 500; "Interview with Mrs. House," n.d.," f 10, b 131-82, FPMS; *Mosby v. Mosby*, case 2876 (1913), CirCtCh, Adams Co., MS; telephone interview of Osborne Reaves, Mar. 25, 2016.

7 Deposition of Robert Jackson in *Jackson v. Jackson*, Feb. 16, 1922, Mecklenburg County Chancery Causes, 1922-019CC, LV; *Conrad v. Conrad*, case 30512 (1912), EDC. Federal statistics, which did not disclose race, indicate about two-thirds of all divorces went to women. Glenda Riley, *Divorce: An American Tradition* (Oxford University Press, 1991), 79.

8 Deposition of Jessie Hopkins, Sept. 10, 1942, in *Reaves v. Reaves*, CirCtCh, Cumberland Co., VA..

9 Deposition of Paschal Green, Nov. 9, 1872, in *Green v. Green*, CirCtCh, Amelia Co., 1872-003, LV; deposition of Stephen A. Douglas, Aug. 19, 1872, in *Thomas v. Thomas*, case 2773, EDC; *Ricks v. Ricks*, CirCtCh, Isle of Wight Co., 1909-032; record in *Purnell v. Purnell*, Court of Errors & Appeals, New Jersey, vol. 413 (1907), 36-39, 71, NJLL; deposition of Mary J. Wheeler, Lonnie OConner, May 20, 1893, both in *McKenney v. McKenney*, case 14431, EDC. For a similar pattern among white women in the early 1800s, see Laura F. Edwards, *The People and Their Peace: Legal Culture and the Transformation of Inequality in the Post-Revolutionary South* (University of North Carolina Press, 2009), 169–201.

10 Deposition of Mary E. Scott, Jan. 8, 1879, in *Chase v. Chase*, case 6537, EDC; deposition of Ed Gore in *Walker v. Tansel*, CirCtCh, Morgan Co., IL, Jacksonville; deposition of Annie Davis, Oct. 7, 1884, in *Smith v. Smith*, case 9037, EDC; deposition of Sam Delk, Apr. 8, 1899, in *Branch v. Branch*, Isle of Wight Chancery Causes, 1899-006, LV; deposition of Jupiter White, Apr. 8, 1873, in *Francis v. Francis*, LVRC; *Bundy v. Bundy*, case 346, 1911-079, Rockingham Co., LV; Austin Sarat and William L. F. Felstiner, *Divorce Lawyers and Their Clients: Power and Meaning in the Legal Process* (Oxford University Press, 1995), 85–107.

11 Virginia Code 1942 §§5103-5104; Vernier, *American Family Laws*, vol. 2, 140–41.

12 "A Fish Story," 1 *Virginia Law Register*, n.s., 559 (1915–16); "Divorce Upon Conditions," *Ohio Law Bulletin*, vol. 54 (1909), 72; "In Wholesale Lots," *West Publishing Company's Docket*, vol. 2 (Nov. 1915), 1455–56; Reva B. Siegel, "'The Rule of Love': Wife Beating as Prerogative and Privacy," YLJ 105, no. 8 (1996), 2134–41; Nancy MacLean, *Behind the Mask of Chivalry: The Making of the Second Ku Klux Klan* (Oxford University Press, 1994), 35, 152–53; Alexander Keyssar, *The Right to Vote:*

The Contested History of Democracy in America (Basic Books, 2000), 111–12, 390–96 (table A.15); Emily Bazelon, "Will Florida's Ex-Felons Finally Regain the Right to Vote?," *New York Times Magazine*, Sept. 26, 2018.

13 Michele Mitchell, *Righteous Propagation: African Americans and the Politics of Racial Destiny after Reconstruction* (University of North Carolina Press, 2004), 82–85; RP, Apr. 9, 1890; *Savannah Colored Tribune*, Apr. 22, 1876; E. Franklin Frazier, *The Negro Family in the United States* (University of Chicago Press, 1939), 510; Hartog, *Man and Wife*.

14 Hartog, *Man and Wife*, 33; Laura F. Edwards, *Gendered Strife and Confusion: The Political Culture of Reconstruction* (University of Illinois Press, 1997), 58–59; Cheryl D. Hicks, *Talk with You Like a Woman: African American Women, Justice, and Reform in New York, 1890–1935* (University of North Carolina Press, 2010), 182–203.

15 Deposition of Julia Freeman in *Freeman v. Freeman*, CirCtCh, Mecklenburg Co., 1912-035CC; *Robinson v. Robinson*, case 30509 (1912), EDC; *Saunders v. Saunders*, CirCtCh, Mecklenburg Co., 1912-024CC; *Such as Us*, 265; *Russell v. Russell*, case 23011 (1901), EDC. For a white example, see *Ferguson v. Ferguson*, case 23047, EDC.

16 Transcript of Record at 4–8, 11, *Harrington v. Taylor*, 36 S.E.2d 227 (N.C. 1945) (No. 594), NCSA. On *Harrington's* use in modern casebooks, see Dylan C. Penningroth, "Race in Contract Law," PLR 170, no. 5 (2022), 1207, 1243–45. Transcript of Record at 29, *Harrington v. Taylor*, 40 S.E.2d 367 (N.C. 1946) (No. 593), NCSA.

17 Kali Nicole Gross, "African American Women, Mass Incarceration, and the Politics of Protection," JAH 102, no. 1 (2015), 30–33; Penningroth, "Race in Contract Law," 1207–9.

18 Virginia Code 1942, §5103; deposition of Mack Walker in *Wimbish v. Wimbish*, CirCtCh, Mecklenburg Co., 1873-051CC; petition, in *Goodwin v. Goodwin*, case 2388 (1889), CirCtCh, Lafayette Co., MS; petition in *Coleman v. Coleman*, case 1783 (1902), CirCtCh, Adams Co., MS; *Morris v. Morris*, case 519 (1893), CirCtCh, Pulaski Co., IL; *Young v. Young*, case 1611, CirCtCh, Pulaski Co., IL. When states mentioned sodomy as grounds for divorce, they likened it to adultery. James Schouler, *A Treatise on the Law of Marriage, Divorce, Separation and Domestic Relations* (Matthew Bender & Co., 1921), vol. 1, §1067; vol. 2, §1674.

19 Frederick Hoffman (1892) and William Hannibal Thomas (1906), quoted in Mitchell, *Righteous Propagation*, 82–83; deposition of Rave Coleman, Jan. 28, 1886, in *Freeman v. Freeman*, case 9446, EDC.

20 On Black mobility during Jim Crow, see Robin D. G. Kelley, *Hammer and Hoe: Alabama Communists During the Great Depression* (University of North Carolina Press, 1990), 36–37; Edward L. Ayers, *The Promise of the New South: Life after Reconstruction* (1992; Oxford University Press, 2007), 154, 197–98; Mia Bay, *Traveling Black: A Story of Race and Resistance* (Harvard University Press, 2021), 3–4. Deposition of Louisa Prather, Nov. 27, 1912, in *Thomas v. Thomas*, case 31254, EDC; petition of Phillis Gatewood, Dec. 30, 1901, in *Gatewood v. Gatewood*, case 23033, EDC;

deposition of Fairchild Mitchell, Apr. 20, 1932, in *Mitchell v. Mitchell,* case 78647, enrollment no. L-96-471, Superior Court of New Jersey, Public Information Center, Trenton; *Pettus v. Pettus,* CirCtCh, Mecklenburg Co., 1912-01CC.

21 On spouses who stayed behind, see *Johnson v. Johnson,* case 23035 (1901), EDC; *Foster v. Foster,* CirCtCh, Albemarle Co., 1881-011CC. For similar examples among whites, see Sophie Holdengraber, "A Study of the Family Separated as a Result of Emigration," MA thesis, University of Chicago, 1928, 75–81, 95–106, 149–50. Deposition of D. H. Jones, Feb. 13, 1915, in *Alexander v. Alexander,* CirCtCh, Mecklenburg Co., 1915-007CC ("never coming back here"). See also Darlene Clark Hine, "Rape and the Inner Lives of Black Women in the Middle West: Preliminary Thoughts on the Culture of Dissemblance," *Signs* 14 (Summer 1989), 913–15. On job and housing discrimination straining Black marriages, see Hicks, *Talk with You Like a Woman,* 142–49; depositions of Robert E. Gilchrist and Richmond Weaver, both in *Freeman v. Freeman,* case 9446, EDC.

22 On migratory divorce, see Hartog, *Man and Wife,* 18; 317 U.S. 287 (1942); [Scovel Richardson], "Notes and Comments," *National Bar Journal* 3 (1945), 304–12; John J. Griggs Jr., "The Role of 'Conflict of Laws' in Matrimonial Actions," *National Bar Journal* 4 (1946), 114–24; S[amuel] S. M[itchell], "Divorce—Foreign Decree," *National Bar Journal* 6 (1948), 155–59. On Black newspapers' coverage of it, see "Court Holds 'Mail Order' Divorce Is Invalid," PC, Dec. 20, 1930; "One-Day Wife Gets Freedom in Mexico," NYAN, Oct. 7, 1931; "Mexican Divorce For Joe, Marva?" PC, Feb. 12, 1949; "Edna Mae Sheds Sugar Ray In Mexican Divorce," CD, Oct. 2, 1962; "Quick Mexican Divorces," PC, Jan. 12, 1935. On Sutton, see "Prominent Harlemites' Marriages Questioned," NYAN, Oct. 3, 1964; Percy Sutton, "New York's Divorce Laws; Will They Ever Change?" NYAN, Jan. 1, 1966. On perception of divorce as right, see Hartog, *Man and Wife,* 281–82.

23 *The Virginia Code of 1942* (Michie Co., 1942), 1, pt. 2, §5103, 1946; Revised Statutes of New Jersey (The State of New Jersey, 1937), title 2, ch. 50, §2; William A. Occomy, "Execution, Acknowledgment and Delivery of Deeds," PC, Dec. 17, 1949 (wife in South). On multistate property in divorce, see Robert M. Gantt to William I. Gosnell, Sept. 22, 1949; "Annie" to Virginia Caldwell, Sept. 20, 1949, both in "Caldwell v. Caldwell," DNWG; T. Carter Franklin to Mr. Willie Taylor, Apr. 3, 1945; handwritten list labeled "Beauty Shop Supplyes," n.d., both in *Willie v. Otha Mae Taylor* but housed in f "Foster v. Foster," 1946, WAITS; William I. Gosnell to C. Jerry Gates, May 11, 1949, *Caldwell v. Caldwell,* DNWG. See also *Moss v. Moss,* case 81501 (1941), CirCtCh, Sangamon Co., IL.

24 On marital property, see testimony of Bythia Brown, *Brown v. McWilliams* case 1451 (1909), CirCtCh, Coahoma Co., MS; answer and cross-bill, Oct. 2, 1922, *Pegues v. Pegues,* case 4852, CirCtCh, Marshall Co., MS; Frazier, *Negro Family,* 526. On nineteenth-century free women's assertion of separate property, see Suzanne Lebsock, *The Free Women of Petersburg: Status and Culture in a Southern Town, 1784–1860* (W. W. Norton, 1984), 54–111; Basch, *Framing American Divorce,* 108.

25 Testimony of Gladys Spinner, Dec. 18, 1930, *Spinner v. Spinner* (1930), ended case 3308, CirCtCh, Albemarle Co., Charlottesville, VA; testimony of R. W. Sadler, Jan. 26, 1933, *Spinner v. Spinner* (1932), ended case 3411, CirCtCh, Albemarle Co., VA; answer and cross-bill, petition, both in *Collins v. Collins* (1923) and decree, Apr. 20, 1923, CirCtCh, Coahoma Co., MS. This might or might not have been completely true, but it was certainly clever; her argument made her out to be B. J.'s landlord and turned B. J. into a mere tenant at "sufferance," whom she could evict at any time. Original bill of complaint, Sept. 29, 1942, *Lee v. Lee* (1942), CirCtCh, Coahoma Co., MS ("joint enterprise").

26 *Reaves v. Reaves,* Sept. 29, 1942, Order Book 10, 403, CirCtCh, Cumberland Co., VA; "Foster v. Foster," WAITS; original bill, Sept. 23, 1943, in *Upchurch v. Upchurch,* case 7366 (1943), CirCtCh, Coahoma Co., MS; *Cherry v. Cherry,* case 2941 (1932), CirCtCh, Pulaski Co., IL.

27 Handwritten notes, probably by RPA, dated June 5, 1943, in file "James Perry," 1943–44, RPA; Duke to Geraldine Hill, Nov. 4, 1950; untitled transcription of Dictaphone-recorded client interview, Oct. 26(?), 1950, both in f "Geraldine v. Matthew Hill," 1948–51, DUKES; W. J[?]. Wynn to Waits, Sept. 20, 1949, in Robert E. Crofton: Divorce-1949, WAITS ("moderate"; white couple). On lawyers' coaxing, see Dallas F. Nicholas to John A. Cook, Feb. 18, 1943, in "Ruth v. John Cook," DNWG ("alimony or support"); W. E. Duke to Nettie May Washington Evans, July 8, 1952, in "Roy v. Nettie Evans," DUKES. Ruth Cook to Nicholas, April 16, 1943, in "Cook, Ruth," DNWG ("so unfair").

28 "Order Dismissing," Nov. 18, 1952, in *Cobb v. Cobb,* case 9943, CirCtCh, Coahoma Co., MS.

29 For median earnings, see https://census.gov/data/tables/time-series/demo/income-poverty/historical-income-people.html. For lawyer fees, see Jerome Shuman, "A Black Lawyers Study," *Howard Law Journal* 16 (Winter 1971), 287, table 26. On judicial lenience, see Blake, *Road to Reno,* 236–37.

30 Matthew Hill to Geraldine Hill, Aug. 16, 1949, typescript copy, in "Geraldine v. Matthew Hill"; Walter Brooks to Susie Brooks, n.d., in "Susie Brooks," 1942–44, RPA. See also Grace Sweeney Jones to RPA, Dec. 14, 1942, in "Robert Jones," 1942–43, RPA.

31 Bacon to STMA, Apr. 19, 1943, "Mary Bacon," 1943–45, STMA. See also *Myrtle Upchurch v. Mariland Upchurch,* case 6806 (1941), CirCtCh, Coahoma Co., MS; Hicks, *Talk with You Like a Woman,* 216–17. On white women's complaints of marital sexual violence, Elaine Tyler May, *Great Expectations: Marriage and Divorce in Post-Victorian America* (University of Chicago Press, 1980), 106–7. For sensationalist Black press coverage, see "Threadgill Must Pay Alimony—Or Else!" PC, Oct. 1, 1938; D'Weston Haywood, *Let Us Make Men: The Twentieth-Century Black Press and a Manly Vision for Racial Advancement* (University of North Carolina Press, 2018), 15–16, 81.

32 Decree, May 23, 1912, in *Josephine Butler v. Smith Butler* (1912), CirCtCh, Morgan

Co., Jacksonville, IL. See also testimony of Ed. B. Gore, n.d., in *Walker v. Hutchinson et al.* (1922), case 2218, CirCtCh, Pulaski Co., Mound City, IL; Hartog, *Man and Wife,* 310, 282.

33 Answer of Catherine Davis, in *William v. Catherine Davis,* case 9437, EDC ("vile").

34 "Negro Minister Says Police Abused Him," *Minneapolis Morning Tribune,* Sept. 4, 1958, 1, 15; "King 'Manhandling' Has Shocked Nation, Eisenhower Is Told," *Philadelphia Tribune,* Sept. 9, 1958, 1; "Rev. Martin King Claims Police Brutality in Arrest," *Daily Boston Globe,* Sept. 4, 1958, 1; "Negro Cleric Is Arrested in Loitering," *The Sun* [Baltimore], Sept. 4, 1958, 4. The *Chicago Daily Tribune* (Sept. 4, 1958, A6) did mention the hatchet and Davis's adultery accusation.

35 *Johnson Publishing Co. v. Edward Davis,* 124 So. 2d 441, 445–46 (Ala. 1960); Richmond Smiley interview, Dec. 28, 1983, f 769; handwritten notes by Taylor Branch on *Birmingham World,* Dec. 3, 1958, f 279, both in Taylor Branch Papers, #5047, SHC ("shocked"); "Jury Rejects Abernathy Charges," *Montgomery Advertiser,* Nov. 22, 1958 ("rights of my people"); "Leaders give Abernathy a big vote of confidence," *Afro,* Dec. 6, 1958 ("unnecessary ordeal"). See also "Rev. Abernathy Rejects Bid to Take Lie Test: 'The Scheme Won't Stop Our Fight He Tells Afro,'" *Afro,* Nov. 29, 1958, 1.

36 J. Mills Thornton III, *Dividing Lines: Municipal Politics and the Struggle for Civil Rights in Montgomery, Birmingham, and Selma* (University of Alabama Press, 2002), 613n136; Krista Johnson, "Montgomery's Ben Moore Hotel has a complicated past, uncertain future," *Montgomery Advertiser,* Jan. 10, 2019; Taylor Branch, *Parting the Waters: America in the King Years, 1954-63* (Simon and Schuster, 1988), 237–41, 245–46 ("soon . . . forgotten"). Abernathy, as well as King's confidant James Farmer, alleged—and rationalized—infidelities by King. Ralph David Abernathy, *And the Walls Came Tumbling Down: An Autobiography* (Harper & Row, 1989), 470–75; interview of James Farmer by Taylor Branch, Nov. 18, 1983, f 611, scan 18, Taylor Branch Papers, SHC, https://finding-aids.lib.unc.edu/05047/#folder_611#1.

37 Thomas C. Holt, *The Movement: The African American Struggle for Civil Rights* (Oxford University Press, 2021), 4–6.

38 "Negro Jailed After Attack On Leader Of Bus Boycott," *Montgomery Advertiser,* Aug. 30, 1958; "City Hearing On King Case Slated Today," *Montgomery Advertiser,* Sept. 5, 1958 ("the King case").

CHAPTER 11: "JUST LIKE ANY OTHER CASE WITH DAMAGES"

1 *Brown v. Board of Education of Topeka,* 74 S.Ct. 686, 692 (1954); interview of Thurgood Marshall, Dec. 28, 1973, f 65, b 4, KLUGER (emphases removed). Compare Richard Kluger, *Simple Justice: The History of Brown v. Board of Education and Black America's Struggle for Equality* (1975; Vintage, 2004), 316, 713. One man asked the

NAACP to take his worker's compensation case on contingency, offering to split the value of his claim. George Price to NAACP, Feb. 8, 1944, NAACP Papers, Legal File, Labor, "O," 1945–47, part 13C, reel 7.

2 Christopher W. Schmidt, *Civil Rights in America: A History* (Cambridge University Press, 2021), 65–73; John Dittmer, *Local People: The Struggle for Civil Rights in Mississippi* (University of Illinois Press, 1994), 302; Clayborne Carson, "Civil Rights Reform and the Black Freedom Struggle," in *The Civil Rights Movement in America*, ed. Charles W. Eagles (University Press of Mississippi, 1986), 19–32; Thomas F. Jackson, *From Civil Rights to Human Rights: Martin Luther King, Jr., and the Struggle for Economic Justice* (University of Pennsylvania Press, 2007); Barbara Ransby, *Ella Baker and the Black Freedom Movement: A Radical Democratic Vision* (University of North Carolina Press, 2003), 368–69.

3 Kenneth W. Mack, "Rethinking Civil Rights Lawyering and Politics in the Era before Brown," YLJ 115, no. 2 (2005), 280–99; Risa L. Goluboff, *The Lost Promise of Civil Rights* (Harvard University Press, 2007), 23–25; Robert E. Cushman, "Civil Liberties," and John Dickinson, "Civil Rights," both in *Encyclopaedia of the Social Sciences*, ed. Edwin R. A. Seligman and Alvin Johnson (MacMillan, 1930), 509–15; Schmidt, *Civil Rights*, 66–75.

4 Kenneth W. Mack, "Bringing the Law Back into the History of the Civil Rights Movement," LHR 27, no. 3 (2009), 661.

5 *To Secure These Rights: The Report of the President's Committee on Civil Rights* (Government Printing Office, 1947), 6, 146; Harry S. Truman, Special Message to the Congress on Civil Rights, Feb. 2, 1948, 1948 Pub. Papers, 121–26.

6 On the tightening link to Equal Protection Clause, see Goluboff, *Lost Promise*, 230–31; [Thurgood Marshall, Gloster B. Current, and Roy Wilkins], "NAACP Civil Rights Handbook" (Apr., 1953), 5, *Papers of the NAACP, Part 15: Segregation and Discrimination, Complaints and Responses, 1940–1955, Series B: Administrative Files*, Library of Congress; Schmidt, *Civil Rights*, 50–51.

7 On "second-class citizenship," see "The Great National Convention," *North Star*, Aug. 11, 1848; Address by Dr. Ralph J. Bunche, July 1, 1951, Papers of the NAACP, Part 01: Supplement, 1951–1955, Group II, Series A, General Office File, Records of Annual Conventions, 42d Annual Convention. June 26–July 1, 1951), frame 94; Martin Luther King Jr., "The Rising Tide of Racial Consciousness," in *A Testament of Hope*, 148; "U.S. No Place for Second Class Citizenship—Ike," *Jet*, June 5, 1953, 5.

8 Michael J. Klarman, *From Jim Crow to Civil Rights: The Supreme Court and the Struggle for Racial Equality* (Oxford University Press, 2004), 377–81; Goluboff, *Lost Promise*, 1–6, 238–70; Derrick A. Bell Jr., "Serving Two Masters: Integration Ideals and Client Interests in School Desegregation Litigation," YLJ 85, no. 4 (1976), 470–516; Tomiko Brown-Nagin, *Courage to Dissent: Atlanta and the Long History of the Civil Rights Movement* (Oxford University Press, 2011), 391–403.

9 Hardy Lott to JOE, June 30, 1947, f 2-5, b 2; Lott to JOE, Aug. 11, 1947, both

in EASTLAND (settlements); Arthur M. Schlesinger Jr., *Robert Kennedy and His Times* (1978; Mariner, 2002), 234 ("big government"); *Carrie Brown v. Prudential* (1947),DNWG (brokered payout).

10 On brokering real estate sales to Black buyers, see JOE to State Highway Department, July 26, 1937, f S-Miscellaneous, b 4; JOE to Evelyn Smith, Dec. 10, 1936; JOE to Brown Speir, Mar. 10, 1939; JOE to Bettye C. Shinn, Aug. 11, 1938, all in f S-Miscellaneous, b 4, EASTLAND. On securing insurance and veterans' payouts for Black clients, see Edgar B. Van Wagoner, Asst. Sec., Surrender Division, to Green, Mar. 10, 1938, f G-Misc., EASTLAND; JOE(?) to Veterans Administration, May 18, 1936, EASTLAND. On personal-injury suits, see JOE to Stevens Bros. & The Miller-Hutchinson Co., Nov. 13, 1939, f S-Miscellaneous, b 4, EASTLAND; "Statement," in f 2-16, b 2, EASTLAND (trucking company); *Vashti Ganges v. Baltimore Transit* (1948), DNWG. For examples of other notable white supremacists with Black clients, see *Tademy v. Scott et al.*, 157 F.2d 826 (1946); *City of Jackson v. Clark,* 152 Miss. 731 (1928) (Ross Barnett); "Lester Mitchell v. Pearline Mitchell Divorce," 1936–1938, WAITS.

11 Mack, "Rethinking Civil Rights Lawyering"; Joseph William Singer, "Legal Realism Now," *California Law Review* 76, no. 2 (1988), 468–71; Roscoe Pound, "Law in Books and Law in Action," *American Law Review* 44, no. 1 (1910), 15; *Plessy,* at 1143.

12 Goluboff, *Lost Promise,* 84–85, 167–72, 16; Brown-Nagin, *Courage to Dissent,* 2.

13 Mack, "Rethinking Civil Rights Lawyering," 277–81; Mack, *Representing the Race,* 39; R. L. P., "Commentary: Negro Members of the Alabama Bar," *Alabama Law Review* 21 (1968–1969), 306, 311; "The Negro Lawyer in Virginia: A Survey," *Virginia Law Review* 51 (1965), 521, 532, 537-470; Barbara Marie Guillory, "The Career Patterns of Negro Lawyers in New Orleans," MA thesis, Louisiana State University, 1960, 17–18, 43–44; Jerome Shuman, "A Black Lawyers Study," *Howard Law Journal* 16 (Winter 1971), 227n7; G. Franklin Edwards, *The Negro Professional Class* (Greenwood Press, 1959), 135. On the rise and fall of the Black corporate law firm, see David B. Wilkins, "'If You Can't Beat 'Em, Join 'Em!' The Rise and Fall of the Black Corporate Law Firm," SLR 60 (2007–2008), 1733–1801.

14 W. E. B. Du Bois, "Postcript: Legal Aid," *Crisis* 34, no. 7 (1927), 239–40 ("as a whole"); "Outline of Procedure for Legal Cases—NAACP Branches, Sept., 1943," Thurgood Marshall, General, 1942–43, Legal File, NAACP Papers.

15 Mack, *Representing the Race,* 241–44; "Negro Lawyer in Virginia," 532–33; "Negro Members of the Alabama Bar," 328; Fitzhugh Lee Styles, *Negroes and the Law in the Race's Battle for Liberty, Equality, and Justice under the Constitution of the United States* (Christopher Publishing House, 1937), 157–65; Guillory, "Career Patterns of Negro Lawyers in New Orleans," 37–40 ("impossible" cases); Mack, *Representing the Race,* 52–54, 61–82; Report of Attorney A. T. Walden, Sept. 8, 1955, f 2, b 1, Walden Papers, AHM; *Prince Hall Masonic Bldg. Ass'n v. Howard,* 36 Ga. App. 169 (1926); Mack, *Representing the Race,* 148–49.

16 Aaron C. Porter, "The Career of a Professional Institution: A Study of Norris,

Schmidt, Green, Harris, Higginbotham, and Associates," PhD diss., University of Pennsylvania, 1993, 197 ("hard core"); "Negro Lawyer in Virginia," 51 *Virginia Law Review* (1965), 537.

17 Mark V. Tushnet, *Making Civil Rights Law: Thurgood Marshall and the Supreme Court, 1936–1961* (Oxford University Press, 1994), 28; "Outline of Procedure for Legal Cases," NAACP Papers, Part II: Legal File 1940–1955, b 2:B110, f 3; "Memorandum from Thurgood Marshall to Legal Staff," Feb. 16, 1949, Thurgood Marshall, General, 1948–50, Legal File, NAACP Papers.

18 "Arguments Before the Court: Enforceability of Restrictive Covenants," 16 United States Law Week 3221 (Jan. 20, 1948); Mark Tushnet, "Lawyer Thurgood Marshall," SLR 44, no. 6 (1992), 1289 ("mere property rights"); undated bulletin titled ". . . To Secure for Negroes Their Basic Civil Rights," 9, pt. II, b II-B-110, Outline of Procedure for Legal Cases, 1940–44, NAACP Papers ("basic"); Howard University Bulletin, vol. 38 (Howard University, 1939), 222; Mack, "Rethinking Civil Rights Lawyering," 287. On court dockets in Wisconsin, see James Willard Hurst, *The Growth of American Law: The Law Makers* (1950; Lawbook Exchange, 2004), 159–60, 309.

19 Melvin I. Urofsky, *Louis D. Brandeis: A Life* (Pantheon, 2009), 8–10; Clyde Spillenger, "Elusive Advocate: Reconsidering Brandeis as People's Lawyer," YLJ 105, no. 6 (1996), 1448, (quotation); Charles H[amilton] Houston, "Tentative Findings Re Negro Lawyers," 3, 6, uncorrected version, Jan. 23, 1928, Rockefeller Archive Center, Sleepy Hollow, NY. Thanks to Kenneth Mack for giving me a copy of this document. Houston to Marshall, Sept. 21, 1935, and Marshall to Houston, Sept. 23, 1935, Cases Supported-University of Maryland, Sept. 3–30, 1935, I-D-93, NAACP Legal File.

20 Penningroth interview of James Baber, Dec. 5, 2016. Supreme Court Justice Hugo Black started his career similarly. John P. Frank, *Mr. Justice Black: The Man and His Opinions* (Knopf, 1949), 15–16. "Negro Members of the Alabama Bar," 313 (church); interview of James Nabrit Jr., f 74, b 4, KLUGER ("where the money was"); Guillory, "Career Patterns of Negro Lawyers in New Orleans," 36 (grand opening); Mack, *Representing the Race*, 139 ("legal drudgery"); Kenneth Walter Mack, "A Social History of Everyday Practice: Sadie T. M. Alexander and the Incorporation of Black Women into the American Legal Profession, 1925–1960," *Cornell Law Review* 87 (Sept. 2002), 1463 ("community service").

21 A. Leon Higginbotham quoted in Porter, "Career of a Professional Institution," 143 ("bread- and-butter practice"). See also "Wichita's Business and Professional Index," *Negro Star*, Jan. 4, 1929. Shuman, "Black Lawyers Study," 239 ("neighborhood practice"); Tushnet, *Making Civil Rights Law*, 10 (garnishing); interview of A. Briscoe Koger, 407, f 67, b 4, KLUGER ("two for nothing"); Kluger, *Simple Justice*, 182 ("through the door"). On seeking institutional clients, see A. T. Walden to Rev. A. P. Morris, Sept. 2, 1960, f 13, b 1, Austin Thomas Walden Papers, Atlanta History Museum; Porter, "Career of a Professional Institution," 185–96.

22 Kluger, *Simple Justice,* 182 ("the little man's lawyer"); Derrick Bell, "An Epistolary Exploration for a Thurgood Marshall Biography," *Harvard BlackLetter Journal* 6 (1989), 55.

23 Kluger, *Simple Justice,* 131–37 (LDF's plan); Houston to Marshall (1935), quoted in Mack, *Representing the Race,* 38 ("cashing in"); Guillory, "Career Patterns of Negro Lawyers in New Orleans," 41–42; Shuman, "Black Lawyers Study," 253, 256 ("demonstration"); "Negro Lawyer in Virginia," 536, 541. See also Edwards, *Negro Professional Class,* 137. Martin Luther King Jr., "The Law Is Majestic," July 31, 1965, King Center Online.

24 Philip R. Lochner Jr., "The No Fee and Low Fee Legal Practice of Private Attorneys," LSR 9 (Spring 1975), 446–47; interview of Albert Matthews, June 24, 2008, Center for Oral History Research, UCLA Library, https://static.library.ucla.edu/oralhistory/pdf/masters/21198-zz001d0qd1-5-master.pdf?_ga=2.28707838.374803678.1659719327-1558287721.1659719327.

25 Houston to RPA, Dec. 5, 1947, "Southern Railway System," STMA; "Statement on Krushchev Visit," in f "Commonwealth v. Barefield," 1957, STMA; f "Estate of Edward J. Burke," 1954, STMA; "Oliver Brown (1954)," RPA. Based on conversations with accessioning and current staff members at University of Pennsylvania Archives and Records Center, I am confident that the Series VII files are largely in the order maintained by the Alexander firm. For the Nicholas & Gosnell arrangement, see www2.law.umaryland.edu/marshall/specialcollections/nicgosnell/introduction.html (accessed Aug. 19, 2022).

26 Interview of William H. Hastie, June 18, 1971, f 40, b 2, KLUGER ("lead and teach"). On torts, see Charles Houston to STMA, Sept. 28, 1943, Southern Railway System, STMA, Penn; Barbara Young Welke, *Recasting American Liberty: Gender, Race, Law, and the Railroad Revolution, 1865–1920* (Cambridge University Press, 2001), 358–69; Myisha Shuntez Eatmon, "Public Wrongs, Private Rights: African Americans, Private Law, and White Violence During Jim Crow," PhD diss., Northwestern University, 2020. On origins of the doll tests, see Pauli Murray, *Song in a Weary Throat* (1987; Liveright, 2018), 285–86, 328–30.

27 On segregation as moral wrong, see Martin Luther King Jr., "Our God Is Able," sermon at Dexter Avenue Baptist Church, Montgomery, Ala., Jan. 1, 1956, MLK Papers, https://kinginstitute.stanford.edu/king-papers/documents/our-god-able. On Scott, see *Sun Oil Co. v. Bennett,* 125 Tex. 540, 84 S.W.2d 447 (1935); Kluger, *Simple Justice,* 390; interview of Inza Brown, n.d., f 11, b 1, KLUGER ("protect blacks"); interview of Esther Brown, May 31, 1969, f 10, b 1, KLUGER ("for nothing").

28 Kluger, *Simple Justice,* 408–10; Tushnet, *Making Civil Rights Law,* 43; Fred Shuttlesworth, "An Account of the Alabama Christian Movement for Human Rights" (1959), appendix B in Jacquelyne Mary Johnson Clarke, "Goals and Techniques in Three Negro Civil-Rights Organizations in Alabama," PhD diss., Ohio State, 1960, 138, 153. For discussion of this quotation and Shuttlesworth's activities

generally, see Andrew M. Manis, *A Fire You Can't Put Out: The Civil Rights Life of Birmingham's Reverend Fred Shuttlesworth* (University of Alabama Press, 2010), 214–15.

29 Alexis de Tocqueville, *Democracy in America,* transl. Henry Reeve (J. &. H. G. Langley, 1841), vol. 1, 304; "Lakeside Colored Special Consolidated School District ($100,000.00)," Aug. 7, 1950, WAITS; Bickerstaff to Dr. W. L. Jacquith, Director Mississippi State Hospital, Aug. 24, 1953, Bickerstaff Collection, Z.2281, MDAH.

30 Interview of Henry Marsh, Dec. 5, 2016 (Tucker's skill in partitions); deposition of William Allen, Dec. 8, 1949; William Allen to Rev. Earl Hoxter, Feb. 28, 1947, and Allen to Hoxter, Mar. 15, 1947 (brokering real estate) all in "Allen v. Christ Methodist Church," DNWG; Richard R. W. Brooks and Carol M. Rose, *Saving the Neighborhood: Racially Restrictive Covenants, Law, and Social Norms* (Harvard University Press, 2013), 135–36 (blockbusters' complex position).

31 Findings of the Board, Mar. 16, 1954, in "Peters, John F. (Tavern)," f 1, b 6A3, DNWG. See also Brown-Nagin, *Courage To Dissent,* 419. Porter, "Career of a Professional Institution," 163 ("breakthrough"); Rev. William Jackson to Whom It May Concern, Nov. 23, 1951; E. A. Pollard [of Pollard's Funeral Home] to Atlanta Police Committee, Nov. 24, 1951 ("keep down crime"), both in f 11, b 12, Walden Papers, AHM.

32 Civil Rights Act of 1964, title II, §201 ("discrimination or segregation"); Civil Rights Act of 1968, at U.S.C.A., title 42, §3604 (fair housing); Lyndon B. Johnson, "Special Message to the Congress on the Right to Vote, March 15, 1965," Public Papers of the Presidents of the United States 1965, 287–91; Bruce Ackerman, *We the People,* vol. 3: *The Civil Rights Revolution* (Harvard University Press, 2014), 135–37.

33 Interview of Oliver W. Hill Sr. by Ronald E. Carrington, Nov. 13, 2002, transcript, VFC.

34 Interview of Sen. Henry L. Marsh III by Ronald E. Carrington, Mar. 20, 2003, transcript, VFC; interview of Henry Marsh by author, Dec. 5, 2016.

CHAPTER 12: CIVIL RIGHTS, INC.

1 This extended and expanded a one-day boycott organized by an existing group, the Women's Political Council. The Montgomery Improvement Association, Entity ID no. 774-072, Alabama Secretary of State. On the procedure for corporate filing, see Act No. 578, *Alabama Laws,* vol. 2 (Skinner Printing Co., 1955), §28, 1263–64. Articles of Incorporation of the Montgomery Improvement Association, Book 33, 55, Montgomery County Probate Records Office, Montgomery, AL.

2 Act No. 578, *Alabama Laws,* vol. 2, §32, 1265; By-Laws of the Montgomery Improvement Association, CRMA, www.crmvet.org/docs/orgsdocs.htm#docsmia; David J. Garrow, *Bearing the Cross: Martin Luther King, Jr., and the Southern Christian Leadership Conference* (Vintage, 1986), 22–24, 71; Martin Luther King Jr., Testimony to the Democratic National Convention, Committee on Platform and Resolutions, Chicago, IL, Aug. 11, 1956, KPP.

3 Clayborne Carson, *In Struggle: SNCC and the Black Awakening of the 1960s* (Harvard University Press, 1981), 25–26, 66–70, 133, 304–5; Barbara Ransby, *Ella Baker and the Black Freedom Movement: A Radical Democratic Vision* (University of North Carolina Press, 2003), 173; Southern Christian Leadership Conference, Inc., control no. 0A01668, Georgia Corporations Division, Office of the Georgia Secretary of State; John Lewis, *Walking with the Wind: A Memoir of the Movement* (Simon & Schuster, 1998), 291 (decision making by consensus), 296 ("more structure").

4 Lewis, *Walking with the Wind,* 292; Robert Charles Clark, *Corporate Law* (Little, Brown, 1986), 22.

5 Lewis Garnett Jordan, *Negro Baptist History, U.S.A.* (Sunday School Publishing Board, N. B. C., 1930), 122–25; interview of Peter Dave, transcript, 36–37, BTV; interview of Alexander McAlister Rivera Jr., transcript, 11, BTV.

6 Richard Kluger, *Simple Justice: The History of Brown v. Board of Education and Black America's Struggle for Equality* (1975; Vintage, 2004), 23; Theodore Rosengarten, *All God's Dangers: The Life of Nate Shaw* (1974; University of Chicago Press, 2000), 156; Neil R. McMillen, *The Citizens' Council: Organized Resistance to the Second Reconstruction, 1954–64* (1971; University of Illinois Press, 1994), 32. On CCIA's unincorporated status, see Civil Rights—1959, Hearings Before the Subcommittee on Constitutional Rights, Senate Committee on the Judiciary, 86th Cong., 1st Sess., pt. 1, vol. 3 (1959), 526–29. On the drawbacks of unincorporated co-op structure, see "Report of Part of the Committee on Classification and Terminology," Business Lawyer (ABA) 5 (Nov. 1949), 74–77; Code of Laws of South Carolina, 1952, Annotated (Michie Co., 1960), §10-215.

7 Carter G. Woodson, "The Negro in Our History," CD, June 2, 1923, 14; Woodson, "The Negro in New York," *Negro History Bulletin,* vol. 5 (Nov. 1941), 28–34.

8 Greta De Jong, *You Can't Eat Freedom: Southerners and Social Justice after the Civil Rights Movement* (University of North Carolina Press, 2016), 62–63. For a suggestive example of these conversations, see Elaine DeLott Baker, "The Struggle Was the Flame," 411–12, in *Hands on the Freedom Plow: Personal Accounts by Women in SNCC,* ed. Faith S. Holsaert et al. (University of Illinois Press, 2010), 411–12.

9 Articles of Association of North Bolivar County Farm Cooperative (A.A.L.), Book 168, 35–38; De Jong, *You Can't Eat Freedom,* 92; New York Department of State, Division of Corporations, DOS ID 197985; William Sturkey, "'Crafts of Freedom': The Poor People's Corporation and Working-Class African American Women's Activism for Black Power," *Journal of Mississippi History* 74, no. 1 (Spring 2012), 25–60. See also Minion K. C. Morrison, *Aaron Henry of Mississippi: Inside Agitator* (University of Arkansas Press, 2015), 174–88.

10 De Jong, *You Can't Eat Freedom,* 94; Alabama Secretary of State, Business Entity Records, Entity ID Number 000-797-811 (Southwest Alabama Farmers Co-operative); Crystal R. Sanders, *A Chance for Change: Head Start and Mississippi's Black Freedom Struggle* (University of North Carolina Press, 2016), 44; Examination of the War on Poverty, Hearings before the Subcommittee on Employment, Manpower,

and Poverty of the Committee on Labor and Public Welfare, United States Senate, 90th Cong., 1st sess., pt. 2, Jackson, MS (Government Printing Office, 1967), Appendix II, 754 (describing CDGM's somewhat complex corporate structure); Sanders, *Chance for Change,* 70 (Tougaloo); Charter of Incorporation of Freedom City Development Fund, Inc., Aug. 20, 1970, Book 183, 47, Business Services, Mississippi Secretary of State (Freedom City); Charter of Incorporation of Freedom Farms Corporation, Incorporated, May 13, 1970, Book 182, 334, Business Services, Mississippi Secretary of State; Monica M. White, *Freedom Farmers: Agricultural Resistance and the Black Freedom Movement* (University of North Carolina Press, 2018), 73–80 (Freedom Farms); Robyn C. Spencer, *The Revolution Has Come: Black Power, Gender, and the Black Panther Party in Oakland* (Duke University Press, 2016), 119–20, 130–31 (Black Panthers' incorporation); Donna Jean Murch, *Living for the City: Migration, Education, and the Rise of the Black Panther Party in Oakland, California* (University of North Carolina Press, 2010), 173–83 (Panther-incorporated initiatives); *The Black Panther Party: Service to the People Programs,* ed. David Hilliard (University of New Mexico Press, 2008), 61; "Free Shoe Program," *The CoEvolution Quarterly* (Fall 1974), 43 ("on becoming a nonprofit"); Tom Adam Davies, "Black Power in Action: The Bedford-Stuyvesant Restoration Corporation, Robert F. Kennedy, and the Politics of the Urban Crisis," JAH 100, no. 3 (2013), 736–60 (Bed-Stuy Renewal Corp.); Thomas J. Ward Jr. and H. Jack Geiger, *Out in the Rural: A Mississippi Health Center and Its War on Poverty* (Oxford University Press, 2017), 10–36; Charter of Incorporation of the International Order of Twelve, of Knights and Daughters of Tabor in Mississippi, Feb. 24, 1903, Business Services, Mississippi Secretary of State (Tufts-Delta Health Center).

11 Randall Kennedy, "Martin Luther King's Constitution: A Legal History of the Montgomery Bus Boycott," YLJ 98, no. 6 (1989), 1029–31, 1046–54; Mark V. Tushnet, *Making Civil Rights Law: Thurgood Marshall and the Supreme Court, 1936–1961* (Oxford University Press, 1994), 310–11; Derrick A. Bell Jr., "Serving Two Masters: Integration Ideals and Client Interests in School Desegregation Litigation," YLJ 85, no. 4 (1976), 494; *NAACP v. Button,* 371 U.S. 415 (1963).

12 Tushnet, *Making Civil Rights Law,* 283–300; *New York Times v. Sullivan,* 376 U.S. 254 (1964); Taylor Branch, *Parting the Waters: America in the King Years, 1954–63* (Simon and Schuster, 1988), 579–80.

13 Kennedy, "Martin Luther King's Constitution," 1042–43; *King v. Lewis,* 188 Ga. 594 (1939); Interview of Peter Dave, transcript, 37, BTV.

14 On members' assumptions, see Risa L. Goluboff, *The Lost Promise of Civil Rights* (Harvard University Press, 2007), 192; Mrs. Lester Pleasant to NAACP, Dec. 11, 1943, NAACP Papers, Legal File, Labor, "O," 1945–47, part 13C, reel 7; [E. Frederick Morrow], speech at 37th annual conference of NAACP, Cincinnati, OH, June 1946, 8, NAACP Papers, pt. 1, reel 11; "Under the Lash . . . ," CD, Dec. 13, 1941, 13; Kluger, *Simple Justice,* 395. On resentment of farm co-ops, see Herbert Black, *People and Plows Against Hunger: Self-Help Experiment in a Rural Community*

(Marlborough House, 1975), 39; E. L. Anderson to Jackson, Mar. 13, 1962, Jackson Papers, CHM; James Forman, *The Making of Black Revolutionaries* (Macmillan, 1972), 139–40.

15 Clotilde Ferguson to Board of Directors, Oct. 28, 1938; affidavit of Caroline Bembry, Oct. 28, 1938, both in "Clotilde Ferguson," STMA; Andrew M. Manis, *A Fire You Can't Put Out: The Civil Rights Life of Birmingham's Reverend Fred Shuttlesworth* (University of Alabama Press, 2010), 224; Carson, *In Struggle,* 147–48; Davies, "Black Power in Action," 746–48.

16 Elsie James to Armstrong Board, July 5, 1939; typewritten notes of meeting, ca. 1939, both in "Clotilde Ferguson," STMA (italics added). On white associations' resistance to scrutiny, see Kent Greenawalt, "Hands Off! Civil Court Involvement in Conflicts over Religious Property," CLR 98, no. 8 (1998), 1843–1907; Douglas Laycock, "Towards a General Theory of the Religion Clause: The Case of Church Labor Relations and the Right to Church Autonomy," CLR 81 (November (1981), 1373–78.

17 Vernita D. Wimbush to Bunton, July 27, 1966, f 7, b 11, Bunton Papers, Schomburg; Business Entity Detail for Christian Methodist Episcopal Church, no. 246599, Office of Secretary of State, Tennessee.

18 Ula Yvette Taylor, *The Promise of Patriarchy: Women and the Nation of Islam* (University of North Carolina Press, 2017), 76.

19 Barbara Dianne Savage, *Your Spirits Walk Beside Us: The Politics of Black Religion* (Harvard University Press, 2008), 56; Benjamin Elijah Mays and Joseph William Nicholson, *The Negro's Church* (Institute of Social and Religious Research, 1933), 100–101; St. Clair Drake and Horace R. Cayton, *Black Metropolis: A Study of Negro Life in a Northern City* (Harcourt, Brace, 1945), 612; Manning Marable, *Malcolm X: A Life of Reinvention* (Viking, 2011), 102, 75–79; Taylor, *Promise of Patriarchy,* 89, 91–92, 113–17. The possession and use of contraceptives was held to be a constitutional right in *Griswold v. Connecticut,* 381 U.S. 479 (1965). That right is now under attack. *Dobbs v. Jackson Women's Health Organization,* 142 S.Ct. 2228, 2301 (2022) (Thomas, J., concurring).

20 Interview of Ella Baker by Eugene Walker, Sept. 4, 1974, 53, SOHP (pretty ornaments); Savage, *Your Spirits Walk Beside Us,* 56; Cheryl Townsend Gilkes, " 'Together and in Harness': Women's Traditions in the Sanctified Church," *Signs* 10 (Summer 1985), 690–95; Mays and Nicholson, *Negro's Church,* 100–101; Drake and Cayton, *Black Metropolis,* 612. For the "co-signe[d]" quotations, see Margaret Lewis, "Along the Kings Highway," *Afro,* Dec. 19, 1942, 15. *The Encyclopaedia of the African Methodist Episcopal Church,* comp. Richard R. Wright (Book Concern of the AME Church, 1947), 362; Charles S. Spivey, *A Tribute to the Negro Preacher* (Wilberforce, 1942), 163–64, 171–72; V. M. Townsend, *Fifty-Four Years of African Methodism: Reflections of a Presiding Elder on the Law and Doctrine of the African Methodist Episcopal Church* (Exposition Press, 1953), 37.

21 *Providence Baptist v. Superior Court,* 40 Cal. 2d 55 (1952) (emoluments); *Bouldin v.*

Alexander, 82 U.S. 131, 140 (1872) ("the organization"); Council minutes, June 26, 1867, Record in *Alexander v. Bouldin,* case 1054, EDC ("rush for the Books"); www.crmvet.org/docs/parksmin.htm (Parks as secretary); transcript, Oct. 3, 1968, *Baugh v. Thomas,* docket C-1938-67, New Jersey Superior Court, Appellate Division, Essex County, vol. 4117 (1969–1970), NJLL; affidavit of Alexander Reaves, March 14, 1968, *Baugh v. Thomas,* Supreme Court Briefs (reel SM-48), case A-47-69, NJSA. On membership packing, see *Walker Memorial Baptist Church v. Saunders,* 285 N.Y. 462 (1941); *Travers v. Abbey,* 104 Tenn. 665 (1900). On women keeping church books, see "Annual Service of the Deacons Board," Mar. 25, 1951, First Baptist Church of South Orange, NJ (in author's possession); Penningroth interview of Adunni Slackman Anderson, Oct. 9, 2020 ("knew everything," cousin to Baugh); *Providence Baptist,* at 59; Mays and Nicholson, *Negro's Church,* 104, 190–91, 281; Anthea D. Butler, *Women in the Church of God in Christ: Making a Sanctified World* (University of North Carolina Press, 2007), 159; Record in *Rakestraw v. McCluskey,* f 6331, 01737, GSA; affidavit of Catherine Bell, July 1, 1958, *Olivet v. Jackson,* 57C 9490, CCA. A hierarchical denomination would "pack" the conference. See also *Sims v. Greene,* 76 F. Supp. 669, 675 (1947). Pastor Edgar Thomas had moved to expel another member, for worshiping too demonstratively. Unlike Baugh, she could not afford a lawyer. Standing in the choir one Sunday, frustrated by her lack of recourse, she took off her shoe and threw it at Thomas. Penningroth interview of Adunni Slackman Anderson, May 1, 2023.

22 Townsend, *Fifty-Four Years of African Methodism,* 69; Record in *Moorman v. Goodman* (1960), vol. 1382, 5–6, 9–10, New Jersey Superior Court, Appellate Division, NJLL; "'Strong Man' of A.M.E. Church Confident on Eve of Trial!," PC, July 27, 1957; Reverdy C. Ransom, *Preface to History of A.M.E. Church* (A.M.E. Sunday School Union, 1950), 199–200; Sadie T. M. Alexander to My Dear Bishop Baber, Sept. 25, 1960, Union AME, b 34, STMA; *Watson v. Jones,* 80 U.S. at 728; Benjamin Mays, "Reflections on the National Baptist Convention," PC, Oct. 5, 1957.

23 "Rev. Jackson Supported by 1,500 Olivet Members," *Afro,* Dec. 11, 1954, 3; Complaint, June 28, 1957, *Olivet v. Jackson,* 57C 9490 (Clerk of the Circuit Court Archives); Benjamin Michel telephone interview by Penningroth, Sept. 11, 2018; Petition for Certification, July 16, 1969, *Baugh v. Thomas,* Supreme Court Briefs.

24 *Jones v. State,* 44 N.W. 658, 659 (1890) (white church) ("valuable privilege"); *Bentle v. Ulay,* 175 Ind. 759 (1911) (white church) ("indirectly"); *Everett v. First Baptist,* 6 N.J. Misc. 640 (1928) (white church) ("involved"); Sydney R. Wrightington, *The Law of Unincorporated Associations and Similar Relations* (Little, Brown, 1916), 210 (civil right of property).

25 Zechariah Chafee Jr., "The Internal Affairs of Associations Not for Profit," HLR 43, no. 7 (1930), 997–99; Roscoe Pound, "Equitable Relief against Defamation and Injuries to Personality," HLR 29 (1916), 677–78. Though their footnotes don't disclose it, these passages cited Black church and lodge cases. Samuel D. Warren and Louis D. Brandeis, "The Right to Privacy," HLR 4, no. 5 (1890), 193–220;

Morton J. Horwitz, *The Transformation of American Law, 1870–1960: The Crisis of Legal Orthodoxy* (Oxford University Press, 1992), 145, 151 ("propertizing"); "Protection of Membership in Voluntary Associations," YLJ 37 (1928), 377 (citing *U.S. v. First Colored Baptist*, 13 F.2d 296 (App. D.C. 1926)); Pound, "Liberty of Contract," 479; Pound, "Equitable Relief against Defamation and Injuries to Personality," 681; *Jones v. State*, 44 N.W. 658 (1890), 659 ("valuable privilege," white church); *Everett v. First Baptist Church of Sussex*, 6 N.J. Misc. 640 (1928) ("involved," white church); *Bentle v. Ulay*, 175 Ind. 759 (1911) ("indirectly," white church, dictum); Chafee, "Internal Affairs," 999–1007.

26 "Rev. Jackson Supported by 1,500 Olivet Members," *Afro*, Dec. 11, 1954, 3; Complaint, June 28, 1957, *Olivet v. Jackson*, 57C 9490, CCA; Michel interview by Penningroth; Petition for Certification, July 16, 1969, *Baugh v. Thomas*, Supreme Court Briefs; *Baugh v. Thomas*, 56 N.J. 203, 208 (1970).

27 For material that reflects an expansive view of a court's power to protect members' right of membership, see *Gray v. Christian Society*, 137 Mass. 329 (1884) ("common justice," white church); *David v. Carter*, 222 S.W.2d 900 (1949) (white church); and "Civil Rights of a Church Member Who Has Been Deprived of Membership," *University of Pennsylvania Law Review and American Law Register* 71 (Jan. 1923), 161–65. For material that reflects a narrow view of a court's power to protect member's right of membership, see *Taylor v. Jackson*, 50 App. DC 381 (1921); *Clapp v. Krug*, 232 Ky. 303 (1929) (white church); *In re Galilee Baptist*, 279 Ala. 393 (1966); and Laycock, "Towards a General Theory of the Religion Clauses," 1403. For critics' warning, see Abstract of Record, 6, in *Olivet Baptist Church v. Joseph H. Jackson* (1960), ILSA.

28 "Baptists in Wrangle Over Convention Issue," CD, Aug. 22, 1931; Wallace Best, "'The Right Achieved and the Wrong Way Conquered': J. H. Jackson, Martin Luther King Jr., and the Conflict over Civil Rights," *Religion and American Culture* 16, no. 2 (2006), 201–2; "Baptists Curb Top Officers; Re-Elect Jemison for Final Term," CD, Sept. 20, 1952; Sherman Roosevelt Tribble, "Images of a Preacher: A Study of the Reverend Joseph Harrison Jackson, former president of the National Baptist Convention, U.S.A., Inc.," PhD diss., Northwestern University, 1990, 104–7; "Sue Jackson Over Baptist Election," CD, Nov. 30, 1957; "Baptists in Convention, Name Two," *Afro*, Sept. 17, 1960; "Baptists End Six-Day Chicago Meeting," CD, Sept. 15, 1958. William E. Montgomery, *Under Their Own Vine and Fig Tree: The African-American Church in the South, 1865–1900* (Louisiana State University Press, 1993), 335. Leaders of other denominations also exploited spectacle and legal technicalities to cling to power. See Marie W. Dallam, *Daddy Grace: A Celebrity Preacher and His House of Prayer* (New York University Press, 2007), 148; "Ira T. Bryant Loses Big Fight," PC, Jan. 13, 1940.

29 Best, "'Right Achieved,'" 195–98, 201–4; "Rev. J. H. Jackson, Baptist Chief, Sued," CD, Nov. 27, 1954, 1; J[oseph] H[arrison] Jackson, *Unholy Shadows and Freedom's Holy Light* (Nashville, 1967), ix, 124–26; Charles H. King Jr., *Fire in My*

Bones (Grand Rapids, 1983), 79–80. *National Baptist Convention U.S. of America, Inc. v. Taylor,* 402 Pa. 501, 503 (1961); Branch, *Parting the Waters,* 500–507; Tribble, "Images of a Preacher," 115–16.

30 Jackson, *Story of Christian Activism,* 432, xii–xiii; Bell, "Epistolary," 55; Jackson, *Unholy Shadows,* 167, vii–viii, 116–17.

31 Best, "'Right Achieved,'" 199; Tribble, "Images of a Preacher," 75–81; Wright, *Encyclopaedia,* 330–35, 397–400; M. W. Williams and George W. Watkins, *Who's Who among North Carolina Negro Baptists* [. . .] (n.p., 1940), 113, 124; Jackson, *Story of Christian Activism,* 227, 431, 396, 465–73. On ministerial authority in Baptist churches, see Randal Maurice Jelks, *Benjamin Elijah Mays, Schoolmaster of the Movement: A Biography* (University of North Carolina Press, 2012), 206–11.

32 Jackson, *Unholy Shadows and Freedom's Holy Light,* 69; Tribble, "Images of a Preacher," 26–28; 54/169 cases (31%) James Storum, "Building Associations," and "From the Field," both in *A.M.E. Church Review* (1891), 146–51, 334 ("antidote," "accumulating"); *Emancipation Oration! Delivered by Rev. E. K. Love, D.D. At the Emancipation Celebration, at Augusta, Georgia, January 1st, 1891,* 9, Daniel Murray Pamphlet Collection, Library of Congress ("buy land").

33 "Mortgage Burning and Laying of Cornerstone at the Hamlett Temple Christian Methodist Episcopal Church," Nov. 23, 1975, f 17, b 11, Bunton Papers, Schomburg. See also "'In Memoriam' Mary McCleod Bethune," 61, program of Women's International Convention Church of God in Christ (D. J. Young Publishing, 1956), http://digitallibrary.usc.edu/cdm/compoundobject/collection/p15799coll14/id/248746/rec/1; Kevin Yancy and Jerome Metcalfe, "Sign Me Up," in *Celebration Series: For Solo, Choir, Keyboard, and Guitar* (Chicago, 1979); Calvin K. Stalnaker, "The Christian's Obligation," "Stephen C. (Dynamo) Campbell, "Hope," Edward V. Hill, "Go Ye," all in *National Baptist Pulpit* (1969/70), 25, 69–70, 141–42; *Holcomb v. Willis,* CirCtLaw, folder 618, Cumberland Co., VA; Martin Luther King Jr., "I Have a Dream" (1963) and "A Testament of Hope" (1968), both in *A Testament of Hope: The Essential Writings of Martin Luther King, Jr.,* ed. James Melvin Washington (Harper & Row, 1986), 217, 313–28.

34 Jackson, *Story of Christian Activism,* 568–69; "I Will Not Shout," *National Baptist Voice,* 32 (May 1954), 26. On Black property owners' faith in private law, see N. D. B. Connolly, *A World More Concrete: Real Estate and the Remaking of Jim Crow South Florida* (University of Chicago Press, 2014); Kenneth W. Mack, "Rethinking Civil Rights Lawyering and Politics in the Era before Brown," YLJ 115, no. 2 (2005), 303; James R. Ralph Jr., *Northern Protest: Martin Luther King, Jr., Chicago, and the Civil Rights Movement* (Harvard University Press, 1993), 77–78; "It Pays to Take Them to Court," PC, June 27, 1959; Ralph David Abernathy, *And the Walls Came Tumbling Down: An Autobiography* (New York, 1989), 5–6; Russell Rickford, "'We Can't Grow Food on All This Concrete': The Land Question, Agrarianism, and Black Nationalist Thought in the Late 1960s and 1970s,"JAH, 103 (March 2017), 956–80.

35 Best, "'Right Achieved,'" 198.

36 Branch, *Parting the Waters,* 104, 109–10, 114–17; Martin Luther King Jr., "Recommendations to the Dexter Avenue Baptist Church for the Fiscal Year 1954–1955," in *The Papers of Martin Luther King, Jr.,* vol. 2: *Rediscovering Precious Values, July 1951–November 1955,* ed. Clayborne Carson et al. (University of California Press, 1992), 287–94.

37 Branch, *Parting the Waters,* 5–6, 133, 175; Houston Bryan Roberson, *Fighting the Good Fight: The Story of the Dexter Avenue King Memorial Baptist Church, 1865–1977* (Routledge, 2005), 63, 78.

38 Zelia S. Evans ed., *Dexter Avenue Baptist Church, 1877–1977* (Dexter Avenue Baptist Church, 1978), 204; Martin Luther King Jr., "Guidelines for a Constructive Church," June 5, 1966, *Speeches by Martin Luther King: The Ultimate Collection* (audio CD; BN Publishing, 2015). Emphasis in original.

39 Marable, *Malcolm X,* 242–44, 274–79, 337.

40 "Malcolm X Cries Foul; Muslims Try To Evict Him," *Atlanta Daily World,* June 13, 1964, 7; "'My Next Move—' Malcolm X: An Exclusive Interview," NYAN, May 30, 1964, 1; Marable, *Malcolm X,* 335–37. Les Payne and Tamara Payne, *The Dead Are Arising: The Life of Malcolm X* (Liveright, 2020), 436, 450-51.

41 On the Nation's conflicting stance toward the use of civil rights rhetoric and litigation, see Marable, *Malcolm X,* 153–54, 208–10, 252–58.

42 James Alan McPherson, "'In My Father's House There Are Many Mansions—and I'm Going to Get Me Some of Them Too': The Story of the Contract Buyers League," *Atlantic Monthly* 229 (Apr. 1972), 66 (biblical confrontation); Jeffrey Michael Fitzgerald, "The Contract Buyers' League: A Case Study of Interaction between a Social Movement and the Legal System," PhD diss., Northwestern University, 1972, 128–32 ("solid rock"); "An Oral History with Hartman Turnbow," Aug. 1967, transcript of an oral history conducted by Sue Sojourner, Mississippi Oral History Program, University of Southern Mississippi, 20 ("take the church away"); Deanna M. Gillespie, "'First-Class' Citizenship Education in the Mississippi Delta, 1961–1965," JSH, 80 (Feb. 2014), 122 ("put more money"); Vernita D. Wimbush to Bunton, July 27, 1966, f 7, b 11, Bunton Papers, Schomburg.

43 Kenneth W. Mack, *Representing the Race: The Creation of the Civil Rights Lawyer* (Harvard University Press, 2012), 38–60, 111–12, 136–50. On the Black lawyers' professional lives, see Tomiko Brown-Nagin, *Courage to Dissent: Atlanta and the Long History of the Civil Rights Movement* (Oxford University Press, 2011), 25–29. On the "mythological clarity" of the Birmingham church bombing, see Branch, *Parting the Waters,* 892. "Civil Rights Movement Sites: Dexter Avenue King Memorial Baptist Church, Montgomery," *UNESCO World Heritage Centre,* https://whc.unesco.org/en/tentativelists/5241/; C. Eric Lincoln and Lawrence H. Mamiya, *The Black Church in the African American Experience* (Duke University Press, 1990), 289–308; Gilkes, "'Together and in Harness.'"

CHAPTER 13: THE NEW PROPERTY

1 James N. Gregory, *The Southern Diaspora: How the Great Migrations of Black and White Southerners Transformed America* (University of North Carolina Press, 2005), 330, Table A.1.

2 Emergency Land Fund, "Legal Documents Preparation: A Proposal for Grant Assistance" (1975), quoted in Alec Fazackerley Hickmott, "Black Land, Black Capital: Rural Development in the Shadows of the Sunbelt South, 1969–1976," *Journal of African American History* 101, no. 4 (2016), 521; Leo McGee and Robert Boone, *A Study of Rural Landownership, Control Problems and Attitudes of Blacks toward Rural Land* (Tennessee State University, 1976), esp. 126–27; Roy Reed, "Blacks in South Struggle to Keep the Little Land They Have Left," NYT, Dec. 7, 1972, 39, 53; The Emergency Land Fund, "The Impact of Heir Property on Black Rural Land Tenure in the Southeastern Region of the United States," Report Submitted to U.S. Department of Agriculture, Farmers Home Administration (1980), https://hdl.handle.net/2027/coo.31924067935720, 115, 121, 289–91, 467; Anthony Griggs, "How Blacks Lost 9,000,000 Acres of Land," *Ebony,* Oct. 1, 1974, 97, 100.

3 On "passing," see Nella Larsen, *Passing* (Knopf, 1929); Daniel J. Sharfstein, "The Secret History of Race in the United States," 112 YLJ 1473, 1476, 1490 (2003); Cheryl I. Harris, "Whiteness as Property," HLR 106, no. 8 (1993), 1710–13. For a fuller discussion of legal professionals' handling of race, see Dylan C. Penningroth, "Race in Contract Law," PLR 170, no. 5 (2022), 1199–301.

4 Interview of Thomas Holcomb (1976); Penningroth interview of Osborne Reaves, Mar. 25, 2016; 1950 Census; Penningroth interview of Osborne Reaves and Penelope Baskerville, July 5, 2003.

5 On Black homeowners' associations, see Thomas J. Sugrue, *The Origins of the Urban Crisis: Race and Inequality in Postwar Detroit* (Princeton University Press, 1996), 188–94, 204–207; Will Cooley, *Moving Up, Moving Out: The Rise of the Black Middle Class in Chicago* (Northern Illinois University Press, 2018), 72, 84–90; N. D. B. Connolly, *A World More Concrete: Real Estate and the Remaking of Jim Crow South Florida* (University of Chicago Press, 2014), 241–45; STMA to Rev. L. Marshall Watts, Apr. 17, 1974, Union AME, STMA. On Black attitudes toward city planners, see St. Clair Drake and Horace R. Cayton, *Black Metropolis: A Study of Negro Life in a Northern City* (Harcourt, Brace, 1945), 205–6; Wendell E. Pritchett, "Where Shall We Live? Class and the Limitations of Fair Housing Law," *Urban Lawyer* 35, no. 3 (2003), 424; Tomiko Brown-Nagin, *Courage to Dissent: Atlanta and the Long History of the Civil Rights Movement* (Oxford University Press, 2011), 63–64; "'There Is No Compromise': Total Freedom or Total Oppression," *Black World/Negro Digest* 12, no. 12 (1963), 25–31 (Baldwin interview).

6 W. Edward Orser, "Secondhand Suburbs: Black Pioneers in Baltimore's Edmondson Village, 1955–1980," *Journal of Urban History* 16, no. 3 (1990), 245 ("When you're black"). See also Brown-Nagin, *Courage to Dissent,* 420–21; Richard K.

Kerckhoff, "A Study of Racially Changing Neighborhoods," *Merrill-Palmer Quarterly* 4, no. 1 (1957), 34 ("the kind of people who"). On whites' invocation of "neighborhood character," see Supriya Yelimeli, "Landmarking Fails for 130-Year-Old Berkeley House in Passionate Debate over Housing, History," *Berkeleyside,* Aug. 7, 2020; Conor Dougherty, "The Great American Single-Family Home Problem," *New York Times Magazine,* Dec. 1, 2017. On Blacks' invocation of it, see Cooley, *Moving Up,* 72.

7 Pritchett, "Where Shall We Live?," 464; Mara S. Sidney, "Images of Race, Class, and Markets: Rethinking the Origin of U.S. Fair Housing Policy," *Journal of Policy History* 13, no. 2 (2001), 181–214; Public Law 90-284, 82 Stat. 73, codified at 42 U.S.C.A. §§3601–19, 3631.

8 Eva Baxter to Nicholas, ca. 1960, and Nicholas to Eva Baxter, Oct. 23, 1961, in f "Baxter, Eva," DNWG; Prudential Insurance Co. to Mrs. Carey E. Brown, Oct. 1, 1947; Gosnell to Joseph Rosenthal, Esq., Oct. 21, 1947, both in f "Brown, Carrie E. v. Prudential Ins. Co. of America," DNWG; A. Pearce King, Claim Manager, to Green Harris, Oct. 23, 1946, in f "Rev. Green Harris," DNWG; Nicholas to William A. Duvall Scaffolding Co., June 29, 1948, in f "Rev. Green Harris," DNWG. On the role of mid-level state and federal bureaucrats in promulgating the idea of a right to welfare, see Karen M. Tani, *States of Dependency: Welfare, Rights, and American Governance, 1935–1972* (Cambridge University Press, 2016).

9 Certified copy dated May 18, 1960, of certificate of marriage dated Apr. 28, 1915; Bureau of the Census to Annie Louise Holcomb, Oct. 4, 1960; delayed certificate of birth, Jan. 3, 1961; Certificate of Social Insurance Award, Old Age Benefit, Apr. 29, 1964, Department of Health, Education, and Welfare, document in author's possession; "Insurance Man Blues," Sonny Boy Williamson: *Complete Recorded Works,* vol. 2, 1938–1939, Document Records, DOCD-5056.

10 Lawrence S. Root, "Employee Benefits and Social Welfare: Complement and Conflict," *Annals of the American Academy of Political and Social Science* 479 (1985), 109. Fred K. Foulkes and Henry M. Morgan, "Organizing and Staffing the Personnel Function," *Harvard Business Review,* May-June (1977), 148.

11 Charles F. Russ, Jr., "Should the Personnel Department Be Abolished?" *Personnel Journal* (June 1985), 80 ("personnel gal"); Beth W. Ghiloni, "The Velvet Ghetto: Women, Power, and the Corporation," in *Power Elites and Organizations,* ed. G. William Domhoff and Thomas R. Dye (Sage, 1987), 21–36; Sharon M. Collins, "Black Mobility in White Corporations: Up the Corporate Ladder but out on a Limb," *Social Problems* 44, no. 1 (1997), 64 ("mainstream"); Russ, "Should the Personnel Department Be Abolished?," 81 ("almighty"). On the feminization of HR, see Patricia A. Roos and Joan E. Manley, "Staffing Personnel: Feminization and Change in Human Resource Management," *Sociological Focus* 29, no. 3 (1996), 245–61; Barbara Reskin and Patricia A. Roos, *Job Queues, Gender Queues* (Temple University Press, 1990), 169. Women held 45 percent of the manager/specialist jobs and 88 percent of the clerk/assistant jobs. Occupations generated from IPUMS by Derek Burk; population calculated on IPUMS 5 percent 1980 sample.

On companies hiring Blacks to staff personnel offices, see Jennifer Delton, "Before the EEOC: How Management Integrated the Workplace," *Business History Review* 81, no. 2 (2007), 285, 90.

12 Susan Hessemer, "Baskerville and Flewelling: There's a Benefit To Knowing These Two Personnel Employees," *Rider [College] Communiqué*, Mar. 26, 1990, 3. In the welfare bureaucracy, this would roughly correspond to the type Celeste Watkins-Hayes calls "social workers." Celeste Watkins-Hayes, *The New Welfare Bureaucrats: Entanglements of Race, Class, and Policy Reform* (University of Chicago Press, 2009), 54–60.

13 Testimony of Mary Woodson, 59, Record in *Hannah v. Woodson*, LVRC; testimony of Felix Brown, in *Brown v. McWilliams*, case 1451, CirCtCh, Coahoma Co., Clarksdale, MS.

14 Charles A. Reich, "The New Property," YLJ 73, no. 5 (1964), 733–87.

15 Johnnie Tillmon, "Welfare Is a Women's Issue," *Ms.* (Spring 1972), 111–16; Reich, "New Property," 751–71. Reich focused on what he called "government largess" and did not discuss employment benefits offered by private organizations.

16 Tani, *States of Dependency*, 223, 256–57, 260–69; Tillmon, "Welfare Is a Women's Issue," 111–16; Chris Myers Asch, *The Senator and the Sharecropper: The Freedom Struggles of James O. Eastland and Fannie Lou Hamer* (University of North Carolina Press, 2008), 227; Clarence Thomas, *My Grandfather's Son: A Memoir* (Harper, 2007), 73.

17 Marcia Chatelain, *Franchise: The Golden Arches in Black America* (Liveright, 2021), 13–14, 204–209, 295n65; Brian Callaci, "Control Without Responsibility: The Legal Creation of Franchising, 1960–1980," *Enterprise & Society* 22, no. 1 (2021), 161; C. M. Griffis, Inc., Entity No. 856230, Calif. Secretary of State; Articles of Incorporation, Kinsman Development Corp., B665-454, Feb. 26, 1970, www.businesssearch.ohiosos.gov.

18 Callaci, "Control Without Responsibility," 169, 161–62; Chatelain, *Franchise*, 157, 162, 190–206, 252–57; Reich, "New Property," 735–42; "Black History Isn't Just a Thing of the Past," *Ebony* (Feb. 1980), 65.

19 Gerald Posner, *Motown: Music, Money, Sex, and Power* (Random House, 2002), 38, 146, 182, 206, 217–20, 234.

20 *Johnson v. Berry*, 228 F.Supp. 2d 1071, 1072–73 (2002); K. J. Greene, "Copynorms, Black Cultural Production, and the Debate over African-American Reparations," *Cardozo Arts & Ent. L.J.* 25, no. 3 (2008), 1199n126; "McCullough Files Suit for $35,000," PC, Aug. 25, 1962; Marie W. Dallam, *Daddy Grace: A Celebrity Preacher and His House of Prayer* (New York University Press, 2007), 170; Taylor Branch, *Parting the Waters: America in the King Years, 1954–63* (Simon and Schuster, 1988), 696; William A. Rutherford to Board of Directors, May 8, 1968, King Center online; Tim Appelo and Stephen Galloway, "Oscars: How 'Selma' Filmmakers Made a Movie About MLK Without Using His Words," *Hollywood Reporter*, Dec. 16, 2014.

21 For example, see Record at 161, *Gilmer v. Brown* (1946), LV. See also Hendrik Hartog, *Someday All This Will Be Yours: A History of Inheritance and Old Age* (Harvard

University Press, 2012); Adrienne Monteith Petty, *Standing Their Ground: Small Farmers in North Carolina since the Civil War* (Oxford University Press, 2013), 180–81; Charles W. Anderson Jr., "The South's Challenge to the Negro Lawyer," *National Bar Journal* 3, no. 1 (1945), 39.

22 Ira Katznelson, *When Affirmative Action Was White: An Untold History of Racial Inequality in Twentieth-Century America* (W. W. Norton, 2005), 42–44, 113–41; Nancy F. Cott, *Public Vows: A History of Marriage and the Nation* (Harvard University Press, 2000), 174–751; Pete Daniel, "The Legal Basis of Agrarian Capitalism: The South since 1933," in *Race and Class in the U.S. South*, ed. Melvyn Stokes and Rick Halpern (Berg, 1994), 79–102. On NAACP declining to help claim New Property, see George Price to Prentice Thomas, Aug. 10, 1943; Thomas to Price, Aug. 27, 1943, both in NAACP Papers, Legal File, Labor, "O," 1945–47 (asking help with workmen's comp denial); Edward R. Dudley to Mrs. Lester Pleasant, Dec. 18, 1943, NAACP Papers, Legal File, Labor, "O," 1945–47 (bus driver's claim to regular route). On other lawyers developing "welfare rights" concept, see Felicia Kornbluh, *The Battle for Welfare Rights: Politics and Poverty in Modern America* (University of Pennsylvania Press, 2007), 66–68.

23 Katznelson, *When Affirmative Action Was White*, 120 (Oliver Brown's GI benefit); Amzie Moore to Maurice McCrackin, Apr. 1, 1963, Correspondence, 1963–1964, Mss 551, b 1, f 5, Wisconsin Historical Society, FSDC. Moore to U.S. Attorney H. M. Ray, Nov. 14, 1963; Moore to Carl and Ann Braden, Nov. 14, 1963, both in Correspondence, 1963–1964, Mss 551, f 5, b 1, FSDC; Amzie Moore to Jim Dombrowski, Oct. 20, 1963, Correspondence, 1963–1964, Mss 551, f 5, b 1, FSDC; Andrew W. Kahrl, "The Power to Destroy: Discriminatory Property Assessments and the Struggle for Tax Justice in Mississippi," *Journal of Southern History* 82, no. 3 (2016), 600.

24 Kahrl, "Power to Destroy," 594; John Dittmer, *Local People: The Struggle for Civil Rights in Mississippi* (University of Illinois Press, 1994), 333–35.

25 Rev. Maurice McCrackin [Operation Freedom] to Amzie Moore, Jan. 13, 1963, FSDC; Barbara Ransby, *Ella Baker and the Black Freedom Movement: A Radical Democratic Vision* (University of North Carolina Press, 2003), 286. Richard R. Hasbrouck to Amzie Moore, Sept. 30, 1964, Correspondence, 1963–1964, Mss 551, f 5, b 1, FSDC ("prevailing"); Ronald Goodman [Chairman, Operation Freedom] to Amzie Moore, Jan. 16, 1964, Correspondence, 1963–1964, Mss 551, f 5, b 1, FSDC; Moore to McCrackin, Apr. 1, 1963, Correspondence, 1963–1964, Mss 551, f 5, b 1, FSDC (sending information about trust deeds, tax payments, and salaries).

26 "Memo: re, A Contract to provide Bail Bonds for Civil Rights Workers," n.d., Misc. COFO and SNCC material, Sally Belfrage Papers, 1962–1966, FSDC; McCrackin to Moore, Jan. 13, 1963. This reliance wasn't new. See Robin D. G. Kelley, *Hammer and Hoe: Alabama Communists During the Great Depression* (University of North Carolina Press, 1990), 52.

27 Andrew Wiese, *Places of Their Own: African American Suburbanization in the Twentieth Century* (University of Chicago Press, 2004), 85, 145–47; Emmett J. Scott, "Additional

Letters of Negro Migrants of 1916–1918," JNH 4, no. 4 (1919), 461; Wiese, *Places of Their Own,* 77–78, 88; Roland L. Freeman, plate 62, *Southern Roads/City Pavements: Photographs of Black Americans* (International Center of Photography, 1981); Thomas J. Sugrue, *The Origins of the Urban Crisis: Race and Inequality in Postwar Detroit* (Princeton University Press, 1996), 39–40; "Mayor launches project: Ghetto farmers get land," CD, Mar. 19, 1975, 21 (thanks to Robert Kutchin for this reference); Edna Lewis, *The Taste of Country Cooking* (Knopf, 1976), 174–75; Verta Mae [Grosvenor], *Vibration Cooking: Or the Travel Notes of a Geechee Girl* (Doubleday, 1970), xiv.

28 [Grosvenor], *Vibration Cooking,* 28. On the religious aspects of Black migrants' sense of themselves as sojourners, see Wallace D. Best, *Passionately Human, No Less Divine: Religion and Culture in Black Chicago, 1915–1952* (Princeton University Press, 2005), 23–24. By 1999, two-thirds of America's Black-owned farmland—more than five million acres—was owned by Black people who did not farm. Thomas W. Mitchell, "Destabilizing the Normalization of Rural Black Land Loss: A Critical Role for Legal Empiricism," *Wisconsin Law Review* 2005, no. 2 (2005), 577; *The Impact of Heir Property on Black Rural Land Tenure in the Southeastern Region of the United States* (Emergency Land Fund, 1980), 62–64; interview of Ella Baker by Casey Hayden and Sue Thrasher, New York, Apr. 19, 1977, G-0008, SOHP.

29 Interview of Mrs. Vance, 1932, FPMS; Arnetha H. Brown to Osborne Reaves, Feb. 9, 1989, in Osborne Reaves's possession; Ransby, *Ella Baker,* 31; interview of Ella Baker by Sue Thrasher and Casey Hayden; Emmett J. Scott, "Additional Letters of Negro Migrants of 1916–1918," JNH 4, no. 4 (1919), 462; James A. Jacobs, "Dexter Avenue King Memorial Baptist Church," Historic American Buildings Survey, http://lcweb2 .loc .gov/pnp/habshaer/al/al1300/al1325/data/al1325data.pdf; Interview of Henry Smith, Aug. 29, 2018, notes ("fellowshipping"); Scott, "Additional Letters of Negro Migrants of 1916–1918," 463. Emphasis added. Interview of Henry Smith, Feb. 21, 2018. For similar accounts of migrant family visiting, see Kimberley Phillips, *Alabamanorth: African-American Migrants, Community, and Working-Class Activism in Cleveland,* 1915–45 (University of Illinois Press, 1999), 137–38, 141; Lewis, *Taste of Country Cooking,* 118, 209.

30 On southern burials and expenses, see interview of Penelope Baskerville, Mar. 30, 2008. See also E. Franklin Frazier, *The Negro Family in the United States* (University of Chicago Press, 1939), 530, 532; [Grosvenor], *Vibration Cooking,* 21; Letter from Annie H. Mosely, Sept. 16, 1961, *Holcomb et al. v. Willis et al.*, f 618, CirCtLaw, Cumberland Co., VA.

31 Lewis, *Taste of Country Cooking,* xiii–xv ("spirit of pride"); [Grosvenor], *Vibration Cooking,* 4; Russell Rickford, "'We Can't Grow Food on All This Concrete': The Land Question, Agrarianism, and Black Nationalist Thought in the Late 1960s and 1970s," JAH 103, no. 4 (2017), 967; J[oseph] H[arrison] Jackson, *A Story of Christian Activism: The History of the National Baptist Convention, U.S.A., Inc.* (Townsend Press, 1980), 568–69; Thomas, *My Grandfather's Son,* 22–26; Addison Gayle Jr., "The Black Aesthetic 10 Years Later," *Black World/Negro Digest* 23, no. 11 (1974), 22–23; Alice Walker, "Lulls," *The Black Scholar* 7, no. 8 (1976), 11.

32 Anthony Griggs, "How Blacks Lost 9,000,000 Acres of Land," *Ebony,* Oct. 1, 1974, 97; Leo McGee and Robert Boone, *A Study of Rural Landownership, Control Problems and Attitudes of Blacks toward Rural Land* (Tennessee State University, 1976), 138; Rickford, "'We Can't Grow Food on All This Concrete,'"967–68; Hickmott, "Black Land," 514.

33 "Impact of Heir Property," 114–26; Eleanor Clift, "Black Land Loss: 6,000,000 Acres and Fading Fast," *Southern Exposure* 2, nos. 2 and 3 (1974), 109; Hickmott, "Black Land," 521; McGee and Boone, "Study of Rural Landownership," 126–27; Roy Reed, "Blacks in South Struggle to Keep the Little Land They Have Left," NYT, Dec. 7, 1972, 39, 53; "Impact of Heir Property" 115, 289–91, 467; Thomas W. Mitchell, Stephen Malpezzi, and Richard K. Green, "Forced Sale Risk: Class, Race, and the Double Discount," *Florida State University Law Review* 37, no. 3 (2010), 617; Lizzie Presser, "The Dispossessed: Inside the Crisis of Black Land Loss," *New Yorker,* July 22, 2019, 28–35 (extensively quoting Mitchell); Ta-Nehisi Coates, "The Case for Reparations," *Atlantic,* June 2014, 54–71.

34 Penningroth interview of Henry Smith, Aug. 9, 2015; Penningroth interview of Henry Smith, Dec. 4, 2016; deposition of Arnetha Brown, Aug. 8, 1961, *Holcomb et al v. Willis.* Smith's conclusion about who paid the taxes seems at least somewhat supported by other evidence. Arnetha Brown To Who It May Concern, Sept. 16, 1961, and J. F. Lipscomb To Who It May Concern, Sept. 16, 1961, both in *Holcomb v. Willis.* Commissioner's Report, Sept. 15, 1961; Supplementary Report of Commissioner, Sept. 18, 1961, both in *Holcomb v. Willis.*

35 Penningroth interview of Henry Smith, Aug. 9, 2015; Penningroth interview of Henry Smith, Dec. 4, 2016.

36 Bill of Complaint, Mar. 5, 1962, *Holcomb v. Holcomb Smith et al.,* file 636, CirCtLaw, Cumberland Co., VA. On the Fergusons' land holdings and the difficulty of proving ethical violation, see Penningroth interview of Henry Smith, Aug. 9, 2015.

37 Bill of Complaint, Nov. 24, 1967, *Mary Maria Holcomb v. Lucille Ferguson et al.,* file 917, CirCtLaw, Cumberland Co., VA. Thomas Holcomb joined the suit as a cross-complainant. Cross-bill, Feb. 10, 1972, *Holcomb v. Ferguson.*

38 Cross-examination by McVey, Record at 46, 51, *Holcomb v. Ferguson;* testimony of Arnetha Brown, Record at 31–32, *Holcomb v. Ferguson.* Until recently, many states permitted cotenants wide latitude to compel a judicial partition. Thomas W. Mitchell, *Historic Partition Law Reform: A Game Changer for Heirs' Property Owners* (U.S. Department of Agriculture Forest Service: 2019). Testimony of Thomas Holcomb, Record at 46, 49–50, *Holcomb v. Ferguson.* Thomas Holcomb said he told Carter to stop specifically because Carter had mishandled the sale of another parcel: "'He ain't paid me for that first land. What do I want him to sell more land for?'"

39 Record at 13–16, 18–19, 21–26, 59, *Holcomb v. Ferguson.*

40 At the July hearing, Judge Dortch asked Tucker and McVey to submit briefs on "the issue of proceeding after being instructed by the client not to." No briefs are

in the file. His decree said only that the complaint wasn't sufficiently supported by the evidence. Decree, Oct. 8, 1974, Record at 49, *Holcomb v. Ferguson.*

41 Abraham Clark Freeman, *Cotenancy and Partition* (Bancroft-Whitney Co., 1886), 719 (citing *Irvin v. Divine,* 7 T.B.Mon. 246 (Ky.App. 1828), holding that judge, not commissioners, must decide whether it was necessary to sell a group of slaves rather than divide them in kind). Migrant population statistic is from Gregory, *Southern Diaspora,* 333, table A3. Thanks to Rabia Belt for this insight. Record at 59, *Holcomb v. Ferguson* ("poor substitute"). Mitchell, "From Reconstruction to Deconstruction," 513–17; Comment, "The Role of the Judicial Sale in Preventing Uneconomical Parcellation of Inherited Land," *University of Chicago Law Review* 23, no. 2 (1956), 343–51.

42 Interview of Shirley Sherrod, transcript, 17, BTV; Penningroth interview of Mrs. Ponder, October 2010; interview of Henry Smith, Dec. 4, 2016.

43 Penningroth interview of Henry Marsh, Dec. 5, 2016; "All U.S. Supreme Justices O.K. Civil Rights Vote Act," CD, Mar. 8, 1966; Frank R. Parker, *Black Votes Count: Political Empowerment in Mississippi after 1965* (University of North Carolina Press, 1990), 99. The case was *Allen v. State Bd. of Elections,* 268 F.Supp. 218 (E.D. Va. 1967).

44 Toni Morrison, "Unspeakable Things Unspoken: The African American Presence in American Literature," *Michigan Quarterly Review* 28, no. 1 (1989), 11–12.

45 Laura Kalman, *Yale Law School and the Sixties: Revolt and Reverberations* (University of North Carolina Press, 2005), 24–28, 111, 119, 175, 181 (2007); *University of Pennsylvania Law School Bulletin* (1971–1973), 68–69; Jeffrey M. Fitzgerald, "The Contract Buyers League and the Courts: A Case Study of Poverty Litigation," LSR 9 (winter 1975), 182–83; Record of the University of North Carolina at Chapel Hill, School of Law (1970), 37–38; Judith Welch Wegner, "The Changing Course of Study: Sesquicentennial Reflections," *North Carolina Law Review* 73 (1995), 734–35; Harvard Law School Catalogue (1967–68), 81–82.

46 Richard Delgado, "The Imperial Scholar: Reflections on a Review of Civil Rights Literature," PLR 132 (1984), 561; Derrick Bell, "The Price and Pain of Racial Perspective," *Stanford Law School Journal* 16, no. 6 (1986), 5; Wegner, "Changing Course of Study," 747.

47 For a fuller discussion, see Dylan C. Penningroth, "Race in Contract Law," PLR 170, no. 5 (2022), 1199–301.

48 *Williams v. Walker-Thomas Furniture Co.,* 350 F.2d 445 (D.C. Cir. 1965). The casebook likened such contracts to "an urban sharecropper system." Lon L. Fuller and Melvin Aron Eisenberg, *Basic Contract Law,* 3rd ed. (West, 1972), 596–605 ("low-income market"). Thanks to Professor Curtis Reitz for recalling the Contracts casebook he used that year and for generously sharing his memories of teaching at Penn Law during the early 1970s. Homer Kripke, *Consumer Credit: Text—Cases—Materials* (West Pub. Co., 1970); Weekly Premium Receipt Book Progressive Life Insurance Company, Industrial Department, in the name of A[nnie] L. Holcomb, insuring life of Penelope Baskerville (approx. 1966) (on file with author).

49 James A. McPherson, "The Black Law Student: A Problem of Fidelities," *Atlantic Monthly,* Apr. 1970, at 94, 96, 100.

50 Robert Browne, "Black Land Loss: The Plight of Black Ownership," *Southern Exposure* 2 (Fall 1974), 115.

51 Myrlie Evers, *For Us, the Living* (Doubleday, 1967), 14; email from Brenda Russell to author, Sept. 24, 2020; Katharine Q. Seelye, "Juanita Abernathy, a Force in the Civil Rights Movement, Dies at 87," NYT, Sept. 13, 2019; Les Payne and Tamara Payne, *The Dead Are Arising: The Life of Malcolm X* (Liveright, 2020), 9, 54–55, 63–68; U.S. Department of Commerce, Bureau of the Census, Fifteenth Census of the United States: 1930: Population Schedule for Alabama, Montgomery County, Pine Level, 2A; Ransby, *Ella Baker,* 14, 31; Ralph David Abernathy, *And the Walls Came Tumbling Down: An Autobiography* (Harper & Row, 1989), 5–7, 21–22, 30–31; Shirley Sherrod interview, transcript, 15, 21, BTV; Interview of Ella Baker by Sue Thrasher and Casey Hayden; interview of Ella Baker by John Britton, Washington, DC, June 19, 1968, https://www.crmvet.org/nars/baker68.htm (accessed Feb. 4, 2023).

52 For activists drawing on rights of everyday use, see Dittmer, *Local People,* 30, 100, 106, 180–81, 188, 190–91. The pattern probably went back earlier. See Kelley, *Hammer and Hoe,* 52. Typed notes of interview of Harry Briggs, Nov. 29, 1971, f 9, b 1, KLUGER; Clayborne Carson, *In Struggle: SNCC and the Black Awakening of the 1960s* (Harvard University Press, 1981), 75, 79; Kahrl, "Power to Destroy," 596–97; interview of Sam Block by Joe Sinsheimer, Dec. 12, 1986, https://www.crmvet.org/nars/js_block_oh-r.pdf (accessed Feb. 4, 2023); Charles M. Payne, *I've Got the Light of Freedom: The Organizing Tradition and the Mississippi Freedom Struggle* (University of California Press, 2007), 128–29, 209; interview of Peter Dave (1994), transcript, 37, BTV; Abernathy, *And the Walls Came Tumbling Down,* 349–50, 353. Clarence Thomas claims his grandfather "routinely put up his property . . . to bail student protesters out of jail." Thomas, *My Grandfather's Son,* 31.

53 Dittmer, *Local People,* 30, 46–48, 253, 280, 358; interview of Billie Flemming, Oct. 22, 1971, f 30, b 2, KLUGER; Typed notes of interview of Harry Briggs, Nov. 29, 1971, f 9, b 1, KLUGER; interview of Rev. Joseph A. DeLaine, f 23, b 2, KLUGER.

54 Payne, *I've Got the Light of Freedom,* 113, 209, 220–21, 279; Dittmer, *Local People,* 188–91.

55 Anne Moody, *Coming of Age in Mississippi* (1968; Dell, 1976), 313; Payne, *I've Got the Light of Freedom,* 255; Dittmer, *Local People,* 191. Ransby [*Ella Baker,* 410n2] modifies this position. See also interview of Ella Baker by Sue Thrasher and Casey Hayden and interview of Ella Baker by John Britton.

56 *The Marcus Garvey and Universal Negro Improvement Association Papers,* vol. 7, ed. Robert A. Hill (University of California Press, 1983), 791; Daniel Patrick Moynihan and Nathan Glazer, *The Negro Family: The Case for National Action* (Office of Policy Planning and Research, U.S. Dept. of Labor (March 1965), preface; Michael Harrington, *The Other America: Poverty in the United States* (Macmillan, 1962), 14–17; *Brown v. Board of Education of Topeka,* 347 U.S. 483, 494, 74 S.Ct. 686 (1954).

57 "An Oral History with Hartman Turnbow," 20 [interview by Sue Lorenzi Sojourner, Aug. 16, 1967], Mississippi Oral History Program, University of Southern Mississippi, https://usm.access.preservica.com/uncategorized/SO_6893f202-4f08-4273-8138-d69aecf450ec; "A [Partial] Transcript of a Recorded Interview with Miss Ella Baker [. . .],"interviewed by John Britton, transcript retyped by Kathy Emery, 1968, *The Civil Rights Documentary Project,* https://www.crmvet.org/nars/baker68.htm; Ella Baker, quoted in *Moving the Mountain: Women Working for Social Change,* ed. Ellen Cantarow (Feminist Press, 1980), 62; Thrasher and Hayden interview of Ella Baker, 4–5, 18–20, 39–41, 57; Britton interview of Baker; Ransby, *Ella Baker,* 36–37; Sherrod interview, transcript, 22, 35, BTV. The family metaphor has long been useful to powerful people. See Dylan C. Penningroth, "The Claims of Slaves and Ex-Slaves to Family and Property: A Transatlantic Comparison," AHR 112, no. 4 (2007), 1039–69. Of course, I don't discount Sherrod's sincerity, but the laborers may have seen things differently.

58 Payne, *I've Got the Light of Freedom,* 216–18, 361. See also James Meredith, *A Mission from God: A Memoir and Challenge for America* (Atria, 2012), 30; Evers-Williams, *For Us, the Living,* 304, 331. On the lynching of Black women, see Crystal Feimster, *Southern Horrors: Women and the Politics of Rape and Lynching* (Harvard University Press, 2011), 235–39.

59 According to one current author, the remedy of "self-help" to a continuing trespass is "surprisingly unexplored by the law." James Charles Smith, *Law of Neighbors,* §3:22, July 2022 update. For analogues relating to straying livestock, see 12 A.L.R. 3d 1103 (1967); *Bruister v. Haney,* 102 So. 2d (1958) (white case); *Seven Day Wholesale Grocery v. Jarvis,* 202 Miss. 446 (1947) (Jarvis was Black); Robert C. Ellickson, "Of Coase and Cattle: Dispute Resolution among Neighbors in Shasta County," SLR 38, no. 3 (1986), 666.

60 *State v. Shack,* in Jesse Dukeminier et al., *Property* (Wolters Kluver, 2014), 106–8; Emily Prifogle, "Rural Social Safety Nets for Migrant Farmworkers in Michigan, 1942–1971," LSI 46, no. 4 (2021), 1022–61; *Cedar Point Nursery v. Hassid,* 141 S.Ct. 2063 (2021).

61 On denim, see Sara Wood, " 'The Thousand and One Little Actions Which Go to Make up Life': Civil Rights Photography and the Everyday," *American Art* 32, no. 3 (2018), 74. Zellner, quoted in Payne, *I've Got the Light of Freedom,* 208, 213–14 ("no shit"); Suarez, quoted in Payne, *I've Got the Light of Freedom,* 176 ("natural ass"). See also interview of Matt Suarez by Tom Dent (1977), quoted in Dittmer, *Local People,* 188; and Anne Moody, *Coming of Age in Mississippi* (1968; Dell, 1976), 331. See also Theodore Rosengarten, *All God's Dangers: The Life of Nate Shaw* (1974; University of Chicago Press, 2000), 3–4.

62 James Forman, *The Making of Black Revolutionaries* (Macmillan, 1972), 422; [Michael Thelwell], "Mississippi's Metaphysical Mystics—A Sect Wrapped Up in a Clique within a Cult (a thumbnail sketch of the New Revolutionary Vanguard)," [November 1964], King—SNCC Position Papers & Reports, undated (Mary E. King papers, 1962–1999, Z: Accessions, M82-445, b 1, f 19), https://content

.wisconsinhistory.org/digital/collection/p15932coll2/id/24623/rec/4. See also Payne, *I've Got the Light of Freedom,* xviii; Carson, *In Struggle,* 155; "The 1964 Civil Rights Law and What It Means to You!," unsigned pamphlet, Civil Rights Movement Archive; Black, *People and Plows,* 145n 3.

63 Penningroth, *Claims of Kinfolk,* 114–16; Anne Fleming, "The Rise and Fall of Unconscionability as the 'Law of the Poor,'" *Georgetown Law Journal* 102, no. 5 (2014), 1412–20; "SNCC: Structure and Leadership," Aug. 1963, www.crmvet.org/docs/sncc63-1.pdf; Congress of Racial Equality: Mississippi Fourth Congressional District, *Freedom Primer No. 3: The Right to Vote and the Congressional Challenge,* 1965, 9, Wisconsin Historical Society, https://cdm15932.contentdm.oclc.org/digital/collection/p15932coll2/id/41536; Ella J. Baker, "Bigger than a Hamburger," *Southern Patriot,* vol. 18 (May 1960); Ransby, *Ella Baker,* 254, 319; Brown-Nagin, *Courage To Dissent,* 249. Of the sampled civil cases for 1952 and 1962, Black plaintiffs lodged 16% (171/1,056), and 23% (77/333) of those in Mississippi.

64 Nancy MacLean, *Freedom Is Not Enough: The Opening of the American Workplace* (Harvard University Press, 2008), 5–6; Jacquelyn Dowd Hall, "The Long Civil Rights Movement and the Political Uses of the Past," JAH 91, no. 4 (2005), 1240. See also Martha Biondi, *To Stand and Fight: The Struggle for Civil Right in Postwar New York* (Harvard University Press, 2003), 15–16; Glenda Gilmore, *Defying Dixie: The Radical Roots of Civil Rights, 1919–1950* (W. W. Norton, 2008), 2, 9; Risa L. Goluboff, *The Lost Promise of Civil Rights* (Harvard University Press, 2007), 269–70; Thomas J. Sugrue, *Sweet Land of Liberty: The Forgotten Struggle for Civil Rights in the North* (Random House, 2008), xvi.

65 Kenneth W. Mack, "Rethinking Civil Rights Lawyering and Politics in the Era before Brown," YLJ 115, no. 2 (2005), 258; Goluboff, *Lost Promise of Civil Rights,* 15, 238–70; Brown-Nagin, *Courage to Dissent*; Penningroth, "Race in Contract Law," 1216–69; E. Allan Farnsworth, "Contracts Scholarship in the Age of the Anthology," *Michigan Law Review* 85 (April-May, 1987), 1409, 1439–40; Grant Gilmore, *The Death of Contract* (1974; Ohio State University Press, 1995), 61–62; Richard Danzig, "*Hadley v. Baxendale:* A Study in the Industrialization of the Law," *Journal of Legal Studies* 4, no. 2 (1975), 275.

66 For two egregious examples of judicial ransacking, see *Dred Scott v. Sandford,* 60 U.S. 393, 403–27 (1857); *New York State Rifle & Pistol Association, Inc. v. Bruen,* 142 S.Ct. 2111, 2125–26, 2174–81 (2022). Kim Forde-Mazrui, "Learning Law through the Lens of Race," 21 *Journal of Law & Policy,* no. 1 (2005), 21; Kimberlé Williams Crenshaw, "Toward a Race-Conscious Pedagogy in Legal Education," *National Black Law Journal* 11 (1988), 2, 9–10; Lani Guinier, "Of Gentlemen and Role Models," *Berkeley Women's Law Journal,* vol. 6 (1990–91), 93–94; Memorandum from Amalee Beattie, Isabel Cortes, Amanda Miller, and Blaine Valencia to Berkeley Law Curriculum Committee & Dean Erwin Chemerinsky (Aug. 17, 2020); Kimberlé Williams Crenshaw, "The First Decade: Critical Reflections, or a Foot in the

Closing Door," *UCLA Law Review* 49, no. 5 (2002), 1353. For a fuller discussion, see Penningroth, "Race in Contract Law," 1201–6.

67 Morrison, "Unspeakable Things Unspoken," 14.

CONCLUSION

1 Robin D. G. Kelley, "'We Are Not What We Seem': Rethinking Black Working-Class Opposition in the Jim Crow South," JAH 80, no. 1 (1993), 103.

2 John Dittmer, *Local People: The Struggle for Civil Rights in Mississippi* (University of Illinois Press, 1994), 1, 71, 75, 127–37, 146–57, 174–92, 205, 219–24, 243, 253, 333, 395–99; Taylor Branch, *Parting the Waters: America in the King Years, 1954–63* (Simon and Schuster, 1988), 512, 548–49, 633; David Halberstam, *The Children* (Random House, 1998), 230–34, 428–29, 487, 502–503; David J. Garrow, *Bearing the Cross: Martin Luther King, Jr., and the Southern Christian Leadership Conference* (Vintage, 1986), 378–96; Gene Roberts, "Mississippi Reduces Police Protection for Marchers," NYT, June 17, 1966, A33. Earlier activists had marched on court-houses, too. See Hasan Kwame Jeffries, *Bloody Lowndes: Civil Rights and Black Power in Alabama's Black Belt* (New York University Press, 2009), 39–55; Robin D. G. Kelley, *Hammer and Hoe: Alabama Communists During the Great Depression* (University of North Carolina Press, 1990), 31, 123, 153, 156, 213.

3 Kenneth W. Mack, "Rethinking Civil Rights Lawyering and Politics in the Era before Brown," YLJ 115, no. 2 (2005), 256–354; Risa L. Goluboff, *The Lost Promise of Civil Rights* (Harvard University Press, 2007), 16–50; Christopher W. Schmidt, *Civil Rights in America: A History* (Cambridge University Press, 2021), 66–68.

4 *Parents Involved in Community Schools v. Seattle School Dist. No. 1*, 551 U.S. 701, 748 (2007).

5 Dorothy E. Roberts, "The Supreme Court 2018 Term—Foreword: Abolition Constitutionalism," HLR 133, no. 1 (2019), 7–11; Patrisse Cullors, "Abolition and Reparations: Histories of Resistance, Transformative Justice, and Accountability," HLR 132 (2019), 1685; Transcript, Barack Obama's Race Speech at the Constitution Center, Mar. 18, 2008; Michelle Alexander, *The New Jim Crow: Mass Incarceration in the Age of Colorblindness* (New Press, 2010); Dorothy E. Roberts, "Constructing a Criminal Justice System Free of Racial Bias: An Abolitionist Framework," *Columbia Human Rights Law Review* 39 (2007), 261–85. See also John Hope Franklin, "Slavery and the Martial South," JNH 37, no. 1 (1952), 36–53. Jamelle Bouie, "Undemocratic Democracy," *New York Times Magazine*, Aug. 18, 2019, 50–55. Bouie, "The Supreme Court Is Just Doing What the Supreme Court Does," NYT, Feb. 11, 2022.

6 Lydia Saad, Jeffrey M. Jones, and Megan Brenan, "Understanding Shifts in Democratic Party Ideology," *Gallup* (Feb. 19, 2019), https://news.gallup.com/poll/246806/understanding-shifts-democratic-party-ideology.aspx; Theodore R. Johnson, "How the Black Vote Became a Monolith," *New York Times Magazine*,

Sept. 16, 2020; *Kelo v. City of New London, Conn.*, 545 U.S. 469, 522 (2005), Thomas, J., dissenting; Tiya Miles, "The Black Gun Owner Next Door," *New York Times Magazine,* Mar. 9, 2019.

7 Heather Ann Thompson, *Blood in the Water: The Attica Prison Uprising of 1971 and Its Legacy* (Vintage, 2016), xiii–xvii; Larry Copeland, "Former King secretary to auction MLK papers," *USA Today,* Oct. 16, 2013; Kimberly M. Welch, *Black Litigants in the Antebellum American South* (University of North Carolina Press, 2018), 6–8, 223–24.

ILLUSTRATION CREDITS

xxi Image provided by Deidre D. Martin, Clerk of Court, and staff.

3 The Colonial Williamsburg Foundation. Gift of Dr. and Mrs. Richard M. Kain in memory of George Hay Kain.

8 The Library of Virginia.

23 The New York Public Library.

43 Cumberland Baptist Church Record Book, 1856–1896. Cumberland County (Va.) Reel 88, Local government records collection, Cumberland County Court Records. The Library of Virginia, Richmond, Virginia 23219.

126 Potter and Potter Auctions/Gado, via Getty Images.

140 Photograph by Stephen M. Penningroth.

157 Martin Dain Collection, Special Collections, University of Mississippi Libraries.

158 Martin Dain Collection, Special Collections, University of Mississippi Libraries.

161 Library of Congress, Prints and Photographs Division, FSA/OWI Collection, LC-USF34-052768-D.

166 Holsinger Studio Collection, ca. 1890-1938, Accession #9862, Special Collections, University of Virginia, Charlottesville, Va.

168 Library of Congress, Prints & Photographs Division, FSA/OWI Collection, LC-DIG-fsa-8a41490.

171 Will of John Dennis, Chancery Cause no. 4226, Office of Chancery Clerk of Lafayette County, Oxford, Mississippi.

175 The Miriam and Ira D. Wallach Division of Art, Prints and Photographs: Photography Collection, The New York Public Library.

194 Courtesy of Theodore Rosengarten.

203 Courtesy of Margaret Smith.

204 Negro Population, 1790–1915. Department of Commerce, Bureau of the Census (Washington DC: 1918), p. 570.

205 Negro Population, 1790-1915. Department of Commerce, Bureau of the Census (Washington DC: 1918), p. 569.

234 Z/2299.000, Gwin and Mounger Records, folder 27, box 6. Courtesy of the Archives and Records Services Division, Mississippi Department of Archives and History.

240 National Archives and Records Administration, Washington DC.

249 Charles Moore, via Getty Images.

255 Library of Congress, Prints and Photographs Division, FSA/OWI Collection, LC-DIG-ppmsca-51775.

275 Book 33, Page 55; Records and Recording Department, Montgomery County, Alabama Probate Court.

285 *St. Paul Recorder*, Oct. 13, 1961.

286 *Pittsburgh Courier*, Dec. 19, 1959, Pittsburgh Courier Archives.

293 Afro Newspaper / Gado, via Getty Images.

298 Charles Moore/Premium Archive via Getty Images.

316 Roland L. Freeman, *Southern Roads/City Pavements: Photographs of Black Americans* (New York: International Center of Photography, 1981), plate 62.

317 Roland L. Freeman, *Southern Roads/City Pavements: Photographs of Black Americans* (New York: International Center of Photography, 1981), plate 72.

319 Penguin Random House; from the personal collection of Dylan C. Penningroth.

328 Library of Congress, Prints & Photographs Division, FSA/OWI Collection, LC-USF34-052684-D.

338 From the Randall (Herbert) Freedom Summer Photographs [Collection], University of Southern Mississippi.

345 Print no. 439, Winfred Moncrief Photograph Collection (PI/1994.0005), Courtesy of the Archives and Records Services Division, Mississippi Department of Archives and History.

347 Print no. 13, Winfred Moncrief Photograph Collection (PI/1994.0005), Courtesy of the Archives and Records Services Division, Mississippi Department of Archives and History.

347 Print no. 20, Winfred Moncrief Photograph Collection (PI/1994.0005), Courtesy of the Archives and Records Services Division, Mississippi Department of Archives and History.

INDEX

Page numbers in *italic* refer to illustrations.
Page numbers after 364 refer to notes.